CANADIAN PROVINCIAL POLITICS

CANADIAN PROVINCIAL POLITICS

The Party Systems of the Ten Provinces

SECOND EDITION

Edited by

Martin Robin

Dept. of Political Science

Simon Fraser University

Prentice-Hall of Canada, Ltd., Scarborough, Ontario

Canadian Cataloguing in Publication Data

Main entry under title:

Canadian provincial politics

Includes bibliographical references.
ISBN 0-13-113233-4

1. Political parties – Canada – Addresses, essays, lectures. 2. Provincial governments – Canada – Addresses, essays, lectures.* I. Robin, Martin, 1936-

JL195.C35 1978 329'.00971 C78-001058-2

Prentice-Hall, Inc., Englewood Cliffs, New Jersey
Prentice-Hall of Australia, Pty., Ltd., Sydney
Prentice-Hall of India Pvt., Ltd., New Delhi
Prentice-Hall International, Inc., London
Prentice-Hall of Japan, Inc., Tokyo
Prentice-Hall of Southeast Asia (PTE.) Ltd., Singapore

Cover design: Peggy Heath

ISBN 0-13-113233-4

1 2 3 4 5 W 82 81 80 79 78

Printed and bound in Canada by Webcom

Contents

Preface

The purpose of this volume is to provide a survey of party politics in Canada at the provincial level. The book is not concerned with exploring the complexities of Canadian federation, or with describing the operations of the formal institutions of government. The focus, instead, is on the history, structure and determinants of the party systems of each of the ten Canadian provinces.

The essays, originally written for the first edition of *Canadian Provincial Politics*, have been revised and updated for the second edition by their individual authors. The sole exception is the Ontario chapter, now written by Professor Norman Penner of Glendon College, York University. All the essays have been modernized, incorporating the events and alterations of recent years. As editor, I have imposed no rigid constraints on the style and approach of the various contributors, who remain united in the common purpose of providing an original analytical survey of the party system in each of Canada's provinces.

Martin Robin

ALBERTA
Politics of Consensus*

J. Anthony Long and F. Q. Quo

The 1971 Conservative victory that ended 36 uninterrupted years of dominance by the Social Credit Party in Alberta was not entirely unexpected. Most political analysts expected the Conservatives to do well, but what took many by surprise, however, was the decisiveness of the victory —the Progressive Conservatives won 49 of the 75 seats in the Legislative Assembly. The electoral performance of the Tories in the 1975 election, in which the party won 69 of the 75 seats, however, surprised no one in the province. In contrast with the high voter turnout in 1971 (72 per cent) Albertans were rather apathetic in 1975 (59 per cent). In many respects, the 1975 election was not a choice among parties. Rather it was a vote of confidence in the Lougheed leadership. In essence, Albertans were asked if they would support Premier Lougheed's strong position in the feud against Ottawa over oil and gas prices. The Progressive Conservative slogan of "Vote for Alberta" used during the campaign dominated the minds of Albertans when they went to the polls, and they did not fail to give Lougheed's "Alberta first" policy a clear mandate.

The Social Credit Party has never recovered from the 1971 defeat. For the most part it has failed to be an effective opposition in the legislature. Werner Schmidt, leader of the party and notable mainly for his unsuccessful attempts to obtain a seat in the Legislative Assembly, was not strong enough to maintain authority over his Social Credit colleagues in the legislature. The 1975 election marked the first time that the Social Credit Party did not field candidates in all constituencies, leaving 5 constituencies uncontested. The Party leadership also failed to convince some of its own M.L.A.s to run on the Socred platform. While campaign efforts focused on Mr. Schmidt, many candidates ignored their

* The authors are grateful to David Elton, Department of Political Science, University of Lethbridge, for his assistance and criticism in the drafting of this revised edition. Acknowledgement is also made for financial assistance from the Canada Council and the Research Committee of the University of Lethbridge for the original research of this paper.

leader and ran their own shows by personally appealing to their constituents, claiming that their ability to represent the voters was better than their opponents'. The Social Credit platform which emphasized lower interest rates, free enterprise, and more equitable sharing of revenue with municipalities, held little magnetism for the voters. Schmidt's personal defeat in the previously safe Social Credit constituency of Taber-Warner by Tory newcomer Bob Bogle signalled the end of his leadership. Bob Clark, a long-time M.L.A. was eventually selected party leader.

The goal of the New Democratic Party in the 1975 election was not to win a majority of the seats, but rather to become the major opposition in the legislature. With this more realistic strategy, the N.D.P. campaigned against the Socreds as much as it did against the Conservatives. Emphasizing public ownership of utility companies, a government-run auto insurance scheme and a dental care program for children, the N.D.P. was unable to dent the Conservative appeal. Even its strong position on the Syncrude Development, which was virtually ignored by the Tories, appeared to have little appeal for the voters and when the election was over, the N.D.P. remained an opposition of one. Interestingly, however, N.D.P. candidates came second in most northern Alberta and Edmonton constituencies. In light of the fact that there was only a minor increase in the total N.D.P. popular vote, the Party's second position in many constituencies can be interpreted as relating directly to the Social Credit and Liberal parties' weak performance rather than an increase in popular support for the N.D.P. itself.

When the expected 1975 election was announced the Liberal party was recovering from its perennial leadership problem, but under its new leader, Nick Taylor, the party managed to field 46 candidates and increase its popular vote to 5 per cent compared with the 1 per cent it had received in the 1971 election. What success the Liberals had in the 1975 election must be treated as a greater recognition by the electorate of the Party's activity in provincial politics, and the relative novelty of the "Alberta Option," an industrial strategy which emphasized heavier reliance upon primary industry and more controlled development of non-renewable resources such as coal, oil, and natural gas. Whether this acknowledgement can be translated into future votes remains to be seen.

The 1975 provincial election results stand as the epitaph for the Social Credit Party in Alberta and signal the beginning of a new period of one-party dominance in Alberta politics.

Historical Background

When the first provincial legislature met in 1906, the opposition had barely enough members to move and second debate on the Speech from the Throne.[2] Leaders in the assembly of the Northwest Territories had insisted that the welfare of the Territories take precedence over party politics. They particularly opposed any attempt to extend federal politics into the Territories. Although party lines were drawn between Liberals and Conservatives after Alberta came into being, the first provincial election found little disagreement between the parties. Both Liberals and Conservatives supported a successful campaign to amend the separate school system clause of the federal legislation creating the province so that it would not contravene the provisions made for minority rights in the Territorial Ordinances of 1892 and 1901. Another important issue, the question of the ownership of Crown lands, found all parties in the province agreed that the lands should belong to the province rather than the federal government, although some Liberals felt a money grant in lieu of lands would be an acceptable settlement.

This "united front" lasted for some time under the leadership of Liberal premier A. C. Rutherford. Writing about the 1909 election, the Provincial Librarian recorded: "On the important questions of the hour there was little difference in the policies of the two parties."[3] But the Alberta and Great Waterways Railway Company scandal of 1910 divided the Liberal party, providing an opportunity for the Conservatives to become a viable opposition. The scandal revolved around the sale of bonds for railway construction to the J. P. Morgan Company of New York, which resold the bonds at a considerable profit. This resulted in rumors that some members of the government received a share of the profits and eventually led to a split in the Liberal cabinet. Rutherford, unable to unite his cabinet, resigned and a new government was formed under A. L. Sifton. Aided by some loss of public confidence in the Liberals, Conservative strength rose from 5 to 32 per cent of the legislative seats in the 1913 election (see Table I).

The scandal also planted the seed of "anti-partyism" in the minds of many Alberta voters. The invasion of the Nonpartisan League movement from North Dakota during the later years of the 1910s fertilized the growth of the anti-partyism and eventually led to the capture of power by the United Farmers of Alberta in 1921.[4]

THE UFA GOVERNMENT (1921–1935)

When formed in 1909, the UFA was not intended to be a political party. Its original purpose was to provide farmers with local recreational and educational facilities. Politically, the organization purported to be no more than a pressure group for farm interests. As late as 1917, Henry Wise Wood, the leader of the UFA, still preferred working within the old party system to building a new one by UFA members: "The machine is all right if it is run right, and it will be easier to run it right than it will be to build another one—another party."[5] It was not until the fall of 1919 that Wood began a vitriolic polemic against the party system and the advocacy of his theory of group government. Wood regarded the party

TABLE I
Legislative Seats and Percentage of Popular Vote by Political Party

Total No. of Seats	Election	Social Credit			Liberal			Conserv-ative			UFA			CCF/NDP			Others			Total Popular Vote
		No. of Seats	% Pop. Vote	% Seats	No. of Seats	% Pop. Vote	% Seats	No. of Seats	% Pop. Vote	% Seats	No. of Seats	% Pop. Vote	% Seats	No. of Seats	% Pop. Vote	% Seats	No. of Seats	% Pop. Vote	% Seats	
*1905	25				23	61	92	2	35	8								4		23,336
1909	41				36	59	88	2	32	5							3	9	7	50,004
1913	56				38	49	68	18	45	32								6		96,833
1917	58				34	36	59	19	30	33							5	34	9	151,499
1921	59				14	33	24	1	11	2	38	28	64				6	28	10	298,087
**1926	60				7	27	12	4	23	7	43	41	72				6	9	10	175,137
1930	63				11	25	17	6	14	10	39	39	62				7	23	11	188,219
1935	63	57	54	90	4	23	6	2	6	3		11						5		301,752
1940	57	36	43	63	1	.6	2								11		20	46	35	308,864
1944	57	51	52	89										2	25	4	4	23	7	282,106
1948	57	51	56	89	2	18	4							2	19	4	2	7	4	294,793
1952	61,	52	56	85	4	22	7	1	2	2				2	14	3	2	5	3	298,335
1955	61	37	46	61	15	31	25	3	9	5				2	8	3	4	5	7	378,179
1959	65	61	56	94	1	14	2	1	24	2					4		2	2	3	413,515
1963	63	60	55	95	2	20	3		13						9		1	3	2	403,444
1967	65	55	45	83	3	11	5	6	26	11					16		1	3	2	498,341
1971	75	25	41	33		1		49	46	63				1	11	1		1		637,969
1975	75	4	18	5		5		69	63	92				1	13	1	1	1	1	590,170

* Source: 1905-1921 Election figures: *Canadian Parliamentary Guide*, 1905-1921.
** Source: Government of Alberta, *Provincial Election Returns*, 1926-1975.

system as an autocratic instrument of the moneyed classes and unsuitable to be a democractic movement.[6] In the place of party politics, Wood suggested "group government." In essence the theory of group government argued for a non-exploitive democracy based upon functional representation by occupational groups. Members of the legislature would be considered instructed delegates from the group that elected them.

When the UFA came to power in 1921 it was confronted with the difficulties of applying this theory in a parliamentary system. The UFA itself controlled two-thirds of the seats in the Legislative Assembly and there was no mechanism for selecting representatives from other occupational groups. Consequently, it had to fall back on its own convention organization for political decision-making. That is, the UFA leadership promised that legislation would be shaped not by a coterie of ministers but by a broadly based party convention. Because of the political realities of government, however, leadership passed quickly from the convention to the cabinet. By the early 1930s UFA convention resolutions that called for easing the farmers' debts were repeatedly rejected by the UFA cabinet. Fourteen years of UFA government only demonstrated the incompatibility of direct democracy and a parliamentary system. Unable to reconcile its ideals with the practical demands of administration, the UFA was swept from power in the 1935 election by a fresher populist vision.

THE SOCIAL CREDIT MOVEMENT

The idea of "Social Credit" was not new to Albertans in 1935.[7] During the 1920s the UFA had devoted considerable effort to studying credit reform and publicizing the doctrine that the state should control credit. By giving legitimacy to Social Credit's monetary proposals, the UFA helped pave its way to power. But legitimized or not, these proposals had a magic appeal in the middle of a depression that was, to many western farmers, simply incomprehensible. Social Credit seemed both to explain why the Depression had happened and to offer a solution to it: Major Douglas' so-called "A + B theorem,"[8] which possessed, in the words of C. B. MacPherson, a "false clarity which made it impossible either to understand it or refute it in simple terms" but "an almost hypnotic quality for those who were disposed to believe it and were not accustomed to close abstract reasoning."[9] The economic validity of Social Credit was not, however, as important as its political potency.

But the appeal of Social Credit's monetary theories only partly explains the movement's success. An important reason for that success was the leadership of William Aberhart, who brought to the movement both charisma and a genius for organization and tactics. Using his Calgary Prophetic Bible Institute as his headquarters Aberhart was able to transform his large personal religious following into a political force—and succeeded, moreover, in identifying the philosophy of Social Credit with Christian fundamentalism, offering Social Credit as a "Divine Plan" for the salvation of society.[10] By 1935 Social Credit study groups had spread into nearly every part of the province. In addition to providing political instruction these groups also served as important sources of funds.

Aberhart campaigned under the slogan: "Vote for results, not schemes." He rejected the UFA's notion of delegate democracy and argued instead for government by plebiscite—something quite the opposite. The electorate, he said, had the right to indicate generally, through its elected representatives, what it wished its government to do, but the choice of means and the execution of policy were properly functions of the government alone. "Don't try to tell your government everything they should do," he warned his followers. "The minute you start to talk about the policing of the country you are out of order."[11] The government would not itself formulate legislation, however; instead it would hire experts in various fields to make and execute policy in accordance with the government's interpretation of the popular will. In exchange for their right to demand "results" from his government and its hired experts, Aberhart told Albertans, it was their "duty" to support that government.

Whether or not many Albertans understood the implications of Aberhart's theory of government, or were even aware of that theory—the Social Credit platform was published only a few days before the 1935 election[12]—the election returns demonstrated both the success of his campaign strategy and the desperation of a poverty-stricken province.

But aside from a half-hearted solicitation of expert advice from Major Douglas, the new government made no effort to implement Social Credit. Neither the promised $25 a month dividend nor a new economic order seemed to be forthcoming. In the spring of 1937 some "faithful" Socred backbenchers refused to support the government's proposed budget. This insurgence forced the government to establish a Social Credit Board and to appoint a commission of experts charged with the implementation of Social Credit doctrines. The Alberta Social Credit acts were, however, either invalidated by the Supreme Court as *ultra vires* or disallowed by the federal government.[13] By 1939 it was evident that Social Credit could not be implemented.

TRANSFORMATION OF THE SOCIAL CREDIT MOVEMENT (1944-1967)

Although the Aberhart Government was able to blame the federal government rather than its own unwillingness for the failure of Social Credit, it lost some popularity. In the 1940 election the number of Social Credit seats dropped from 57 (out of a total of 63) to 36 (out of 57) and the party's share of the vote from 54.2 to 42.9 per cent. Liberals and Conservatives joined forces in many constituencies to defeat Socred candidates. Running as Independents, these fusion candidates captured 20 seats with 45.1 per cent of the popular vote. Although the advent of World War II and the return of some measure of prosperity helped the Social Credit government to survive this election, in spite of its abandonment of Social Credit economics, it clearly had to find a new justification for its existence.

In the 1944 election campaign it found a formula that has served it faithfully in every election since: evocation of the threat of socialism and the promise of clean government. The 1944 campaign was lead by E. C. Manning, Aberhart's most trusted disciple, who succeeded to the party leadership upon the death of the master in 1943. The inspiration of the 1944 anti-socialist campaign was the rise of the Co-operative Commonwealth Federation (CCF), but after the war the world situation encouraged the government to identify a larger enemy: international communism. Fear of communism, or what seemed to be communism, was strong enough to rally many Albertans behind the SC government. Thus, in the spectrum of political ideologies, Social Credit can be said to have moved from a kind of right-wing populism to a more orthodox conservatism.

However, what a political party professes does not necessarily correspond to what it does. In spite of its statement that Social Credit is "a free individual enterprise movement opposed to Socialism and all other forms of Statism," the Socred government in practice created a welfare state. In 1967 it spent $446 *per capita* for public services, compared to a national average of $333 *per capita*.[14] The government continually opposed proposals for the release of the state-owned Alberta telephone system to "free individual enterprise."[15] It established a Human Resources Development Authority in order to realize the potential of Albertans who are socially and economically depressed. Premier Harry Strom endorsed a guaranteed national income plan similar to the Social Credit monetary proposals of the 1930s.[16] On the other hand, the government was generous to large resource development industries to the point where it was often criticised as being "soft" on oil and mining companies. Its labor legislation, moreover, has been characterized as extremely illiberal.

From one election to another Social Credit of Alberta depended more and more on its administrative record as a government that served the people rather than on its appeal as a party of particular doctrine. "The major function of any government," according to the official statement of the Alberta Socreds, "is to bring to people the results which the people want in the management of their affairs."[17] Because of the revenues it harvested from the oil fields, the Socred government was able to give considerable "results" without resorting to such unpopular devices as a sales tax and extensive deficit financing. This earned it much credit for its "management." Until the 1967 election Social Credit received a majority of the popular vote in every election except those of 1940 and 1955.[18]

But the 1967 election alerted the Socreds to an erosion of their popularity. The metropolitan areas are attracting newcomers with new outlooks. The younger generation, with no memory of the Great Depression is full of new dreams. The old image of Social Credit means little to these groups. Federally, Social Credit seems to be finished. It has never recovered from Diefenbaker's sweep of the West in 1958.[19] But before his retirement from the premiership and the Socred leadership in 1968, E. C. Manning made a last attempt to establish his ideology, if not his party, in federal politics. The social-conservatism advocated by Manning in his *Political Re-alignment: A Challenge to Thoughtful Canadians*[20] caused much speculation that the premier of Alberta would soon enter the federal political scene. In essence, Manning argued for a pragmatic, conservative approach to government. Moreover, he felt there were already too many federal parties and that his suggested approach should be adopted by one of the existing major parties. Since the Progressive Conservative party was at that time faced with the problem of choosing a new national leader, the interpretation that the Premier was making himself available seemed reasonable. But the Progressive Conservative response was barely audible. In his speech at the 1967 Social Credit Convention, Manning blamed this lack of interest on the undemocratic machine of the Conservative party and the unfavorable treatment of his party by the mass media. The failure of this attempt to use the existing Conservative party as a vehicle for his social-conservative ideology convinced Manning and many Socred leaders that Social Credit as a national political force was dying. The episode resulted in the desertion of the party by Socred politicians at the federal level and also led the party to decide against making any province-wide bid for seats in Parliament. In the 1968 federal election Social Credit candidates ran in only three constituencies and they received little official support from their party. All of them lost. But the myth of social-conservatism remains a ready-made justification for those who support the Conservative party federally but Social Credit provincially.

Before leaving office, Manning also gave some thought to modernizing the provincial party. There were two important aspects to his reform strategy: to attract the younger generation, and to extend Socred strength in the urban centers. But it was left to his successor, Harry Strom, to try to realize these ends. The creation of a Ministry of Youth, the appointment of young Socreds to the cabinet, and the establishment of a regional party office in Calgary were some of his efforts. These instruments of reform, however, proved to be ineffectual, for in the 1971 election the Conservatives won most of the urban seats and appear to have attracted a great number of young voters.

THE GOVERNMENT AND OPPOSITION IN RECENT YEARS

No significant opposition to Social Credit emerged until the assumption of the Progressive Conservative leadership by Peter Lougheed, a Calgary lawyer. Though the Progressive Conservatives won only six seats in the 1967 general election, they enlarged that number to ten by winning two by-elections and absorbing two seats from other parties.[21] This increase culminated in their victory in the 1971 election. It is obvious that Lougheed is a capable leader and campaigner. A 1969 publication of the Progressive Conservative Party entitled *Winning the Election* showed that the party had done a great deal of research into the techniques of organizing and campaigning.[22] The material includes suggestions for day to day campaign schedules, examples of vote probability in each poll of a sample constituency, and word-by-word formulas for making and answering telephone calls. Intensive policy seminars were conducted and brainstorming sessions for candidates and party officials were scheduled far in advance of the election. The party successfully impressed the voters that there was a need for a change in government and that it was the only rival of Social Credit with any real chance of success. Because of the weaknesses of the other opposition parties, the Conservatives attracted many of those who were discontented with the dominance of Social Credit. But the party itself has confessed that "party labels are misleading."[23] Like Social Credit, the Progressive Conservatives have professed a belief in free enterprise and in the idea that the main function of a provincial government is to administer "welfare in relation to need without detracting from human dignity."[24]

The major challenge that has confronted the Conservatives since they assumed control of the government has been the management of the province's natural resources. The energy crisis of the early 1970s and the rise of oil prices on the international market has placed Alberta with its abundant resources at the centre of national concern. The plan of the Conservative government has been concentrated on the long-range investment of revenue surplus from oil and gas.

Premier Lougheed has appealed to Albertans for their support for his plan to invest income from non-renewable resources in projects that will still produce when the non-renewable resources are depleted. Moreover, to ensure continuous exploration and development, the Alberta government has taken steps to refund the province's share of the federal tax on royalties to the oil companies and also to reduce royalty rates under certain conditions as well as work out a joint venture with Ontario and the federal government to develop the Athabasca tar sands. The relatively mild nature of the criticism directed at the Premier, indicates that he is in firm control of the province's affairs. Moreover, the repeated attempts to draft Premier Lougheed as the national Progressive Conservative leader has only served to add more popularity to the already well-accepted Premier.

The Liberals are the most impotent party in Alberta provincial politics. This is evidenced by the fact that they fielded only 46 candidates during the last election, and won only 5 per cent of the popular vote. The image of Liberals as eastern, pro-American lawyers and professionals has alienated Albertans, who identify their province as western, agrarian, and culturally British. Historically, the party has been troubled by a lack of unity and capable leadership. In the years since Michael Maccagno left the leadership for an unsuccessful venture in the 1968 federal election, the Alberta Liberals have had several leaders. In 1971, behind-the-door negotiations between the party leader at that time, Jack Lowery, and ex-Premier Strom led to an attempt by the former's own party executives to censure him. Bob Russell, the previous leader, was unsuccessful in his bid for a legislative seat in 1971 and offered little hope of resurrecting the party in provincial politics. A new leader, Nick Taylor, was selected in the spring of 1974. It was Taylor who developed the Party's 1975 campaign with its emphasis on the quality of life. More importantly, however, Taylor's scheme to build up the Alberta provincial Liberals at the grassroots level is a correct diagnosis for a party that does not really have any provincial roots. If Nick Taylor retains his commitment, the Liberal Party may manage to capture a few seats in the provincial legislature. On the other hand, Taylor may go the way of his predecessors, who considered provincial elections as trial runs for their entry into federal politics.

The New Democratic Party (N.D.P.), like the Liberals, is oriented more towards national than provincial politics. Although the old CCF supporters were unhappy with the soft line adopted by the provincial N.D.P.'s founding convention,[25] the N.D.P. is nevertheless the most doctrinaire party in the province, with the result that its policies and its leaders' statements have at times been rather impractical in terms of provincial politics. After two unsuccessful bids to win a seat in the Legislative Assembly, Notley was finally elected by a narrow margin. The only previous N.D.P. member in the Legislative Assembly was defeated in the 1967 election after an attempt to destroy the Socred image of "honest government."[26] The support of the trade unions alone is not sufficient to elect N.D.P. candidates in most constituencies since there are very few constituencies in which organized labor boasts a majority.[27] Unlike its counterparts in the other prairie provinces the Alberta N.D.P. has been unable to attract the support of the rural voters. The fact that its popular vote increased by only two per cent in the last election suggests that, while it may criticize the Conservative policies, it is very unlikely that it will become a significant opposition force.

Party Organization: From Political Movement to Party Politics

Historically, political parties in Alberta as loose multi-goaled federations of voters have been no match for single-goaled mass movements. It is also clear, however, that a political movement cannot perpetuate itself unless it is capable of developing pragmatic policies and building an effective organizational structure.

THE SOCIAL CREDIT LEAGUE

Social Credit reform began at the higher levels of the party's structure, since the party is by far the most organized of the provincial parties at the grass roots level (see Figure 1). A steering committee headed by Raymond Speaker, one of the young Socred leaders and former Minister

FIGURE 1

*Organization of the Alberta Social Credit League**

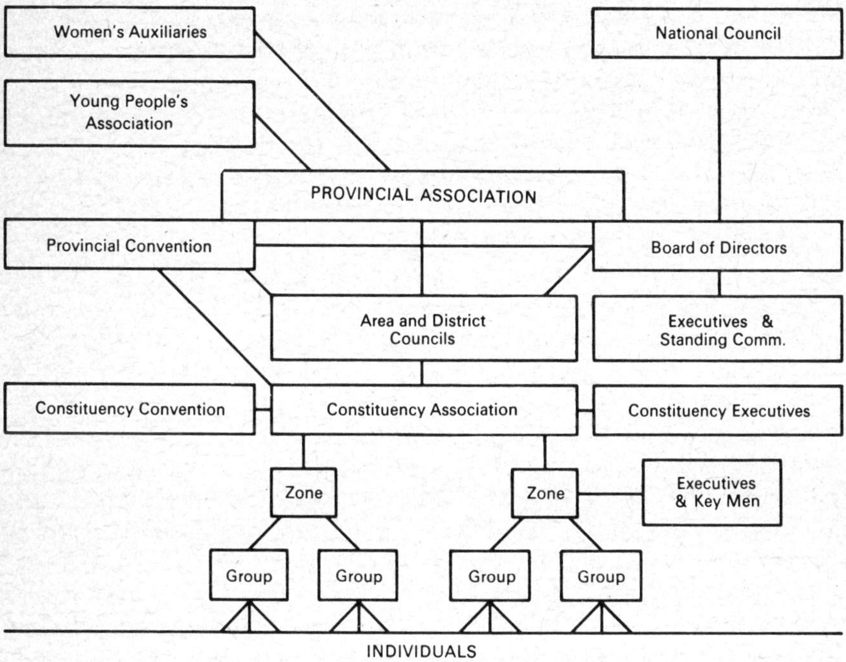

*Based on the constitution of the Alberta Social Credit League.

of Social Development, was in charge of the reorganization task.[29] Its main goal was "to direct the development of a complete political strategy plan for the party and for the government, leading up to the next Provincial General Election."[30] Seven "task forces" were established, each assigned to deal with special aspects of party operation.[31] The main problem was to modernize the old agrarian, religion-oriented Social Credit organization. Not long before the departure of Premier Manning the central organ was divided into two branches, the Alberta Social Credit League and the Political Arm, formerly called the Alberta Social Credit Association (see Figure 2). The League organization, which is under the control of the old guard, is now "historical" in both its influence and its operation. However, in order not to alienate the older generation, Premier Strom introduced the idea of a "second income plan" which may pacify those who retain a nostalgia for the old Social Credit "Money Plan."[22] It is evident that the party made every effort to absorb new blood as well as new techniques of organization. The Political Arm and the new task forces were designed essentially for younger

FIGURE 2

*Central Organ of the Alberta Social Credit League**

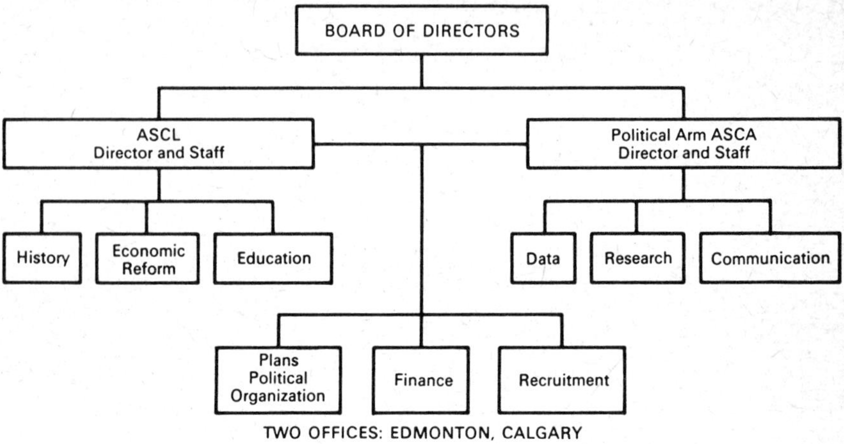

*Supplied by the Alberta Social Credit League.

talents. A key question is whether the Social Credit organization can remain viable when the party is out of power. Already a splintering between the older and the younger members was taking place in early 1970 which should have been taken as a signal of disintegration of the party organization. On leaving office Premier Strom commented that the Socred defeat could be attributed to the many political opportunists who saw the party as an instrument for their personal ambitions. Strom's comment came as a prophecy. In 1975, the party could not field a whole slate for all of the constituencies. Some of the old Socreds ran as independents and many of its "young advisors" conveniently changed their colors.

THE PROGRESSIVE CONSERVATIVES

The task of organizing the Alberta Progressive Conservatives has not been an easy one. Unlike the Social Credit party, which can concentrate its efforts on provincial politics, the Conservatives contest the federal as well as the provincial elections. In recent years, however, the Party has emphasized its operation at the provincial level, more or less leaving federal politics to its national headquarters. As Figure 3 indicates the party organization is based on both provincial and federal constituencies. However, the party constitution clearly charges the provincial leader with the responsibility in provincial politics. The leadership review has to be made "at the first Annual General Meeting of the Association following a *Provincial General Election*" by a secret ballot of the delegates.[33] The

FIGURE 3

*Organization of the Progressive Conservative Association of Alberta**

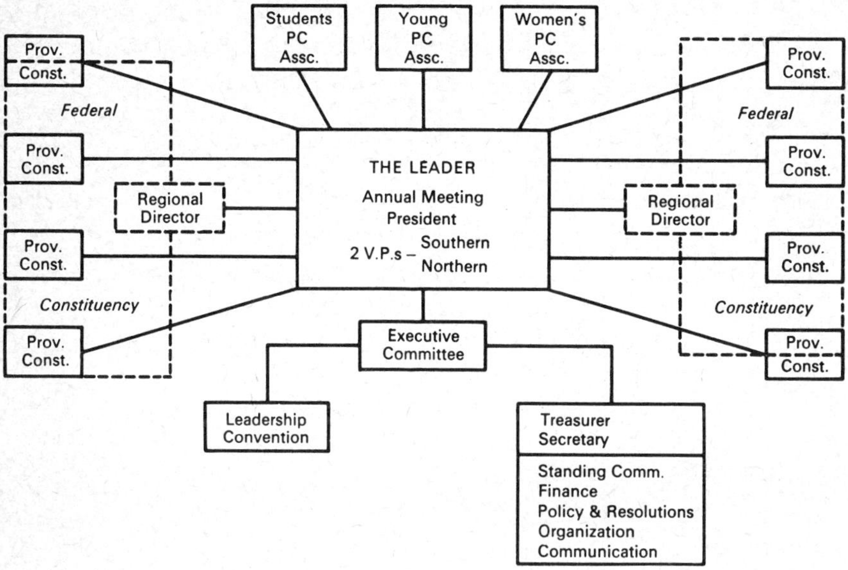

*Based on the constitution of the Progressive Conservative Association of Alberta.

provincial and federal constituency associations operate separately, but with possible duplication in membership and officers. The separate structures not only facilitate the task-oriented operation at the constituency level but also make it possible for those who support other parties federally to join the Tory organization in provincial politics.

THE LIBERALS

As was mentioned earlier, the question of whether to organize the party on the Progressive Conservative model, *i.e.*, separate conventions and structures for the federal and the provincial constituencies, was one issue that split the Alberta Liberal executive in 1970. At present the orientation of the Alberta Liberal organization is to federal rather than provincial politics (see Figure 4). Because of the strong regionalism of Canadian politics a provincial party operating under the direction of its federal counterpart faces many difficulties. What would the position of the Alberta Liberals be should the regional interest conflict with the national policy of the Liberal government in power at Ottawa? On what basis can Alberta Liberals solicit the support of Albertans in provincial elections while the party is in general not "pro-Alberta" in the minds of the voters?[34] In order to improve their showing in provincial elections, the

FIGURE 4

*Organization of the Liberal Association of Alberta**

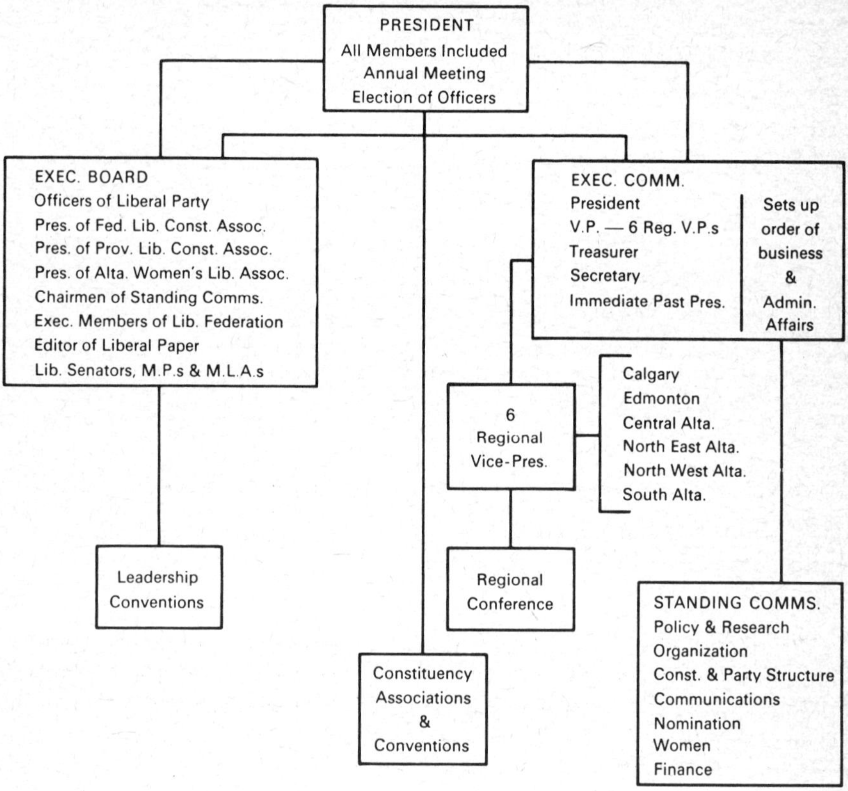

*Based on the constitution of the Liberal Party in Alberta.

Alberta Liberals would have to develop an organization, leaders, and policies independent of the federal party. This would, however, rule out any likelihood of the provincial party riding to power on the coat-tails of its national counterpart.

THE NEW DEMOCRATIC PARTY

Although as a provincial party the Alberta N.D.P. is supposed to be "fully autonomous," the supremacy of the federal party is repeatedly emphasized in the constitution of the N.D.P. Members, candidates, officers, and even the provincial convention, rhetorically proclaimed "the supreme governing body," are expected to act in consistency "with the constitution and principles of the Federal Party."[35] Although the party

FIGURE 5

*The Alberta NDP Organization**

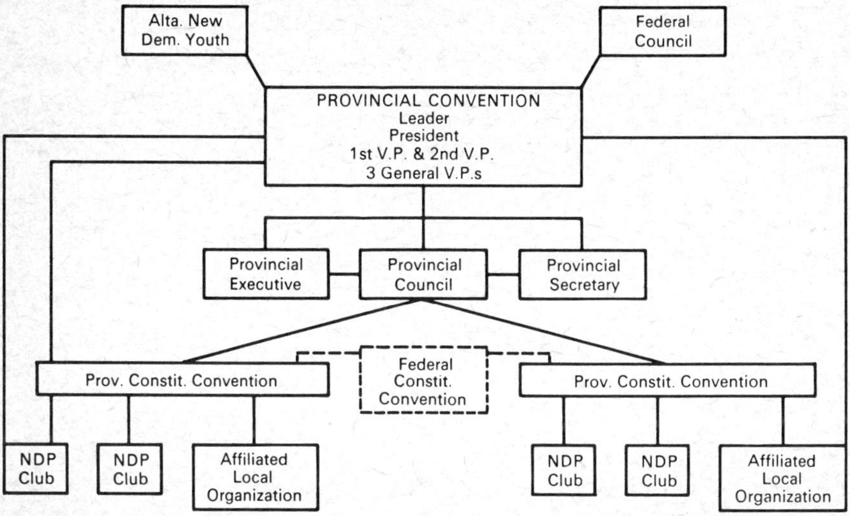

*Based on the constitution of the Alberta NDP.

insists upon democratic practices, such as pro-rated representation of each local unit in the Provincial Convention (see Figure 5), the Provincial Council retains the authority to nullify a nomination made by a constituency convention "if the interests of the federal or provincial party are involved."[36] The provision for disciplinary action by "warning, reprimand, or suspension for any cause" also indicates the centralist tendency of the N.D.P. structure.

In contrast with the Liberal and the Progressive Conservative parties which are loose federations of voters, the Alberta N.D.P. appears militant. Its constitution stipulates that "four or more members in any polling division . . . shall without fail" organize themselves "to see to it that every effort is made and every safeguard taken to ensure the success of its candidate at the poll."[37] Emphasis on an action-group organization is reflected in the N.D.P. clubs, which promote not only political but also "social and educational purposes." The Alberta N.D.P. also makes provision for affiliated membership, evidently created for trade unions. This involves group membership with the provision that an individual member may opt out. As of 1971, the affiliated member organizations seem to be more effective in local political activity than the regular units of the N.D.P. In light of the political tradition in Alberta, the provincial N.D.P. cannot attract significant electoral support until it achieves autonomy.

Bases of Electoral Support

Until recently empirical research into the voting patterns in Alberta provincial elections and the social characteristics of provincial political party supporters has been lacking. Most studies of the Alberta electorate have dealt with the distribution of voter support among federal political parties,[38] and have contributed little to our understanding of Alberta provincial politics in the past because of the traditionally high incidence of alternate voting among the Alberta electorate.[39] As a consequence, most interpretations of Alberta politics have rested on speculative historical generalizations about the nature of support for the different Alberta provincial parties. In general, there has been a tendency to assume that Social Credit drew its strength mainly from the small towns and the countryside; the Liberal party from the urban, professional sector; the N.D.P. from the workers and the intellectuals; and the Progressive Conservative party from the urban middle class and farmers.

Data obtained in three studies of the Alberta electorate, however, and a close study of recent provincial elections indicate that these generalizations are inadequate, obscuring what is in fact the relatively heterogeneous nature of electoral support for each of the provincial political parties and ignoring recent trends in provincial politics. In the following two sections we will examine the social and geographical cleavages in electoral support for each of the provincial parties.

SOCIAL CHARACTERISTICS

The analysis in this section is based partly upon data taken from two surveys of the Alberta electorate conducted during the late 1960s, but relies more heavily on an extensive survey conducted shortly after the 1971 election through the cooperative effort of Alberta's three universities.[40] All three surveys utilized a recall method, with the respondents' demographic data correlated with their recollection of previous voting behavior. Taken collectively, these surveys are highly indicative and represent the most accurate picture yet obtained of provincial party supporters. Moreover, they enable us to develop a comparative profile of the patterns of support before and after the landmark 1971 election, which brought about the first shift in governing authority within the province in 35 years.

For purposes of analysis, we have classified the social characteristics of the Alberta electorate in terms of the demographic variables ordinarily used in the study of voting behavior: age, education, occupation and social class. The data in this latter category derive from the respondent's own perception of his or her social class, correlated with social and economic background data on the respondents.

The age group data from the three surveys reinforce the popular impression that Social Credit has historically derived a large part of its vote from older age groups. The percentage of electoral support given to the Social Credit party rises with the age of the voters. This generally concurs with the hypothesis that many people who supported the Social Credit party in its initial rise to power have remained constant in their party identifications. The percentage of defectors to the Tories in the 1970s from the older age cohorts has been significantly less than from the lower age groups. There is little question that youth perceived the Social Credit government as being tired and unimaginative and turned to the Conservatives. On the other hand, Conservative support appeared to be distributed evenly among all age groups, with the exception of the 65 and over group. Even in this category, however, Conservative support was slightly higher than that given to the Social Credit party. Electoral support by age for the N.D.P. and the Liberal party was scattered throughout the age cohorts. Both parties received slightly higher percentages of the vote from the middle-age and younger groups.

Occupation and education are integrally related in determining social class and usually should be considered as a composite with social class in analyzing political behavior. As Table III indicates, Social Credit support in the 1971 election was highest among the non-professional occupations and the retired. As could be expected, professionals were much more likely to vote Conservative than Social Credit. The shift of a substantial portion of the farm vote from the Socreds to the Conservatives has to be regarded as one of the most important features of the 1971 election. While farmers have voted for the Conservatives in federal elections, they had remained basically loyal to the Socreds at the provincial level previous to 1971. The loss of the farm vote represented the crumbling of the major bastion of Socred strength. Actually, Social Credit lost much of its electoral support in all occupational categories to the Conservatives. Not unexpectedly, Liberal support was negligible among farmers, white collar and skilled workers. The greatest Liberal support, in the 1971 election, appeared to be from the retired, professional and blue collar occupational categories. Among the latter groups are probably new arrivals to Alberta from eastern Canada, and the usual assortment of lawyers and other professionals who have historically dominated the provincial Liberal organization. The occupational breakdown of support for the provincial N.D.P. agrees with the general impression that the New Democrats are weakest among professionals and retired persons. The fact that the N.D.P. received some support from every occupational group indicates that in Alberta, at least, it is not just a party of the poor.[41]

The education data show that voters with less formal education were more inclined to vote Social Credit. Socred support tended to be lowest among university-educated, and highest among individuals with only a grade school education. The Conservatives attracted large numbers of

TABLE II

Party Support by Age

Age	Progressive Conservative	Social Credit	Liberal	New Democratic	Did Not Vote
18-25	46.7%	15.2%	1.6%	8.7%	27.7%
26-35	50.0%	25.0%	1.0%	5.4%	18.6%
36-45	43.1%	29.3%	0.0%	6.9%	20.7%
46-55	54.2%	25.0%	2.8%	9.7%	8.3%
56-65	49.5%	33.0%	1.8%	7.3%	8.3%
over 65	33.3%	36.4%	0.0%	3.0%	27.3%

Alberta 1971 Electoral Study

TABLE III

Party Support by Occupation

Occupation	Progressive Conservative	Social Credit	Liberal	New Democratic	Did not Vote
Professional	65.6%	21.9%	1.6%	2.3%	8.6%
White Collar	49.0%	26.1%	0.0%	8.3%	16.6%
Skilled Workers	39.7%	23.8%	0.0%	9.5%	27.0%
Blue Collar	43.4%	25.4%	1.7%	7.5%	21.9%
Farmers	59.7%	16.4%	0.0%	9.0%	14.9%
Retired	35.3%	45.1%	2.0%	5.9%	11.8%

Alberta 1971 Electoral Study

TABLE IV

Party Support by Education

Education	Progressive Conservative	Social Credit	Liberal	New Democratic	Did Not Vote
Grade 9 and below	37.3%	29.9%	2.0%	7.0%	23.8%
High School	51.3%	25.2%	1.1%	6.5%	15.9%
Vocational & Technical	50.0%	25.0%	0.0%	7.3%	17.7%
University	54.8%	19.9%	1.4%	9.6%	14.4%

Alberta 1971 Electoral Study

TABLE V

Party Support by Social Class

Social Class	Progressive Conservative	Social Credit	Liberal	New Democratic	Did Not Vote
Upper	52.9%	35.3%	0.0%	5.9%	5.9%
Middle	51.9%	24.7%	1.8%	6.3%	15.4%
Working	43.7%	26.2%	_.7%	8.5%	20.8%
Other	61.5%	15.4%	0.0%	7.7%	15.4%

Alberta 1971 Electoral Study

voters at all educational levels, with its greatest support, proportionately, coming from university graduates. Not unexpectedly, both the Liberal and New Democratic parties' support tended to be polarized in the low and high educational group categories.

Social class data from the 1971 electoral study generally correlate with the relationships found between occupation and education on one hand, and party identification on the other. Conservative strength transcended all social classes, with a tendency for the party to receive more extensive support from the upper and middle classes. The Liberal party, once again, appears to have received its greatest support from the middle class. The N.D.P. vote is scattered throughout all social classes, which supports our previous argument that there are no class-based parties in Alberta. Our social class data deviate slightly from the previous data when they show that Social Credit support declines as class status declines. A possible explanation for this anomaly might be social class misidentification on the part of the respondents, which would have the effect of skewing Social Credit support toward the higher social classes.

When analyzed on a longitudinal basis, the three studies reveal that a wholesale defection of voters to the Conservatives from the Social Credit party occurred during the 1971 and 1975 elections. Tentatively, we suggest that the changes in party allegiance can be traced to a perceptual shift by members of the various social and economic groups. While the Social Credit Party was conceived as a good governing party prior to 1971, during the 1971 election most voters perceived, for different, if not conflicting, reasons, that the Socreds were no longer capable of governing in their best interest. For those voters, the Conservatives stood as the only viable alternative, because the Liberal Party and N.D.P. were far too weak to present any meaningful challenge to the Social Credit government.

The preceding analysis also shows that popular assumptions concerning the social bases of provincial party support in Alberta tend to over-

TABLE VI

*Province-wide Vote by Party**

	S.C.			Lib.			P.C.			N.D.P.		
Election Year	% Major Urban**	% Small Urban***	% Other Districts	% Major Urban	% Small Urban	% Other Districts	% Major Urban	% Small Urban	% Other Districts	% Major Urban	% Small Urban	% Other Districts
1944	23	5	72	–	–	–	–	–	–	25	5	70
1948	25	8	67	32	5	63	–	–	–	24	6	70
1952	28	9	63	27	5	68	100	–	–	32	4	64
1955	31	8	61	41	4	55	68	15	17	31	6	63
1959	34	8	58	39	4	47	43	9	48	48	3	49
1963	38	8	54	47	8	45	54	9	37	48	6	46
1967	41	8	51	53	9	38	62	9	29	44	6	50
1971	47	7	46	45	19	36+	55	5	40	52	6	41
1975	35	10	55	68	6	26	51	6	43	49	5	46

* Source: Government of Alberta, *Provincial Election Returns.*

** Includes voters in the Calgary and Edmonton constituencies.

*** Includes voters in the Lethbridge, Red Deer, and Medicine Hat constituencies.

\+ In 1971 the Liberals only received 6475 votes in total. 1660 of these votes were received by one man, Russell in St. Alberta; which accounts for 26% of the party total.

compartmentalize the Alberta electorate. When considered in terms of demographic variables, Alberta voters appear to exhibit a high degree of catholicity. Although different provincial parties can expect to receive a higher percentage of votes from certain socio-economic groups, these margins are not significant enough to divide the electorate on a class basis. The fact that all parties received a fairly even proportion of electoral support from all socio-economic groups indicates not only a lack of class voting, but also that in emerging as the dominant party within the province, the Conservatives have extended their electoral base and should be able to rely upon a "politics of consensus" within the Alberta electorate. It is a consensus in a society which is no longer dominated by the small independent farmer, but one that has become socially and economically heterogeneous.

GEOGRAPHICAL BASES OF PARTY SUPPORT

Like most other Canadian provinces Alberta has experienced increasing urbanization. At present nearly 50 per cent of its population resides in

TABLE VII

*Percentage of Vote by Party in Major Urban, Small Urban, and Rural Areas**

	Major Urban Districts**					Small Urban Districts***					All Other Districts				
Year	Social Credit	Liberal	Conservative	CCF/NDP	Other	Social Credit	Liberal	Conservative	CCF/NDP	Other	Social Credit	Liberal	Conservative	CCF/NDP	Other
1944	43			22	35	47			20	33	56			27	17
1948	49	20		15	16	66	15		19		58	17		21	4
1952	50	19	12	14	5	74	18		8		58	24		14	4
1955	40	35	17	7	2	53	20	20	7		50	30	3	9	8
1959	51	15	28	6	.3	64	7	27	2		57	14	21	4	4
1963	49	22	16	11	2	57	21	15	7		59	17	9	9	6
1967	38	12	34	15	.2	44	13	30	13		51	9	17	18	5
1971**	38	1	49	12	.04	47	3	39	11		44	.9	44	11	.1
1975	13	7	67	13	.53	27	4	59	9	.13	22	3	59	13	2.2

* Source: Government of Alberta, *Provincial Election Returns.*

** Indicates voters in Calgary and Edmonton constituencies.

*** Indicates voters in the Lethbridge, Red Deer, and Medicine Hat constituencies.

the two major urban centres, Calgary and Edmonton.[42] Alberta has always had a comparatively large urban population, but the ratio of urban to rural population has shifted considerably in the last decades, a shift accentuated by the absolute decline in population in many rural areas of the province. The effect of this population shift is that new patterns of urban-rural distribution of electoral support for the provincial parties have emerged.

Over the span of the last several decades an increasing proportion of each party's total vote has come from Calgary and Edmonton. As Table VI indicates, between the elections of 1952 and 1975, the proportion of total Social Credit vote from these areas increased by 7 per cent, Liberal support by 41 per cent, and N.D.P. vote by 17 per cent. The relative growth of Progressive Conservative strength should be traced from 1959, because in the 1952 election the party ran no candidates in rural constituencies and in 1955 it contested only 15 constituencies in addition to those in Calgary and Edmonton. Since 1959 the urban proportion of its total vote has increased by 8 per cent. The breakdown of electoral support by area given in Table VII, however, shows that the growth of the Conservative vote in Alberta's major urban centers has been far more rapid than for the other parties, to the point where the Conservatives are now the dominant urban party, having won all seats in Edmonton and Calgary in the last election. Table VII also indicates that the Tories' province-wide strength increased and that the party captured the most votes in every geographical category. With the successful invasion of the rural ridings, a traditional stronghold of Social Credit, the Conservatives appear to have solidified a province-wide base of electoral support. The Liberal party managed to make moderate gains in all parts of the province, while the N.D.P. vote remained steady, except for a slight increase in the northern districts. The proportionate distribution of each party's strength will become increasingly important in assessing its fortunes in future Alberta provincial politics.

Conclusion

Our analysis of contemporary Alberta provincial politics suggests that it is no longer possible to view the Alberta party system solely in the context of Macpherson's theory of a "quasi-party" system.[43] Although his *Democracy in Alberta* still represents the best historical explanation of the rise of political movements in Alberta, his quasi-party thesis, which argues the existence of one dominant party within a homogeneous electorate, had greater validity two decades ago than it does today. It is doubtful whether the two conditions necessary for the existence of a quasi-party system—quasi-colonial status and a predominately *petit-bourgeois* society—still exist in Alberta. Although the recent confrontations between Ottawa and Edmonton may give the impression that Albertans still consider themselves as having a "quasi-colonial status" within the Canadian political and economic systems, there is little question that Albertans are confident of their own ability to develop the province's natural resources. Moreover, Alberta voters seem satisfied with having their representation in Ottawa channeled through the traditional national parties. Although Alberta still confronts the national government in the areas of grain marketing, allocation of tax revenue, language rights, and other issues, the effects of these conflicts on provincial politics vary greatly from one election to another. Disputes between Ottawa and the provincial governments have been a rather common phenomenon of Canadian federalism in recent years and cannot be considered peculiar to Alberta. Regarding the second condition, the majority of the present Alberta electorate cannot be characterized as having an "independent producer outlook." The last two decades have witnessed an extensive diversification of the Alberta economy.[44] The number of Albertans engaged in farming is continually declining, while the resource extraction, service, and light manufacturing industries are expanding. Accompanying this economic diversification is the growing trend toward urbanization and the development of political attitudes more characteristic of urban voters. The Alberta of today is a socially and economically heterogeneous society. Consequently, Macpherson's homogeneous class theory as the basis for a quasi-party system needs substantial modification. Very little class voting exists. All provincial parties attract some votes from every socio-economic group in the Alberta electorate. The fact that the Social Credit party drew, prior to the 1971 election, a larger proportion of support from each of these groups than any of the other provincial parties indicates that its electoral success was not due primarily to an image as a party of the *petit-bourgeois*, but rather that it governed sufficiently well to satisfy most of the social and economic groups in the Alberta electorate.

It can be argued that the political structure of Macpherson's quasi-party system only partly exists in the present Alberta political system. Lipset is basically correct in his contention that the large legislative majorities in Alberta political history have been partly the result of the opposition vote being divided among a number of parties.[45] As we have pointed out above, moreover, the size of a legislative majority can also be related to the degree of maldistribution in the electoral system. Rural areas have until the last election always been over-represented in the Alberta legislature and Social Credit has been the major beneficiary of this maldistribution.[46]

For a dynamic interpretation of the recent history of party politics in Alberta we suggest the use of the "developmental approach," designed originally for the study of developing political systems.[47] The main advantage of applying the developmental approach to Alberta is that changes in provincial politics can be explained in light of the necessity of the party system to adapt itself to a modernizing society. The demise of Social Credit as an ideological movement and its transformation into a success-oriented administrative party with a differentiated structure is a reflection of this adaptation process. This process is of course conditioned and directed by the strong tradition of democracy in Alberta. That is, democracy is a framework within which the development of the Alberta party system must take place. Albertans may respond favorably to a charismatic leader in times of unusual social stress, as they did to William Aberhart, but they do not hesitate to demand that charisma be accompanied by pragmatic governing ability. Furthermore, a strong identification with the rest of Canada also limits the directions party politics will take. Albertans did not seriously threaten to separate from Confederation during the 1930s, nor does it seem likely that they will do so in the future.[48] Within these limiations one can draw a meaningful analogy between the course of political development in Alberta and a developing nation.

Another advantage of such an approach is that it complements Macpherson's quasi-party thesis by adding to it an explanation of recent developments in Alberta provincial politics. That is, the quasi-party system should be considered as a stage in the development of the Alberta party system, a stage the party system has now passed beyond. Finally, the developmental approach may facilitate comparative study of provincial politics in Alberta and in other provinces. Instead of over-emphasizing the idiosyncrasy of Alberta provincial politics, the developmental approach may provide common measures for cross-provincial comparison.

Endnotes

[2] The Alberta Act came into effect on September 1, 1905. The first provincial general election was held on November 9, 1905. For a description of the first legislature see Archibald O. MacRae, *History of the Province of Alberta* (Calgary: Western Canada History Co., 1912), p. 90.

[3] John Blue, *Alberta: Past and Present* (Pioneer Historical Publications Co., 1924) I, p. 122-125.

[4] For the spread of the Nonpartisan League movement in western Canada, see Paul F. Sharp, *The Agrarian Revolt in Western Canada: A Survey Showing American Parallels* (Minneapolis: University of Minnesota Press, 1948).

[5] H. W. Wood, "The Price of Democracy," *Grain Growers' Guide*, June 20, 1917, quoted in Macpherson, *Democracy in Alberta*, p. 38.

[6] *Ibid.*, pp. 40ff.

[7] The background and development of the Social Credit Movement in Alberta have been studied quite extensively under a program sponsored by the Canadian Social Science Research Council. Publications resulting from the program most pertinent to the problems discussed in this paper include: C. B. Macpherson, *Democracy in Alberta: Social Credit and the Party System*, 2nd ed. (Toronto: University of Toronto Press, 1962); J. R. Mallory, *Social Credit and Federal Power in Canada* (Toronto: University of Toronto Press, 1954); W. E. Mann, *Sect, Cult and Church in Alberta* (Toronto: University of Toronto Press, 1955); L. G. Thomas, *The Liberal Party in Alberta: A History of Politics in the Province of Alberta, 1905-1921* (Toronto: University of Toronto Press, 1959); and J. A. Irving, *The Social Credit Movement in Alberta* (Toronto: University of Toronto Press, 1959).

[8] The "A + B Theorem" argues: 1. that the cost of every unit produced consists of (A) all payments made to individuals either in the form of wages, salaries, or dividends and (B) all payments made to organizations either for raw materials, bank interests or other external costs; 2. therefore the price of goods has to be at least A + B; 3. however, only A creates purchasing power and since A is less than A + B, not all goods can be purchased; thus 4. in order to ensure that all products be purchased, purchasing power in the amount of B has to be created; and 5. this new money created can be distributed to consumers as social credit or to producers as subsidies for their lowering of prices.

[9] Macpherson, *Democracy in Alberta*, pp. 108-111.

[10] Irving, *The Social Credit Movement*, p. 338.

[11] *Alberta Social Credit Chronicle*, August 16, 1935.

[12] Macpherson, *Democracy in Alberta*, pp. 149-160.

[13] The Dominion of Canada disallowed 12 Alberta Provincial Acts, 11 of which dealt with Social Credit monetary legislation. In 1938 the acts were declared *ultra vires* by the Supreme Court. See R. MacGregor Dawson, *The Government of Canada* (Toronto: University of Toronto Press, 1964) and Mallory, *Social Credit and Federal Power.*

[14] *Alberta: The Tax Haven* (Edmonton: Alberta Social Credit League, n.d.).

[15] The motion to transfer the government-owned Alberta telephone system to private enterprise has been repeatedly objected to by the leaders and consequently rejected in the Social Credit Conventions.

[16] *Calgary Herald*, November 1, 1969.

[17] Orvis A. Kennedy, *Principles and Policies of Social Credit* (Edmonton: Alberta Social Credit League, 1965).

[18] The 1955 election centered around the issue of the honesty and integrity of some Social Credit M.L.A.s. J. H. Prowse, the Liberal leader, led the accusations. In the constituencies where the Liberals did not run candidates they supported coalition candidates with other parties against Social Credit. Social Credit lost 10 per cent of its popular support.

[19]

	1957 Federal Election		*1958 Federal Election*	
	Seats	*% of Vote*	*Seats*	*% of Vote*
Social Credit	13	37.8	0	21.6
Progressive Conservative	3	27.6	17	59.9

[20] E. C. Manning, *Political Realignment: A Challenge to Thoughtful Canadians* (Toronto: McClelland & Stewart, Ltd., 1967).

[21] One Liberal and one Independent M.L.A. joined the Progressive Conservative caucus.

[22] *Winning the Election* (Edmonton: Alberta Progressive Conservative Association, October, 1969).

[23] *Ibid.*

[24] Peter Lougheed, "Guideposts of the Progressive Conservative Party of Alberta," ratified by the Annual Meeting of the party in November 1967.

[25] At the NDP of Alberta Founding Convention there were 172 union delegates, 98 New Party Club delegates, and 85 CCF delegates. See Gad Horowitz, *Canadian Labour in Politics* (Toronto: University of Toronto Press, 1968).

[26] The NDP member of the Legislative Assembly, Mr. G. Turcott, attacked the Socred government for misuse of public funds and improper activities on the part of two Socred cabinet members. The incident led to the appointment of a Judicial Inquiry Commission. (See a special edition of *The Alberta Democrat*, Vol. I, No. 9 (January 1968) for details of the event.) The NDP fought the 1967 general election campaign by challenging the honesty of the Socred government.

[27] During the 1967 election the NDP received approximately $20,000 in campaign contributions from trade unions. See Peter Hill, "The Alberta New Democratic Party" (unpublished paper, University of Lethbridge, 1968.)

[28] The 1969 Alberta Legislative Assembly lowered the voting age to nineteen.

[29] *Re-organization of the Alberta Social Credit League*, a publication for internal circulation made available to the authors through the courtesy of Mr. Orvis Kennedy, the president of the League.

30 *Ibid.*, p. 2.

31 They include the Planning and Programming Task Force, Financial Task Force, Membership Task Force, Data Task Force, Policy Review Task Force, Communication Task Force, and League Task Force.

32 At the 1969 Annual Convention of the Social Credit League Louis Kelso, from the United States, was a guest speaker. The "Kelso plan" is based on the argument that labor is no longer the main principal means for creating individual wealth and the individual's "right" to capital and investment is therefore in need of government protection. The plan proposes government loans to wage earners for investment, the dividends to become a second income for the individual and his family. It met with an enthusiastic response from old Social Crediters, who found a similarity between the plan and their old dream.

33 *Constitution of the Progressive Conservative Association of Alberta*, Article 13.

34 Robert Russell, "Alberta Needs an Independent Liberal Party," *Edmonton Journal*, January 14, 1970. See also, "Liberals Told: Only Move Left Can Save Party," *Ibid.*, November 10, 1969, referring to the so-called John Hotton paper, which advocates a move toward a "social democrat" position and a Liberal organization independent of its national counterpart; and "Alberta Liberals Consider Cutting Their Federal Ties," *Ibid.*, February 28, 1970.

35 See the *Constitution of the Alberta New Democratic Party*, Articles 5 (3), and 11 (1).

36 *Ibid.*, Article 18(9).

37 *Ibid.*, Article 16(3).

38 See Frederick C. Engelmann and Mildred A. Schwartz, *Political Parties and the Canadian Social Structure* (Scarborough, Ontario: Prentice-Hall of Canada, Ltd., 1967); Robert R. Alford, "The Social Bases of Political Cleavage in 1962," in *Papers on the 1962 Election*, John Meisel, ed. (Toronto: University of Toronto Press, 1964), pp. 203-234; S. Peter Regenstreif, "Some Aspects of National Party Support in Canada," *Canadian Journal of Economics and Political Science*, XXIX, No. 1, (February 1963), pp. 59-74; and Wallace Gagne and Peter Regenstreif, "Some Aspects of New Democratic Urban Support in 1968," *Canadian Journal of Economics and Political Science*, XXXIII, No. 4 (November, 1967), pp. 529-550.

39 See F. Q. Quo, "Split-Ticket Voting in Alberta," a paper delivered at the 40th Annual Meeting of the Canadian Political Science Association, Calgary, June 5, 1968.

40 The first survey was carried out by F. Q. Quo for his study on alternate voting patterns among Alberta voters. The second was conducted by David K. Elton in conjunction with his study on electoral perception of federalism. Both studies used the proportional random probability sampling technique. The third survey was part of the broader Alberta 71 project, carried out jointly by the University of Alberta, the University of Calgary, and the University of Lethbridge.

41 Regenstreif also makes this point about the federal N.D.P. See "Some Aspects of National Party Support in Canada," p. 62.

42 Statistics Canada, *1971 Census of Canada*, I (1-1.1), February 1973.

43 Macpherson, *Democracy in Alberta*, pp. 237ff.

[44] The following socio-economic indices clearly indicate the changes which have taken place in Alberta in recent decades:

	1931	1961	1971
Population engaged in agriculture	56.41%	25.16%	15.10%
Net value of production: agriculture	52.85%	18.70%	16.30%
Population living in urban areas	31.10%	63.90%	72.43%

As of 1966 the oil industry provided 27 per cent of the productive value of industries in Alberta. Alberta Bureau of Statistics, *Alberta Industry and Resources*, 1973.

[45] Seymour Martin Lipset, "Democracy in Alberta: Part I," *Canadian Forum*, November 1954, pp. 175-177.

[46] See John Anthony Long, "Maldistribution in Western Provincial Legislature: The Case of Alberta," *Canadian Journal of Political Science*, II, No. 3 (September 1969), pp. 345-355.

[47] G. A. Almond and G. Bingham Powell, *Comparative Politics: A Developmental Approach* (Boston: Little, Brown and Company, 1966).

[48] See David K. Elton, "Electoral Perception of Federalism: A Descriptive Analysis of the Alberta Electorate," a paper presented at the One Prairie Province Conference, May 10-13, 1970, Lethbridge.

BRITISH COLUMBIA The Company Province

Martin Robin

Social Structure

The British Columbia party system has evolved from and reflects a unique social environment. Frequently designated a fragment of western Canadian society, British Columbia is as distinct in social structure and party politics as it is in ideology and culture. British Columbians are westerners, but they share little in common with the prairie provinces. They are Canadians, but only half-heartedly attached to their loose and variegated federation. British Columbians cultivate and feed on a sense of uniqueness and they are aided in their narcissistic idolatry by the great Rocky Mountain divide which separates this remarkable land of mountains, forests, and sea from the flattened land mass to the east.

Prairie politics in Canada have been indelibly stamped with the ideology of agrarianism. Industrialism, with its concomitant changes in class structure, is a late-comer to the Canadian prairies, and the western provinces, outside of British Columbia, have been until the Great Depression predominantly rural expanses populated by independent commodity producers. In all three provinces, Manitoba, Saskatchewan, and Alberta, indigent farmers banded together in social and economic organizations to oppose the railways, the urban middlemen, and the eastern financial interests that controlled the institutions and made the decisions that affected their lives as consumers and producers. They organized politically as well to oppose the major national parties traditionally responsive to the eastern financial and industrial interests. The center of gravity of the Progressive movement was in the Prairies and the contemporary culture and politics of these provinces, although markedly changed from an earlier day, still bear the certain stamp of agrarianism.

The British Columbia frontier differs from the Prairie frontier. The latter was settled by independent commodity producers who owned the means of production they worked with, produced agricultural commodities for sale to a largely external market, and refrained from employing wage labor except on a small scale. British Columbia society developed as a corporate frontier and the agrarian sector has always played a smaller part in the economy, society and politics of the province than has its equivalent in the Prairies.

The British Columbia economy is peculiarly dependent, directly and indirectly, on the extraction of natural resources, particularly forest and mineral. The primary industries, producing goods for export, form the hub of the economy, Auxiliary industries which supply goods to the other industries of the province, and the consumer-oriented industries, are both dependent on the primary industries. The auxiliary industries exist only to service the basic industries, and without the income and employment provided by these two classes, the local consumer-oriented industries would have no market.

The shape of the British Columbia economy has not altered since the turn of the century. The fortunes of different industries have risen and fallen with economic expansion. The relative importance of agriculture and fishing has declined while others such as petroleum and natural gas, has flourished. But the structure of the economy, tied to the foundations of the primary-resource-extractive industries, has remained unaltered. British Columbia has long been a "company" province and the large enterprise, rather than the small family homestead, is the dominant shape on the social landscape. Scattered throughout the province are company towns, single-enterprise communities subsisting on the activities of resource extraction which provide the goods for an economy serviced and administered by the heavily populated area of metropolitan Vancouver.

Along with the rise of an industrial economy based on resource extraction there has grown a labor movement stronger and more articulate than most in Western Canada.[1] Agrarianism has colored the economy and culture of the prairie provinces. The labor movements in all three provinces, with the possible exception of Manitoba, have been relatively weak and wielded little effective political power. In British Columbia, there grew steadily, from the onset of industrialism, a political labor movement intent on checking the powers of the employing class in a company-dominated province. Carried by radical British and American workers, socialism emerged as a viable ideology around the turn of the century, at a time when the movement was weak and ineffective in most other Canadian provinces.

Large-scale production and the structure of employment in the coal and metal mining industries ensured that industrial unionism, with its radical ideology, was well represented within the provincial labor movement. The British workingmen who first led the unions and worked the coal mines of Vancouver Island were not the highly skilled and exclusive artisans who dominated the trade assemblies of Ontario during the 1880s. They were men from the north of England who brought to Canada organizational skill and a marked propensity toward independent politics characteristic of the English and Scottish northern mining communities. Equally militant were the many American workers who provided the early constituency of radical unions like the Western Federation of Miners. The frontier labor conditions prevailing in the metal mining areas of the Pacific Northwest shaped the outlook and temperament of many of the miners who settled in the B.C. interior. The employing class's views of property rights were narrowly and rigidly defined. The proliferation of company towns, the struggles of the hardrock miners, the millmen and smeltermen within the bowels of the earth, the rapid proliferation of militant employers' associations and the frontier tradition of violence as a solution to social conflicts, contributed to the creation of a "heritage of conflict" between capitalists and workers.[2]

The legacy of class opposition, forged over decades of struggle, persists today and colors the ideology of contemporary workers. The coastal labor movement is highly politicized. Labor has unabashedly engaged in partisan politics, not simply the Gompersian variety of rewarding friends and punishing enemies, but ideological politics. The question of labor's political action, together with a host of issues arising from working-class participation, form enduring themes of the British Columbia political culture.

British Columbia labor leaders have acted politically, in both pragmatic and ideological ways, because they perceived that the problems the workers faced were insoluble except by state intervention through partisan alignment. Workers organized politically to overcome problems and lessen insecurities which could not be remedied by industrial organization alone. The problems facing coast workers were legion and their political response was correspondingly strong. The perceived insecurities of coast workers stemmed from a variety of causes and circumstances. The province has been subject to waves of immigration—Oriental, central and eastern European, and American—which have created an unstable labor market. For decades, trade unions sought to restrict the influx of Oriental immigrants, who were used by the employing class to break strikes and lower wage rates in mining and other employments.

The insecurity that many workers felt in the face of foreign labor was reinforced by the employment and wage fluctuations of a specialized resource-based economy responsive to and dependent upon the vagaries of external markets. A much larger percentage of the wage income of British Columbians, as compared to Canada as a whole, derives directly from the export of goods and services and is subject to the rise and fall of world prices. Construction, mining, and lumber workers have been particularly vulnerable to seasonal and cyclical unemployment and to high job turnover. Workers quickly understood that the problems of cyclical unemployment could not be solved by union action alone. During depressed periods large groups of unemployed were radicalized and when conditions improved they brought their militant ideology into the organized labor movement.[3] Workers became equally restive during inflationary periods, when real income fell. Socialist and labor parties enjoyed their greatest support during periods of rising prices rather than during periods of recession.

Large sections of British Columbia industry have been prone to conflict and the frontier conditions which obtained in the American Pacific Northwest and Mountain states were equally in evidence across the international boundary. The maritime, mining, longshoring, and lumber industries were plagued by harsh conditions: a high accident rate, geographical and social isolation, a high turnover rate, and unstable family circumstances. The closed nature of many homogeneous single-industry mining communities with no middle-class to mediate industrial conflict, in which class lines were clearly drawn, contributed to the development of an intense working-class consciousness freed from the restraints of traditional conservative institutions like the church, family, and an "enlightened middle class." A significant portion of the west coast labor force has been located in non-urban areas where little contact is maintained with the urban middle classes. Workers in these outlying communities developed an intense group consciousness, a cohesive isolation experienced by miners, loggers, and fishermen who lived and worked on "the periphery of modern society."[4] Many of the employers in these industries tended to be robust newly-risen capitalists intent on extracting as much surplus profit as circumstances would allow. Men like James Dunsmuir, proprietor of a vast industrial empire on Vancouver Island at the turn of the century, were captains of industry untroubled by a conservative ethic of social obligation.

The industrial class struggle in British Columbia has necessarily involved a struggle for political power. The early union of industrial captains and political parties was fruitful and the state was used to create and consolidate company empires which flourished in the frenetic business environment of the mountain province. Many labor leaders quickly realized that what the state granted the state could take away, and they worked to curb business' hold on government by exerting influence within the non-socialist parties through support of "independent" candidates sympathetic to labor's claims. A significant section of the labor movement has, for many decades, by-passed the non-socialist parties and candidates altogether, and channeled the resources of organized labor into support for socialist parties.

In contrast to the labor movement in the coastal province, and to the farmers' movements in the other western provinces, British Columbia agrarians have never paraded a myth of social regeneration and have rarely strayed from the quiet confines of the major non-socialist parties in their search for economic redress.[5] The major struggle in the fractured coastal community, aside from regional disputes of varying intensity, has been the class struggle between worker and capitalist. The British Columbia agrarians have not viewed themselves as an oppressed class and have refrained from importing or creating on their own a social philosophy, or myth of agrarianism, which would articulate their desire for a new golden age of blissful cultivation. Thomas Jefferson, William Jennings Bryan, and Henry Wise Wood have received a cold reception in the sunny orchards of the Okanagan and pretty greenery of Saanich.

In a society as industrialized as British Columbia, the farming class has rightly never seen itself as a majority, or as being synonymous with "the people." Farmers have been reluctant to parade under the banner of "agrarian power" or any other physiocratic slogans. In Alberta and Saskatchewan, the farmers' movements spoke for a large majority of the population and both provinces were governed for years by farmers' parties. The outstanding feature of the class composition of these provinces has been the high number of independent commodity producers which, in Alberta, formed about 48 per cent of the gainfully employed occupations between 1921 and 1941, while in British Columbia the same number in 1941 stood at no more than 13.1 per cent, a figure which declined to 4 per cent in 1961.[6] Independent commodity producers in Alberta continued to outnumber industrial employees and, in 1941, farmers constituted about 45 per cent of the gainfully employed and industrial employees 41 per cent. Since the beginning of the century, industrial workers in British Columbia have greatly exceeded the farmers in number.

An indebted rural peasantry or tenantry, or an impoverished rural proletariat have been traditional seed-beds of discord. British Columbia farmers stress ownership: only 4.1 per cent of the farms were rented in 1961. Approximately 85 per cent of the farm operators in 1961 held the title to their land with 75 per cent of the total number of farms free from mortgages or agreements for sale. British Columbia agriculture resembles in some respects the farm regions of the Maritimes, another area of rural political quiescence, with a large number of farms being on a small scale or part-time. Since farming in British Columbia is still basically a family affair, the wage bill related to gross output is not high and the rural proletariat remains a small inarticulate group.

Farming in British Columbia has been a relatively successful operation and the ample monetary returns cooled whatever ardor agrarians may have had for social reform. Favorable climatic conditions and cost structures have allowed common B.C. farm commodities like fruit, milk, and vegetables to compete successfully in foreign markets, and the internal market for these commodities has been stable. Tree farming and ranching attracted capitalistically oriented farmers, some of whom began operations with substantial investments. Their native conservative sentiments were reinforced by the discipline of occupations that placed a premium on patience and long-term planning.

British Columbia agriculture is highly varied and the great regional and occupational diversity has retarded the development of common rural culture and group consciousness. Unlike Saskatchewan, where farmers were common residents of a great wheat culture, the perceived particular interest of regional rural groups, wedded to a common employment, superseded any generalized conception of the farmers as a class, with a separate class interest. "Strictly speaking," wrote Louis Aubrey Wood in his pioneering study of Canadian farm movements, "the physical characteristics of British Columbia and the diversity of its farm occupations have been, and still are, the main hindrances to an evolution of class-consciousness among its rural dwellers."[7]

There is considerable diversification both within and between the major agricultural areas of the province concentrated in the Peace River, Okanagan, Vancouver Island, and Lower Fraser Valley regions. The Peace River region is the grain basin of the province with over 68 per cent of all acreage devoted to the growing of wheat, oats, and barley. The Okanagan is intensively farmed and highly diversified. In the north, the emphasis is on livestock, cultivated grains, grass, and commercial vegetable and potato growing. From the northern limit to Kelowna the emphasis is on apple production. Specialized crops such as fruit trees and vegetables are grown on the irrigated lands throughout lower Similkameen and the Okanagan valleys. The Okanagan provides for 90 per cent of all fruit production in the province and is a major supplier of hot-weather crops such as tomatoes, peppers, etc. The Lower Fraser Valley is the major vegetable producing area and also the principal center of small fruit production. A wide variety of cereal, fruit, and vegetables are grown on Vancouver Island. Dairy production is scattered in the Okanagan, Lower Fraser Valley, and Vancouver Island regions while beef cattle are raised in the Cariboo region.

The types of farmers that settled and cultivated these agricultural regions varied considerably but they generally shared an ideological and cultural conservatism which effectively prevented any fusion or cooperation between the farm and labor movements. The fruit farmers were described by Lord Grey as "par excellence Nature's Gentlemen," and when radical American unions began to expand in the interior at the beginning of the century, Grey confessed to Laurier that he looked to the fruit growers "to save the situation." Bruce Hutchison, in his *Unknown Country*, described many of the Okanagan farmers as gentlemen Tories living in "cheerful well-groomed towns" and possessed of rich fields and fat cattle. "Here is a refuge . . . here is the true sanctuary of British Columbia. Here is a distinct race of men, basically English, running the largest fruit industry in the British Empire."[8] There settled in the Okanagan, as well as in certain areas of Vancouver Island like Duncan, Victoria, and Saanich, many remittance men and other delinquent colonial offshoots of the British upper class. A. G. Bradley wrote of attractive districts in the Cowichan valley where retired military and naval men, "or what is generically known as the younger son"[9] lived comfortably on small incomes or pensions and casually farmed. The *Week* reported in 1905 a large influx of remittance men whose "real home is in British Columbia which seems to afford them their real resting place."[10] The British influx into British Columbia's agricultural regions had the opposite effect of the migration from the "old country" into urban and industrial areas. The British worker formed the vanguard of coastal trade unionism and provided a ready radical constituency for union organizations in industries like coal mining. Rural areas in the Okanagan and on the Island, on the other hand, provided the gathering place for strange and exotic remnants of the British upper classes.

While the Peace River and Lower Fraser Valley regions contained fewer refined escapees from imperial England, and could even boast of a share of Alberta and Prairie radicals, most residents of these areas remained as conservative as their Okanagan and Island counterparts. "From Chilliwack to the Sea," Bruce Hutchison wrote, "the Fraser's earth has bred the kind of folk who live in the St. Lawrence Valley and are different in their life and in their ownership of land from the cereal farmers who work the open stretches of the prairies . . . these are peasants in the old fashioned and best sense of the term—people who love and cling to the soil, and maintain its virtues, asking no more than the fruits of their labour, but people who enjoy a standard of living high among the farmers of America . . . "[11]

The high standard of living of British Columbia farmers derived not merely from careful cultivation and favorable market conditions. Since the 1920s, the farmers have been accommodated by the major parties and agrarian lobbyists have gained a host of important legislative enactments. Coast farmers have not formed class organizations campaigning under broad slogans of social reform, but they have organized interest groups like the British Columbia Fruit Growers' Association and the Fraser Valley Milk Producers' Association which effectively regulated standards of production and shaped the course of government legislation. A number of premiers—Oliver and Tolmie, for instance—were drawn from the rural classes. The over-representation of the rural interest in the electoral system, a conservative device up to the present day, has assured the presence of vocal spokesmen for the rural interests in the legislature. Traditionally a major voice in the early Liberal and Conservative parties—and today effectively represented by the governing Social Credit party—the farmers have steadfastly refrained from engaging in any futile third party ventures. The province of British Columbia, according to Louis Aubrey Wood, remained until 1917, "entirely outside the sphere of influence of agrarian movements in Canada ... " Both the populist and progressive movements found little favor in rural British Columbia and the few radicals who propagated the faith of Henry Wise Wood and his predecessors could never find a wide and meaningful audience. A few locals of the Grange sparked and sputtered briefly in the years preceding World War I. A more important venture occurred after the war when the United Farmers of British Columbia briefly flirted with a motley and dissident bag of crank Conservatives in the ill-fated Provincial Party, which quickly passed from the provincial scene following its defeat in the 1924 provincial election.

The quixotic and half-hearted Provincial Party venture attested to the essential bankruptcy of British Columbia rural progressivism. Unlike the Prairie Progressives, British Columbia farmers "seemed to see nothing in the nature of party as had developed in the province to account for the conditions against which they were protesting."[12] What the farmer seemed to be campaigning for was a party of "moderately honest people," and the slogan of the Provincial Party, "turn Oliver out and don't let Bowser in," amply testified to the ideological vacuousness of the movement. Third party adventurism failed basically in rural areas because the farmers had been able to wrest substantial gains from the major parties. "Largely because the various agricultural interests," Edith Dobie wrote in her pioneer survey of B.C. parties, "have been organized and reasonably successful in gaining their demands upon the government, third parties have not played so large a part in British Columbia as in the prairie provinces."[13] Premier John Oliver played Mackenzie King to the rural Progressives in the late 1920s. The Oliver government recognized the power of the farmers and devised many policies to aid them. The *Province* reported on August 31, 1929, that "... the legislature has swelled the statute books with enactments for the relief of the farmers."

Today the farm communities receive priority treatment from the Social Credit government. The farmers enjoy, in addition to special land purchasing rights, a variety of fiscal concessions (especially under Property and Income Tax laws), special credit facilities, technical and marketing assistance, certain direct subsidies to agricultural products, and a large number of privileges and priorities not available to other industries. Provincial legislation relating to forest, water, game, trespass, motor vehicles and so on, all provide special privileges to farmers.

Political Culture

British Columbia has long been a fractured community. The major divisions in coast society are class and regional. A religious or racial cleavage, such as exists in Canada as a whole between the English and French, or in the province of Quebec between the two groups, has never taken root in the ethnically polyglot coast community. This is not to suggest that ethnic and religious differences do not exist, or fail to motivate people politically. Party support varies among the different ethnic groups and religious and ethnic questions occasionally bubble to the surface as did the Catholic school question during the historic 1952 election. But class, rather than religious or ethnic identification, seems a greater determinant of political preference, and ethnic and religious issues have not been major political questions dividing the political parties. British Columbia's separation from Canada is not a religious or ethnic difference, and group splits within the province revolve more around regional and economic issues than around ethnic or religious questions. Only one of the two ethnic elements which have divided federal and provincial politics in Canada—the English—is present in any number in British Columbia. The French-Canadians remain a tiny group little different in number and consciousness from other exotic specimens which honeycomb the province.

It is difficult to say which cleavage, class or regional, is more critical in determining the structure of British Columbia politics. Divided as it is into distinct and separate cultural and geographic entities, enjoying different rates of growth and histories, and only slowly brought into greater union through the expansion of the provincial communication system, British Columbia is a society rife with xenophobia, with antagonisms between regions whose residents often rely only on the honeyed words of the party politician or the insular prose of the local press to gain mutual knowledge. The manipulation of regional antagonisms is a prime requisite of any successful coast politician and the Social Credit party have proved themselves experts in this ancient political game. The earliest significant split was between the Island and Mainland and rivalry between the two regions provided ample fuel for politicians in the decades following Confederation. Subsequent population explosions increased the claims of new regions for representation and legislation. British Columbia today displays a high degree of concentration with more than two-thirds of the population crowded into the Lower Mainland region. Although it has made significant inroads into the Lower Mainland region since 1952, an advance which assured its retention of power, the Social Credit party has enjoyed great and consistent support in the rural interior, in the north, and in the metropolitan area of Victoria. The Vancouver area has never been the happiest hunting ground for the governing party.

British Columbia exhibits a high degree of nodality and the conflict between the center and the periphery is a nagging fact all politicians have to take into account. Metro Vancouver, the central place of the economy, exists in a state of symbiotic tension with the hinterland. The city of Vancouver is the administrative center of the provincial economy, the locale of the regional head offices of the leading business firms and financial institutions. Here too are concentrated the major auxiliary service industries and distribution facilities. The port and major overland transportation routes all radiate from the metro area. Whatever its role as a provider of services for the producers of the interior, Vancouver is often seen by the plain folks in non-urban areas as a threatening parasite, rather than a symbiotic partner, and politicians like Phil Gaglardi were careful to preserve this view.

Regional and class divisions have both contributed to the persistence of a tenuous community in British Columbia whose residents share little else than the vague conviction that coast society is somehow different, and better endowed than the rest of the country. Otherwise there are few effective bonds tying estranged groups into greater communion. An important factor guaranteeing the persistence of the tenuous community is the high immigration rate. In 1961 more than half of the local residents were born outside the province. Existing at the periphery of the western frontier, British Columbia has served as a magnet for persons discontented with their lot, personally, economically, and politically. Being a high income region, the province is an obvious attraction for fortune seekers and for ordinary people seeking a modest improvement of their standard of living.

British Columbia provides a safe home for the acquisitive spirit. From the days of Captain Vancouver when the white men came and traded utensils for otter with the Indians, to the 1850s when the province was flooded with "off-scour-rings of the world" in search of gold, up to recent years when rustic buccaneers like Ben Ginter built strange empires in the northern wilderness, the province has provided a haven for fortune seekers, boodle hunters, and promoters with questionable pasts and devious ways. Poets and plunderers have sung hymns of praise to the beauty and fleshly delights of the pacific land and celebrated the opportunity for every man there to become a king. While many perished in the uncertain hunt for the golden calf, and still more languished in a state of proletarian torpor from which they had tried desperately to escape, not a few became rustic capitalists who wielded their new power with the brash abandon of the parvenue. "Hobos in evening clothes," Joseph Martin described a motley gang of businessmen in Rossland, the early Johannesburg of British Columbia.

It is a common view that buccaneer capitalists, striving in a competitive state of nature, prefer that state which governs least. Capitalists have traditionally warned of the danger of state intervention, but the action they have decried is the sort that redistributes opportunities and incomes in favor of the lower classes. Intervention that guarantees further opportunities and greater incomes for the upper classes has never met with much opposition but, on the contrary, has enjoyed considerable favor in Canada as a whole and in British Columbia in particular. Neither God, nor the exceptional financial or industrial talents of particular individuals who claim to be favored by God, created the great bulk of corporate wealth in British Columbia. It arose instead from the monopolistic advantages conferred by governments on favored persons through mineral grants, forest management licences, utility franchises, land grants, public contracts and so on.[14]

The British Columbia government has been the grantor and regulator of the greatest material prizes this economy has to offer and businessmen have striven, in large measure successfully, to influence governments as a prelude to capturing economic resources. From the earliest days of the province, they went about the task of buying governments with the same audacity displayed in purchasing lands or floating companies. Without a friendly government, Oriental labor could not be imported at lower wage rates, unions could not be easily combatted, or timber licences and railway charters gained in ample number. "The people will always accept a railroad," commented one knowing local observer at the turn of the century, "if it is vigorously thrust down their throats." Corporate investment in politics has always yielded ample returns.

The political intervention of corporate business, with the resultant buying and selling of politicians, early debased the level of political morality in coast politics. In British Columbia, there is a curious tension between the inherited British ideal of constitutional and representative government operating through a parliamentary system, and a furious commerce intent on creating its own rules and rendering the political system subservient to its goals; a conflict perceived early by observers like Frances MacNab, who in his *Handbook for Settlers*, attributed the coast's acquisitive spirit to the presence of American speculators. MacNab noted that while British Columbia was part of the empire of Great Britain, the province was similar to parts of the southern United States or California "... inasmuch as there is a sudden enormous increase of wealth in a country whose constitution is scarcely hatched, whose system of administration is half-fledged, and whose laws have to be framed without the light of previous experience."[15] MacNab felt that the experience of older states like Britain could not "offer much assistance in solving the political and economic problems relating to a highly advanced commerce which invariably shows a determination of establishing and creating a code for itself."[16]

The code dictated by the furious commerce, which shaped political institutions in its own image, was not a pretty one, and British Columbia is possessed of a politics as corrupt as any in the country. Since the inception of self-government, scarcely an administration has survived without a serious financial scandal and British Columbians have become so accustomed to scandal during good times that the fate of governments seems unaffected by the financial misdemeanors of its ministers. W. A. C. Bennett's Social Credit government survived a number of serious scandals, until its defeat in 1972, on issues other than political morality.

In 1958, Robert E. Sommers, former Minister of Lands, was convicted and sent to prison for being part of a conspiracy to accept bribes while serving as a minister of the Crown. The Sommers scandal had received full publicity for over two years, yet a by-election held in Sommers' Trail constituency soon after his conviction was easily won by Socred Donald Brothers, a lawyer who had managed Sommers' campaigns.[17]

British Columbians are tolerant of corruption in prosperous times. During depression periods, however, the masses wax restive. The apprehensions of the working class were aroused early in the province's political history and socialism as a political philosophy and movement became a strong indigenous force at the very onset of industrialism. To the poets and plunderers, British Columbia is a province of promise, but to many who tasted the familiar fruits of exploitation and unemployment, it became a province of disappointment. Two philosophies and value systems exist in opposition within the coast society and are reflected in the party system. An acquisitive individualism, which advertises a dynamic approach to the development of natural resources through private enterprise is opposed by a strong collectivism, engrained in the strong trade union and socialist movements, who maintain that private enterprise tends to exploit resources, human and material, wastefully and immorally. The opposed philosophies are represented in the major political parties: the Social Credit Party, imbued with the religion of growth, and the New Democratic Party, taken with the values of collectivism. The parties, of course, are not nearly as polarized as their ideologues insist. Social Credit, if only for pragmatic electoral reasons, lives comfortably with the welfare state while the N.D.P. searching for the center vote, has admitted, in word and deed, the viability of the mixed economy.

In the elusive search for votes, Social Credit has so far been the more effective competitor. The Socreds have successfully advertised and sold the ideal of stable government in a society divided by regional and class loyalties, where a multitude of parties have flourished in a changeful climate. Stable government, in British Columbia, implies strong executive leadership described by some as a legacy from Britain, where deferential norms in the social system reinforce strong leadership in the political system reflected in the legitimacy of cabinet government. But, in British Columbia, it is more likely due to the effects of an acquisitive frontier culture. Action not deliberation, results and not methods, are important in a society where the British respect for parliamentary form has been undermined by the frontier's thrust to possess and hold no matter what. Not the freedom of the masses to deliberate or dictate, but the liberty of the political and economic elite to act and get results is respected by people concerned with achievement to the exclusion of rights. Over the years of Socred rule, the opposition and the press caused little stir among the electors when they ranted about government by Order-in-Council, a weak legislative committee system, the absence of a Hansard, and truncated legislative sessions. Like the corporate elite, the political lieutenants get things done and place little value on accountability to a deliberative assembly.

Finally, the stable government ideal in British Columbia, where socialism is a bogey as well as a movement, promises a favorable investment climate. Majority, free-enterprise government ensures the expansion of new investment frontiers, and the perpetuation of a legal environment favorable to corporate business. Both public order and the good life depend upon the pacification of the wants of all classes which, the free enterprise elite maintains, can be achieved through the free flow of capital into the province, providing employment and high wages for the workers as well as profits for the employers. The proper function of a stable government is to protect property, facilitate the investment flow through grants of timber and mining rights, ensure a "reasonable" tax structure and restrict and control unions as much as possible.

In the eyes of the governing business elite, socialist politicians and labor leaders have been ardent proponents of instability. Equally obstructive has been the federal government, which has served as a favorite whipping boy of provincial politicians. By doing battle with the federal authorities, the Socreds and their predecessors prey on and activate regional sentiments and deflect internally divisive sentiments on to an external enemy. The community created is an artificial community, a unity that exists only in opposition to the federal government. The community is tenuous because regional sentiments in British Columbia are not, as in Quebec, passionately held. British Columbia has a distinct society, history, and political tradition, and it has a unique ethos. But British Columbians are not ardent anti-federalists and anti-nationalists. Their separatist sentiments are not reinforced by ethnic, religious, or national differences. Quebeckers see themselves as a nation, a conquered nation, and French Canadians are concerned with the preservation of their language and culture. British Columbia is an ethnic hodgepodge with a majority of the contemporary population born outside of the province. When claims are pressed on the federal authorities, they are couched in material rather than cultural or nationalist terms. British Columbia wants "better terms" and a fair deal, rather than an opportunity to develop its cultural personality. Being more regional than cultural, coast separatist sentiments are only mildly held, but they have been prone to effective manipulation by resourceful premiers who, in arduously tilting at federal windmills, pre-empt feelings of regional patriotism and isolate opposition groups as alien apologists of a hostile external authority.[18]

Historical Development

From 1856 until the entry of British Columbia into Confederation, British Columbia was ruled by a governor and legislative council not responsible to an elected legislative assembly. But the 14th article of the Terms of Union pledged the Dominion to the establishment of a system of responsible government and the Constitution Act of 1871 provided for the creation of an assembly of 25 to be elected by a system of oral nominations and open voting.

The achievement of responsible government in British Columbia did not usher in an age of mass democracy. The legislature, in the decades following B.C.'s entry into Confederation, was composed largely of acquisitive merchants, lawyers, industrial and landed proprietors, whose wealth derived chiefly from investment in land, transportation, mines, lumbering, salmon canneries, and flour mills. The ruling dynasties busied themselves with fighting the federal government over railway and other matters, distributing timber and mining rights, and issuing railway charters to friends, or friends of friends. Sectional splits, between island and mainland, were salient until the turn of the century.

Federal and provincial politics were pursued along different trails and under different labels. "All British Columbia asks is justice," wrote the *Daily British Colonist* in 1876. "She seeks alliance with neither political party in the East . . ."[19] Members of parliament were local lobbyists who attached themselves to the federal bandwagon and received the patronage necessary to assure their further election. Since the Dominion government, with the exception of the Mackenzie interlude, was Conservative, the bulk of M.P.s were Conservative. So were most of the provincial cabinet ministers, despite the absence and perceived irrelevance of party labels. Provincial elections were not fought on party lines with federal labels, although federal legislators participated in local elections. Although all government majorities and cabinets had a preponderance of Conservatives, so did the opposition groups. Federal Liberals could also be found scattered among both the government and opposition supporters. Mr. J. P. Booth, a strong federal Liberal, was a supporter of the provincial government throughout the 1890s. The leading oppositionists during the same period, Messrs. Beaven, Semlin and Cotton, were federal Conservatives, although they counted among their supporters a number of Liberals. Provincial Liberal sentiment increased with the Laurier victory of 1896, when for the first time since the province's entry into Confederation, British Columbia returned a contingent to the House of Commons predominately Liberal in complexion.[20]

British Columbia appeared to survive nicely without firm party lines and federal labels in provincial elections up to the year 1898, when the Turner government failed to return with a majority. During the next five years, a succession of legislative turnovers and weak regimes threatened the viability of the old system of "group government" and "composite cabinets" and contributed to the emergence of the "party line movement" among Liberals and Conservatives who constituted themselves in separate federal and provincial associations and abandoned the principle of composite government. The shift towards partyism was a response to rapid industrial growth which exerted unbearable pressures on the informal system of group alignments. As population poured into new areas opened by the railways, the province became balkanized, the forces for political cohesion weakened, and the need for discipline and executive control increased. "Conditions in this province," a local Liberal wrote to Laurier, "are not and have not been favorable to the development of a party leader. Our population is divided into a number of communities, more or less isolated, and there is almost none of that daily intercourse between the various sections, which is possible in the more compactly settled sections of the East. Hence it is that the man who is looked upon as a leader in one section, sees no reason why he should concede why some other man in some other section should be his leader, and as yet no one has displayed the qualifications which command support from all sections."[21] During the late 90s, the province suffered from the blight of localism. Elected representatives acted as sponsors for interested industrial promotors and maintained intensely local affiliations. Governments were loose coalitions of interested M.L.A.s whose loyalties to party and principle were secondary to their commitment to local interests. So long as governments changed in kaleidoscopic fashion and House members crossed the floor at whim, industrial promoters, whether in the mining, railway, fishing or lumber industries, were reluctant to invest for fear of changed conditions. Railway contracts were made and unmade, mining laws passed and altered. Investments could not be planned and undertaken where the legal environment was not predictable. The proponents of B.C.'s new party line politics in the early years of the 20th century, were determined to "make the land one which the British and Canadian investor could come to with a surety that his undertaking would not be crippled by quibbling legislative enactment or his enterprise hampered by injurious imposts."[22] The primary function of government, in the eyes of businessmen and politicians, was to protect private property and provide a stable investment climate; and the primary issue in British Columbia politics became, as the *Colonist* reported in 1902, "stable government against the forces of disorder." The growth of a radical and articulate labor movement, whose political spokesmen flourished in a fluid legislature of contesting groups, contributed to the need for a system of disciplined parties campaigning under familiar and standardized labels. The proposal to firm up party lines and introduce federal labels in provincial elections, the

Canadian Annual Review reported in 1901, was favored by both Liberals and Conservatives as a means of escaping from a powerful conflict along labor union and anti-labor union lines.

Richard McBride's Conservative victory in 1903 began a period of Tory ascendancy that lasted until the 1916 provincial election. Under the premier's strong leadership, the Tories became the party that guaranteed stability and growth through the encouragement of railway development, Asiatic exclusion, timber alienation, and better terms for British Columbia through the application of methodical "Fight Ottawa" policy. The majority was steadily increased in all provincial elections preceding World War I. Briefly dependent upon the support of the two Socialist M.L.A.s, Parker Williams and J. H. Hawthornthwaite, following the 1903 election, the Tories were able to gain an absolute majority in the 1907 election in which 27 Conservative members were returned. In the 1909 election McBride swept back into power with a large majority in a campaign that witnessed the defeat of all opposition members save two Liberals and two Socialists. Liberal representation was reduced to nil in the 1912 provincial election, but the Tory ascendancy was rudely halted in the provincial election of 1916. The resignation of Premier McBride, his succession by the heavy-handed W. J. Bowser, the recession of 1913-1915, which resulted in a high rate of unemployment and acute industrial failures, and the new winds of progressive reform focusing on the issues of women's suffrage, temperance, and honest government, conspired to bring down the Conservatives.

The 1916 election was important not merely because it ended Conservative rule, but because the Liberals, who organized and channeled the new urban progressive forces, gained a majority and formed a government in a legislature in which they had had no representation since the preceding election. The Socialist Party of Canada, whose two representatives formed His Majesty's Loyal Opposition following the 1912 election, had missed a golden opportunity to firmly establish itself as a replacement for either of the major parties. Observers like Ramsay Macdonald, who visited the coast province in the years before the outbreak of the War, were convinced that conditions were then ripe for the Socialists to gain power. But internal divisions within the Socialist party, aggravated by the party's sectarianism, the increasing alienation of the Socialist elite from organized labor, together with the virulent anti-labor and Socialist scare campaigns launched by the press on behalf of the political and economic elites, ensured that the Liberals, who effectively reorganized after the 1912 debacle, channeled the rising tide of protest against the Conservative party along moderate and gradualist lines. The 1916 election witnessed the rejuvenation of the British Columbia Liberal party, which elected 37 members to the provincial legislature as compared to only 10 by the prostrate Conservatives.[23]

The resurgence of the Liberal party was not, however, complete enough to destroy the protest vote, which was strong in the years preceding the war and revived with the return to normalcy following the end of hostilities. The Liberals won 26 of the 47 seats in the election of 1920 but the Tories raised their total to 14 and Labour elected four candidates. The protest vote in the 1924 election, which exceeded 35 per cent of the total ballots cast, was split between Labour and Socialists on the one hand, and the curious Progressive-Conservative alliance known as the Provincial Party on the other. The Provincial Party resulted from a temporary alliance of dissident Conservatives who resented the re-election of W. J. Bowser as leader at the 1922 provincial convention, a smattering of Tory farmers who felt that rural interests were being neglected by both major parties, and dissatisfied businessmen and millionaires like General A. D. McRae who bellowed about corruption and "injected a shot of gold cure" into the infant party to ensure its survival for at least one election. Provincial Party supporters believed that "there was an underground sewer connecting the two old parties," and campaigned earnestly for "honest and economical government" by a party free of any unsavory ties with the corrupt federal parties. Although only three candidates were elected, the Provincial Party gained 24 per cent of the popular vote and achieved the short-run objective of keeping Oliver out and not letting Bowser in. The defeat of both major party leaders and the high protest vote testified to the extent of the electoral cynicism in postwar years. The CCF explosion in the following decade, and the Social Credit rise 20 years later, both stemmed from a similar disillusionment with the prevailing structure of partisan politics by alienated social groups both left and right.

The ascendancy of the Conservative liberalism of John Oliver ended in the 1928 provincial election. By then, the Provincial Party had quietly expired and the Conservatives had temporarily laid aside their daggers to elect Simon Fraser Tolmie as party leader. Tolmie led the Tories to victory against the Liberals headed by John Duncan MacLean, who as a successor to Oliver after the 1927 convention, failed to kindle any enthusiasm among electors for policies basically similar to those of the former premier.

The Liberal defeat in the election preceding the Depression was a godsend because the Tories were left holding the reins of government at a time of serious social dislocation. The Tolmie government proved unable to meet the challenge of unemployment and falling prices and when election day approached in 1933 the Conservatives were in the worst condition they had ever been in. Faced with a great clamor for reform, but possessed of few ideological tools or policies to mend the social fabric, the Conservative party faced the election as an amorphous and dissident mass rather than as a cohesive and purposeful organization. The provincial executive of the Conservative association decided, to take no official part in the impending election campaign, allowing the local associations to fight the election under an assortment of odd labels.[24]

The desolate state of the Tories made things easy for the rejuvenated Liberals, now led by the able and urbane T. D. Pattullo, who campaigned on a reform new deal program of "work and wages" which promised a new social order through progressive labor legislation, social welfare supports, increased aid to municipalities, state health insurance, a public utilities commission, and an economic council which promised to mobilize expertise to the cause of social reform. The Premier described his program as "practical idealism" as opposed to the visionary socialism of the resurrected Socialist Party.

The 1933 election was a watershed because it resulted in the elevation of a socialist party to major status, a new position briefly relinquished in the subsequent election, but thereafter maintained up to the present day. The major fight in the campaign was not between Grits and Conservatives, who were politically bankrupt, but between the Liberals and the CCF, which broadened and deepened its base in the early depression years.

Because an institutionalized left had existed in the decades preceding the Depression, the new task of reconstruction was easily accomplished. At the outset, the Socialist Party of Canada was the sole party affiliate of the new CCF, but the Reconstruction Party, which grew out of the League for Social Reconstruction, a middle-class radical group, soon became a second party affiliate. The Reconstruction Party combined in August 1933 with the various unaffiliated CCF clubs organized by an energetic doctor named Lyle Telford to form the Associated CCF Clubs of B.C. These, in turn, merged with the Socialist Party of Canada two years later to form the CCF. The 1933 election was conducted under various labels by the socialist candidates, who won seven seats and 31.5 per cent of the popular vote.

Pattullo liberalism survived, with varying success, until after the provincial election of 1941. The reform ardor of the new regime cooled with experience in office and as opposition to the progressive reforms of people like George Pearson and George Weir increased within the legislative caucus. The Liberals were returned with 31 seats in the 1937 election and the Tories, who sheathed their knives at their 1936 convention long enough to elect Dr. F. P. Patterson as party leader, replaced the CCF as the second largest party in the legislature by winning eight seats to the Socialists' seven. The drop in CCF support was facilitated by a serious schism within the party at the 1936 provincial convention, which adopted a radical program in opposition to party leader Robert Connell, an Anglican minister and Victorian gentleman who inadvertently stumbled into a party dominated by proletarian Marxists. Connell, together with three other M.L.A.s, left the CCF and created their own party, the Social Constructives, which was supposed to be true to the principles of the Regina Manifesto, betrayed, the Constructives claimed, by sinister Communists within the CCF.

The brief Tory advantage over the CCF ended in the election of 1941, a fateful contest which resulted in the union of the old parties in opposition to the growing socialist threat. Pattullo liberalism began to falter badly after the 1937 election and the reform vigor needed to command a society in ferment slowly dissipated. The abandonment of relief payments to unemployed single men, the failure to implement the comprehensive medical insurance scheme long advocated by progressive Liberals, and the ineffective fight with oil companies over rising gasoline prices, were evidence that the "practical idealism" dramatized by the slogan "work and wages" had somewhere faded in the long trek through the hard Depression. Liberal representation was reduced from 31 to 21 in the 1941 election, the Tories increased their support to 12, and the CCF, with restored party unity, elected 14 representatives and gained 33 per cent of the popular vote. Faced once again with the socialist threat, businessmen and politicians within both old parties began to pressure for a coalition to ensure stable majority government. The coalition idea was heatedly opposed by Pattullo, a curious constitutional Grit whose hatred of the Conservatives exceeded any fear of the CCF. Pattullo felt that the CCF was a party of well-meaning idealists that could be effectively checked by a progressive center party. But Pattullo lost the fight and resigned after the Liberal convention of December 1941, which supported the principle of coalition with the Tories. Foremost in the minds of the coalitionists was the task of avoiding a quick election, contested by three parties, which the CCF could win. The Liberals needed Tory support to stay in power but the price of support was cabinet representation. When John Hart assumed the premiership in December 1941, one of his first tasks was to find a place for his Conservative colleagues.

The coalition arrangement worked admirably in the next two elections and the CCF found itself engaged in two-party contests in constituencies with strong socialist support.[25] The CCF won only 10 seats in the 1945 election but would probably have attained power had it not been for the coalition arrangement. In 21 of the 48 electoral districts, CCF candidates received between 40 and 50 per cent of the vote; a percentage high enough to win in most three-way election contests.

The coalition device was equally effective in the 1949 election, which witnessed a diminution in CCF representation and popular support. The election contributed to the development of a defeatist mentality that often characterizes parties that have been political bridesmaids too long. Once again, a coalition platform was constructed, a collective war chest gathered, joint nominations effected in dual ridings, and saw-offs arranged in single-member ridings, with one or the other party organization performing the nomination function.

But the very success of the coalition arrangement contributed to its abandonment before the fateful 1952 election. The CCF dragon began to appear less awesome than in older days and the temptation to go it alone correspondingly increased among politicians who still thought jealously in partisan terms. The coalition was constructed and made workable by John Hart and R. J. Maitland, but when Maitland died in 1946 and Hart resigned a year later, two new leaders were chosen—Herbert Anscomb by the Conservatives and Byron Johnson by the Liberals—who were considerably less enamored of the coalition. The Tories complained of too few cabinet posts and were incensed at the retention of the coveted Attorney-General portfolio by the hated Gordon Wismer. They were equally upset by the pressure to move left by the Liberals who sought to take the wind out of the socialists' sails by instituting a hospital insurance scheme. As it turned out, the scheme was badly maladministered and the principle of comprehensive free coverage quickly abandoned. Federal Liberals and Conservatives were never very happy with the coalition and their persistent opposition began to meet with results after the 1949 election. Matters were aggravated in 1945 and 1949 when federal and provincial elections were held in the same year and, in the case of 1949, practically at the same time. Federal candidates were upset when they discovered their local association had lapsed in ridings controlled in provincial elections by the other party.

Few in British Columbia were surprised, therefore, when Byron Johnson dissolved the coalition by firing Tory leader Herbert Anscomb as Minister of Finance in January 1952. Facing the prospects of an election replete, once again, with three-party contests, Liberal and Conservative politicians were fearful of a CCF victory through a split in the free enterprise vote; an apprehension that was a major determinant of the formation of the coalition in the first place. The coalition politicians wanted both a dissolution of the partnership and a CCF defeat in the impending election and were convinced that this could be achieved by the institution of a system of alternative voting. During the 1951 legislative session, amendments were made to the Provincial Elections Act providing for the replacement of the old simple majority type by a system of preferential voting known as the alternative vote. Their expectations were clear and simple. The CCF would be able to gain an absolute majority on the first ballot in only a few constituencies. The electorate, enamored of free enterprise, would deny the socialists second preferences. Grits would specify Tories as a second choice and Tories would specify Grits as their second preference. The CCF would be robbed of victory by the miraculous workings of the new voting system. "Without the alternative vote," declared Attorney-General Wismer, "it would have been possible for one party which wanted to upset our whole system to have become the government on a minority vote."

The coalitionists were partly correct. The CCF was unable to beat the system and remained the major opposition party with 18 seats and

34.3 per cent of the popular vote. But both the Liberals and Conservatives suffered crushing defeats: the Liberals gained 6 seats and 23.5 per cent of the vote and Conservatives won 4 seats and 9 per cent of the vote, a meager total which they barely exceeded in subsequent elections. The victor was the strange new Social Credit party, which elected 19 candidates and proceeded to form the government.[26]

The rise of the Social Credit party to power is a simple tale of persverance and luck. Before 1950, Social Credit remained an inconsequential movement with a tiny following. Although all provincial elections since 1937 were contested by Social Credit nominees of sorts, few candidates gained sufficient votes to save their deposits. The new movement underwent numerous schisms until taken in hand by Lyle Wicks, an ex-railway conductor who perceived that the political vacuum foreseen by T. D. Pattullo was imminent. Wicks and others streamlined the party during the late 40s, excommunicated many of the cranks and troublemakers, and rid the platform of the extremist planks abandoned by the Alberta Social Credit party decades earlier. With the coalition floundering and the electorate still fearful of the Socialist bogey, a golden opportunity presented itself to the new band of reformers. Funds and personnel were sent into the province from Alberta and a successful expansion drive was launched in 1951 in rural areas that counted a high percentage of Alberta emigrants. Devoid of practical political experience, the new movement welcomed, though reluctantly, two dissident M.L.A.s, Tilly Rolston and W.A.C. Bennett, who were only recently converted to the new cause. Bennett, who quarrelled with his Tory party rulers over many issues, had crossed the floor and sat as an Independent in 1951 after unsuccessfully contesting the Conservative Party leadership twice. He rightly perceived the opportunity presented by the new movement.

Social Credit's accession to power was derived less from economic discontent than from political disillusionment due to the constant bickering over patronage questions; the unsavory ties with liquor and other interests openly maintained by Anscomb, Wismer, and others; the bungled hospital insurance scheme; the stalled Pacific Great Eastern railroad enterprise; the ineffective Labour Relations Act; and the credibility of politicians who hurled knives at one another after reclining in an amorous embrace for over a decade. The new party of Christian purity found ready support among the many disillusioned with the old parties but frightened of the CCF.

The mechanics of the alternative voting system favored the Socred parvenus. Liberal and Conservative mutual hostilities were so great that in many constituencies, the second choices of free enterprise voters went to Social Credit candidates instead of to those of the former coalition partners. The Socreds also picked up ancillary support in several key constituencies from CCF voters whose dislike of the coalition party far exceeded any mistrust of the unfamiliar new group which, after all, was opposed to the old politics. The net effect of the ballot system was to channel socialist and free enterprise resentments against the old parties into support for the newcomers. The surprise and disillusionment of the Liberals and Tories, whose best laid plans had gone awry, were matched only by the wild elation of the motley bag of merchants, ministers, salesmen, and real estate agents who made their way into the legislature. The Social Credit party had fought the campaign without an official leader: Ernest Hansell, an Alberta M.P. and president of the National Social Credit League acted as the temporary campaign leader. They had gone to the public on a platform thrust upon them, and accepted without debate, by the Alberta movement which managed, like a marionette show, the entire party convention of April 1952. But the new M.L.A.s, practised in the art of small business, were now faced with the serious task of running a large enterprise. They turned to the successful hardware merchant and experienced Tory politico W.A.C. Bennett for guidance. Bennett accepted the invitation and earnestly applied himself to the hard business of retaining power.

The Contemporary System

The realignment of the provincial party system, begun in the 1952 election, was completed the following year. The Bennett minority government pursued a strategy of early dissolution, courting defeat in order to capitalize on the prevailing public yearning for political stability. Social Credit strategists hoped to appeal early for a majority government in order to "get things done." "Social Credit," *Maclean's Magazine* reported, "has one clear advantage, the average voter's desire for a stable government. No one, not even the Liberal and Conservatives themselves, will go so far as to predict a Liberal or Conservative victory. Therefore, the only non-Socialist government with any hope of a majority is the present Social Credit government."[27] The budget was not yet through and some 80 bills hung in suspension when the government was defeated on a bill involving the so-called "Rolston formula" providing for a new system of school finance. Bennett's calculations proved correct and both Liberals and Conservatives were decimated by the new free enterprisers in the election that followed. The Social Credit majority was increased to 28, Liberal representation fell to four, while the Tories obtained one seat. The CCF representation stood at 14. The alternative ballot system again worked in favor of the Social Credit party. Many CCF electors, shocked by the twisted results of the previous contest, mended their ways and either plumped on their second choice or cast votes for the Liberals. But the movement of supporters away from the traditional free enterprise parties, begun in the 1952 contest, became a landslide. Both Grit and Tory voters rushed to vote for the Social Credit candidates. The new system was wisely abandoned by the Social Credit party in favor of the simple majority system in time for the 1956 election.

What emerged in the early 1950s was a party system different in structure and composition from any in the country. British Columbia was the only province in which the two federal minor parties became major parties in the legislature. Some preferred to label the new system, a protest party system. But this designation is far from accurate. The strange band of protesters campaigning under a vague platform imported and swallowed whole in 1952 soon became a conservative party although, admittedly, an unorthodox one, and the traditional balance of the party system between left and right was preserved. According to W.A.C. Bennett, what occurred in British Columbia in the mid-1950s was a "return to the two party system . . . a Socialist party on the one hand and our Social Credit free enterprise party on the other."[28]

The Social Credit explosion in British Columbia bore some similarities to the earlier one in Alberta. Both movements grew rapidly in the period immediately preceding their advent, both exploited mass sentiments of disillusionment with politics, both contained significant elements, though in different proportions, of religious zealots who sought to purify the fetid political world. But the differences between the two movements exceeded their similarities. Social Credit in Alberta was born in the Depression and purported, in its protest phase, to provide a populist Utopian answer to the extreme deprivations people were experiencing. Although power had a sobering effect on Social Credit governors, the Alberta party, from the top down, contained a good sprinkling of monetary fetishists who believed that all social and economic ills could be solved through adjustments in the monetary system, just as some wayward chiropractors are convinced that most human body ills can best be treated through manipulation of the spinal column. The Alberta party became a prosperity party only after the Depression and the happy discovery of oil which transformed Alberta into an affluent province. The chiliastic strain in the Alberta movement, expressed through the charismatic person of Aberhart, was powerful and the party in its early phases was a political emanation of a personal religious movement built up by Aberhart through his church radio broadcasts.

The British Columbia movement, despite its mushroom growth, was more politically orthodox than its Alberta counterpart. The party came to power during a period of relative prosperity and received support from groups in both rural and urban areas free from severe economic stress. Bennett was not a charismatic messiah born to free the masses from economic slavery. Economic renovation, though of a different variety, was the exclusive province of the CCF, which had advocated socialist ideas for decades. Coming to power almost two decades after the Alberta group, British Columbia's Social Crediters and their supporters were well aware of the conservative effects of power and responsibility on the Alberta government. The 1952 platform, handed down from Alberta, talked about voluntary hospital insurance, old-age pensions, better tax rental arrangements and a "pay as you go" policy in provincial expenditures, but there was nothing said about revamping the financial system or instituting a technocratic system of government by experts. Alberta was cited in the 1952 campaign and beyond, not as a reform Utopia, but as an affluent, well-run, and debt-free province; the model of a well-run business enterprise but hardly the petty bourgeois paradise conjured up by Major Douglas. British Columbia Social Credit triumphed despite the absence of a charismatic leader like Aberhart who exploited the feelings of despair in a society of scarcity and unemployment. Ernest Hansell lent a certain religious flair to the 1952 campaign, but after the election he left the provincial party and government to W.A.C. Bennett, a recent party supporter ignorant of Major Douglas' theories, who had distributed hardware rather than grace most of his life. "I make you only one promise," Bennett informed the electors before the 1953 election, "if you vote Social Credit, we will give you good government."[29] Finally, British Columbia Social Credit was not a religious movement and the fundamentalist strain in the party, still present today, is much less accented than in the Alberta party. "Social Credit was regarded by Mr. Aberhart as a way of life," Ernest Hansell told the farmers in Vernon in May 1952, "it is a subject involving the destiny of the human race."[30] But to the many thousands of Liberals and Conservatives who cast their votes for the new party, and to W.A.C. Bennett, who lived most of his life as a Conservative, the new party was merely a vehicle for attaining power and for keeping the CCF out in the cold.

It is true, however, that the fundamentalist strain was present at the time of the party's accession to power, and still provides residual gloss today. Party conventions are opened with hymns, and candidates are careful to present Social Credit as a Christian party, especially in sectarian constituencies like Chilliwack where religious feelings are strong. "I don't know as much about your party as I should," Tilly Rolston told a nominating convention in 1952, "but I believe in a return to honest Christian principles in government."[31] The Christian orientation of the Social Credit party is sharply contrasted by party zealots with the alleged atheism of the NDP. Despite the subsidence of the wave of religiosity which spilled into the interior in 1952 at the behest of Alberta sorcerers like Hansell, Social Credit continued to receive strong support in areas with a high representation of sectarian religionists and recruited a small and dwindling section of its elite from the fundamentalist clergy. Included among the group of 1952 swept into the legislative assembly were three fundamentalist preachers: Reverend Charles W. Parker

(Church of Nazarene), and Reverends H. D. Frances and P. Gaglardi (Pentacostal Assemblies). About one-third of the caucus of 19 elected members was affiliated with fundamentalist sects: four were Baptist M.L.A.s and two were affiliates of the Holiness movement. By 1955, fundamentalist representation in the caucus was restricted to two members of the Pentacostal Assemblies and one Full Gospel member. There were no Baptist M.L.A.s. A study made of clergymen in the Vancouver area in 1959 revealed that ministers affiliated with the smaller denominations preferred Social Credit to the other major parties.[32] Electoral support remains high for Social Credit in areas like Chilliwack, Langley, and the Cariboo, with their relatively high proportion of religious sectarians. But the religious element was never as predominant in the caucus as in Alberta, where the high priest Aberhart was succeeded as party leader by his charismatic apprentice Manning, the first graduate of Aberhart's Prophetic Bible Institute. Much of the Alberta leadership cadre was recruited from fundamentalist ministers and lay preachers. As late as 1965, seven Alberta M.L.A.s could be counted as members of radical sects (Evangelical Free Church, Christian Science, Latter Day Saints), while another seven were of Baptist persuasion. The predominant part of the British Columbia Social Credit caucus is affiliated with the Anglican and United Churches and the movement represents, both in terms of elite recruitment and electoral support, a coalition of the former Anglican elements, United Church supporters, and the rising fundamentalist sects.

But religion is not a major factor in British Columbia politics. Religious affiliations are not as determining of a political preference as in other parts of the country and religious issues have rarely provided the stuff and substance of political debate. A more important element is economic position which is a key determinant of voting in British Columbia as in Ontario, two regions where class voting, according to Alford and others, has been among the highest in the country.

There have been current in British Columbia three theories about Social Credit's relation to the class system: one advertised by Socred elite, the second finding favor among liberal critics of the governing party, and the third held by the traditional socialist opposition. According to the Bennetts, and their principle colleagues, Social Credit is not a class party but a people's party. Like the United Nations, the party draws support from many and diverse groups and walks of life and, like the good King Solomon, the government dispenses justice and favors in fair proportion to all sections of the realm. In the eyes of the Bennetts, the opposition parties are exclusive class parties; only Social Credit is an inclusive party that represents and cares for the masses as opposed to the classes. "The aim of the Social Credit government," W.A.C. Bennett stated in the 1953 campaign, "is to enlist the united support of British Columbians who believe in a free way of life, and we will oppose equally as strongly the forces of monopoly and the forces of socialism."[33] Past Liberal critics of the governing party, confused and dazzled by Social Credit's sometimes idiosyncratic style, prefer to define Social Credit not as a political and legislative coalition which represents different groups and balances one interest against the other, but as an unpredictable band of latter-day Poujadists and political nihilists who have no purpose in mind except to retain power and do so by cynically waging war on all established elites whether of the left or right. The Socialist critique abjures both views and defines Social Credit in a more traditional way as primarily a spokesman and representative of the established economic elites, both within and without the province.

The Bennett claim for Social Credit must be taken with more than a few grains of salt. Without a reasonable spread of regional class support, Social Credit would not, of course, have retained power as long as it has. A primary base of party support, from the very onset of the growing movement in 1950 until the present day, has been the rural constituencies. Conservative farmers and small businessmen have rarely deserted the Socreds and the party counts its greatest strongholds in rural areas, retaining strong support in the towns as well as in the ranching and farming areas of regions in the interior. Chilliwack, Cariboo, the Fraser Valley, North and South Okanagan, and North and South Peace River, form traditional bastions of Social Credit support. These areas, since the Social Credit explosion, have never been centers of acute rural unrest.

High Social Credit representation in non-urban strongholds has been aided by a persistent discrepancy in constituency sizes. Rural and sparsely populated interior areas like North and South Peace River have been over-represented in the legislature; the Lower Mainland area, with over 70 per cent of the population, has been under-represented. Until the 1966 redistribution, it was possible for one party to sweep the rural areas and leave the ridings in Greater Vancouver, New Westminster, and Victoria with no representation on the government side of the House. There were as many voters registered in the three largest provincial ridings—Point Grey, Vancouver East, and Delta—as there were in 26 non urban ridings. The three urban districts elected only seven M.L.A.s, the 26 non-urban seats elected 26 M.L.A.s. One vote in Atlin counted for thirty in Vancouver East. Thirty per cent of the voters in Vancouver received only nine members or 17.3 per cent of the legislative representation. Recent redistributions have considerably lessened discrepancies, but interior constituencies remain over-represented.

Interior ranchers, farmers and small businessmen have been a primary base of Social Credit support and the Bennett governments have actively fostered and defended the interests of these groups. The Socreds, from the very outset, enthusiastically pursued a politics of *bouts de chemin* in a province where inter-regional communication is minimized by hostile geographical barriers. Numerous highway extensions were constructed and rebuilt on both the mainland and Vancouver Island; the Trans-Canada Highway was completed, with substantial federal aid, linking Vancouver with the western rim of the Rockies, while bridges and tunnels were built to provide key links in the road system; the ferry system was taken over by the government, upgraded with new equipment, and expanded to serve outlying coastal communities; the Pacific Great Eastern Railway, now the B.C. Railway, was completed and extended, after decades of intrigue, scandal, and embarrassments for previous governments, linking the productive mineral basins of the north and central interior with Vancouver.

Transportation construction has made good politics. The tourist industry is indebted to the government for good roads. Contractors have filled the party coffers with contributions and many working men, provided with jobs in periods of high prosperity, have ignored NDP propaganda and voted for the government. Trucking competition with the railroads has been facilitated and transportation costs reduced. The improved transportation system contributed to the development of a series of small regional service centers close to centers of resource extraction. The service industries are the mecca of the small businessman and the rapid expansion of cities like Prince George, Kamloops, and Chilliwack during past decades coincides with their emergence as strongholds of Social Credit support. Outlying and isolated communities in the north and coastal areas have been indebted to the government for transportation links, whether by ferry or by road, and expressed their gratitude through the ballot box. British Columbia's historic rural bias in road building has left Greater Vancouver with a poorly developed transportation system without rapid mass transit.

The political acceptability of expensive road construction has been facilitated by the bookkeeping practices of a government whose founder delighted in accounting double-talk. Highway and bridge construction are costly and involve a high level of government borrowing, but growing indebtedness has been minimized to the public by classifying the debts of government agencies as "contingent liabilities." Protestations about being debt-free are belied by the huge indirect debt incurred through borrowing agencies like B.C. Hydro. But the idea of a balanced budget and a debt-free province, widely advertised by the Bennett dynasty, caters to an old faith in financial status heartily endorsed by the bingo set inhabiting the Legion halls of Kamloops and Dawson Creek.

Social Credit's marriage with the old middle class has been a tranquil affair which belies the excited accusation of some critics that the governing party has blindly waged war at different times on all sections of the population and against all established elites. The British Columbia Federation of Agriculture, and other agricultural interest groups, the sundry

Chambers of Commerce, the assemblies of businessmen, real estate and insurance salesmen, and learned societies of notary publics have rarely tasted the Socred whip but, on the contrary, have provided the active supporters from whom the party recruits electoral supporters, party activists, and its political elite.

More problematic has been the Socred's relationship with sections of the new middle class and the higher professions which were barely represented in the new governing elite in 1952. The government of Bennett the Elder slowly incorporated new professional elements in the mid 1960s but there persisted tensions and mistrust well into the next decade when spiralling inflation, and the growing political awareness and sophistication of professional groups such as teachers, social workers, hospital employees and civil servants eventually led to bitter confrontations with the government and contributed heavily to the Socred defeat in the 1972 election.[34] Since returning to power in 1975, the Socreds, infused with new managerial psychology and aided by a buttressed civil service, have "modernized" somewhat and are more open to suasion by and bargaining with professional associations.

The one social group which the Socreds have fought, consistently and zestfully, has been the organized labor movement. The Social Credit platform in the 1952 election contained few references to labor problems and the candidates returned were not elected on a wave of anti-labor sentiment. Having gained power, however, the government of small businessmen soon ran full steam into a trade-union movement, strong and militant by national standards. Labor leaders were incensed with the developing course of government labor legislation designed to restrict the organizational power of unions. The first major Social Credit labor legislation, the Labour Relations Act, known as Bill 28, was passed in 1954. It provided fines and penalties for a union and its officers for contravening the new restrictive provisions regarding the legality of strikes and it decreased the power of the Labour Relations Board established under the province's Industrial Conciliation and Arbitration Act of 1947, in favor of the Minister of Labour and the courts. A second major bill, 43, was passed in 1958, forbidding the secondary boycott, limiting picketing to a union or plant directly involved in a strike, and making the unions liable entities in offences committed by individual members in strike situations. The secretary of the militant I.W.A. described the act as "another Pearl Harbor attack by the Social Credit government" and one which brought the province a step closer to fascism. Labor leaders, who believed the only way to change the law was to change the premier, consolidated politically and moved closer to the NDP in order to better oppose the new legislation. The government responded by bringing in Bill 42, which forbade the use for political purposes of any money collected in unions by payroll deduction. Organized labor also collided with the government over Bill 33, passed in 1967, which established the principle of compulsory arbitration in essential industries; a bill described by labor leaders as a "club over the head of every employee and every worker's family in B.C." Since returning to power in 1975, the Socreds' war with the labor leadership has cooled somewhat and the government has done little (as of March, 1977) to alter the new industrial relations framework introduced by the NDP.

In defence of his labor legislation, Bennett the Elder advanced a peculiar Okanagan variant of Marxism which agreed with Marxists that workers were exploited, but violently disagreed about the identity of the exploiters. To Social Credit ideologists, the exploiters of labor are union leaders rather than capitalists. The function of the state is not to save the worker from the capitalist but to rescue him from his leader. Left to their own devices in a prospering society in which private enterprise freely pursues its ends, workers may live and work in a state of blissful contentment. As it is, they are constantly misled by their leaders who impose their own political aims on the unsuspecting masses. Social Credit politicians have by-passed labor leaders and appeal directly to the masses. The government bitterly fought and restricted the organizational demands of labor, which enhance the power of labor leaders, and at the same time wooed the masses with political sweets like the Homeowner's and Home Purchase Grants, medicare, and annual vacations with pay. Social Credit has not been entirely unsuccessful in its bid for the labor vote. Workers who enjoyed high wages and prosperous times, who saw little benefit from belonging to a union, who joined unions through closed or union shop regulations, who resented the proliferation of union bureaucracies, who disliked having their dues channeled to support an opposition party, quietly cast their vote for Social Credit leaders, whose anti-establishment style had, in the past, struck a sympathetic chord with their own feelings of alienation.

Social Credit's relations with sections of big business have been strained and difficult on occasion but the party has basically performed the functions expected of all free enterprise parties in British Columbia: to provide a favorable investment climate for businessmen fearful of the demon of Socialist expropriation. The Social Credit movement was not, at the outset, a creation of the business tycoons who had found a safe abode in the Liberal-Conservative coalition, a marriage that big business avidly encouraged in the early 1940s as an answer to the Socialist threat. Until 1950-1951, the Social Credit party was an assemblage of cranks and monetary faddists who feared the domination of the financial interests as much as they quaked at the thought of a Socialist state. Party leaders like Hansell and W.A.C. Bennett at times used the theory of Invisible Government, with its moral overtones of deceit, corruption, and graft, to exploit the realistic observations and suspicions of ordinary people that political parties were facades that hid the real rulers from public view. "There is a government," Ernest Hansell told the citizens of Vernon in 1952, "more powerful than governments, this great monetary power that knows no international boundaries. That is what we are attacking, and everyone who opposes Social Credit is either ignorant of that power or a party to it." Bennett knew as well as Hansell the fears of ordinary people when he promised during the 1953 campaign that Social Credit would "oppose equally as strongly the forces of monopoly and the forces of socialism."[35] Catapulted into power by a swift and peculiar conjunction of circumstances, and devoid of initial support from any established interests, the Social Credit regime found itself free of any incurred political obligations. The new men of power ruled a domain rich in resources and conferred privileges on favored barons in return for oaths of allegiance and economic support. The coffers of the Liberal and Conservative parties were rich in funds in the 1949 and 1952 elections, but by 1953, the sad moans of Grit and Tory money collectors were heard everywhere. "Many large and small industries are awaiting the outcome of this election," Bennett informed the electors in 1953. "If the Social Credit government has a good working majority new industries will be commenced with increased payrolls and benefit to all...The issue is clear: it is Social Credit or chaos." Businessmen got the word and fell into line to the point where party collector Al Williamson could admit at his trial a few years later that he had not been refused once in his many requests for funds from assorted businesses. Campaign contributions went into a fund administered by Einar Gunderson and W.A.C. Bennett known as the British Columbia Free Enterprise Educational Fund; which was in no way accountable for receipts and expenditures to Social Credit conventions or party organization. The surviving remnants of the Liberal and Conservative parties have been starved for funds since the 1953 election.

Big business hitches its star to the Social Credit government not because of customary partisan predispositions, but because Social Credit is the only effective alternative to the NDP. A shift of support back to one of the floundering old parties is liable to have a short run effect of returning to power a New Democratic government through a split in the free enterprise vote.

As it is, the Socreds have rendered good services to the business community by controlling a head-strong labor movement, keeping the tax incidence "reasonable," expanding the economic infrastructure and framing a regulatory structure consistent with the aims of big business. And businessmen have shown their gratitude for the services rendered.

When Social Credit lost power in 1972, leading business politicians worked behind the scenes to head off attempts to create a "unity" party or revive either of the old free-enterprise, Liberal or Conservative parties.

A proven vehicle of business defence and governing competence, with substantial roots in the electorate, the Socreds were favored over the competing Liberals and Conservatives as the most likely instrument of NDP removal. Encouraged by board room support, Bennett the Younger reconstituted Social Credit as the anti-socialist coalition party by enticing an array of dissident Liberals and Conservatives into their camp including such notables as Pat McGeer, G. Gardom, Allan Williams, Bill Vander Zalm, Jack Davis and Hugh Curtis. The result was a further erosion of residual Liberal and Conservative strength and a return to power of the Socreds in the polarized election of 1975.

In defeating the Barrett government, the Socreds slowed the drift toward a greater collectivism which developed under B.C.'s first socialist regime. State intervention, of course, is nothing new to British Columbia where Bennett the Elder's "little government" became itself a large interest in the economy and society. B.C. Hydro, B.C. Ferries and the B.C. Railways testified to the extent of the development of state capitalism under the Social Credit regime as did the bevy of welfare measures, including Medicare, which were necessary and expedient reforms in a welfare-conscious society.

During the NDP interlude, however, state intervention took on a new pace and direction. The socialists, in contrast to the Elder's Main Street proclivities, modernized the bureaucracy, infused new young talent into the civil service, heightened the participation of experts in government, and engaged in a spurt of legislative activism unseen since the days of Pattullo. Public auto insurance was implemented, to the consternation of the insurance companies. A land commission regulated the use and sale of land in farm areas. The old inactive Public Utilities Commission was replaced by a B.C. Energy Commission while the new B.C. Petroleum Corporation was empowered to buy, sell and otherwise deal in petroleum and natural gas. The Mineral Royalties Act pinched the mining industry which sponsored and financed a lively anti-government publicity campaign. The Ocean Falls plant and townsite were bought out from Crown Zellerbach while Canadian Cellulose Limited, a new crown corporation, took over the major holdings of Columbia Cellulose in the pulp and paper industry. In the area of industrial relations, a new labor code was drawn up and collective bargaining rights extended to civil servants. Pharmacare and Mincome were key reforms in the welfare field.

A major effect of the Barrett government's activism was to antagonize powerful business interest groups and promote a polarization of both parties and the electorate. Nor were the socialists aided in their bid for re-election by the state of the economy which suffered the twin blights of unemployment and inflation. When the socialists finally went to the people in December 1975, they found themselves in a two-party fight with the rejuvenated Socreds infused with a host of Liberal and

Conservative renegade notables as well as former NDP M.L.A. Frank Calder. The Liberal converts brought the Socreds some old elusive high-priced waterfront seats like Vancouver Point-Grey and West Vancouver Howe Sound. Equally beneficial to the Socreds were shifts in the voting patterns in Lower Mainland working and middle class suburbs like Burnaby-Willingdon, Burnaby South, Coquitlam and Surrey where many upwardly mobile voters and inflation-conscious condominium dwellers deserted the socialist government.

Elections, within the foreseeable future in British Columbia, are likely to continue as two-party contests. Both Liberals and Conservatives are left with tiny fragments of the popular vote and minimal legislative representation. But the streamlined Socreds, led by Bennett the Younger, are well aware that long governmental tenures, of the W.A.C. Bennett sort, are unlikely as long as the economy splutters.

Endnotes

[1] For background information on B.C. labor politics see Martin Robin, *The Rush for Spoils* (Toronto: McClelland and Stewart, 1972), pp. 23-35 and Paul Phillips, *No Power Greater* (Vancouver: Boag Foundation, 1967).

[2] V. H. Jensen, *Heritage of Conflict* (Ithaca, N.Y.: Cornell University Press, 1950), p. 11.

[3] Phillips, *No Power Greater*, p. 162.

[4] S. Jamieson and P. Gladstone, "Unionism in the Fishing Industry in British Columbia," *Canadian Journal of Economics and Political Science*, Vol. XVI, Feb. 1950, p. 2.

[5] Robin, *The Rush for Spoils*, pp. 34-40.

[6] C. B. Macpherson, *Democracy in Alberta* (Toronto: University of Toronto Press, 1953), p. 15 and J. J. Richter, "The Developing Pattern of British Columbia Agriculture," Inventory of the Natural Resources of British Columbia, *British Columbia Natural Resources Conference*, 1964, p. 153.

[7] Louis A. Wood, *A History of Farmers' Movements in Canada* (Toronto: Ryerson Press, 1924), p. 307.

[8] Bruce Hutchison, *The Unknown Country* (Toronto: McClelland and Stewart, 1948), p. 269.

[9] A. G. Bradley, *Canada in the Twentieth Century* (London: 1903), pp. 409-410.

[10] October 28, 1905.

[11] Bruce Hutchison, *The Fraser* (Toronto: Clarke Irwin & Co., 1950), p. 210.

[12] Edith Dobie, "Party History in British Columbia, 1903-33," *Pacific Northwest Quarterly*, 1936, p. 158.

[13] *Ibid.*

[14] Robin, *The Rush For Spoils*, Chapters 2-5.

[15] Frances MacNab, *British Columbia for Settlers* (Chapman and Hill Ltd., 1898), p. 9.

[16] *Ibid.* p. 5.

[17] See Martin Robin, *Pillars of Profit* (Toronto: McClelland and Stewart, 1973), Chapter 7.

[18] Robin, *The Rush For Spoils*, pp. 42-48.

[19] M. J. Dwyer, "Laurier and The British Columbia Liberal Party, 1896-1911" (M.A. Thesis, U.B.C., 1961), p. 25.

[20] Robin, *The Rush For Spoils*, p. 81.

[21] As quoted in M. J. Dwyer, *Op. Cit.*, p. 111.

[22] As quoted in T. A. Gregg, "Canadian Celebrities," *The Canadian Magazine*, Vol. 23, 1904.

[23] Robin, *The Rush For Spoils*, p. 164.

[24] *Ibid.*, Chapter 9 for an account of the Tory decline and defeat.

[25] Robin, *Pillars of Profit*, Chapters 3 and 4.

[26] *Ibid.*, Chapter 5.

[27] June 1, 1953.

[28] *Vancouver Sun*, Sept. 20, 1956.

[29] *Ibid.*, June 2, 1953.

[30] *Vancouver Province*, May 31, 1952.

[31] *Ibid.*, May 3, 1952.

[32] Walter Ellis, "Some Aspects of Religion in British Columbia Politics," (M.A. Thesis, U.B.C., 1959), p. 85.

[33] *Vancouver Sun*, June 2, 1953.

[34] Robin, *Pillars of Profit*, Chapter 10.

[35] *Vancouver Sun*, June 2, 1953.

MANITOBA
Ethnic and Class Politics

Thomas Peterson

> *It might be argued that the low level of class voting in Canada implies that it is in the forefront of a trend in all of the Anglo-American countries away from class politics ... I suggest, on the contrary, that class voting in Canada is less than should be expected in a country with its type of stratification, and that therefore class voting may be expected to increase if social changes follow certain paths.*[1]

The development of party politics in Manitoba has been influenced by the interaction of two social and economic classes. One of these has generally been more prosperous and culturally more secure. Most of its members were of British origin and many of them originally came to the province from Ontario. For almost a hundred years, this class controlled political and economic power. The second or lower class was more heterogeneous. It was comprised of diverse cultural groups including working-class immigrants from Britain, various other immigrants of non-British origin and the province's native Indians and Métis. The members of this class were generally poor and submissive. By the 1960s, the ethnic and other divisions within this lower class were declining. There were indications of assimilation in some cases, and more militant political attitudes in others. This contributed to a polarization of party politics partly along class lines. Also, the traditional ruling group showed signs of age and its capacity for maintaining control wavered. As a result, there emerged a new political environment in which the two rival classes were more equally matched.

One of the initial bases of the province's class division was the uneven distribution of good land. When the glaciers of the Ice Age passed over north-eastern Manitoba, they left it scarred and barren.

Along the Shield's southern edge, extending diagonally from Lake of the Woods in the southeast to the Swan River Valley in the northwest, are numerous marshes, bogs, and gravel ridges. Coarse stones litter the fields, and the soil is shallow and poor. The area to the south and west, comprising about one-seventh of the province, is more attractive. Rolling plains extend from the Red River valley to the western prairie uplands. The soil is fine textured and fertile, average temperatures are higher, and spring rains more reliable.[2] When they first saw his region, La Vérendrye and his sons were struck by its beauty:

> *It is all very level, without mountains, all fine hard wood with here and there groves of oak . . . everywhere there are quantities of fruit trees, and all sorts of wild animals . . . the savage tribes are there very numerous. There are some magnificent plains . . . Trees grow only on the banks of the rivers and the prevailing kinds are white oak, elm, ash . . . bass and birch. All the rest is prairie, with here and there clumps of oak and wild plum.*[3]

When Manitoba became a province in 1870, the population numbered about 13,000 and consisted mainly of Indians and Métis. After Louis Riel's failure to secure their rights, they were forced to move further west or north into the Shield. Their claims to the southern region were extinguished by treaties in 1871 and their eviction completed by 1890.[4]

The British settlers who displaced them came mainly from Ontario:

> *Nearly all were practical farmers with means, a few were graduated of the Ontario Agricultural College at Guelph, and they brought to the parklands . . . a high degree of agricultural experience and skill.*[5]

Others came directly from Great Britain:

> *Including among their numbers graduates of British universities, and, as well, people of sufficient means to permit of their living the life of the English country gentlemen, so far as it might be lived on the prairies, these settlers, by their love of good books, art, music, flowers . . . made a contribution to the life of Manitoba.*[6]

A local history of Carman, a British settlement begun in 1878, later commented on the removal of the original inhabitants:

> *The time . . . was not favourable for the Métis, who were such a contented people . . . Today there is not one Métis left from the many that used to be here. They dispersed in all directions.*[7]

During the winter of 1891, an editor reported that "an untutored child of the Plains came into the *Free Press* on Saturday and left the following letter":

> *We are very poor. Simpson (an Indian commissioner) told us at the Lower Fort that the treaty would not be broken so we hope the authorities will keep their word. We are kept from killing moose and those who have no crop will starve. We have no school house nor anything which the Queen promised us.*[8]

Ebenezer McColl, the local Indian agent, responded that the Indians were "most indolent and improvident" and that their annuities had already been increased from three to five dollars.[9]

During the 1870s and early 1880s, a few non-British immigrant groups also arrived in the province. About fifteen hundred Icelanders, obliged by an active volcano to emigrate, moved into a bleak district north of the provincial boundary alongside Lake Winnipeg and named their new community Gimli, meaning Paradise. Escaping Czarist conscription, an estimated seven thousand German-speaking Mennonites settled south of Winnipeg along the American border. An English visitor to their community reported:

> *The Mennonites do not give a great impression of cleanliness... the same roof covers the horses and the chickens and rest of the family. As a race they are thrifty and industrious but their neighbours say that the women do most of their work. The great drawback of the Mennonites seems to be their poverty.*[10]

To the northwest, a party of Hungarians settled at Stoney Creek, which came to be called Huns' Valley. From Quebec, a few French-Canadians came to St. Boniface and villages in the southeast. Also about 350 Jewish refugees from Russia spent a winter in makeshift sheds in Winnipeg and then moved north to a barren Interlake settlement at Narcisse. After watching Jewish women "picking up odds and ends of food and clothing" in Winnipeg streets before their migration north, a writer concluded:

> *A more helpless and useless lot never crossed the Atlantic.... It will cost our people more to keep them than to send them back to Europe.*[11]

By the mid-1880s, the province's ethnic and class structure was thus being established by the pattern of immigration and settlement. A relatively prosperous British majority occupied much of the best land in the southwest while various non-British minorities were located in poorer areas.

In the first years after Confederation, political parties were little more than primitive factions.[12] With federal help, a stable Conservative ministry was formed in 1878. Its leader was John Norquay, a 300-pound Métis who could astonish English visitors with a high-kicking Red River jig. To the British immigrant settlers from Ontario, confidently rooted in a rural Grit tradition, Norquay seemed little better than a federal puppet: as their settlements grew, his government weakened. He narrowly won re-election in 1886 but lost the new British ridings. The next year, their dissatisfaction with federal railway policy drove him to desperate efforts to borrow money for the construction of a provincial railway.[13] His failure forced his resignation and he died 18 months later. Ontario democracy triumphed.[14] The new Liberal premier was Thomas Greenway, a prosperous farmer originally from Centralia, Ontario. After winning the election of 1888, his government took decisive action against the French minority. The printing of government documents in French was ended and public financial support withdrawn from Catholic schools. The French sought help from the courts and the federal Conservative cabinet but without success. The Greenway government remained secure, partly by appointing clerks to control the voters' lists and by a gerrymander in 1892.[15]

Only after the federal Liberal victory of Wilfrid Laurier in 1896 did Greenway become suspect to his British supporters. Under federal pressure, he agreed to permit limited Catholic religious instruction and the use of languages other than English in Manitoba public schools. A new Conservative newspaper now accused him of "treachery and hypocrisy" and condemned "the special privileges now enjoyed by the French."[16]§ More vigorous Conservative leadership was provided by Hugh John Macdonald, son of former Prime Minister John A. Macdonald, from Kingston, Ontario.[17] He blamed Greenway for the federal Liberal immigration policy directed by Clifford Sifton, one of Greenway's former ministers, and warned that "the wholesale importation of undesirable immigrants," particularly from Eastern Europe, threatened the province's newly asserted British character. His speeches on this issue secured a good response:

> *Discussing Mr. Greenway's approval of Galician and Doukhobor immigration, Mr. Macdonald made a vigorous protest against importing this class of immigrants in reference to immigrants of Anglo-Saxon racial stock.*
>
> *His remarks on this point were received with prolonged applause.*
>
> *The people of the West, at any rate, are not going to place the government of this intelligent and British community at the mercy of a horde of Slavs.*[18]

The *Manitoba Free Press*, in which Sifton purchased a controlling interest,[19] defended the Liberals by claiming that the Conservatives were really to blame for the "foreign colonies" in Manitoba since Slavic immigration had begun in 1892.[20] But Macdonald won the election by capturing most of the British ridings in the southwest. To the extent that they were politically active, the ethnic minorities tended to vote in separate blocs. Many of the Mennonites regarded any government as a threat and their religion opposed holding public office. Few welcomed the right to vote and a small turnout in their district of Rosenfeldt elected Wilhelm Hespeler, the German consul in Winnipeg, as an Independent. The contest in Gimli was narrowly won by a former Conservative immigration agent, Baldwin Baldwinson, who answered charges that he bribed his way to victory by claiming "it was the Liberals who sold themselves."[21] For the French, survival required solidarity:

> *D'un commun accord les électeurs, conservateurs comme libéraux, ont cru qu'il ne fallait pas introduire ces divisions dans nos luttes provinciales... Notre peuple est trop faible pour se payer le luxe de luttes fratricides.*[22]

They voted Liberal in 1899 partly because of Laurier's appeal and partly because they expected Greenway to win and thought they would be safer on the winning side.[23] Nine months after the election, Macdonald resigned and was succeeded by Rodmond P. Roblin, a grain merchant in Carman originally from Picton, Ontario. To the Catholic clergy, Roblin's accession was reassuring and he shortly secured French allegiance. Like Macdonald, however, he considered foreign immigration objectionable:

> *He regarded it as of vital importance that Canada should exercise the greatest care in the selection of those admitted to her shores. The folly of paying agents and corporations a bonus for using the dragnet through Europe to gather those who could be induced to settle in Canada, regardless of all considerations of suitability, appeared to him as not only dangerous to the future state but absolutely un-British.*[24]

Paradoxically, his government came to be based upon the support of non-British immigrants.

Between 1901 and 1911, the province's population nearly doubled, becoming almost half a million.[25] Thousands from Central and Eastern Europe were settled by immigration officials along the fringe of existing northern settlement on "marginal lands which demanded much more work and gave fewer returns than any of the lands hitherto settled."[26] Clifford Sifton later commented:

> *For thirty years Canadian and British settlers had been coming to Manitoba, but none would go on those lands where I as a boy with my father, who was a railway contractor, had sunk into the swampy muck. Perhaps it was hardly fair to place those people there but it was... like their old home and they went there willingly.*[27]

Albert Smith, a Methodist minister in the northwestern town of Dauphin, witnessed the arrival there in 1898 of the first Ukrainians who "were conducted by government agents" to homesteads further north in "an area of low, cheap land covered with willow scrub."[28] The remoteness and hardship of these new communities confirmed their natural disposition: they became isolated by poverty as well as language.[29] As the province thus became more clearly divided along ethnic and class lines, so did Winnipeg become two distinct cities. The more prosperous British families moved southward and westward along the Assiniboine River and built impressive homes amid boulevards and parks in the new districts of Crescentwood and River Heights. Much of the city's north end, in contrast, became a noisy, crowded ghetto. In 1906, a delegation of ladies from the Winnipeg Ministerial Association, accompanies by a private detective, visited a Jewish district, identified as "Jerusalem number one," and reported back to a meeting:

> *Forty-five families inhabited a very small space, living in a manner that was to say the least disgraceful. Diseases of all kinds were common.... It was just the spot for a plague to begin and sweep over the city, and it was a providence that such had not occurred.*[30]

After discussing the possibilities of confining the immigrants to an industrial farm or at least curbing their beer consumption, the meeting went on to hear a lecture on "The Christology of Paul." James Woodsworth, a Methodist minister from Ontario who organized missionary work in Winnipeg's north end, also characterized some of the new immigrant groups:

> *Even those who detest 'foreigners' make an exception of Germans, whom they classify as 'white people like ourselves'.*
>
> *Most of the Poles who reached this country are peasants or workingmen...far from the best class. They are poor, illiterate, and with a code of morals none too high....*
>
> *The Galician figures, disproportionately to his numbers, in the police court and penitentiary. Centuries of poverty and oppression have, to some extent, animalized him.*
>
> *The large majority of Jews...come here wretchedly poor... and yet in some way they exist and make money....* [31]

Having come from villages where vestiges of feudalism persisted, most of these immigrants tended to be deferential to authority, fearful of giving offence, and more than willing to cooperate with their new government.

On this foundation, Premier Roblin and his minister of public works, Robert Rogers, built a powerful party machine. Undecipherable Slavic names made voters' lists elastic and impersonation unchallengeable. In 1914, the *Free Press* investigated voter registration at Komarno, a village in the Interlake district:

Wasyl Krucekowski appears again on the same list as Wasyl Kluczkowski.... Alex Cymbaluk blossomed forth twice as Alex Cybulak. John Blowatczuk admitted that he was on the list again as John Glavacz. Leon Ukramik was first on the list as Leon Szpakowski.... There were dozens of others like him. A large measure of the credit for this is freely given to F. S. Szablewski, the debonair land inspector, whose success in "organizing" is giving him a "stand-in" with the bosses of the Conservative machine.[32]

Platoons of such inspectors exchanged kegs of beer for votes. Contributions squeezed from government contractors paid the bills, newspapers multiplied and fattened on government printing orders, and when necessary, most of the annual road appropriation for the province could be spent in one district to win a difficult by-election, as was done in Gimli in 1913.[33] Above it all, Premier Roblin invoked Biblical phrase and patriotic sentiment to roast his opponents. Proclaiming that "in Western Canada all roads lead to Winnipeg,"[34] his government initially showed great energy. An agreement with the Canadian Northern secured another grain outlet to the lakehead in 1902, and resulting competition cut freight charges. Before 1905, Roblin almost acquired the North-West Territory as a Manitoba empire, and despite the local popularity of reciprocity in the 1911 federal election, he delivered 8 out of 10 Manitoba seats to the Conservatives and won a massive northward extension of the provincial boundary in 1912. Pioneering in public ownership, he bought out Bell Telephone in 1907 and three years later launched a public grain elevator scheme that became a fiscal nightmare. Economic growth and prosperity, based in part on the abundance of cheap immigrant labor, were unprecedented. But even so, provincial expenditures threatened to become unmanageable. Roblin himself was wearing out: his platform performances became unpredictable, his rhetoric more florid. After Rogers entered federal politics, the party organization also faltered. Its final glory was the 1914 election victory. With only a minority of the popular vote, it won a majority of seats by sweeping the non-British ridings.

In their frustration, the Liberals urged higher public morality and attacked the foreign immigrants for being constitutionally inferior, if not depraved. A temperance movement, undeterred by Roblin's defence of saloons as centers of good-will, blamed electoral corruption on immigrant vice. After observing the 1914 campaign, a Presbyterian minister reported:

They come to Canada and huddle themselves off in colonies and are subject to evil influences. From the conditions in which they live, they are brought up to expect remuneration for their votes. Unfortunately it is difficult, I have found, to separate drink from the foreigners. During this election, it was not an uncommon sight

> *to see these new arrivals lying around soaked in whiskey that was carried in suitcases by ardent politicians. Thousands of foreigners have been given the ballot who have certainly no right to it, and thousands of intelligent women have been denied the right.*[35]

Illustrating a common tendency to unite the emerging question of female suffrage with the need to curb immigrant influence, there was hearty agreement with the Britisher who declared: "Surely my wife is more capable of voting than the ignorant Galician."[36] Another non-British group was treated with humor:

> *The wildest excitement prevails among the Indians . . . over the election campaign. On Thursday, the whole thing was made plain by the arrival from Winnipeg of a party of expert naturalization and registration operators, who explained that the scheme is to put through bogus naturalization papers making the Indians citizens.*
>
> *One group will have their faces darkened and will be naturalized and registered as Hudson Bay Railway sleeping car conductors; other groups will be naturalized as newcomers to this country from continental Europe.*[37]

When the government tried to assist urban Catholic schools and in 1913 admitted a French-Canadian to cabinet, it incurred the wrath of the Orange Lodge, which joined the Liberals in attacking Roblin. The onset of World War I increased these racial and religious tensions. North and east of Winnipeg, there had developed a substantial settlement of German Catholics just prior to the war.[38] After their newspaper advised them to return to Germany, the *Free Press* reacted by charging it with "active and flagrant treason" and also warned that "agitators have imported into this country the lingo and catch cries of the nationalist crusade in Galicia."[39] The war placed both East European and German immigrants on the defensive, while Mennonites henceforth identified themselves as being of Dutch origin.

In 1915, a scandal involving the construction of the provincial legislative building finally finished Premier Roblin's political career. He was forced to resign and in the resulting election the Liberals won almost every seat. Their leader was Toby Norris, a farmer and auctioneer who had come to Manitoba from Brampton, Ontario, and settled near Brandon in the southwest. Women were given the right to vote in 1916 and became an important source of Liberal support. Regarding non-British women, Nellie McClung, a leading suffragette, advised that there was nothing to fear:

> *Mrs. McClung declared she was not afraid of the way in which the foreign women of Manitoba would cast their vote. She knew many of the Mary's and Annie's among the foreign-born women and she*

> *loved their honest faces. The women who had fought for suffrage would take upon themselves the task of instructing their foreign-born sisters in the duties and privileges of citizenship.*[40]

The persistence of sharp racial divisions was shown by the conflict in 1917 over Quebec's opposition to conscription. At a mass rally in Winnipeg's Walker Theatre, Mrs. Edward Brown, wife of the provincial treasurer, declared:

> *It is a proud boast for anyone who can say today: I am of the British race, I am of Canada! I have absolute confidence in the people of Canada, outside of the unspeakable French-Canadians.*[41]

In this spirit, the Norris government moved to accelerate assimilation of the non-British groups. Primary school attendance became compulsory and the use of languages other than English in the public schools was prohibited. To escape the school law, about 6,000 Mennonites, a third of their community, emigrated to Mexico and Paraguay after 1918.[42] The Ukrainians made little protest since they were internally preoccupied with a deepening struggle between Greek Catholic and Greek Orthodox congregations.[43] But for the French, protection of their language became an overriding goal that absorbed their attention to the virtual exclusion of all else, and a new educational association, allied with clerical leaders, replaced their political representatives as guardian of the group's survival.[44]

Other reforms also cut against the non-British minorities. With the establishment of a Civil Service Commission empowered to hire on the basis of competitive examinations, their access to jobs by the back door of patronage was blocked. A new electoral system of transferable ballots which was designed to ensure that winning candidates had majority support proved advantageous to the more experienced British voters. A temperance referendum, that split the electorate along ethnic lines, was won by the British; and after moderate control reportedly failed to curb drunkenness in the non-British districts, it was followed by total prohibition in 1920. The problem of absorbing or containing the foreign element invariably became entangled in such questions. To provincial Liberal leaders, reform and assimilation seemed nearly synonymous: the non-British evidently needed civilizing and in practical terms this meant that they needed to be Anglicized. Few of the non-British were in a position to oppose this view and many indeed welcomed and pursued Anglicization as a step toward economic survival. Beyond this ethnic issue, the Norris government also introduced other reforms including allowances for deserted or widowed mothers, improved workmen's compensation for industrial injuries, more effective factory inspection and a fair wage board to consider requests for higher pay. It proved unwilling to recognize collective bargaining rights, however, and on this issue rising working-class discontent shortly erupted.

Protest came from British workingmen in Winnipeg. After forming a labour party in 1895, they entered the 1899 provincial election with resolutions advocating free compulsory education, a minimum wage and a maximum 48-hour work week, abolition of child labor, orderly negotiation of wage disputes, public ownership of utilities and abolition of the federal Senate.[45] Arthur Puttee, a printer from Folkestone, England, won a labor seat in a federal by-election in 1900 and held it until 1904.[46] The first labor victory in provincial politics was in 1914, when Fred Dixon, an engraver who arrived from England in 1904, won in Winnipeg Centre. Like Puttee and Dixon, other labor leaders were also recent immigrants from Britain: William Ivens came in 1896, John Queen in 1906, Bob Russell in 1911 and R. J. Johns in 1912. Dixon was joined in the legislature in 1915 by Richard Rigg, a Methodist preacher and bookbinder, who immigrated from Lancashire in 1903.[47] But despite this common background, disputes occurred within the movement and splinter groups appeared, such as a socialist party in 1902. Another limiting factor was the non-British working-class group, considered more an economic threat than a possible political ally. The Winnipeg Trades and Labour Council made this clear in 1899:

> *A protest was sent to the Dominion government against the expenditure of public funds for the wholesale importation of Galicians and Doukhobors to this country and thus bringing unjust competition against the industrial classes . . . (with immigrants) accustomed to starvation wages.*[48]

As heavy immigration continued over the next decade and a half, so did similar complaints.

Far from going to a labor party, most non-British voting support was captured early by the Liberals and Conservatives. Both parties organized Jewish political clubs in Winnipeg in 1896. The first Jewish political representatives were Conservative businessmen: Moses Finkelstein and Altar Skaletar, elected as city aldermen in 1904 and 1912. The Liberals countered by launching the *Canadian Israelite* and their efforts secured the 1910 election to the provincial legislature of Solomon Hart Green, a prominent lawyer originally from New Brunswick.[49] Both parties sent speakers to address Jewish meetings on such topics as "Courage," "Our Patriotism," and "Equal Suffrage for All."[50] Labor candidates made no such appeal and their early successes in the north end came from British working-class support, in spite of non-British opposition. Thus Richard Rigg's victory in 1915 was possible partly because the Jewish vote split between Green and Elias Levinson, a prominent Conservative lawyer from Australia appointed Crown prosecutor in 1912. When Rigg resigned to contest a federal seat in 1917, the Jewish vote again elected a Liberal, Robert Jacob, although there was uncertainty about his background:

> *At some meetings, Mr. Jacob has been referred to as a Hebrew, the speakers evidently thinking that he is of Hebrew extraction. To this Mr. Jacob has had to explain that he is an Englishman by birth.*[51]

In 1917 a radical Jewish upholsterer, A. A. Heaps, won election as an alderman, but at the provincial level there was no Jewish representation from 1915 to 1927, when Captain William Tobias, a prominent city "lawyer and sportsman" was elected as a Conservative.[52]

A similar pattern of allegiance developed in the Slavic community. From the outset, its newspapers were directed by Conservative and Liberal publicists. When the Liberals organized the *Canadian Farmer* in 1903, John Dafoe, editor of the *Free Press*, wrote to Clifford Sifton:

> *Our Galician paper has at last made its appearance. J. Obed and John Appleton with the assistance of a Galician interpreter are keeping an eye on the matter that goes into it. It has been thought desirable to keep contentious matters out of the first few issues: later on we shall give a few knocks to the Tories.*[53]

In 1910, another paper, the *Ukrainian Voice*, was organized by a school teacher, Taras Ferley, who won as a Liberal in Gimli in 1915. By this time, Ukrainians were under attack from two sides. As aliens, many were disfranchised, interned and suspended from applying for naturalization.[54] For their service as pawns of the Roblin machine, they were also blamed for its corruption. To escape this stigma, a new Ukrainian political club emphasized in awkward English its dedication to a higher level of politics:

> *The lack of such organization has been painfully felt in the past by Ruthenian-Ukrainians themselves as on account of such a state of affairs existing, there has not been clear political ideas and from this, quasi politicians drew advantages of all kinds through their persistency in the bartering of people, entailing disgrace for the whole nation.*[55]

Similarly, the *Canadian Ruthenian*, a Conservative and Catholic paper formed in 1911, now disavowed its previous political association which it blamed on the "French Mafia":

> *Every true Ruthenian-Ukrainian considers it from now on his sacred duty... to protest against the running of a Ukrainian paper by the French with the following words: Down with the French Conservative hirelings.*[56]

Thus, when under political attack, one ethnic group would seek respectability by attacking another.

For their part, the French sought respite by retreating from partisan politics altogether. The only other numerically significant non-British group, the Icelanders, became increasingly Liberal, particularly after the appointment of Thomas Johnson, a prominent attorney, to the Norris cabinet in 1915 and the placing of a statue of one of their national heroes, Jon Sigurdson, on the legislative grounds. By the end of the war, the roster was virtually complete: the major parties, especially the Liberals, enjoyed the allegiance of most foreign voters, both rural and urban. In Winnipeg, the lower class was thus divided into British workers prepared to protest economic conditions and non-British workers, amounting to almost a third of the city population, who were either intimidated and politically inert, or securely harnessed to the support of the existing system. This ethnic division shaped the outcome of the city's crisis in 1919.

By early 1918, trouble was imminent. The cost of living index had doubled during the war from 137.5 to 290.9, while wages increased only about 20 per cent.[57] The government fair wage board's hesitant recommendations nonetheless encountered business opposition. When it raised the minimum wage for female restaurant employees by 50 cents to $12.50 a week, owners protested:

> *It means that we will have to raise prices . . . and higher prices will deprive the girls of the generous tips the girls now receive.*[58]

Wage increases sought in most trades were about 15 or 20 cents an hour, amounting to raises of 20 to 30 per cent. When these were rejected, a series of strikes began in the spring of 1918 and unrest mounted to desperation the following winter. A typical delegation to the premier complained just before Christmas that "married men with families were finding it impossible to live on $75 a month."[59] As mass protest meetings developed, the federal government sent 200 cavalry to reinforce the police.[60] The first riots began in January. They attacked the non-British who were blamed for the low wages and lack of jobs:

> *The outbreak developed into a general display of feeling against foreigners, who were supposed to be of alien enemy sympathies, and about a score of buildings, principally stores in the central and northern parts of the city, suffered at the hands of mobs, which were composed of returned men and youths. In the attack . . . a number of people of foreign nationality were somewhat severely mauled.*[61]

In February a provincial alien board began deportation proceedings against foreigners and the department of education gave assurance that it was "stamping out" foreign languages in the schools.[62] Unemployed veterans forced "bohunks" on downtown streets to kneel and kiss the Union Jack and obliged Premier Norris to send a telegram to Ottawa:

> *Deputations of returned soldiers... urging immediate internment and deportation of alien enemies. Also want all property belonging to aliens confiscated.*[63]

In this atmosphere, when a new wave of strikes began in May, the non-British became the scapegoat. To no avail did one group insist that "we have always been loyal and law-abiding citizens of this country and shall always stand for the preservation of peace and order."[64]

By early, June, the *Free Press* asserted that the strikes were a lesson to workers to avoid "subjugation to the mass of rough labor, mostly foreign born," and, focusing on the interrupted delivery of milk, charged that the strike leaders "have deprived the babies of this town of milk; that is they have condemned a very large percentage of them to death—did the Returned Soldiers, in all their overseas experience, ever hear of a more Hunnish trick than that?"[65] The *Winnipeg Citizen*, issued by a businessmen's committee, went further:

> *Are Austrians, enemies of Canada, to be allowed to attempt to murder loyal soldiers, heroes, true Britishers upon the streets of Winnipeg?*
>
> *There is no middle ground. Let all this twaddle about "collective bargaining" drop in the face of bloodshed!*
>
> *There is anarchy and revolution abroad in Winnipeg... and organized labor has been betrayed into a position which gives the alien enemies, the Austrians and the Germans, cowards that they are, the chance to do their bloody work.*

Sam Blumenberg, one of the few non-English spokesmen active in the strike, was singled out for criticism:

> *Agitator Blumberg (sic), the man who is keenly interested in turning "wage slaves" into automobile owners... is not noted as a worker himself. In fact he never slaves at anything unless it is on a platform with an alien audience where he slaves for an hour in broken English to tell them that they are the salt of the earth and that the earth belongs to them.*[66]

James Woodsworth, who returned to the city on a lecture tour and helped raise money for strikers' families, later commented:

> *Without hesitation I say that there was not a single foreigner in a*

position of leadership, though foreigners were falsely arrested to give color to this charge.... In short it was the biggest hoax that was ever 'put over' any people![67]

While the strikes came to be called a general strike, whatever coordination they had was improvised and haphazard. The *ad hoc* leaders fumbled through the crisis and "never made the slightest effort" toward militant action.[68] Their paper, the *Western Labour News*, repeatedly tried to escape the alien taint and the charge of plotting revolution:

Keep your heads. Keep away from troublemakers. Leave no loophole for the other side to foment trouble.

Don't play their game. Keep out of their trap. Keep quiet.

The workers are dissatisfied, but they are not revolutionists. And their (sic) will be no revolution.

Beware of the stump orator who jumps on a box and talks Bolshevism. Beware of the fellow who tries to raise a row... because he is a stool pigeon.

The bosses love the alien when they can use him to break strikes. In fact in many cases he was brought here for that purpose.

Who brought the alien to Canada? It was not the workers. They opposed it by might and main. We will support all efforts on the part of the authorities to deport all the undesirable aliens.[69]

Yet the opposition persisted in its charges of "murderous assaults by riotous aliens,"[70] and ultimately the tactic proved successful. On June 21, cavalry armed with baseball bats and revolvers charged a gathering of strikers, some carrying placards that declared "Britons Never Will Be Slaves." A spectator was killed outright and about 25 others were injured. Five days later, the strike collapsed, its leaders in prison and its press banned.

The use of racism in breaking the strike further isolated the non-British. Foreign agitators were blamed for the trouble, although, as an objective inquiry later concluded, its basic causes were low wages, high living costs, unemployment and the evident class division in the city.

Winnipeg unfortunately presents a prominent example of these extremes. There has been, and there is now, an increasing display of carefree, idle luxury and extravagance on the one hand, while on the other is intensified deprivation. The generally cold indifference of the one section to the condition of the other and the display of luxury aggravate this feeling of social disparity into one of active antagonism by the one class against the other.[71]

But Winnipeg labor leaders themselves came to accept the claim that the strike was a foreign-inspired aberration and became apologetic:

The Winnipeg Trades Council has fulfilled in no mean or small way the real function of a labor institution. Its deflection in 1919 was due to very unusual and abnormal circumstances. Made subversive to the propaganda passion and prejudice arising out of a world war, its existence was for a time seriously threatened. It has however regained its poise, conscious by far of its greater mission in seeking to direct the thought of the workers into a more correct interpretation of those relations necessary between capital and labor in industry.[72]

Except for a few Jews who pioneered in organizing the garment workers, leadership in the trade union movement remained overwhelmingly British. In the 1920 provincial election, 11 Labor representatives, of whom 10 were British, won seats in the legislature. Reorganized as the Independent Labor Party in 1921, the group included Fred Dixon as leader, several railway workers such as Arthur Moore, George Palmer and Charles Tanner, a teacher, William Bayley, and Albert Smith, a Methodist minister in Brandon. The strike made these labor representatives more wary of foreign support, which could clearly be used to discredit their movement. For the non-British, the strike's lesson was that whether they were agitators on not, aliens were the first target of reprisal. The threat of deportation became an effective deterrent. Thus the strike widened the ethnic division within the poorer class. With only a limited base of support, labor representation in the legislature by 1927 declined to three members.

Rural newspapers in the British southwest were virtually unanimous in condemning the strikers and in criticizing the provincial government for not taking sterner measures. All the jurors who convicted the strike leaders of seditious conspiracy were farmers.[73] Disgruntled also by declining postwar grain prices, and encouraged by farmers' political activity in Alberta and Ontario, a number of farmers entered as non-party candidates in the 1920 election and 12 won election. This cost Premier Norris his majority but he remained in office two more years. Political allegiances became confused, with former Liberals now sitting as Farmers and sitting Liberals continuing to desert Norris. One of the latter blamed him for the strike in fairly typical terms:

Unrest and discontent threaten the institutions and production of the country.

The recent general strike was nothing short of a revolution.

The policy of the Norris government . . . was to do nothing but sit and wait.[74]

On the alien question, W. R. Wood, secretary of the United Farmers of Manitoba, "forcibly emphasized the need of elevating the foreigner to the higher ideals of Canadian citizenship."[75] A Ukrainian elected in the northwest riding of Ethelbert as a Farmer candidate made a similar point defending "the foreigners" as "not inferior" but merely lacking opportunities, and stressed their loyalty to the Crown.[76]

House divisions generally saw the Farmers, under the leadership of William Robson, voting with the Conservatives, under Winnipeg lawyer John Haig, in urging economy and attacking alleged extravagance, while the Labor group generally supported the Norris government's program. One attitude shared by Farmers and Labor was a rejection of the old parties. Dixon was one of the first to express what later became a common theme in the legislature:

> *Increasing numbers of people consider this body nothing less than a glorified municipal council, and there is no more room for party politics in this house than in a municipal council, and the sooner we get that into our heads the better.*[77]

To the Conservatives, this offered a way to escape the Roblin scandals. As for the Liberals, they had long solicited non-partisan support as a reform movement and since 1918 had identified themselves with the federal Unionists. But at a provincial convention in April of 1922, they narrowly voted to rejoin the Dominion Liberal party, and became vulnerable to charges of surrender to Ottawa and of "putting provincial interests in the back seat."[78] The delegates also split over the desirability of an "aggressive immigration policy" and the teaching of French in the public schools. A resolution on the latter issue produced stormy and prolonged debate:

> *D. R. MacLean said the resolution should be voted down, as he thought it meant the thin edge of bilingualism.*
>
> *A Ruthenian delegate appealed for justice saying if the French people were entitled to recognition so were the Ruthenians who had done as much proportionally in the war as the French (Shouts of No! No!). F. L. Davis suggested this . . . would certainly mean the loss of some seats to the Liberal party. Many were now in doubt but if the resolution was passed they would be irretrievably lost.*[79]

After the Norris government was defeated in the legislature in 1922, the United Farmers won a majority in the election. Party government was apparently ended. Yet the reality was little changed: the new ruling group was substantially the same as the old one—farmers of British origin from the southwest of the province supported by businessmen of British origin in south Winnipeg. This durable alliance now governed under a new name.

A new proportional system of representation in Winnipeg exploited the division within the lower class. Instead of marking a simple "X" on his ballot, the voter was now asked to number his choices on a long ballot listing 35 or 40 candidates for the 10 city seats. Among inexperienced voters, this created a confusion that as often as not worked to the disadvantage of Labor candidates.[80] In 1920, for example, the Liberals and Conservatives won six city seats with 44 per cent of the popular vote in the city, while Labor candidates, with 56 per cent of the city vote, won only four seats. Answering critics of the system, a *Free Press* editorial claimed that it helped keep Labor representation down:

> *Whatever is wrong with the old parties it is certain that Proportional Representation is not responsible for their woes. It is instead about the best friend they have got.*[81]

Coalition was effective in other ridings, such as Brandon, where Albert Smith was defeated in 1922 by a "fusion" candidate, Dr. E. H. Edmison, supported by both Liberals and Conservatives. Also, a 1920 statutory ratio, making each rural voter the equivalent of two city voters, assured the over-representation of the British farming districts in the southwest. Thus the Farmers' majority in 1922 was based on only one-third of the popular vote.

After their victory, the farmers persuaded John Bracken to be premier. Like them, he was of Ontario British stock: his father's farm near Brockville was reputed to be "one of the finest in Leeds County."[82] He came to Manitoba in 1906, and rose through agricultural extension work to head the Manitoba Agricultural College by 1920. Spartan by temperament, he probably remains the only premier to have swum in Hudson Bay and sprinted up and down the stony northern shoreline in September.[83] A visitor at a political meeting in a south-western town compared him to "a Baptist preacher, perhaps because of his black tie and solemn expression" and was impressed that his dry exhortation on the need for disciplined economy "had the undivided attention of everyone in the hall."[84] Another observer commented:

> *He comes of Irish Presbyterian stock . . . who neither make jokes nor feel comfortable when they encounter wit. Incessant and laborious campaigns with the dry minutiae of provincial business have not exasperated his imagination, because he is not imaginative. He is an earnest young man . . . quite without frills.*[85]

The basis of the Bracken government was the claim that good government was mainly a matter of careful administrative husbandry. That government should above all be firm, cautious, and conservative was the lesson drawn from the 1919 disorders. Both the prosperous business interest in Winnipeg and the farmers of the southwest shared the same goals: economy and stability.[86] Premier Bracken became custodian of the *status quo*. Remaining close to agriculture, he became also a prosperous landholder, owning by 1928 a 2,000-acre farm and after his retirement a 1,000-acre ranch estate in the Ottawa Valley.

Primary emphasis during the Bracken years was on the virtue of self-denial. The legislature became preoccupied with sin. Through the efforts of Mrs. Edith Rogers, wife of the president of the Crescent Creamery Company in Winnipeg and first woman elected to the legislature, smoking was prohibited in the legislature chamber.[87] Former suffragettes now scolded flappers and counselled that skirts should be longer. A newly-elected farmer expressed his view of the motion picture industry:

> *Personally, I would like to see the moving picture industry wiped out. One of the reasons for illegitimacy is that people are living so fast in these times.*[88]

The government established a censorship board with extensive authority:

> *The board shall not approve any film or slide depicting scenes of an immoral or obscene nature, or which indicate or suggest lewdness or indecency, or marital infidelity, or showing the details of murder, robbery or criminal assault, or depicting criminals as heroic characters; and the board shall refuse to approve any other picture which it may consider injurious to public morals.*[89]

Other issues stirring debate included the need for stringent limits on horse racing, whether evolution should be taught in the public schools, the need to arrest any child under sixteen found on city streets after 9 p.m., and reported orgies on Sunday excursion trains to Lake Winnipeg beaches. Liquor also roused spirited discussion, as when a provincial police commissioner claimed that 95 per cent of bootleggers were Jews engaged in a world-wide conspiracy to overthrow Christian values.[90] Total prohibition proved unworkable, since thousands of gallons of liquor were sold through drug store prescription; and after a referendum, the government permitted beer sales under careful regulation:

> *Every brewer who manufactures beer in the Province of Manitoba shall on every Wednesday make to the commission a return in writing showing in separate detail each and every sale of beer made by him during the successive six days terminating with the Saturday immediately preceding. Such return shall show (a) the name and address of each purchaser* [*etc.*].[91]

Such questions of morality practically monopolized party politics, partly because the province's political system was securely in the control of the relatively prosperous class and other issues could not readily arise.

In a listing of about 700 prominent Manitoba citizens in 1925, the great majority were British.[92] Obituaries during the period show the same pattern. Alexander McLaren, proprietor of several hotels, came to Winnipeg in 1874 from Perth, Ontario. James Ashdown, a millionaire hardware merchant, came to Winnipeg in 1868 after working in his father's store in Weston, Ontario. William McMillan, a founder of the Dominion Elevator Company and the Winnipeg Grain Exchange, came to Winnipeg in 1875 from Pickering, Ontario. His brother, Daniel McMillan, accompanied the Wolseley expedition to expel Louis Riel and, after serving as provincial treasurer in the Greenway government, was knighted and appointed Lieutenant-Governor by the Laurier government. In a similar pattern, James Aikins, son of one of John A. Macdonald's cabinet ministers, came to Winnipeg in 1879 from Grahamsville, Ontario, became a major owner of downtown real estate, a director of Great West Life Assurance, the Imperial Bank of Canada, and other companies, and finally was appointed Lieutenant-Governor by the Borden government in 1916. Likewise, Theodore Burrows came to Winnipeg in 1875 from the Ottawa Valley, prospered with his uncle, the first Dominion land agent in Winnipeg, became head of numerous lumber and mortgage companies, and in 1926 was appointed Lieutenant-Governor to succeed Aikins. James Richardson, a director of numerous financial and grain companies, came to Winnipeg in 1912 after experience in the family business in Toronto. George Galt, nephew of Alexander Galt, another of John A. Macdonald's ministers, came to Winnipeg in 1881 from Toronto and within six years was president of the Winnipeg Board of Trade, as well as president or director of several financial and insurance enterprises. His view of politics was straightforward:

> *If we in Canada would reflect more on our blessings and think less about our real or imaginary grievances, we would all be a happier and more self-reliant people.*[93]

Of the same mind was Sir Augustus Nanton, son of a law partner of Alexander Galt in Toronto, who came to Winnipeg in 1881 and became a financial partner of Hugh Osler, son of Sir Edmund Osler of Toronto.

When Nanton was appointed president of the Dominion Bank of Canada in 1924, he delivered a characteristic warning:

> *In my opinion, the greatest peril which confronts Canada and especially this city is the teaching we hear of that is going on behind closed doors. This should be done away with. We welcome all good citizens from foreign lands but if they do not believe in the Christian religion, nor intend to keep our laws, they should be asked without delay to return from whence they came.*[94]

Most of these prominent citizens were members of Winnipeg's Manitoba Club, Canadian Club, and St. Charles Country Club, all clubs for successful persons of British origin. Hugh Robson, who succeeded Norris as

Liberal leader in 1927 and was later appointed to the Manitoba Court of Appeal by the federal Liberal government of Mackenzie King, was a member of this group. So was the Conservative leader from 1922 to 1933, Fawcett Gowler Taylor, who in the latter year was appointed to the Manitoba Court of King's Bench by the federal Conservative government of R. B. Bennett. Former prominent politicians, such as Hugh John Macdonald, Clifford Sifton, and Robert Rogers, were also members, as were the province's leading jurists, such as Thomas Mathers and Daniel Macdonald. So were the province's two leading editors, John Dafoe of the *Free Press* and R. L. Richardson of the *Tribune*, both of whom, like most of this group, came to Winnipeg from Ontario. The *Free Press*'s bitter attacks on the Winnipeg strike were, according to his biographer, to be expected from Dafoe, who "had joined the Winnipeg establishment and took some pride in the fact that the boy from the backwoods was now an accepted member of the Manitoba Club."[95] Several cabinet ministers, such as William Clubb and Richard Craig, the Attorney-General, were also members. The British group from Ontario thus comprised a ruling class, although it claimed that class politics was undesirable. Craig, for example, advised immigrants:

> *A government composed of one class is not democratic, but autocratic. Today we require a government of all the people, elected by the people and not by any one class.*[96]

To the non-British, the attractiveness of this ruling class was a major incentive for Anglicization. The shame they felt in not being English is well expressed in a novel about Winnipeg in the 1920s by a writer of non-British origin. It tells of Sandor Hunyadi, the son of Hungarian immigrants, who tries to become an English businessman. At 12, looking for a job as a gardener, he first visits the English neighborhood south of the Assiniboine River:

> *In a daze, he moved down the street. The boulevards ran wide and spacious to the very doors of the houses. And these houses were like palaces, great and stately, surrounded by their own private parks and gardens.*

After securing a job from an impressive English matron, he exults:

> *He was going to work for her, and so in a sense he belonged to her house and some of this high splendid arrogance of hers would be his too. This is the way it should be, he thought. This was how the rich English should act, this was the way they should look, dignified and cool-eyed and distant.*[97]

After growing up, Sandor changes his name to Alex Hunter and tries to succeed as a rent collector. The novel's conclusion is gloomy: despite his effort to become like the English, "Hunter" fails in business and retreats into despair.

A primary concern of the British ruling group was to protect itself from taxation. Hence the provincial government pursued rigorous thrift, keeping annual expenditure to $10 million or less and producing budgetary surpluses year after year in the 1920s. Costs were held down particularly in the areas of health, education, and welfare. Of $5,000 appropriated for child welfare in 1921, for example, $420 was actually spent;[98] seven years later, the grant for two child welfare agencies was increased to $787.60.[99] On taking office, one of the Bracken government's first actions was to cut provincial allowances for widowed and deserted mothers, despite a mass protest meeting at Winnipeg's Grace Church.[100] Responding to briefs from the Winnipeg Board of Trade and a Taxpayers' Association protesting education costs, even though 104 schools closed for lack of funds in 1923, the government appointed a special commission to recommend further economies.[101] The school population increased by 15,000 between 1921 and 1928, but the provincial appropriation for education remained virtually constant and declined as a proportion of total expenditure.[102] In 1928, Miss Charlotte Whitton was appointed to appraise the administration of provincial welfare and her report stressed the adverse consequences of rigid cost reduction. Visiting a provincial charitable home for the infirm, she found 435 persons from under five to over seventy jammed into two inadequate buildings without any nursing staff.[103] The next year the provincial grant for the home was raised by $40, but three years later was reduced by $807.[104] After noting that the average monthly wage in Winnipeg in 1928 was $108.25, and that the minimum monthly subsistence budget for a family of four was $88.00, the Whitton report listed numerous case histories of families below this minimum, one example being "case no. 1937: father, 49, born in Poland, illiterate, incapacitated from osteo-arthritis; mother, 44, illiterate; four children—girl, 16; girl, 11; girl, 8; boy, 5," who lived on a monthly income of $40.00.[105]

Regarding public health services, hospital directors repeatedly stressed the need for more financial support. The government's response, as in the 1927 Speech from the Throne, was to reassert the necessity of "lessening the ever-increasing cost of public health activities."[106] That the poorer living conditions of the non-British immigrants were reflected in higher incidence of disease and early death received comment in both official and professional reports:

> *As persons of Ukrainian origin are usually regarded as robust, the rather high percentage of deaths of Ukrainian fathers at comparatively early ages may cause some concern as to whether hygienic and social conditions of their family life can be improved.*[107]

> *Scandinavians [in Manitoba] appear to be susceptible to tuberculosis. This is attributed partly to lower resistance and partly to poor housing conditions.*
>
> *Manitoba's French-Canadians have a high death rate from diphtheria (22.2 deaths per 100,000 as against 9.8 per 100,000 for the whole province). Winter epidemics are common among them and the factors relating to these outbreaks are overcrowding in the homes and inadequate sanitation.*
>
> *The typhoid morbidity rate among the (province's) Mennonites is 44.4 per 100,000 as against 16.0 per 100,000 for the province.*[108]

In 1928, the Bracken government passed an Old Age Pensions Act, but it seemed that few of the poor survived long enough to qualify for it. It granted monthly pensions of $20 for persons over 70 years of age who had resided in Canada for at least 20 years. Both Liberals and Conservatives opposed the pension as too costly, since the province's share of the cost was to be raised by a supplementary property tax levy; but as one newspaper noted, the total cost involved was not great and the help it provided for the elderly was "better than nothing at all."[109]

The onset of the Depression in the fall of 1929 reinforced the government's determination to reduce public expenditure. When the stock market crashed, Premier Bracken was away on a European tour. He returned shortly and instituted a program of paring costs everywhere possible, to the extent of cutting the *per capita* daily bread allowance of mental patients from 11.99 to 11.68 oz.[110] In the province's northern territories, where the number of orphans whose other relatives could not assume responsibility for them doubled between 1929 and 1930, the monthly allowance for each child was cut in half to ten dollars.[111] This policy held firm against requests for help from the increasing numbers of unemployed. On a winter afternoon during the 1931 session, for example, 4,000 assembled outside the legislative building and their leaders conferred at length with the premier. Shortly after six, when it was already getting dark, he returned to the legislative chamber where the MLAs awaited him "amid a profound silence."[112] Other meetings sometimes became violent, as in the summer of 1935, when a number of unemployed seized and briefly occupied a soup kitchen.[113] With 25 per cent of its work force unemployed, Winnipeg by 1932 was reported as having the second highest urban *per capita* unemployment rate in Canada.[114] By 1937, the number of persons seeking relief in the province had reached 115,155, or a sixth of the population.[115] Since many were non-British, deportation was used to reduce relief costs. A reporter who lost his job in 1930 and had to apply for relief recorded the impact of this threat:

> *I came to appreciate for the first time the tremendous advantage it was to be a Canadian Anglo-Saxon in Winnipeg. And as time*

> *passed, the advantage widened when, as if racial intolerance was not enough, a new terror for the New Canadians began to stalk the land in the form of Immigration Officers with deportation orders in their hands.*
>
> *The foreign born... sought more and more to melt into the background, say nothing, hear nothing....*
>
> *Ours was a society with a well-defined pecking order of prejudice. On the top were the race-proud Anglo-Saxons.*[116]

Those eligible for relief earned it in such make-work projects as removing dandelions from the boulevards of south Winnipeg. In the city's north end, the housing of the unemployed was officially described in a 1939 report, which gave examples:

> *One house on Barber St.—no bath, no furnace, and not even a single sink—yet no less than twelve men are living in the basement, seventeen men, women and children are huddled in rooms on the first floor and eleven more persons are crowded in beneath the eaves on the second story.*[117]

That some were worse off was indicated by reports through the decade of corpses found in various places, such as that of an unemployed man who died of starvation in the spring of 1939 in a freight car in the CPR yards.[118] Outside Winnipeg, the relatively poorer areas settled by non-British immigrants in the northwest, in the interlake district, and to the southeast were dotted with abandoned homestead shacks and had the highest incidence of municipal disorganization, tax delinquency, and subsistence living standards.[119] Without much success, the Bracken government sought after 1932 to reduce urban unemployment by launching a back-to-the-land resettlement program sending relief families into these areas with monthly allowances from eight to fifteen dollars, depending on family size, payable for a maximum of 12 months, after which the families were to be self-supporting.[120] To cover the cost of these relief programs, the government imposed a flat 2 per cent wage tax, which a federal royal commission later termed "the heaviest income tax on low income groups in North America."[121] In contrast, the tax rate on the Winnipeg business community, according to an independent survey by Assessment Appraisers Ltd. of Toronto, was substantially lower than in other major Canadian cities.[122]

The poorer class provided little opposition to the Bracken government's policies. The French minority, preoccupied with preserving its religion and language, generally supported the government, and constituency contests were due more to the personal rivalry of candidates than to party differences. A form of quasi-seigneurial paternalism developed under the leadership of a small clique closely aligned with the French

Catholic clergy and successively represented in the cabinet by Albert Préfontaine, Sauveur Marcoux, and Edmond Préfontaine. Only after 1936 did some French express an economic protest by voting Social Credit, largely because of the example of *Béret Blanc créditisme* in Quebec.[123] Associated with the French in the Roman Catholic Church was the Polish community, so politically inactive that a recent history of it concludes simply that "Polish participation in the public life of Manitoba has been so far insignificant."[124] In 1932, a convention of citizens of Polish origin briefly considered running an independent "national" candidate to secure group recognition but, like the French, decided it would be better to be loyal to the government in office.[125] The more numerous Ukrainian community was divided into Greek Orthodox and Greek Catholic factions, which sometimes, as in 1927, promoted rival candidates.[126] A few Ukrainians were more radical: in 1932, when D. M. Elchesen, backed by a group of Conservative British businessmen, tried to address a north end meeting, he was shouted down with cries of "Traitor! You've gone over to the bosses!"[127] Generally, however, the Ukrainians tried to avoid offending the government:

> *Canadian Ukrainians do not have any influence. We are poor and need political help. Ukrainian farmers and workers depend for their livelihood on the more powerful. This forces us to support a politically influential party. Affiliation with small radical parties brings us Ukrainians only discredit and ruin.*[128]
>
> *All signs show that the Bracken government will remain in power. This means that we have to elect candidates put forward by the governing party. . . . Candidates from parties making strange and impossible promises will bring us no advantage, only national dishonour.*[129]

Like the French, the Ukrainians were primarily concerned with having one or two respectable national representatives on the government side. Serving in this capacity through the 1930s and after were a prosperous lumber and implement dealer, Nicholas Hryhorczuk, and a former police interpreter, Nicholas Bachynsky. Again like the French, and like some Icelanders in the Interlake district, a few Ukrainians tried to protest by voting Social Credit in 1936, but with little effect.

Most vulnerable of these non-British groups was the German-speaking community. Circumspect since the First World War, it approached politics cautiously, and when it ventured to criticize the government, it was usually to request it to be true to its principles and to practice careful economy.[130] The group was divided into Catholics, Lutherans and Mennonites with the latter further split on their degree of orthodoxy. To escape Soviet collectivization, a new wave of relatively less conservative Mennonites came to the province during the late 1920s. They entered politics more readily than had their predecessors and Dr. C. W. Wiebe won election in 1932 as a Bracken supporter from the riding of Morden-Rhineland. By that time, Hitler's rise caused new divisions in the German community. A poem in a local German newspaper applauded his success:

> *Reach forth your hand to Adolf Hitler! Adolf! Let us grasp your hand!*[131]

Winnipeg was reported to be the "headquarters of the Canadian Union of Fascists," the German consul was claimed to be organizing Nazi cells, and brown-shirted Mennonites marched in the streets.[132] "Mysterious tappings" in the legislative building aroused fear of Nazi sabotage, but armed guards who searched "every nook and cranny" discovered that the sounds were being caused by maintenance carpenters.[133] Repeating the pattern of the First World War, such allegations of sedition obliged Manitobans of German origin to reaffirm their loyalty, as in an official statement issued by the local German-Canadian League:

> *Nazis constitute but a small minority... German settlers here in the vast majority are loyal to Canada and to democracy.*[134]

The rise of Naziism in the 1930s was comparable in its effect on Manitobans of German origin to that of the Bolshevik revolution on Manitobans of East European origin: both groups were obliged to be unobtrusive in provincial politics.

In 1932, under pressure from their federal leaders, the Liberals entered a coalition with the Bracken Progressives. After the election of that year sustained the government, two prominent Liberals, Ewan McPherson, a barrister, and J. S. McDiarmid, a south Winnipeg lumber merchant, joined the cabinet. The Conservatives remained outside the coalition but provided little opposition. The party was led from 1932 to 1936 by W. Sanford Evans, a wealthy Winnipeg publisher and grain merchant, who was succeeded in the latter year by Errick French Willis, a prosperous farmer in the southwest and son of the former Conservative leader R. G. Willis. Both Evans and Willis criticized the government primarily for not cutting expenditures and taxes further. On the latter's election as leader in 1936, for example, he declared that "technical advice had been obtained from an expert chartered accountant to show that a million dollars could be saved" by pruning government expenses.[135] The Conservatives publicly received testimonials of support from Winnipeg's business community, as in 1932 when 100 prominent businessmen published a statement pledging their support for the party,[136] and this enabled the Liberal-Progressives to distribute pamphlets to the ethnic groups declaring that the Conservative party "is not good for the poor people—it only helps those who are already rich."[137] But there was little real difference between prosperous farmers such as Willis and Bracken or between prosperous businessmen such as McDiarmid and Evans, and the two parties frequently voted together in the legislature. In 1936, it appeared that opposition would come from Social Credit, which unexpectedly won five seats in poor non-British districts in the north. When the movement's leader, Dr. Stanley Fox, joined the Bracken coalition after the election, some of his former supporters held meetings which expressed their sense of having been betrayed:

> *"Between 80 and 90 per cent of those who voted Social Credit voted, not for Social Credit, but as a protest against the Bracken government", Robert Gissing, Gimli delegate, complained. Cries of "Hear! Hear!" greeted his remark.*[138]

After Dr. Fox became involved in court proceedings on a personal matter,[139] he was succeeded by non-British representatives such as Miss Salome Halldorson, J. M. Montagnon and William Lisowski. But as a protest movement, Social Credit failed to regain its original momentum.

Hence the only consistent opposition to the Bracken government came from the Independent Labor Party and its successor after 1933, the Manitoba Cooperative Commonwealth Federation.[140] Showing little change from election to election, the party platform regularly urged, as in 1932, increased relief, public health and unemployment insurance, public ownership of natural resources and major industries, and increased taxes on higher incomes.[141] The party's predominantly British character gave it political legitimacy while reflecting the cultural conservatism that generally characterized labor politics in this period.[142] Most of its leaders—John Queen, Seymour Farmer, who succeeded Queen in 1935, James Woodsworth, and Stanley Knowles—were of British origin. Exceptions included Jews such as J. A. Cherniack, elected ILP treasurer in 1928, and Marcus Hyman, an Oxford-trained barrister, elected in Winnipeg in 1932 and 1936, and a Ukrainian, Joseph Wawrykow, elected for the ILP in Gimli in 1936 partly because he was the only Ukrainian candidate in the contest. Otherwise almost all ILP-CCF candidates in 1936, as well as those signing their nomination papers, were English. So also was an avowed independent socialist, Lewis St. George Stubbs, who topped the poll in Winnipeg's proportional representation list in 1936 and retained his seat until he retired in 1949. Most Communist candidates were also British: Leslie Morris, who ran unsuccessfully in 1932, was born in Somerset, England, in 1904, and came to Manitoba in 1920; James Litterick, who won a seat in 1936 and thus became the first Communist MLA in Manitoba, was born in Glasgow and came to Canada in 1925.[143] Remaining steady through the 1920s and the 1930s at about 5,000, the Communist vote was strongest in the city's north end. But it did not significantly increase in the non-British neighborhoods despite the party's emphasis after 1934 on cultural activities in ethnic associations.[144] Instead, among Ukrainians Stalin's purges and policies in the Ukraine caused splits and defections. To the Comintern in Moscow in 1929, the Canadian Communist party's dependence on non-British support seemed a source of weakness.[145] But this association was mutually disadvantageous. The allegiance the party received from a few Ukrainians and Jews came mainly from immigrants who arrived in the 1920s and remained both apart from and an embarrassment to the older non-British group. By lending credibility to the 1919 charge that all foreigners were untrustworthy, their example widened the division between the British ILP-CCF and most of the non-British poor. As a survivor of the period later observed:

> *If you were British, you could be critical of society. But if you weren't they blamed it on your background. You were a Communist. The Communists proved it. So it was best to keep quiet.*[146]

Had there not been a Communist party, drawing publicized "foreign" support, more political cooperation might have developed between the British and the non-British lower class groups. In prejudicing such cooperation, the Communist party in effect assisted the supremacy of the Bracken government. Winnipeg's system of proportional representation in turn enabled a Communist candidate to get elected with a small scattered vote. This made the party a conspicuous if ineffective contender, and kept alive the 1919 specter of alien revolution. The preoccupation of Communist spokesmen with international events similarly served the province's ruling group by seeming to confirm its claim that discontent with local economic conditions was inspired by sympathy for or allegiance to Russia and was therefore unpatriotic if not traitorous. A 1929 address by a Professor Scott Nearing was entitled "The Crumbling British Empire" and claimed that British imperialism would be replaced by American imperialism: "The United States will dominate, rule, exploit and rob the earth."[147] During the 1936 election, Tim Buck, the party's general secretary, spoke on the Spanish civil war, claiming that "in Manitoba, Ontario, Spain and France – the conflict is everywhere the same."[148] Similarly, Litterick's major addresses after his election were on such topics as Hitler's threat to Russia, the justification for the Moscow trials, the need for an embargo on exports to Facist countries, and the dangers of Chamberlain's appeasement policy.[149] This compromised the party after the Nazi-Soviet Pact in 1939. Local Communists were interned under the Defence of Canada Act in 1940 and Litterick was disqualified from holding a seat in the legislature. His final speech was a defence of Soviet foreign policy and an attack on the Canadian war effort.[150] Few non-British voters could afford to share such views; more representative of their attitude was the advice given by Wasyl Swystun to a Ukrainian convention in Winnipeg in 1941, telling them to vote for the Liberal party in office because "we must all be good Canadians."[151]

Premier Bracken responded to the outbreak of war by calling for an all-party coalition, partly on the premise that in wartime political opposition was inappropriate. A similar case was made for the need to present a united front in negotiations with Ottawa, although there is little evidence that the government ever used or mentioned in later federal-provincial conferences the fact that it represented several political parties.[152] By absorbing the Liberals in 1932 and Social Credit in 1936, the coalition device had helped keep the Bracken government in office. It was also the fulfillment of Bracken's philosophy that government was merely a matter of administration, transcending class division and obviating class politics. As applied, however, the doctrine demonstrated itself to be a peculiarly unproductive form of conservatism. One of its first apparent effects was a sharp decline in voting. The turnout of registered voters dropped from 73 per cent in 1932 and 66 per cent in 1936 to 50 per cent in the 1941 election, 56 per cent in 1945 and 54 per cent in 1949.[153] There was a corresponding increase in acclamations: 16 in 1941, 7 in 1945, and 16 in 1949. In some ridings, such as those represented by Errick Willis, the Conservative leader in the coalition, and by Douglas Campbell, a cabinet minister and later premier, there were no elections for 17 years; and in another, represented by William Morton, a coalition cabinet minister, there was no election for 22 years. After Bracken left Manitoba in 1943 to become national leader of the Progressive-Conservative party, he was succeeded by Stuart Garson, an Ontario-born farmer much like Bracken. When Garson joined the federal Liberal cabinet in 1948, he in turn was succeeded by Douglas Campbell, a prosperous farmer similar in background and temperament to Bracken and Garson. Statements by Campbell and Willis during the 1949 election expressed the philosophy with which the coalition justified itself:

> *The provincial government deals with the same matters as municipal councils. The present coalition has eliminated politics from the business of government and has made up for what it lacks in color by gaining in efficiency. We aim to avoid wearying the electorate with partisan political speeches. All the brains do not rest in the heads of one party and therefore it seems logical that by using the process of coalition government, we should select the best men in both the Progressive-Conservative and Liberal parties. Where in the name of common sense is the need for party politics? Isn't it just a case of meeting together?*[154]

Despite the coalition's claimed efficiency, however, its only major accomplishment was a rural electrification program. Its strength lay not in its legislative record but in the alliance of southwestern British farmers and south Winnipeg British businessmen that supported and financed it. This foundation was reinforced by appeals to ethnic groups, as in the address of a cabinet minister to the Polish Combatants' Association pledging the coalition's support for a "free Poland, undivided and independent."[155] Backed by a united dominant class and able to exploit cultural divisions in the lower class, the coalition seemed to have discovered the key to political immortality.

As a passive member of the coalition during the 1941 election, the CCF lost four of its seven seats in the legislature. But after withdrawing the next year, it received a surge of popular support comparable to CCF gains at the same time in Ontario and Saskatchewan. Its candidates, Berry Richards, a mining engineer, and Dr. Dwight Johnson, won two 1943 provincial by-elections in The Pas and Brandon respectively; party membership rose sharply from about 500 in 1942 to over 5,000 in 1944; and the annual budget approached $15,000, permitting the employment of two secretaries and two full-time organizers.[156] In the 1945 election, the party won 34 per cent of the popular vote; but with the system of representation that discriminated against both Winnipeg and the poorer northern ridings, this translated into only 10 seats. From this high point, the party declined. As the Cold War began, a split occurred on the party's attitude toward the Soviet Union and on the advisability of collaboration with the local Communist Labor Progressive Party. Favoring cooperation, Richards and Johnson issued a joint statement:

> *Peace and progress will only be brought about by cooperation with, and understanding of, the Soviet Union, which involves the abandonment of anti-communism and the unity of all progressive forces.*[157]

Both were ultimately obliged to withdraw from the party, and by 1949 both their seats were lost to the coalition. The controversy enabled the *Free Press* to claim that the CCF "has become a political bedlam in which the official views are opposed by a very large minority of Communists—the party is infiltrated today to the point where no one knows where it stands."[158] Such charges made the CCF more conservative. The Communist issue also cost the party what little support it had gained among non-British groups sensitive to charges of being disloyal. A Ukrainian newspaper commended the rejection of left-wing parties:

> *This time, just as in previous elections, many of our people either did not vote or, through ignorance, spoiled their ballots. This is inexcusable, for every vote is a vote for freedom and against communism. It is worth noting however that in our Ukrainian districts in the recent election there has appeared a marked deviation from socialist candidates. This is to be considered a healthy development.*[159]

This attitude was reinforced by a numerically small but influential group of immigrants, mainly from the intellectual, business and professional class, who were displaced by the Soviet occupation of Eastern Europe and brought bitter memories to Canada.[160] This ethnic hostility to Communism hurt the CCF despite its attempts to be respectable. With organizers such as Alistair Stewart and Donovan Swailes, and under the leadership successively of Edwin Hansford and Lloyd Stinson, it barely kept alive, retaining in the 1953 election only five seats with less than 17 per cent of the popular vote.

Another casualty of rising post-war anti-Communism was the Labor-Progressive Party member of the legislature, William Kardash. A veteran of the Mackenzie-Papineau battalion in the Spanish civil war, he won election in Winnipeg in 1941 with about 5,000 votes. After 1945, however, whenever critical international events occurred, his party was attacked. When headlines in 1949 reported a new defeat of Chiang Kai-shek and the charging of "top U.S. Communists" with conspiracy and espionage, demonstrators threw rocks at the LPP office and reduced a party meeting to a riot.[161] Even minor events sparked major reactions, as in 1953, when it was reported that 20 children were attending a Russian-Canadian Society evening class where they were exposed to Soviet textbooks. These allegedly contained poetry:

> *We sing songs about Stalin*
> *We love our Stalin*

as well as the claim that a certain Ivan Polzunov invented the steam engine 20 years before James Watt.[162] Mrs. B. Dyma, president of the Ukrainian Catholic Women's League, called the teaching "vicious poisoning"; Slaw Rebchuk, a Liberal alderman, termed it "malicious propaganda"; and Metropolitan Ilarion Ohienko of the Ukrainian Greek Orthodox church condemmed it as "Godless and evil."[163] Speaking for the government, the Conservative leader Errick Willis added:

> *We and the churches are the strongest fortresses against Communism. Communism should be outlawed.*[164]

When Kardash finally lost his seat in the 1958 election, he was probably right in attributing his defeat to ethnic and religious opposition. As the Communist vote declined and the Cold War appeared to abate somewhat, so did publicity on the threat of subversion or Communist infiltration. The CCF in turn could afford to be less defensive and began to attract more votes from the non-British lower class.

The first effective opposition to the coalition government, however, came from one of its traditional supporters, south Winnipeg's business community, increasingly concerned about the province's slow economic growth and the Campbell administration's evident preoccupation with rural matters. The attack on the coalition was initiated by a group of Conservatives led by Duff Roblin, grandson of Sir Rodmond P. Roblin. A Winnipeg automobile dealer associated with his family's business, he won a seat in south Winnipeg in 1949 as an Independent Conservative, and gathered support from other Winnipeg businessmen such as Gurney Evans, a son of the earlier Conservative leader Sanford Evans. This group helped extricate their party from the coalition in 1950, and four years later Roblin won the party leadership from Errick Willis. His victory in the provincial election that followed in 1958, shortly after John Diefenbaker's landslide federal victory, was almost a foregone conclusion. Ironically, one of the Campbell government's reforms helped defeat it: a 1957 redistribution of legislative seats, carried out by an independent boundaries commission, ended the system of proportional representation in Winnipeg and raised its number of seats in the legislature to 20. Of these, the Liberals retained only St. Boniface, won by Roger Teillet with French Catholic support; while another was held by Winnipeg's Mayor Stephen Juba as an Independent. Otherwise the city polarized along class lines, with the poorer north end voting for the CCF and the wealthier south end voting Conservative.

That the whole province did not similarly polarize in 1958 was partly due to the Liberals' retention of their traditional ethnic appeal in some rural areas, such as the Mennonite district of Rhineland, won by Wallace Miller, the French and German districts of Carillon and La Vérendrye, won by Edmond Préfontaine and Stan Roberts, and the Slavic districts of Springfield, won by William Lucko, Emerson, won by John Tanchak, and Ethelbert Plains, won by Michael Hryhorczuk, son of Nicholas Hryhorczuk, leading Ukrainian representative in the legislature during the 1920s and 1930s. All these districts, with the exception of Rhineland, where Mennonite farmers had prospered, were relatively poor and had been so since their original settlement. In these areas past ethnic traditions still served the Liberal party. The first indication that they were declining came with two CCF victories in similarly poor rural non-British districts. Brokenhead was won by Edward Schreyer, and in the riding of Fisher, Peter Wagner defeated Nicholas Bachynsky, who, like Nicholas Hryhorczuk, had been one of the leading Ukrainian Liberal-Progressive representatives and had been appointed Speaker of the legislature in 1950. Twenty years before the 1958 election, the prospect of having one of its members given such a position had been a potent symbol of ethnic recognition to a Ukrainian newspaper editor:

> *In English parliamentary bodies, the Speaker is called the President of the House, an extremely serious position, almost like a Minister. As their representative, our voters for the Ukrainian nation may be given an opportunity to have the first Ukrainian President of a legislature in the world.*[165]

But it appeared by the late 1950s that the need for ethnic recognition was being replaced by class consciousness. The slow process toward political assimilation extended by degrees into remoter areas and made possible a polarization not only in Winnipeg but across the province.

The Roblin period was a transitional one, with the government containing both conservative and reform elements. Its progressive enterprise was substantially the achievement of the premier himself, assisted by representatives from poorer northern districts such as Dr. George Johnson of Gimli. Provincial expenditures on health, welfare, and education over the decade from 1956 to 1966 increased from $27.5 million to $136.7 million.[166] After overriding rural opposition, schools were consolidated and dramatically improved. The government established a Metropolitan Corporation to coordinate the municipal services in Greater Winnipeg, a Manitoba Development Fund and various advisory agencies to promote economic development, and a Housing and Urban Renewal Corporation. A major highway construction program was instituted and a massive water diversion channel constructed to prevent further Red River floods in Winnipeg. In the north, a new power development was launched and a new mining community established at Thompson. But the province's basic class structure appeared to be affected little by these reforms.

After showing almost no increase during the 1920s and 1930s, provincial income increased sharply in the post-war period. Average weekly wages rose from $40.06 in 1949 to $84.44 in 1967;[167] and *per capita* income in the province rose from $980.00 in 1948 to $2,317.00 in 1967.[168] These gains were partly cancelled by an approximate increase of 50 per cent in the cost of living over the same period.[169] Average income figures, moreover, gave no indication of distribution, since a few large individual incomes could raise the average without any appreciable improvement of individual incomes at the bottom of the scale. Reported income tax statistics, by excluding the non-taxable returns of the poor and the non-monetary expense account and other benefits available to the upper income group, also tended to obscure or underestimate the gap between rich and poor.[170] But even within that limitation, they suggested that the range of income disparities from 1948 to 1968 remained virtually unchanged. In both years, the top 5 per cent of taxpayers reported receiving about 20 per cent of all income, the next 20 per cent received about 30 per cent of the income, while the bottom 75 per cent of taxpayers received the remaining 50 per cent of the income.[171] Taking into account the probably greater opportunities for tax avoidance and untaxed capital appreciation available to the upper income group, it appeared that there was little or no economic class equalization in Manitoba during the post-war period.

The gleaming new Centennial Concert Hall, the new University buildings, and the new luxury motor hotels built in Winnipeg during the Roblin period were remote from the lives of those on lower incomes. Following a tenement fire in which a three-year-old boy burned to death, a Metro statement reported that 5,000 residential buildings in the city deserved to be condemned and torn down.[172] Municipal Affairs Minister Thelma Forbes reported in 1967 that public housing was the "obvious answer" for the estimated 40,000 families in Greater Winnipeg who were unable to buy or rent privately built homes.[173] A slum-school principal tried throughout the period, without success, to persuade the government to locate a community center for children in his neighborhood, and ended by taking a group of his pupils to the new Pan-American swimming pool in the city's south end to see "where the rich people live."[174] At the end of the Roblin years, there was still no hospital in the city's north end, although a public housing development was built alongside the railway tracks in the district. Illustrating the difficulties of those on welfare was the case of a deserted wife with three children who had her rent paid and received a monthly allowance of $95. When evicted by her landlord for complaining about unsanitary conditions, she appealed to city authorities:

> *"Why do I have to suffer this hell?" she shouted. "Why can't you help me?" she asked city aldermen, who sat with their eyes fixed on the table in front of them.*[175]

Conditions had evidently changed little from 1946, when another deserted wife with three children was assigned by welfare officials to a cubicle in the city's old immigration building:

> *As we entered the front door our ears were assaulted by a splitting cacophony of screams, cries, radios, wails and curses. Hordes of children ran yelling down the halls which were strewn with filth from overturned garbage cans... Malodorous smells told of sour bodies, spilled wine, urine...*

In desperation, she too appealed to the city aldermen:

> *"I'm not going to be stuck in some lousy hole... with drunks and bums and filth! My children are not going to be stuck in some godforsaken hole where they don't have a chance."*[176]

At the beginning of the 1960s, it was estimated that over 17,000 city families still lived in extreme poverty. Average annual family incomes ranged from about $3,000 to $5,000 in the central and north end city districts and from about $10,000 to $20,000 in the south end districts of River Heights and Tuxedo.[177] Outside the city, a similar class division obtained, as it had since 1901.[178] The average capital value of Manitoba farms in 1966 was about $45,000, with the districts to the southwest all well above this average and those to the northwest, northeast, and southeast of Winnipeg, where non-British immigrants had settled, all markedly lower.[179] A similar pattern applied in farm size, productivity, and income from sales. In one of the poorest northern areas, the Interlake district, a third of the farms had annual incomes of under $1,200, with correspondingly poor housing, education, and other public facilities.[180]

As families within such districts moved about in search of a better living the old cultural divisions disappeared.[181] The second and third generations of the non-British immigrants became less susceptible to ethnic appeals.[182] Among this younger group, in contrast to the "hesitant conservatism" of their elders, there was a greater drive toward improvement of their material circumstances as well as a skepticism that this could be achieved within the existing system.[183] The ethnic press, whose total circulation declined after 1950, obliging rival newspapers to merge,[184] resisted this change yet admitted it, as for example in the 1959 election:

> *In Ethelbert Plains, the threat to the former Liberal minister, M. N. Hryhorczuk, was not from the Conservatives but from younger Ukrainians who supported the CCF.*[185]

As the young were assimilated, moreover, many changed their names, so ethnic editors became less certain about the origin of candidates:

> *In the last legislature, there were members whose national origin was uncertain. Rumours claimed they were Ukrainian but it was impossible to determine this from their surnames.*[186]

Had the province continued to attract as high a proportion of new immigrants after 1950 as it had in the period before and after the first war, these developments would have been offset by a continuing infusion of ethnic consciousness. But apart from a few hundred Philippine and Italian girls imported to work in the garment industry,[187] the province attracted relatively few immigrants: whereas before 1946, Winnipeg contained almost 9 per cent of all new immigrants in Canada, in the decade of the 1950s this proportion dropped to less than 4½ per cent.[188] Intermarriage also blurred ethnic lines, most notably with the Icelandic group[189] but increasingly through the 1950s and 1960s among the others as well, although orthodox Mennonites and Jews retained high rates of endogamy.[190] Another factor assisting assimilation was the impact of television, extending even to long-isolated rural areas.[191] Rear guard action resisting these forces tended to be ineffective: under pressure from ethic spokesmen, Ukrainian was introduced in 1963 into the Winnipeg school curriculum, but four years later, although there were in the school system approximately 6,000 children of Ukrainian descent, only 73 had been induced to study the language.[192]

In resisting the trend to assimilation and the political advantages accruing from it to a lower-class based party, there developed a more marked alliance between ethnic association leaders and the more conservative political parties. The political implications of even relatively minor ethnic questions were taken into account, as for example in his selection of entertainment for a Conservative convention, a program convenor reported that:

> *It might be advisable to have the Ukrainian choir and dancers, even if they cost more, for purely political reasons.*[193]

Both the Liberals and Conservatives solicited the ethnic vote with speakers, patronage, and status symbols. After the federal Conservative victory in 1958, for example, Gunnar Thorvaldson, a wealthy lawyer of Icelandic origin, who had sat in the legislature from 1941 to 1949 as a Conservative, was appointed to the Senate, where he opposed government assistance to the Interlake area, saying he was shocked at its being considered "underprivileged."[194] A similar appointment, hailed by the Ukrainian press, was that of Professor Paul Yuzyk to the Senate in 1963 after he had long served the party by addressing Ukrainian Catholic meetings on its behalf. Other such Conservative speakers and former candidates included Maurice Arpin, a lawyer of French background, and Daniel Zaharia, a realtor, both of whom were appointed to the University of Manitoba board of governors, and Michael Baryluk, a lawyer and former candidate, supported strongly but unsuccessfully by the Ukrainian press, who was appointed a magistrate in 1968. Another Conservative candidate, Peter Okrainec, emphasized in his 1962 campaign that he had been head marshal of the dedication procession at the 1961 ceremonial unveiling on the legislative grounds of a statue of the Ukrainian poet, Taras Shevchenko.[195] The appeal of such devices was mainly to the middle-aged or elderly, who adhered to tradition despite what in many instances were bleak personal circumstances. An extreme example of this was a 68-year-old Polish laborer and consistent Conservative voter who responded to a university questionnaire on his impression of political campaigns with a vivid statement of his difficulties:

> *Which campaign is the most effective for me I do not know. I have not radio no television no telephone. I never read newspaper. I live like rat in hole.*[196]

Prominent Conservatives, such as the cabinet ministers, Harry Enns, a Mennonite rancher, and Sidney Spivak, a hotel and apartment owner, were in contrast relatively well-to-do, as was the prominent Liberal MLA and later MP, Mark Smerchanski, a geologist and businessman, who expressed firm conservative views throughout the 1960s, urging the need for lower public expenditures and taxes at a Liberal leadership convention in 1961, for example, and vehemently attacking a capital gains tax in 1969.[197] Smerchanski was descended from Ukrainian immigrants who came to Manitoba in 1903 and established a general store.[198] A statement by his father exemplified a central theme of ethnic allegiance in Manitoba's political history:

> *I became a Liberal in 1911. We have seven children and they are all like me good Liberals.*[199]

The pattern appeared to be that those among the non-British groups who prospered or were co-opted into the Liberal or Conservative parties then served those parties by helping them exploit the ethnic traditions and divisions among those still in the lower class. In this way, ethnic leaders helped maintain the political hegemony of the predominantly British upper class which they joined or hoped to join. The gratification of lower class ethnic sentiment thus served as a tactical alternative to social and economic equalization.

In 1967, Roblin resigned the premiership and, after an unsuccessful attempt to enter federal politics, accepted an appointment as executive vice-president of Canadian Pacific Investments Ltd.[200] He was succeeded by Walter Weir, a funeral director from Minnedosa, who was first elected in 1959 and entered the cabinet in 1961. With Weir's accession, the government became markedly more conservative. One of his supporters, Gordon Lawson, an executive of James Richardson Ltd. and director of several companies, expressed the new administration's viewpoint:

> *The power to tax is the power to destroy. The lack of coordinated and controlled spending will result in an impossible burden on the taxpayer. I can't help but be staggered at the future costs of some of these programs.*[201]

With this concern, the Liberal party was in full agreement. Its leader from 1961 to 1969, Gildas Molgat, a Winnipeg businessman of French descent, emphasized the need to restrain expenses:

> *The new premier of Manitoba has vowed that he will hold the line on taxes. I ask him to make sure his promise is not broken.*[202]

As in the 1920s and 1930s, there was little difference between the two parties. Like the Conservatives, the Liberals drew much of their support from the business community of south Winnipeg. Most members of this group were members of the Manitoba Club, still symbolic of exclusive affluence in Winnipeg. The similarity between the two parties was further shown by federal-provincial voting patterns: south Winnipeg, which voted Liberal federally in 1968, voted Conservative provincially throughout the 1960s. Of the two parties, the Liberals received support from more senior corporate executives, particularly in the grain trade, probably because the Liberal federal government had more influence on their affairs. But this difference amounted to little in practice. In supporting the provincial Conservative government's policy of curbing taxation, the relatively wealthy in Winnipeg with few exceptions were united in a community of economic self-interest.

Notwithstanding this support, the Weir government began within a year of its formation to experience serious difficulties. When Weir reversed Roblin's decision and announced that Manitoba would remain out of the federal Medicare program, widespread protest developed, particularly among those on low or average incomes confronted with a 25 per cent increase in the fee schedule of the Manitoba Medical Association. A statement from the Manitoba Association of Social Workers claimed that 200,000 persons in the province could afford no medical insurance whatsoever,[203] and a Manitoba Federation of Labor delegation led a protest demonstration to the legislature. The premier argued against the plan's projected cost and its compulsory nature,[204] but was finally obliged to negotiate the province's entry into the plan. Another difficulty arose after a Toronto consultant, Murray V. Jones and Associates Ltd., reported that living conditions in northern Manitoba were "among the most wretched in Canada."[205] Charging the government with indifference to these conditions, Gordon Beard, the Conservative MLA for Churchill, resigned from the legislature.

His action focused attention on the plight of the province's Indians and Métis. Since surrendering their land claims in the 1870s, they had come near extinction and still barely survived, a minority of about 60,000 that was proportionally larger in Manitoba than in any other province.[206] Their revenues from trapping and fishing were in decline and they were virtually excluded from employment in the new mining centers such as Thompson. With high rates of infant mortality, tuberculosis and malnutrition, their life expectancy was about 34 years. Provincial child care services were available to only about half of those who left their reservations.[207] An estimated 10,000 moved to Winnipeg between 1961 and 1966 and comprised a tenth of all welfare cases.[208] Having been excluded from the franchise from 1885 to 1952, the province's Indians, like the Métis, were unused to voting or any political action. Those who did vote during the 1950s and early 1960s either supported the government or, in the case of some Catholic reservations, voted Liberal. But by 1968, the group's mood was clearly less pliable and more militant.

Similar dissatisfaction with the Weir government was expressed by Manitoba's French minority. Numbering about 80,000, this group remained mainly Liberal through the 1960s, partly because of tradition and partly because of Molgat's appeal, although in some poorer rural areas a few continued to express discontent with their economic circumstances by voting Social Credit.[209] Against this pattern of allegiance, Roblin could make little impression, even though he introduced a program whereby Catholic private schools could use some public school facilities and also allowed up to 50 per cent French language instruction in public schools in predominantly French districts. After Weir's accession, the government was less sympathetic toward the French and the premier repeatedly declared that in his list of priorities the question of language and cultural rights was far below the need for budgetary retrenchment. The Conservative party's campaign in 1969 was directed by a public relations firm, which concentrated on newspaper and television advertising. It involved only relatively minor participation by Premier Wier, who in the final two weeks of the campaign visited a number of rural centers but was otherwise inconspicuous. The theme of the advertising campaign was the need for Weir's continuing determination to restrain public spending, and this message was substantially conveyed by broadcast testimonials from average citizens who endorsed his firmness in resisting claims on the public treasury.

In contrast with the professionalism of the Conservative party, the NDP organization appeared improvised and amateurish. Much of its public impact during the Roblin period was provided by its leader, Russell Paulley. A railway worker, Paulley was able at times to secure press headlines with blunt criticism of the government, but by 1968 he was handicapped by ill-health and a record of election disappointmens. His party executive through the 1960s had to juggle deficits, and despite repeated emergency drives party membership remained low, amounting at the end of 1966 to 3,000, well below provincial CCF membership in 1945 and about a tenth of the party's 1966 membership in Saskatchewan.[210] The campaign manuals which belatedly appeared in 1967 retained much of the old CCF flavour:

> *Ideally, voters can inform themselves about the candidates and the issues. In practice, political parties must help provide this information. Canvassing is by and large a most interesting and pleasurable task. Ours is not to argue, but to meet and persuade.*
>
> *Visitors always want to chat. No matter how pleasant this may be, the candidate must remember that he should be out winning votes, and not passing the time of day with old friends.*
>
> *A good letters-to-the-editor campaign can be most effective, particularly if the local press is prepared to give you a fair break.*
>
> *Billboards can be effective, but their cost virtually rules them out.*[211]

Within the crisis-ridden context of the party's organization, this modest approach availed little; and the most encouraging gain during the 1960s was the gradual increase in the proportion of candidates, delegates and party members from the non-British minorities. An indication of this development was the 1968 candidacy of Sid Green, a Jewish labor lawyer, for the party leadership. Green lost to Paulley by a narrow margin, but it was more significant that for the first time in its history, the province's left-wing party was seriously considering someone of non-British origin as a prospective leader. To the NDP, as to increasing numbers among the younger descendants of non-British immigrants, questions of ethnic and religious background appeared to be of diminishing relevance in party politics. As ethnic and religious traditions exercised less effect in dividing lower class groups from one another, moreover, it became possible for them to coalesce politically in support of a party expressing dissatisfaction with existing inequalities. Even among those of non-British origin who had secured moderate prosperity through relatively accessible occupations such as teaching, the memory of past inequalities and obstacles endured by their parents was in some cases sufficient incentive to support a party committed to reforming the political and economic system.

This pattern provided part of the basis for the 1969 NDP leadership convention. Hastily moved up to June 7 after Premier Weir called the election for June 25, it was a contest between Sid Green and Edward Schreyer, MP for Selkirk. Schreyer won the leadership largely because of his successful record in politics and his expected ability to present an energetic alternative to Premier Weir. His German Catholic and rural origin was also expected to help attract those rural non-British groups already of increasing importance to the party. In the campaign he was assisted by a dozen party organizers from across Canada and by unprecedented NDP expenditures, later estimated by the party president at about $35,000.[212] But the result of the election was largely due to Schreyer's strenuous personal efforts and to the continuing process of change in Manitoba society.[213]

Just as Winnipeg polarized in 1958 so the whole province did in 1969: the poorer ridings in the north and east, whether predominantly Ukrainian, German, Icelandic, French, or Indian and Métis, voted for reform, while the older, mainly British ridings in the southwest voted for the *status quo*. The NDP representation in the legislature rose from 12 to 28 seats, and its share of the popular vote increased from 23 to 38 per cent. Of the 27 seats in Metro Winnipeg, the party won 17, mainly in the poorer north and central districts. Where it penetrated southward as in Crescentwood, won by University of Manitoba Professor Cyril Gonick, the division in poll results similarly reflected the division in the riding between a relatively wealthy neighborhood and one containing more modest homes and lower-income households. Of the two ridings in the city of Brandon, likewise, the poorer one in the east was won by the NDP, while the relatively more prosperous one in the west was retained by the Conservative party. The NDP also won both of the northern mining towns, Flin Flon and Thompson, where better than average incomes were undermined by exceptional living costs and where union spokesmen repeatedly expressed local dissatisfaction with high rents and food prices. In the ridings of The Pas and Rupertsland, similar dissatisfaction in Indian and Métis communities assisted the NDP victory. In the 14 northern and eastern ridings, generally, the NDP secured an average popular vote of 43 per cent; while in the same number of more prosperous ridings in the southwest, it secured only 19 per cent of the popular vote. Reversing this pattern of support, the Conservatives obtained 32 per cent of the vote in the north and east, but retained 47 per cent in the southwest.

This result did not appear to be an "ethnic revolt" in the sense that "ethnics" were "aroused" in seeking "the right they have now earned" to participate in the political process.[214] The ethnic associations, as in the past, were generally conservative in the campaign; some of their spokesmen, such as William Swystun, tried to exploit ethnic feeling on the issue of bilingualism.[215] After the election an ethnic press editor attacked socialism with customary vehemence:

> *Ed Schreyer, who knows a few words in Ukrainian because he grew up in a Ukrainian district, is assuring everyone that he will follow a so-called social-democratic course. Time will tell how far to the left the socialists will go and how far they will lead Manitoba into ruin.*[216]

But the traditional ethnic appeals were now less effective; in the north-south polarization, the separate loyalties and rivalries of individual ethnic communities could no longer be identified. The NDP victory appeared to have been made possible by a decline in ethnic consciousness. Ironically, the major victim of this polarization was the Liberal party, which had served as a vehicle of assimilation for the non-British groups. It was debatable whether by voting according to class the non-British groups in 1969 were necessarily acting more rationally than their predecessors had in voting for the government in office and seeking in that way a measure of security from ethnic discrimination.[217] But the old Liberal party was no longer able to profit from immigrant need for acceptance. Campaigning under the leadership of Robert Bend, who succeeded Molgat as party leader six weeks before the election, the party presented the appearance of an elderly warrior, whose fatigue could scarcely be concealed by Dixieland bands and mini-skirted cheerleaders. Bend himself was a Conservative survivor of the coalition period, and in neither style nor program did he distinguish himself from Premier Weir. Hence the electorate's polarization was assisted by its being presented with two clear alternatives: one conservative and expressed by Weir; and the other more progressive, expressed by Schreyer. A revived and vigorously reform-minded Liberal party could conceivably have secured the lower class vote, and might well have done so under Schreyer's leadership had he and others like him been attracted to it. With the Liberal failure to attract such leadership, however, the NDP became the party of reform for the relatively poorer class as well as for those generally unenthusiastic toward a government which had shown little initiative beyond a repeated commitment to budgetary restraint.

After the election, Weir tried to stay in office by proposing a coalition with the Liberals and offered a cabinet post to Larry Desjardins, the Liberal MLA for St. Boniface. But to the consternation of those who feared the NDP, Desjardins announced instead that he would support Schreyer.[218] Thus assured of a one-vote majority in the legislature, the new cabinet took office on July 15. Reflecting the party's varied support, it included a clergyman, two professors, a credit union manager, a railway shop foreman and a former miner, and was later enlarged with appointments of two teachers and a former policeman. Such a range of occupations hitherto little represented at the cabinet level increased apprehension among businessmen and the more lucrative professions whose members had traditionally administered the province's affairs. But the new ministers proved generally moderate in tone and Schreyer in particular took pains to reassure the business community. As the government's first legislative session opened in August with a lawn party and full ceremonial decorum, it was clear that fears of a socialist revolution were unjustified.

The Schreyer government enacted extensive reform legislation during its first term. In the field of individual rights, it established an ombudsman, a Human Rights Commission and various consumer protection measures. In health care, it promoted community health clinics, abolished medicare premiums and introduced a limited pharmacare program which paid part of the prescription drug costs incurred by the elderly. In housing, it established a rentalsman to adjudicate landlord-tenant disputes, undertook a major expansion of the supply of public housing and provided grants for the renovation of private homes owned by pensioners. In the north, it increased jobs for Indians and Métis on government projects, promoted fishery cooperatives, improved roads and airports and undertook, through a public corporation, to establish a model community at a new mining centre at Leaf Rapids. With respect to municipalities, it assumed much of their welfare costs, paid property tax rebates to home owners and tenants, encouraged further secondary school consolidation and, partly to equalize taxation and services through the metropolitan area, integrated the city governments of Winnipeg into one central administration.[219] All of these measures incurred little opposition criticism except concerning the total costs involved, which doubled provincial expenditure to almost $700 million by 1973.[220]

Even with regard to the long-controversial French minority, there was little debate as street signs and government notices in St. Boniface became bilingual and a French cultural center and teachers' college were established there under joint financing with the federal government. In 1970, in the same spirit, a bill extending the use of French as a full language of instruction in public schools in French areas was passed unanimously.[221]

The main battles between the opposition parties and the NDP were fought over public ownership and fiscal equalization. In 1970, the legislature was reduced to near bedlam and fisticuffs when the NDP established a government monopoly over automobile insurance. After that, nationalization was virtually dropped as too disruptive. Further takeovers of private business were largely inadvertent; struggling companies borrowed money from the Manitoba Development Corporation, then got into more difficulty and eventually surrendered ownership to the government. In January of 1971, a paper factory at The Pas was placed in receivership and later began operation as a public corporation burdened with heavy debts.[222] Other companies following a similar route included a bus factory, a vegetable cannery, an aircraft plant, a fertilizer company and a luxury ship on Lake Winnipeg. All had troubled careers and by the spring of 1973, the MDC reported an accumulated deficit of $40 million.[223] While they provided local jobs, these government wards had little or no effect on the overall income distribution and politically were a source of embarrassment. In seeking to reduce class disparity, government policy was limited to adjusting taxes.

Provincial party politics in Manitoba now approximated the British pattern. Expressed in a relatively civil debate over the "fundamental principle" of hierarchy *vs* equality, the continuing engagement was between rival income groups who competed to protect or improve their respective economic positions.[224] On one side, speaking for upper and upper middle income groups, the Liberal and Conservative parties defended the social hierarchy claiming that it represented the result of individual capacity and effort, that those in the upper ranks had secured their position because of their drive to succeed, and that because such drive was essential to social progress, it should not be jeopardized by government regulation and taxation. On the other side, speaking for lower and lower middle income groups, the NDP claimed that existing inequalities were at least partly the result of different social background, competitive advantage and market power, that those in the lower ranks were there because they lacked these assets, and that in the interest of fairness, government had an obligation to equalize opportunities and living standards. The alternative positions were commonly summarized as "free enterprise" *vs* "social justice", or as "political freedom" *vs* "economic democracy". Because the lower classes were widely, and probably accurately, believed to be numerically preponderant, Liberals and Conservatives deprecated "class warfare" and sought instead to stress the dangers inherent in government expansion; while the NDP, the presumed beneficiary of a straight economic alignment in the electorate, was much readier to focus debate on class disparities. Between party and class, the relationship was reciprocal; voters' perception of economic differences was both a cause and a product of the party system.[225]

In this context, articulate class consciousness was far from widespread; and there remained numerous exceptions to class voting. Young upper class iconoclasts relished the discomfiture of traditional authority and voted for the NDP; whereas elderly lower class traditionalists saw the NDP as an upstart and voted Conservative. Among the poor, there remained those who did not vote at all because they distrusted all authority or were sunk in apathy. Nor was the influence of cultural background completely diminished, though declining political forces, immigrant timidity, religious conservatism and ethnic patronage still persisted as cross-pressures on class voting. Many in the lower class also continued to identify with the Liberal and Conservative parties, in some cases apparently as a form of association with, or deference to, those with superior status; while the NDP drew support from a few in the upper classes who were moved by humanitarian sentiments or sought career advancement by serving the new ruling party. Nor did all issues clearly relate to class. Questions such as administrative competence, fiscal waste and extravagance, the personal appeal of local candidates and party leaders, as well as new concern with energy costs served to blur or override the emerging class alignment. Also, perhaps because of greater access to education, it appeared that more voters were becoming independent of any party. Hence there was no neat division in the electorate along class lines.[226]

Despite its avowed commitment to equalization, moreover, the NDP showed signs of succumbing to institutionalized conservatism. Beset by the demands of every group that considered itself in some way disadvantaged, and sensitive to criticism, it became cautious and defensive. Increasingly image-conscious after assuming office, it hired a public relations agency, Dunsky Advertising of Montreal, which received part of the province's tourism promotion account in the same way that Dalton Camp had earlier been rewarded by Duff Roblin.[227] Nor did some party leaders seem as willing to tolerate the traditional degree of dissent and amateur participation in constitutency associations and provincial council meetings. Except at nominations, constituency meetings were poorly attended and the party continued to lack the consistently broad membership base of its counterparts in Saskatchewan, British Columbia and Ontario. Because effective unionization included little better than half the proportion in more industrial provinces, exceptional influence was wielded by a few strong unions such as the Steelworkers at Thompson and their leaders such as Len Stevens, president of the Manitoba Federation of Labour. Also, since the cabinet was able to reward its supporters with patronage appointments to over 100 boards and commissions as well as various advisory and research agencies, there was little likelihood of the party's resisting control and direction from above. All this suggested that the NDP in office could become at least as oligarchic and professional as the Liberal and Conservative parties. But whether it could do this and still be sensitive to its lower class constituency was unclear.

The 1973 election result closely followed the pattern set in 1969. The NDP won the poorer ridings across the northeast; the Conservatives won the better established ridings through the southwest; the Liberals picked up a few odds and ends along the frontier between the two major parties; and Social Credit, by losing its last surviving seat to the Conservatives, was extinguished. Following a series of recounts and judicial rulings in close contests the NDP retained a majority of 31 seats, to 21 for the Conservatives. Having a Jewish leader, Sidney Spivak, did not hurt the Conservative party: both in Winnipeg and in rural areas, its share of the popular vote rose slightly, evidently at the expense of Social Credit and the Liberals. As for the latter, their vote dropped to 19 per cent. The party initially retained 5 seats, but shortly lost 2 of these in by-elections, one each to the NDP and the Conservatives; and the apparent trend toward a straight two-party system threatened its future survival in provincial politics.[228] Liberal losses were most marked in rural areas, and the party's only gains were in south and central Winnipeg, where a concentrated effort obtained only one secure seat. The overall distribution of its gains and losses suggested that it was losing most heavily in poorer rural areas, to the advantage of the NDP, and where its vote held up in urban areas, this was achieved at the Conservatives' expense, apparently because the two opposition parties were competing for the same vote.[229] This competition helped to keep the NDP in power.

A basic change in opposition strategy came with the election of Sterling Lyon as Conservative leader in 1975. The next year he travelled to B.C. to study how the uniting of anti-NDP forces behind Social Credit had defeated the Barrett government. On his return, the Conservatives directed their tactics to attract right-wing Liberals, and this was assisted by a Liberal move, under a new leader, Charles Huband, to the left, in apparent hope of retrieving "liberal" NDP voters. Meanwhile the Schreyer government became increasingly cautious and introduced few new programs during its second term. By the spring of 1977, private polls showed the Conservatives ahead of the NDP in popularity; and this pattern held firm in the election which followed in October. Lyon campaigned on the need to cut government spending and promised to reduce corporate and personal income taxes. Schreyer offered little, other than an accident insurance scheme and the extension of pharmacare, a prescription drug insurance program, to include dentures and eye-glasses, evidently believing it safer to emphasize the government's past record. For his part, Huband campaigned strenuously, but with a platform which was difficult to distinguish. The election was fought amid signs of imminent economic crisis: prices continued to rise at a rate of over 8 per cent a year; unemployment rose to almost 6 per cent; and the exceptionally cold wet autumn severely damaged crop prospects.[230] The result gave the Conservatives a secure majority with 33 seats, winning 8 from the NDP and 2 from the Liberals, who virtually collapsed to 12 per cent of the vote and only one seat. The pattern was a clear continuation of the two previous elections, with the result determined by the Conservative strategy of polarization of the right, the hard times, the NDP's policy exhaustion after 8 years in office, and its disconcerting record of financial losses, particularly in ill-fated public enterprises.

Over the first century of its development, political competition in Manitoba appeared to have undergone a substantial change of emphasis. From the beginning there had been marked class divisions but these were long overshadowed by cultural issues: the question of evicting or domesticating the Indians and Métis; the question of suppressing and subordinating the French Catholic minority; and the question of excluding or Anglicizing the immigrants from Eastern Europe. The lower classes, comprised of these and other diverse groups, including poorer English-Canadians and immigrants from the United Kingdom, were so internally fragmented that they posed no major challenge to the ruling group. In provinces further west, where there was more immigration from the United States, the influence of "radical" American ideas was probably greater.[231] But Manitoba was occupied earlier and decisively by British immigrants from Ontario who became prosperous entrepreneurs in Winnipeg and highly capitalized wheat farmers in the province's fertile southwest. Agrarian socialism did not attract them.[232] Their advantages were manifold: facility in the dominant language; pre-emption of much of the best land; more investment capital or access to it; better business and commercial connections with Toronto and Montreal; and greater political awareness and experience. It may be mistaken to ascribe to this group the coherence of a homogeneous cultural "fragment" of mid-nineteenth century Ontario,[233] for it contained diverse denominational and regional interests; and rival business interests, both on their own behalf and as agents of competing eastern corporations, fought each other for government patronage and the wealth it provided. Indeed the cultural divisions and political weakness of the lower class permitted those at the top to compete among themselves. Only when threatened by lower class discontent, as in 1919 and 1936, and then reluctantly, did they put aside their differences to meet the threat from below. Their skill in defeating these challenges, their ability to manipulate the ethnic vote, their material advantages and their sheer tenacity gave the Ontario British a remarkable political career in Manitoba.

But like all ruling groups, they eventually wore out. The austere puritanism which drove them to secure political control and family wealth also made them a demographic victim. By the 1920s, when British families were carefully limited to two or three children, the families of French and Slavic Catholics and German Mennonites frequently included a dozen or more children. And the sons of the British were also reduced by disproportionate losses in the two world wars. In particular, many of the old wealthy families in Winnipeg seemingly failed to reproduce themselves: the only survivors in some cases were elderly widows or spinster daughters living alone in decaying mansions. In the rural southwest, aged British pioneers sold their farms to young Mennonites and Ukrainians, and retired to small towns. Some of the group's more ambitious descendants sought opportunity elsewhere, just as their grandfathers had sought it in Manitoba in the 1880s. And their parents' ability to afford higher education for them made them more mobile, more likely to leave an area which could seem cold, dreary and provincial, when compared with the reputed excitement and sophistication of metropolitan life elsewhere.

Winnipeg's business decline was gradual. The opening of the Panama Canal in 1920 diverted grain exports through Vancouver; the rise of farmer-owned elevator companies and the establishment of the Canadian Wheat Board reduced the flow of wealth to the Winnipeg Grain Exchange; the development of automobile and truck transport reduced the importance of its railway facilities; the rise of cities in Alberta and Saskatchewan undercut Winnipeg's position as a distribution center for eastern manufacturers; and as second or third generation inheritors of local businesses proved uninterested or incompetent, more of these were sold to national or foreign corporations. A new transient executive class replaced the old entrepreneurs; its members were as conservative as their predecessors but more cautious about direct involvement and they frequently lacked the personal wealth and free time for politics. Thus Manitoba's traditional ruling group was diminished by many forces.

Meanwhile the descendants of early "aliens" now spoke English, learned to imitate acceptable social behavior and scrimped to get ahead. As some of these succeeded, there developed a new class structure in which cultural origin was largely irrelevant. Ethnicity survived mainly as a nostalgic memory to be celebrated at summer festivals and preserved in museums. The new "elite" was culturally less distinct, and less inclined to copy the upper classes of England: its pursuits were less lavish than those of the earlier period when millionaires built palatial Tudor or Georgian homes, entertained visiting British nobility and rode to hounds over farmers' fields. Upper class entertainment was now more discreet, less flagrantly displayed, more often enjoyed in distant luxury resorts in Mexico and the West Indies. And its income was frequently less secure, drawn from rents from ramshackle apartment blocks whose collapse or condemnation was imminent, from constricted profit margins in marginal enterprises or from loans advanced by eastern finance companies. Such as it was, much of Manitoba's "establishment" was in fact not much better off than the new government technocracy which assailed its "privileges".

Had Manitoba been settled exclusively by British immigrants, a major left-wing party could perhaps have emerged sooner, as it did in Britain, Australia and New Zealand, or in the culturally more homogeneous Scandinavian countries. But the motley lower class immigrant and native peoples in Manitoba long remained a precarious caste of poor outsiders. Preoccupied with survival, they were mainly passive spectators to the conflict between Ontario-born employers and immigrant workingmen from England and Scotland—except when they were recruited to support the *status quo* as docile voters and strike breakers. The course of international politics assisted their exclusion, as German and Slavic minorities were compromised by association with enemy countries, as social reform was identified with "foreign" Communism, and as new immigrants fleeing from Eastern Europe were even more markedly conservative. But by the 1960s the ethnic influence in Manitoba was waning. It survived in occasional reports, as in an interview with an 18-year-old Portuguese girl who came to Winnipeg in 1969:

> *The first two years I worked as a sewing-machine operator in a factory. I used to cry a lot. We were treated like slaves. People put you down because they know you can't get out.... I was lucky I got married and got the chance of being supported....* [234]

And in 1975, a prolonged strike at a Winnipeg bed factory was marked by strikers' complaints about "scabs—many of them East Indians and Filipinos," leading one striker to ask a reporter: "Is that any way for them to start life in Canada?"[235] But reduced immigration made such incidents rare reminders of the past. The province's original immigrant minorities were now relatively secure. By long and prudent service to the ruling class, by the carefully respectable careers of their "national" representatives, and by the progress of assimilation, the survivors of the ethnic experience won acceptance. As discrimination declined, so did ethnic voting. Concern over cultural divisions gave way to concern over continuing economic disparities; and it became possible for those in the lower classes, regardless of origin, to move toward supporting a party which promised to improve their economic condition.

This sequence from ethnic to class politics in Manitoba offered a clue to possible future alignments across Canada. If the country could somehow accommodate its French-Canadian minority and absorb new immigrants from Asia and Africa without revivals of prejudice, a similar trend was at least distantly possible. If it developed, the fate of Manitoba's Liberal party, whose failure to move leftward reduced it to an ambiguous and diminishing "center" position, afforded its federal counterpart a cautionary example. For the present, however, the debate over Quebec separatism, and the security of its non-French minorities, as well as the racist attacks on colored immigrants in Toronto and Vancouver, comparable to what had occurred in Winnipeg when it was a major recipient of immigration, suggested that the passing of ethnic issues from national politics was far from inevitable. So long as they persisted, a left-wing party would probably remain weak. Plato and Aristotle were among the first to note that recruiting a working-class from diverse cultures kept it so internally divided as to be incapable of concerted protest.[236] And the experience in the 1960s of West European countries with the divisive effects of unskilled immigrant labor on lower class political movements indicated that their observations were still relevant.[237]

As for Manitoba's future, the new class politics seemed incapable of achieving significant economic equality. Despite its efforts toward that goal, the record of 8 years of NDP government confirmed the comment that the "possessing classes" had many ways of defending themselves.[238] Noting the respective assets of the rival political groups, the owner of a Winnipeg business suggested the prospective winner:

> *Next to the power of the vote, power is dollars. Money is the finest criterion of where power lies.*[239]

By the 1970s, the struggle was joined; but, at least within the existing institutional structure, it was unlikely to be resolved. Because the Manitoba government, like all the provincial governments except the government of Quebec, had its income tax collected for it by the federal government, and therefore had to adhere to the federal graduated scale, the NDP had little freedom in re-allocating the income tax burden onto higher income groups. Accordingly, it was obliged to resort to complex property tax rebates and cost-of-living credits, designed to benefit poorer families disproportionately. As a Toronto survey of provincial tax rates across Canada indicated, these had some effect in reducing the taxation on the lower income group: in 1976, a family with four members, whose head earned \$8,226 a year, paid lower taxes in Manitoba than in any other province.[240] For families at this level, the benefit was clearly significant. But beyond such incremental modifications, involving a few hundred dollars one way or another, there was little indication of greater equality in the province: wage and pension increases appeared to be largely offset by equivalent or greater increases in living costs. As regards the federal income and price controls program, Premier Schreyer had by 1976 concluded that it was "damn inequitable" and suggested that federal Liberals were unwilling to use it to assist equalization because "the Liberals basically are trying to retain the affection of a certain fashionable elite in the country who make $30,000 a year and more."[241] In a retrospective appraisal of his government's record, he claimed that its main accomplishment was "some greater degree of equality":

> *... We have made progress toward that goal... despite the fact that the subtle general trend has been if anything slightly in the opposite direction. We haven't achieved 2½ to 1, but we've moved some way toward it... We're probably closer to it here than anywhere else in Canada.*[242]

At the same time, he termed general social tendencies toward greater income inequality "disheartening". The only equality in full view, as an immigrant novelist in Manitoba earlier observed, was an equality of ambition to secure a life-style as close as possible to that of the upper classes.[244] Serving this dream, the popularity of provincial lotteries established in the 1970s was as symptomatic of the new social climate as was the emergence of class voting. Even the native people, long regarded as little more than a dormant anachronism, increasingly shared the common aspiration. Asked "What do Indians want?" a Saulteaux descendant born in the remote village of Camperville responded simply:

> *The same thing as everyone else. A color TV set, a car, a nice home, a job and a good education for the children.*[245]

Few if any, it seemed, were willing any longer to forego affluence in order to remain picturesque.

Nor did it seem probable that the developing class rivalry would impair the basic unity of Manitoba society. Compared with the past, the classes were closer in many respects than ever before. The local upper classes were neither as wealthy nor as remote as their predecessors; and the lower classes, assisted by the two decades of postwar prosperity, were neither as poor nor as submerged. Class competition evidently became more acute as rival classes were less sharply distinguished. Perhaps in party politics, as in sports, there had to be a near equality between prospective competitors for there to be even a semblance of a contest. It was likely for this reason that much of the political rivalry occurred between the small business owners and professional groups in the upper middle class on one side and the relatively skilled and organized trade unionists in the lower middle class on the other side.[246] The secure rich and the hopeless poor at the extremes of the social scale were alike in their pursuit of other interests: the rich because they could afford to abstain and the poor because they could not afford to participate.

Whatever the disabilities and limitations of class politics, finally, its development appeared to be an improvement. The moral of Manitoba's political experience seemed to be that only within a culturally integrated society could class rivalry be expressed in orderly party competition. And the earlier task of resolving deep cultural antagonism was evidently the more hazardous. Where class provided the main basis for political alignments, there could be the recurrent recrimination and frustration of the legislative proceedings at Westminster and Paris. But this was preferable to having class divisions so compounded and exacerbated by intransigent ethno-religious hostilities as to erupt into civil violence, as in Belfast and Beirut. In the old attacks on native people, French Catholics and foreign immigrants, Manitoba politics at times came close to sowing the seed of irreconcilable cultural conflict. But by the 1970s, this danger had evidently passed. Having survived the vicissitudes of this process, Manitobans in their second century appeared ready for a more straightforward competition between those inclined to reform and equalization and those who expressed the need for restraint and stability.

Endnotes

[1] R. Alford, *Party and Society* (London: John Murray, 1964), p. 25.

[2] *Economic Atlas of Manitoba*, T. R. Weir, ed. (Winnipeg: Queen's Printer, 1960), pp. 12-13.

[3] Quoted in *The Western Interior of Canada*, J. Warkentin, ed. (Toronto: McClelland and Stewart Ltd., 1964), pp. 44-48.

[4] J. H. Lagasse, *et al.*, *The People of Indian Ancestry in Manitoba, A Social and Economic Study* (Winnipeg: Queen's Printer, 1959), I, pp. 32-35 and pp. 58-67.

[5] W. L. Morton, *Manitoba, A History*, 2nd ed. (Toronto: University of Toronto Press, 1967), p. 179.

[6] M. McWilliams, *Manitoba Milestones* (Toronto: J. M. Dent and Sons, 1928), p. 165.

[7] Carman Centennial Committee, *Up To Now, A Story of Dufferin and Carman* (Altona, Manitoba: D. W. Friesen and Sons, 1967), pp. 7-9.

[8] *Manitoba Free Press* (Winnipeg), February 2, 1891.

[9] *Ibid.*, February 3, 1891.

[10] *Ibid.*, September 2, 1881.

[11] *Winnipeg Daily Times*, August 9, 1882.

[12] R. O. MacFarlane, "Manitoba Politics and Parties after Confederation," *Canadian Historical Association Annual Report*, 1940.

[13] J. A. Jackson, "The Disallowance of Manitoba Railway Legislation in the 1880s" (M.A. Thesis, University of Manitoba, 1945), pp. 90-102.

[14] Morton, *op. cit.*, Chapter 9.

[15] J. Holmes, "Factors Affecting Politics in Manitoba: A Study of the Provincial Elections, 1870-1899" (M.A. Thesis, University of Manitoba. 1936), pp. 94-96. Also see J. A. Hilts, "The Political Career of Thomas Greenway" (Ph.D. Thesis, University of Manitoba, 1974).

[16] *Winnipeg Telegram*, January 26, 1899.

[17] See H. J. Guest, "Reluctant Politician: A Biography of Sir Hugh John Macdonald" (M.A. Thesis, University of Manitoba, 1973).

[18] *Winnipeg Telegram*, July 11, August 11 and September 5, 1899.

[19] M. S. Donnelly, *Dafoe of the Free Press* (Toronto: The Macmillan Company of Canada, 1968), p. 35.

[20] *Manitoba Free Press* (Winnipeg), September 2, 9, and 12, 1899.

[21] Quoted by W. Kristjanson, *The Icelandic People in Manitoba* (Winnipeg: Wallingford Press, 1965), p. 295.

[22] *Le Manitoba* (St. Boniface), January 22, 1896, quoted by R. Turenne, "The Minority and the Ballot Box, A Study of the Voting Behaviour of the French-Canadians of Manitoba, 1888-1967" (M.A. Thesis, University of Manitoba, 1969), p. 35.

[23] *Ibid.*, pp. 42-57.

[24] Hugh Ross, *Thirty-Five Years in the Limelight, Sir Rodmond P. Roblin and His Times* (Winnipeg: Farmer's Advocate Press, 1936), p. 85.

[25] Canada, Dominion Bureau of Statistics, *Census of the Prairie Provinces, Population and Agriculture, 1916* (Ottawa: King's Printer, 1918), p. 22.

[26] *Economic Atlas of Manitoba*, p. 28.

[27] Quoted by V. Lysenko, *Men in Sheepskin Coats* (Toronto: The Ryerson Press, 1947), pp. 123-124.

[28] A. E. Smith, *All My Life* (Toronto: Progress Publishing Company, 1949), p. 27.

[29] C. Dawson and E. Younge, *Pioneering in the Prairie Provinces: The Social Side of the Settlement Process* (Toronto: The Macmillan Co. of Canada, 1940), p. 36.

[30] *Manitoba Free Press* (Winnipeg), October 9, 1906.

[31] J. S. Woodsworth, *Strangers Within Our Gates* (Toronto: Missionary Society of the Methodist Church, Canada, 1909), pp. 100, 136, 141 and 156.

[32] *Manitoba Free Press* (Winnipeg), May 21, 1914.

[33] L. Orlikow, "A Survey of the Reform Movement in Manitoba, 1910-1920" (M.A. Thesis, University of Manitoba, 1955), pp. 136-140; also see A. I. Inglis, "Some Political Factors in the Demise of the Roblin Government" (M.A. Thesis, University of Manitoba, 1968).

[34] R. P. Roblin, *et al.*, *A Handbook to Winnipeg and the Province of Manitoba* (Winnipeg: Sanford Evans, Ltd., 1901), p. 45.

[35] *Manitoba Free Press* (Winnipeg), May 18, 1914.

[36] *Winnipeg Tribune*, February 2, 1912.

[37] *Manitoba Free Press* (Winnipeg), June 27, 1914.

[38] C. Dawson, *Group Settlement, Ethnic Communities in Western Canada* (Toronto: The Macmillan Company of Canada, 1936), p. 277. Regarding the early history of the German community in Winnipeg, see A. Grenke. "The Formation and Early Development of an Urban Community: A Case Study of the Germans in Winnipeg" (Ph.D. Thesis, University of Manitoba, 1974).

[39] *Der Nordwesten* (Winnipeg), August 5, 1914; *Manitoba Free Press* (Winnipeg), August 10, 1914.

[40] *Manitoba Free Press* (Winnipeg), August 14, 1915.

[41] *Winnipeg Telegram*, December 14, 1917.

[42] E. K. Francis, *In Search of Utopia* (Altona, Manitoba: D. W. Friesen and Sons, 1955), p. 187.

[43] O. S. Trosky., *The Ukrainian Greek Orthodox Church in Canada* (Winnipeg: Bulman Bros., 1968), pp. 8-16.

[44] Turenne, *op. cit.*, pp. 101-105.

[45] *Winnipeg Telegram*, July 16, 1899. For an account of the beginnings of left-wing parties, see E. Chisick, "The Development of Winnipeg's Socialist Movement, 1900-1915" (M.A. Thesis, University of Manitoba, 1972).

[46] *Manitoba Commonwealth* (Winnipeg) April 28, 1945; Cp. A. R. McCormack, "Arthur Puttee and the Liberal Party: 1899-1904," *Canadian Historical Review*, June, 1970, pp. 141-163.

[47] *Winnipeg Tribune*, January 28, 1916.

[48] *Winnipeg Telegram*, August 4, 1899.

[49] A. Chiel, *The Jews in Manitoba* (Toronto: University of Toronto Press, 1961), pp. 124-128 and 176-177.

[50] *Ibid.*, p. 155; *Manitoba Free Press* (Winnipeg), July 23, 1915.

[51] *Winnipeg Telegram*, January 12, 1918.

[52] Chiel, *op. cit.*, p. 177.

[53] Dafoe-Sifton Correspondence, November 3, 1903 (Provincial Archives of Manitoba).

[54] Yuzyk, *The Ukrainians in Manitoba* (Toronto: University of Toronto Press, 1953), pp. 177-178.

[55] *Manitoba Free Press* (Winnipeg), July 24, 1915.

[56] *Ibid.*, August 5, 1915.

[57] *Ibid.*, December 16, 1918.

[58] *Winnipeg Telegram*, April 9, 1919.

[59] *Manitoba Free Press* (Winnipeg), December 20, 1918.

[60] *Ibid.*, December 17, 1918.

[61] *Winnipeg Telegram*, January 27, 1919. Also see M. K. Mott, "The Foreign Peril: Nativism in Winnipeg, 1916-1923" (M.A. Thesis, University of Manitoba, 1970).

[62] *Manitoba Free Press* (Winnipeg), February 22, 1919.

[63] *Winnipeg Telegram*, May 2, 1919.

[64] *Manitoba Free Press* (Winnipeg), May 3, 1919.

[65] *Ibid.*, June 6, 1919.

[66] *Winnipeg Citizen*, June 11, 12 and 16, 1919.

[67] Quoted by K. McNaught, *A Prophet in Politics* (Toronto: University of Toronto Press, 1959), p. 116.

[68] D. C. Masters, *The Winnipeg General Strike* (Toronto: University of Toronto Press, 1950), p. 131; cp. D. J. Bercuson, *Confrontation at Winnipeg* (Montreal: McGill-Queen's University Press, 1974), pp. 178-179.

[69] *Western Labour News* (Winnipeg), May 20, 22, 29 and June 4 and 7, 1919.

[70] *Manitoba Free Press* (Winnipeg), June 11, 1919.

[71] *Royal Commission to enquire into and report upon the causes and effects of the General Strike which recently existed in the city of Winnipeg*, H. A. Robson, K. C., Commissioner (Winnipeg: King's Printer, November, 1919), p. 27.

[72] *Winnipeg Trades and Labor Council Legislative Year Book, 1928,*, p. 17.

[73] Masters, *op. cit.*, pp. 70-71 and 121; cp. W. L. Morton, *The Progressive Party in Canada* (Toronto: University of Toronto Press, 1950), pp. 117-118 and 226-227.

[74] *Winnipeg Telegram*, February 3, 1920.

[75] *Manitoba Free Press* (Winnipeg), March 8, 1920.

[76] *Winnipeg Evening Tribune*, March 4, 1921.

[77] *Manitoba Free Press* (Winnipeg), March 22, 1921.

[78] *Ibid.*, April 28, 1922.

[79] *Winnipeg Evening Tribune*, April 26, 1922.

[80] *Manitoba Free Press* (Winnipeg), July 20, 1922.

[81] *Ibid.*, July 25, 1922.

[82] A. G. Dexter, "A Professor in Politics," *Maclean's Magazine*, September 1, 1928, p. 16.

[83] W. J. Healy, "The Flying Prairie Premier," *Western Home Monthly*, December, 1926, p. 42.

[84] *Deloraine Times*, December 8, 1926.

[85] *Manitoba Free Press* (Winnipeg), January 7, 1927.

[86] W. L. Morton, *Manitoba, A History*, pp. 378-379.

[87] *Manitoba Free Press* (Winnipeg), February 10, 1921.

[88] *Winnipeg Evening Tribune*, March 3, 1921.

[89] *Statutes of Manitoba*, 1923, C.1, Sec. 16-20, p. 8.

[90] *Winnipeg Evening Tribune*, February 22, 1922.

[91] *Statutes of Manitoba*, 1927, C. 32, Sec. 18A, p. 77.

[92] W. McRaye, ed., *Pioneers and Prominent People of Manitoba* (Winnipeg: Bulman Bros. Ltd., 1925).

[93] *Manitoba Free Press* (Winnipeg), April 16, 1928.

[94] *Ibid.*, December 17, 1924.

[95] M. S. Donnelly, *op. cit.*, p. 102.

[96] *Canadian Farmer* (Winnipeg) June 15, 1922. This newspaper was published in Ukrainian. The excerpts from it and other Ukrainian newspapers quoted herein were translated by Miss M. Pidhirnyj, whose assistance is gratefully acknowledged, as is the University of Manitoba's provision of funds to pay for the translation.

[97] John Marlyn, *Under the Ribs of Death* (Toronto: McClelland and Stewart, 1957), pp. 75-76. I am indebted to Professor Ed Rea of the University of Manitoba Department of History for drawing my attention to this novel.

[98] *Public Accounts of Manitoba*, 1921, pp. 27 and 114.

[99] *Ibid.*, 1928, p. 166.

[100] *Manitoba Free Press* (Winnipeg), March 23, 1923.

[101] J. C. Hopkins, ed., *Canadian Annual Review*, 1924-1925 (Toronto: The Annual Review Publishing Company, 1925), pp. 402-404.

[102] *Public Accounts of Manitoba*, 1921, p. 31; and 1928, p. 12.

[103] *Report of the Special Commission of Inquiry into Welfare in Manitoba*, Nov. 15, 1928 (Winnipeg: King's Printer, 1928), Part VI, pp. 7-10 (*Whitton Report*).

[104] *Journal of the Legislative Assembly of Manitoba*, 1929, p. 129; 1932, p. 168.

[105] *Whitton Report*, Part III, p. 51.

[106] *Journal of the Legislative Assembly of Manitoba*, 1927, p. 12.

[107] Manitoba, Department of Health and Public Welfare, *Annual Report, 1929* (Winnipeg: King's Printer, 1930), pp. 5-6.

[108] F. W. Jackson, "Racial Origin in Relation to Public Health Activities," *Canadian Public Health Journal*, 1931; cited by C. A. Dawson and E. R. Younge, *op. cit.*, pp. 272-273.

[109] *Winnipeg Tribune*, December 10, 1928.

[110] Manitoba, Department of Health and Public Welfare, *Annual Report, 1930* (Winnipeg: King's Printer, 1931), p. 69.

[111] *Ibid.*, pp. 11-12.

[112] *Winnipeg Free Press*, February 26, 1931.

[113] James Gray, *The Winter Years* (Toronto: The Macmillan Company of Canada, 1966), pp. 157-159.

[114] *Winnipeg Free Press*, November 12, 1932.

[115] Manitoba Economic Survey Board, *Unemployment in Manitoba* (Winnipeg: King's Printer, 1938), pp. 31-32.

[116] J. Gray, *op. cit.*, pp. 131-132.

[117] Manitoba Economic Survey Board, *Interim Report and Findings* (Winnipeg: King's Printer, 1939), II, 325.

[118] *Winnipeg Free Press*, May 6, 1939.

[119] Manitoba Economic Survey Board, *Agricultural Income and Rural Municipal Government in Manitoba* (Winnipeg: King's Printer, 1939), pp. 80-90.

[120] *Winnipeg Free Press*, August 1, 1932.

[121] *Report of the Royal Commission on Dominion-Provincial Relations* (Ottawa: King's Printer, 1940), II, 98-99.

[122] *Canadian Annual Review, 1935-1936* (Toronto: The Annual Review Publishing Company, 1936), pp. 377-378.

[123] R. Turenne, *op. cit.*, pp. 117-129.

[124] V. Turek, *The Poles in Manitoba* (Toronto: Polish Alliance Press, 1967), p. 148.

[125] *Winnipeg Free Press*, May 25, 1932.

[126] *Canadian Farmer* (Winnipeg), June 25, 1927; *Ukrainian Voice* (Winnipeg), July 6, 1927.

[127] *Winnipeg Tribune*, June 10, 1932.

[128] *Canadian Farmer* (Winnipeg), June 8, 1932.

[129] *Ukrainian Voice* (Winnipeg), July 22, 1936.

[130] *Der Nordwesten* (Winnipeg), June 15, 1927.

[131] *Ibid.*, March 1, 1933. I am indebted for the translation to Mr. A. Penner, a graduate student in political science at the University of Manitoba.

[132] *Winnipeg Free Press*, October 22, 1936; F. Epp, *Mennonite Exodus* (Altona, Manitoba: D. W. Friesen and Sons, 1962), p. 324.

[133] *Winnipeg Free Press*, April 12 and 13, 1939.

[134] *Ibid.*, April 21, 1939.

[135] *Ibid.*, July 25, 1936.

[136] *Winnipeg Tribune* May 18, 1932.

[137] *Ibid.*, July 5, 1932.

[138] *Ibid.*, October 20, 1936.

[139] *Winnipeg Free Press*, May 25 and July 7, 1937.

[140] The Manitoba branch of the CCF was formed in 1933, but because of organizational difficulties in changing the official designation, candidates in the 1936 provincial election continued to be identified as running for the ILP. For an account of the Party's development, see Nelson Wiseman, "A Political History of the Manitoba CCF-NDP." (Ph.D. Thesis, University of Toronto, 1975).

[141] *Winnipeg Tribune*, May 17, 1932.

[142] M. Robin, *Radical Politics and Canadian Labour, 1880-1930* (Queen's University, Kingston, Ontario: Industrial Relations Centre, 1968), pp. 276-277.

[143] *Winnipeg Free Press*, July 30, 1936.

[144] D. Rowland, "Canadian Communism: The Post-Stalinist Phase" (M.A. Thesis, University of Manitoba, 1964), pp. 86-90.

[145] W. Rodney, *Soldiers of the International, A History of the Canadian Communist Party, 1921-1929* (Toronto: University of Toronto Press, 1968), pp. 152-153.

[146] Personal interview.

[147] *Manitoba Free Press* (Winnipeg), January 21, 1929.

[148] *Winnipeg Tribune*, July 24, 1936.

[149] *Ibid.*, April 6, 1938; *Winnipeg Free Press*, August 6, 1938 and March 21, 1939.

[150] *Ibid.*, December 18, 1940.

[151] *Ibid.*, March 31, 1941.

[152] M. S. Donnelly, *The Government of Manitoba* (Toronto: University of Toronto Press, 1963), p. 66.

[153] Compiled from the unpublished election reports on file in the office of Manitoba's Chief Electoral Officer, Legislative Building, Winnipeg.

[154] *Winnipeg Free Press*, September 30, October 11, 13, and 18, 1949.

[155] *Ibid.*, October 10, 1949.

[156] Provincial Secretary's Report to the 9th Annual Manitoba CCF Convention, October 24-26, 1944 (Mimeo.). This and subsequent CCF-NDP documents referred to below are in the files of the party at its provincial headquarters in Winnipeg. Permission to examine and use this material was given by the party's executive secretary, Mr. Donovan Swailes, and is gratefully acknowledged.

[157] *Winnipeg Free Press—Winnipeg Tribune*, December 10, 1945 (Joint edition put out during a typographers' strike).

[158] *Winnipeg Free Press*, September 13, 1949; Cp. W. Young, *The Anatomy of a Party: The National CCF, 1932-61* (Toronto University of Toronto Press, 1969), pp. 201-205.

[159] *Canadian Farmer* (Winnipeg), November 23, 1949.

[160] P. Yuzyk, *op. cit.*, pp. 37-38.

[161] *Winnipeg Free Press*, October 14-17, 1949.

[162] *Winnipeg Tribune*, February 28, 1953.

[163] *Ibid.*, March 4, 1953.

[164] *Winnipeg Free Press*, March 27, 1953.

[165] *Ukrainian Voice* (Winnipeg), August 5, 1936.

[166] Manitoba Economic Consultative Board, *Fourth Annual Report* (Winnipeg: Queen's Printer, 1967), Appendix B, Table 12, p. 148.

[167] *Canada Year Book, 1952-1953*, p. 632; and *Ibid.*, 1969, p. 776.

[168] Canada, Dominion Bureau of Statistics, *National Accounts, Income and Expenditure, 1926-1956* (Ottawa: Queen's Printer, 1958), p. 65; and *Ibid., 1967* (Ottawa: Queen's Printer, 1968), p. 36.

[169] *Canada Year Book, 1968*, p. 940.

[170] J. Porter, *The Vertical Mosaic* (Toronto: University of Toronto Press, 1965), pp. 104-112.

[171] Canada, Department of National Revenue, *Taxation Statistics, 1950* (Ottawa: King's Printer, 1950), p. 143; *Ibid., 1970* (Ottawa: Queen's Printer, 1970), p. 113; cp. H. Chorney. "The Political Economy of Economic Growth in Manitoba" (M.A. Thesis, University of Manitoba, 1970), pp. 131-133.

[172] *Winnipeg Free Press*, February 17, 1968.

[173] *Ibid.*, March 7, 1967.

[174] Personal interview.

[175] *Winnipeg Free Press*, November 22, 1968.

[176] From *Laugh Baby Laugh* by Ann Henry, reprinted by permission of the Canadian publishers, McClelland and Stewart Limited, Toronto.

[177] Metropolitan Winnipeg Social Service Audit, *Interim Report* (Winnipeg: Social Service Audit Committee, 1967), Vol. I. Table 10, p. 34; cp. T. G. Nicholson and M. H. Yeates, "The Ecological and Spatial Structure of the Socio-Economic Characteristics of Winnipeg, 1961," *The Canadian Review of Sociology and Anthropology*, August, 1969, pp. 162-177.

[178] Canada, Dominion Bureau of Statistics, *Fourth Census*, 1901, Vol. II, Tables 4, 8, and 36; *Sixth Census*, 1921, Vol. V, Tables 79, 80, and 85; 1961 *Census of Canada*, Bulletin 5.3-1, Tables 14-16 and 18.

[179] Canada, Dominion Bureau of Statistics, *1966 Census of Canada*, Vol. 5, *Agriculture Manitoba*, Table 22.

[180] D. Woodsworth, *et al.*, *Rural Need in Canada, 1965; The Background of Rural Poverty in Four Selected Areas* (Ottawa: Canadian Welfare Council, 1966), pp. 12-19.

[181] *Ibid.*, p. 2.

[182] Cp. V. Kaye, "Political Integration of Ethnic Groups: The Ukrainians," *Revue de l'Universite d'Ottawa*, 1957, pp. 460-470.

[183] M. Stancliff, *et al.*, *A Comparative Study of Value Orientations among Three Ethnic Groups living in the Province of Manitoba*, a study conducted under the auspices of the Province of Manitoba Interdepartmental Committee for ARDA (Winnipeg: University of Manitoba, 1965), pp. 88-89 and 160-162.

[184] For example, the Winnipeg Icelandic newspapers *Heimskringla* and *Logberg* merged in 1959, as did *Der Nordwesten* and *Der Courier* in 1970.

[185] *Canadian Farmer* (Winnipeg), May 25, 1959.

[186] *Ukrainian Voice* (Winnipeg), December 5, 1962.

[187] *Winnipeg Tribune*, September 29, 1967; *Winnipeg Free Press*, November 12, 1968.

[188] Y. Kasahara, "A Profile of Canada's Metropolitan Centres," in B. Blishen, *et al.*, *Canadian Society* (Toronto: The Macmillan Company of Canada, 1965), p. 58.

[189] W. Kristjanson, *op. cit.*, pp. 505-508.

[190] *Report of the Royal Commission on Bilingualism and Biculturalism* (Ottawa: Queen's Printer, 1969), Vol. IV, pp. 92-94 and 287.

[191] *Ibid.*, p. 135.

[192] *Winnipeg Tribune*, April 27, 1967.

[193] Party correspondence on program preparations for the 1964 annual meeting. This and subsequent references from the party files were located and examined with the permission of the party executive director, D. A. Schwartz, whose help is gratefully acknowledged.

[194] *Winnipeg Free Press*, March 11, 1967.

[195] *Ukrainian Voice* (Winnipeg), December 12, 1962.

[196] Personal Letter.

[197] *Winnipeg Free Press*, April 15, 1961; *Ibid.*, November 17, 1969.

[198] *Winnipeg Tribune*, November 15, 1967.

[199] *Ibid.*, April 20, 1961.

[200] *Ibid.*, September 10, 1968.

[201] *Winnipeg Free Press*, May 11, 1967.

[202] *Ibid.*, December 5, 1967.

[203] *Winnipeg Tribune*, February 13, 1968.

[204] Legislative Assembly of Manitoba, *Debates and Proceedings*, March 19, 1968, p. 294.

[205] *Winnipeg Free Press*, April 20, 1968.

[206] H. B. Hawthorn, *et al.*, *A Survey of the Contemporary Indians of Canada* (Ottawa: Queen's Printer, 1966), Vol. I. p. 376.

[207] *Ibid.*, pp. 156-158 and 328-329.

[208] *Winnipeg Free Press*, May 16, 1967; *Winnipeg Tribune*, October 9, 1967.

[209] R. Turenne, *op. cit.*, pp. 152-164.

[210] Minutes of the Manitoba NDP Provincial Council meeting. December 10, 1966. (Quoted with the permission of party secretary, F. Petruic.)

[211] Compiled from various mimeographed campaign guide sheets including *Why Canvass*? (August, 1967) and CCF-NDP *Organization Manual* (1968).

[212] *Winnipeg Tribune*, June 26, 1969.

[213] For a rather more detailed account of the campaign itself, see T. Peterson and P. Barber, "Some Factors in the 1969 NDP Victory in Manitoba," *Lakehead University Review*, Autumn, 1970, pp. 120-133; and T. Peterson, "Manitoba," in *Canadian Annual Review*, 1969, J. Saywell, ed. (Toronto: University of Toronto Press, 1970); and Larry Edward Joseph, "The 1969 Manitoba General Election." (M.A. Thesis, Carleton University, 1971).

[214] D. Swainson, "Ethnic Revolt: Manitoba's Election," *Canadian Forum*, August, 1969, pp. 98-99.

[215] *Winnipeg Tribune*, June 23, 1969.

[216] *Canadian Farmer* (Winnipeg), July 5, 1969.

[217] Cp. A Milnor, "The New Politics and Ethnic Revolt: 1929-1938," in *Politics in Saskatchewan*, N. Ward and D. Spafford, eds. (Don Mills, Ontario: Longmans Canada Ltd., 1968), p. 152.

[218] See Paul Beaulieu, "The Transfer of Electoral Allegiance in Ethnic Politics: A Study of the Voting Behaviour of Franco-Manitobans, 1969-1974" (M.A. Thesis, University of Manitoba, 1976), pp. 39-42.

[219] See Lloyd Axworthy and James Cassidy, *Unicity: The Transition* (University of Winnipeg: Institute of Urban Studies, March, 1974).

[220] Manitoba, Department of Finance, *Budget Address, 1973* (Winnipeg: Queen's Printer, 1973), p. 47.

[221] Legislative Assembly of Manitoba, *Votes and Proceedings*, June 26, 1970, No. 74, p. 8.

[222] See Manitoba, *Report of the Commission of Inquiry into The Pas Forestry and Industrial Complex at The Pas, Manitoba* (Winnipeg: Queen's Printer, 1974), Six volumes; Philip Mathias, *Forced Growth, Five Studies of Government Involvement in the Development of Canada* (Toronto: James Lewis and Samuel, 1971), pp. 124-179; Walter Newman, *How Dr. Kasser Came to Northern Manitoba* (Winnipeg: Newmac, 1976).

[223] Manitoba, Department of Industry and Commerce, Manitoba Development Corporation, *Fifteenth Annual Report, 1972-73* (Winnipeg: Queen's Printer, 1973), p. 13.

[224] Samuel H. Beer, *British Politics in the Collectivist Age* (New York: Alfred A. Knopf, Inc., 1966), pp. 386-387.

[225] Cp. Robert E. Lane, *Political Life* (New York: The Free Press, 1959), p. 178; N. H. Chi, *Class Voting in Canadian Politics* (Ottawa: Carleton University Department of Political Science, August, 1972), pp. 3-4; Richard Ogmundson, "Social Class and Canadian Politics" (Ph.D. Thesis, University of Michigan, 1972), p. 85.

[226] Cp. Jane Jenson, "Party Systems," in *The Provincial Political Systems*, D. J. Bellamy, J. H. Pammett and D. C. Rowat, eds. (Toronto: Methuen Publications, 1976), p. 131, 25 n.

[227] The company established a Winnipeg branch in 1969 and during the three fiscal years from 1970 to 1973 received $840,000 from the government. Manitoba, Department of Finance, *Public Accounts, 1970-1971*, p. 66; *1971-1972*, p. 76; *1972-1973*, p. 87.

[228] John Wilson, "The Decline of the Liberal Party in Manitoba Politics" *The Journal of Canadian Studies*, February, 1975, pp. 24-41.

[229] T. Peterson, "A Regional Analysis: Recent Patterns of Manitoba Voting" *Winnipeg Free Press*, July 14, 1973, p. 20.

[230] *Statistics Canada Daily*, October 12 and 18, 1977; Statistics Canada, *Telegraphic Crop Report*, Field Crop Reporting Series, No. 18, Sept. 22, 1977, pp. 5-6.

[231] Denis Smith, "Prairie Revolt, Federalism and the Party System," in *Party Politics in Canada*, H. G. Thorburn, ed., 2nd ed. (Scarborough, Ontario: Prentice-Hall of Canada, Ltd., 1967), p. 191.

[232] Cp. H. M. Clokie, *Canadian Government and Politics* (Toronto: Longmans Canada Ltd., 1944), p. 94; S. M. Lipset, *Agrarian Socialism*, 2nd ed. (Garden City, New York: Anchor Books, 1968).

[233] Cp. Kenneth D. McRae, "The Structure of Canadian History," in *The Founding of New Societies*, by Louis Hartz, *et al.* (New York: Harcourt, Brace and World, Inc., 1964), pp. 255-258.

[234] *Winnipeg Tribune*, November 29, 1975.

[235] *Ibid.*, October 22, 1975

[236] Plato, *The Dialogues*, translated by Benjamin Jowett (London: Oxford University Press, 1892), Vol. V. p. 159; Aristotle, *Politics*, translated by Benjamin Jowett (New York: Modern Library, 1943), p. 299.

[237] Stephen Castles and Godula Kosack, *Immigrant Workers and Class Structure in Western Europe* (London: Oxford University Press, 1973), pp. 116-179 and 430-460.

[238] Raymond Aron, *La lutte de classes* (Paris: Editions Gallimard, 1964), p. 240.

[239] *Winnipeg Tribune*, November 21, 1975. The speaker, Neil Baker, president of the Winnipeg Supply and Fuel Company, was one of the candidates endorsed by the Group for Good Government in the 1973 election.

[240] *The Globe and Mail* (Toronto), April 23, 1976. The total annual tax, including federal and provincial income tax, health insurance premiums (where applicable), and a standard estimated property tax of $480, and minus any rebates (where applicable), ranged from $1,078 in Ontario to $682 in Manitoba, with the average for the 10 provinces being $886.

[241] Haroon Siddiqui, "Interview with Ed Schreyer" *Maclean's Magazine*, March 22, 1976, p. 8.

[242] Jenni Mortin, Robert Matas and Ron Kustra, "Schreyer: stormy years but few regrets" *Winnipeg Tribune*, January 7, 1977, p. 6.

[243] *Ibid.*

[244] Frederick Philip Grove, *Tales From the Margin*, edited with an introduction by Desmond Pacey (Toronto: McGraw-Hill-Ryerson, 1971), p. 306; Grove is identified as "Felix Greve" by Douglas Spettigue, *FPG, The European Years* (Ottawa: Oberon Press, 1973).

[245] *Winnipeg Tribune*, November 21, 1975.

[246] Cp. Richard F. Hamilton, *Class and Politics in the United States* (New York: John Wiley and Sons, Inc., 1972), p. 218; Gerald Pomper, *Voters' Choice: Varieties of American Electoral Behavior* (New York: Dodd, Mead and Co., Inc., 1975), p. 65.

NEW BRUNSWICK
The Politics of Pragmatism*

P. J. Fitzpatrick

Provincial politics in New Brunswick might best be described as parochial, stagnant, and anachronistic—reminiscent, in some ways, of politics in nineteenth-century Britain before the reform movement. The Liberal and Progressive Conservative parties dominate the political environment without fear of challenge or stimulation by third parties, traditionally sustained by gerrymandering,[2] patronage, and constituencies with hereditary political loyalties kept intact by ancient ethnic and religious antagonisms. Neither party is receptive to the idea, so fashionable elsewhere, of popular participation in government; party leadership is firmly of the opinion that it should lead.[3] But leadership in New Brunswick politics is not a matter of putting forth ideas or initiating well-defined policies. A visitor to the Legislative Assembly in Fredericton is more likely to hear a member advise the Assembly that maple syrup time has come to the Keswick than a debate on French Canada's role within Confederation. Question time in the Assembly is used not to challenge policy, but rather to query ministers about expenditures, in hopes of discovering patronage. Issues, when they are allowed to arise, interest government and opposition alike less on their own merits than as a means to score debating points, often using the most childish tactics.[4] In short, the Assembly functions less as a deliberative body than as an arena for partisan conflict.

Yet the electorate seems satisfied with this arrangement. If there were a felt need in the province for a more progressive or ideological mode of

* Much of the material included here was gathered through discussions with party workers and through following Mr. Van Horne and Mr. Hatfield during the Conservative leadership race in 1966, the Restigouche by-election in 1967, and both Mr. Van Horne and Premier Robichaud during the 1967 general election.

politics, then presumably viable alternatives to the two traditional parties would have arisen. But while the New Democratic Party, for example, may have the support of organized labor in other provinces, labor in New Brunswick seems to feel that it may best further its goals within the traditional two party system.[5] In fact, no third party Members have been elected provincially since 1920, when the United Farmers, contesting 26 of the 48 seats, elected 9 Members by taking 21 per cent of the popular vote.[6]

The NDP's ill success may be attributed largely to the failure of labor to become significantly aware of itself as an interest group, but it may also be due in part to the timidity of the electorate. For although many voters grumble between elections about existing institutions, this discontent often fails to be articulated at the polls, where people feel obliged to obey social, ethnic, or religious rather than political imperatives.[7]

Political Culture

In no other province are the ethnic, religious, and geographic divisions quite so explicit or so closely balanced as in New Brunswick. The correspondence between these divisions and the distribution of political allegiance in the province is almost exact: 59.2 per cent of the population claims British origin, 34.2 per cent is of French extraction, while "others" account for only 6.6 per cent. Roman Catholicism has the adherence of 51.7 per cent of the population, the major Protestant denominations (Baptist, United Church, and Anglican) 40.6 per cent, and other denominations 6.6 per cent.[8] The Liberal party draws strong support from French Roman Catholics and significant support from Irish Catholics. The Conservative party commands the allegiance of most Protestants of British origin but receives only limited Catholic support.

One can draw an imaginary diagonal from Grand Falls in the northwest to Sackville in the southeast: north of this diagonal all districts are either French or mixed, and all but five (two in 1970) Assembly seats are held by Liberals. South of the diagonal the population is predominantly English, and overwhelmingly Conservative.

With the political parties so closely associated with particular patterns of ethnic and religious loyalty, political allegiance in New Brunswick is no casual matter. In certain other provinces, where this correspondence is not so close, a fickle electorate might feel free to cast its votes on the basis of issues and policies; but to a British Protestant New Brunswicker of United Empire Loyalist stock, for example, the idea of voting Liberal might well be unthinkable, an act of cultural treachery equivalent to conversion to Roman Catholicism. The comparative remoteness of government and a political apparatus that is visible to most of the electorate only around election time do much to ensure the unreliability of many voters in, say, Ontario; in New Brunswick, however, the relationship between the individual voter and his party is in many cases one of intimate reciprocity, a mutual loyalty sustained by, among other things, a wide distribution of "honest" patronage.

Within a given constituency, the privilege of dispensing patronage rests primarily with the M.L.A., if of the government party, or the defeated candidate of this party, and with one or two members of the constituency committee. But the efficient operation of the patronage machine demands some degree of co-ordination and centralization. A small office exists in each constituency, manned by a "contact man" whose responsibility is to receive calls requesting temporary help in the area and to determine through the party system and the M.L.A. if a party worker is available. If so, this worker gets the job; if no party worker is available the job may well wait until one is. Patronage of this sort distributes the spoils of political victory to the lowest levels of the party in power and is the tangible reward for diligence and loyalty awaiting the rank and file of the party not in power. The voter is therefore encouraged to make his party affiliation explicit and the party is assured of a large core of active and loyal support. Since the electorate does gain something from this arrangement, there is little complaint against it.

This tolerance extends to patronage in the area of small government contracts and government purchases. During a Liberal administration, for example, a Conservative, finding his small company in danger of bankruptcy through the loss of government sales, might approach a Liberal friend, asking him to run the business at a 5 or 10 per cent commission while the Liberals are in office. Or, one partner in a firm will support the Liberals, the other, the Conservatives; if the Liberals are in office, the Liberal runs the firm and the Conservative partner is "silent." When the Conservatives are in, the roles are reversed. Needless to say, the parties make use of this system when campaign money is needed. The government party approaches the firm with a list of all purchases made from it and suggests an appropriate campaign contribution.

The party in office extends its ties to the electorate by making itself accessible. The citizen with a problem or grievance prefers to approach his M.L.A. or the defeated government candidate in his constituency rather than the more remote and less flexible civil service bureaucracy in Fredericton. He does not regard his M.L.A. as a quasi-ombudsman or as an errand boy for constituency complaints, but he knows that his mediator will solve the problem not by raising it with civil servants, but rather through a quiet chat with the appropriate minister. The M.L.A. is aided in this by provincial statutes giving the minister considerable discretion. Again, the citizen is both rewarded for, and reinforced in, his loyalty to the party.

When politicians lock horns in the Assembly or during a campaign, they are less likely to try to prevail over each other by reasoned arguments than by ridicule. This is, of course, in keeping with the emphasis within the political environment on partisan loyalty at the expense of issues and is completely tolerated by an electorate that perhaps feels closer to the political process because its legislators are unwilling to allow each other any dignity. Thus, during a 1970 budget debate, the Minister of Education could make parenthetical reference to then Opposition Leader Hatfield's apparent reluctance to marry, implying some deficiency in the frontier virtues.[9]

There is a sense in which the vaudevillian element in political controversy serves a kind of diversionary function, offering the electorate the placebo of ferocious spectatorship in lieu of genuine political involvement. The concentration and insulation of power concomitant on this may be clearly seen in the structure of the party organizations.

Party Organization

The rewards extended by a party to its faithful do not include a voice in party decisions. This prerogative is reserved for a select few. But as long as the party is faithful to its traditions and does not startle its constituents with heretical notions, and as long as patronage is forthcoming for loyal service, the rank and file does not resent this exclusion. Both parties hold annual provincial constituency meetings,[10] but usually all the decisions have been made in advance. The leadership decides if it will remain in office; if not, it chooses its successor. At the actual meeting, those present merely concur in the leadership decision, pass a motion of confidence in the provincial party leader, and adjourn.

The New Brunswick Liberal Association,[11] the primary Liberal party organization in the province, consists of representatives from the constituency associations, the Liberal Women's Association, the Young Liberal Association, the university Liberal clubs, and the Liberal M.L.A.s. In all, about forty people are eligible to attend Association meetings, held four or five times a year. But even this inner circle is relatively powerless —or rather its members have power only insofar as it is delegated to them by the party leader who presides over the meetings. His presence and the members' awareness that their political fortunes are his to advance or retard ensure that Association meetings are free of any real activity whatsoever: policy suggestions are not raised, issues go undebated; instead representatives of the various constituency associations read invariably optimistic reports on Liberal strength in their districts, or fruitless squabbles arise between factions or individual representatives, which the party leader smooths over. In short, party decisions are made not by the N.B. Liberal Association, but by the party leader. He may discuss matters with an informal group of advisors—mostly of the parliamentary party and a few of the extra-parliamentary party, some of whom may be in the Association—but the decision is his.

Among the prerogatives of leadership, in both parties, is the choice of candidates. While there is a degree of self-recruitment of candidates for federal elections, at the provincial level the recruitment process is centralized, heirarchal, and formalized—the party leader, abetted by his advisors, makes the final choices and the nominating conventions are arranged accordingly.[12] The leader's prerogative is limited only in that he must be careful not to offend the parochialism of a given constituency. Hence, it is rare that a candidate is "parachuted" into a safe seat, as the electorate would regard as an "outsider" and his success would be doubtful.

Prior to the major revision of electoral boundaries in 1974, a party worker who earned the reward of office but who would not perform well in a single-member constituency was not infrequently smuggled into office, so to speak, by having him run in one of the multi-member ridings.[13] Both parties rationalized the existence of these constituencies by arguing that they made it possible for a candidate who was representative of a group in the minority in that area to gain office—for example, an Irish Catholic could in this way win election in an English Protestant area such as Saint John. More to the point, the parties knew that the electorate rarely split the ticket; one strong candidate in a given constituency could carry several weaker hopefuls to victory on his coattails.

Separate federal and provincial party organizations exist in the province only at the local level, but the frame of reference of the organizations is strictly provincial; only grudging efforts are made in federal campaigns. Ottawa is of interest to the parties mainly as a source of spoils—a senate seat for a member of the party leadership, for example. Or it may be necessary to tap the federal party's campaign chest for a provincial election campaign—especially if the provincial party is in opposition and cannot raise money locally.

As we have seen, the political landscape of New Brunswick has been portioned out more or less equally between the Liberal and Conservative parties, each of which, by identifying itself closely and almost exclusively with one of the province's two dominant ethnic and religious groups, has guaranteed itself a following of hereditary and apparently unshakable loyalty. The passive steadfastness of a substantial part of this electorate is warmed to active support of its party by a broad distribution of patronage or the promise of patronage. As many voters regard politics as a means by which they may express cultural loyalty rather than as merely an expedient means to obtain certain social ends, the politician in New Brunswick need not concern himself greatly with public issues or the formulation of broad policies. His constituents and the rank and file of his party are born into their political loyalties; there is no need for him to secure the loyalty of the former with reforms and social programs or the loyalty of the latter with a distribution of power downward through the party heirarchy. Politics in the province have therefore been characterized by both a freedom from substantial issues and an extremely narrow concentration of decision-making power at the top of the party organizations.

Contemporary Political System

It is perhaps to be expected in a province whose politicians have had no reason to gain experience in the formulation of complex legislative programs that such a program, when it did come to New Brunswick, was proposed by a Royal Commission, given shape by hired experts from outside the province, and implemented by the Liberal government of Premier Louis Robichaud with an awkwardness that exacerbated to a novel degree the ethnic and religious tensions in the province.

In March 1962, a Royal Commission on Finance and Municipal Taxation (commonly referred to as the Byrne Commission, after its chairman, G. Edward Byrne, Q.C.) was appointed to "make findings and recommendations consistent with the public interest and the general welfare of the people of New Brunswick with respect to the whole field of relevent facts, issues and legislation relating to public or municipal fiscal matters within the Province of New Brunswick . . . "[14] The Commission's report and the resultant Programme of Equal Opportunity both threatened the province's ancient parochialism and gave that parochialism opportunity to find its fiercest expression.

The Byrne commission recognized that the system of municipal government in New Brunswick was out of date. The welter of parishes, countries, villages, and cities into which the province was divided was perhaps an adequate scheme of government in a society with an immobile population. But increasing urbanization and resultant displacements of people and capital had rendered the traditional institutions, particularly the county councils, obsolete. Commission studies revealed that while the counties had primary responsibility for education, health, welfare, and the administration of justice, most counties did not have financial resources equal to these responsibilities. The result, more often than not, was a tremendous imbalance in the level of services that the counties could provide. An urbanized county such as Saint John was able to spend $180.79 per capita on municipal expenditures, while a rural area such as Queens County could spend $53.24, a depressed area such as Restigouche only $19.06.[15]

The Byrne Commission stated that the solution to this problem was either to transfer adequate financial resources from the province to the municipalities or, as it recommended, to transfer the general service functions from the municipalities to the province. This recommendation, and its corollary that county councils be abolished, generated political passions the likes of which the province had not previously experienced. When the Liberal government moved to implement these recommendations in the form of the Programme of Equal Opportunity, it was faced with powerful opposition from at least three sources.

While Equal Opportunity was of value to all citizens, its impact as a plan of social change would be greatest in the depressed North Shore. This area was solidly French, Roman Catholic, and Liberal. On the other hand, the Programme would have the least impact in urbanized English-Protestant areas, such as Saint John and Fredericton. But these areas, under-assessed in the past, would carry the greater burden of taxation under Equal Opportunity. Since many people had come to believe implicitly that the Liberal party was an Acadian party, it followed that in much of English New Brunswick the Programme of Equal Opportunity was regarded as a manifestation of a French takeover. The argument that equal services should be available to all citizens regardless of where they lived or the fiscal capabilities of their municipalities fell on deaf ears. English New Brunswick, falling back upon its hereditary allegiance to the Conservative party, saw Equal Opportunity as simply a plot on the part of the Liberals "to rob Peter and pay Pierre." This theme was elaborated upon, with much color, throughout Greater Saint John and the Saint John River Valley, the major areas of Conservative strength, and a latent but never absent hostility to French New Brunswick—and, by association, to the Liberal party—blossomed into virulence. In the midst of all this passion it occurred to almost no one that Equal Opportunity was a policy issue and as such could be constructively criticized.

Before considering other sources of opposition to Equal Opportunity, it may be profitable to examine some of the forms anti-French hostility in New Brunswick may take. The extreme fringe of Francophobia is occupied at present by the Canadian Loyalist Society,[16] an organization located in the Salisbury area.[17] As the Society is not without influence in the province, it is worth quoting one of its pamphlets in some detail:

> *The following letter has been sent to Louis Robichaud. . . .*
>
> *"The Canadian Loyalist Association wish (sic) to congratulate you on the masterful manner in which you have deceived the people of New Brunswick and Canada by leading them to believe that New Brunswick has two official languages.*
>
> *Your senseless, degenerate and ruinous official language act (sic) is one of the worst evils anyone ever tried to perpetuate (sic) on the citizens of this province.*[18]

The pamphlet goes on to accuse the French of a complete takeover of government, an argument summarized in 10 points for the faithful to memorize, and concludes with an attack on the federal leadership:

> *To-day, Canada is in the hands of three Frenchmen, i.e. Trudeau, John (sic) Marchand, and Gerald Pelletier (a hater of all English) and no English speaking person of consequence is attached to the Prime Minister's staff.*
>
> *Trudeau, the legalizer of the sin of homosexuality, is trying to dissolve all ties with BRITAIN and the COMMONWEALTH in exchange for ties with France and Communist China. Trudeau has passed in Parliament Bill C-120 and has in effect by-passed the B.N.B. act (sic) and has imposed upon the country the French language. This bill (sic) is nothing short of LEGALIZED FRENCH COLONIZATION OF CANADA. (Emphasis in the original.)*[19]

While these feelings may be openly expressed only by a fringe group, they may in fact be shared covertly by a significant number of English New Brunswickers.

The second major source of opposition confronting the Liberal party was the municipalities and county councils. The political leadership of the municipalities, realizing that a transfer of functions to the province would reduce their political power, were generally against Equal Opportunity.[20] They found an ally in the English press, notably the *Fredericton Daily Gleaner* and the *Atlantic Advocate*, which argued that Equal Opportunity would destroy local autonomy and lead to over-centralization.[21] This charge was leveled most strenuously against the decision to abolish county councils, despite the fact that the councils were anachronisms in most counties, without adequate financial resources, qualified staff, or effective leadership. But given the patriarchal nature of local politics in the province, the councils were not without influence on public opinion. Sheer tenure gave many councillors strong positions in their communities; though in their sixties and seventies and perhaps out of touch with modern ideas of government, the inertia of 30 or 40 years in office made them difficult to dislodge. The Liberal party underestimated their influence; the Conservatives capitalized on it.

The third major source of opposition to the Equal Opportunity proposals was the business establishment, most notably the Irving interests. The multi-million-dollar empire of K.C. Irving of Saint John, Eastern Canada's most prominent businessman and industrialist, was, understandably, opposed to those provisions of the Programme which threatened the abolition of certain tax and assessment concessions.[22] But the Liberal party did not attract any popular support in the dispute between itself and the industrialist. If anything, it lost support, as a significant number of citizens looked upon Mr. Irving as an economic savior. The electorate did not consider the dispute a battle between its interests and those of the industrialist; their perception was that the man who brought industry to the province was being attacked.

In all its aspects, the Equal Opportunity debate reflected the parochialism of the electorate. The Liberal government hired a number of experts, former senior public servants from Saskatchewan and elsewhere, and created the Office of Government Organization to implement the Equal Opportunity Programme. These experts were denounced throughout the province as "outsiders", and OGO was seen as part of a Machiavellian conspiracy. This attitude was another manifestation of the political culture of the province—a hidebound intolerance of new ideas and a disdain bordering upon abhorrence, of social and political change.[23]

But the debate also had the effect of making visible certain differences in ideology between the Liberal and Conservative parties. While neither party has in its ranks issue-oriented politicians, nor is itself issue-oriented, the Liberals have demonstrated a responsiveness to change that, in effect, gives them a slightly left-of-centre ideology. The Liberals, once advised by the Royal Commission and by outside experts, were prepared to implement a programme with massive implications for social and political change. The idea of redistribution of wealth, accomplished through fair assessment of real property and equalization grants, was abhorrent to the Conservatives. Their feeling was that the depressed areas of the North Shore could improve their position through hard work and immigration, without government intervention. In emphasizing such differences between the parties, the Equal Opportunity debate polarized the electorate even more than it had been polarized in the past. The Liberal party had its image as a French-Catholic party refined and the Conservative party became even more explicitly an English Protestant party.

It is characteristic of New Brunswick's political climate that social inequalities have perpetuated themselves by circumscribing (through inadequate educational and other facilities) the political awareness of those who would benefit most from reform. Consequently, effective change must often be generated at the level of the party leadership and imposed "from above". Even Van Horne is no exception to this rule, since his grass roots support was largely cultivated, and he related to it more as choirmaster than as spokesman. But the principle is more clearly illustrated by the career of Premier Robichaud, who armed a personal belief in the social obligations of the state with the extensive powers of his office.

Besides reflecting its geographical base of power in the province and some elements of Liberal party ideology, Equal Opportunity may have arisen from Robichaud's personal commitments. Robichaud's egalitarianism doubtless grew in part out of his own experience of ethnic and class barriers. Prohibited by lack of funds from attending the University of New Brunswick Law School, he articled in a small law office in Buctouche and eventually passed both the provincial and the U.N.B. law examinations, the latter with high honors. Moreover, his studies at the Social Science School at Laval in the charged political atmosphere of the Duplessis regime doubtless reinforced his commitment to social change.

Besides the Programme of Equal Opportunity mentioned earlier, one of the Robichaud government's most significant reforms was the integration of Acadians into the economic and cultural life of the province. Through legislation and Orders-in-Council, Acadians received senior positions in the public service, a French-speaking Deputy Minister was appointed to the Department of Education, and L'Ecole Normale and L'Université de Moncton were structured to provide post-secondary education to Acadians in their own language. The Official Languages Act of 1968, though not completely proclaimed during the Robichaud administration, also establishes the right to use French in the courts, in the Assembly, and in dealing with the provincial bureaucracy.

Equally important, though perhaps more difficult to effect, were changes in the mechanics of the party system. In 1967, Robichaud introduced collective bargaining for public servants, including those who were hired on a casual-patronage basis. The upshot of this has been that when Conservative patronage committees have attempted to secure the dismissal of casuals appointed by the Liberals, the Canadian Union of Public Employees has stepped into the breech. CUPE has had about 90 per cent success in bringing cases of alleged political firings to arbitration. However, there has been considerable opposition to CUPE, both from local patronage committees and from much of the populace. The reaction of one Charlotte County M.L.A. is perhaps typical: "... doing away with the patronage system—where those who work for you are favoured by you when you are in power—wouldn't that be doing away with the democratic system?"

In the summer of 1966, a new element was added to this pattern of polarization and reciprocal hostility: the return to New Brunswick and New Brunswick politics, after an absence of six years, and the subsequent elevation to the leadership of the Conservative party of J. Charles Van Horne. During his 15 months as Tory leader, Van Horne had a profound, if contradictory impact on the political system of the province. His rise to power illustrated that the establishment in the Conservative party could be thwarted; his successful by-election in Restigouche,[24] or more specifically his style of campaign, reduced even further his party's limited orientation to issues; his motions in the fifth session of the 45th Assembly momentarily changed the nature of his party and at the same time made it easier for the Liberal government to introduce its language legislation;

his campaign style during the 1967 general election introduced the ultimate wheeler-dealer, non-issue-oriented politician; his presence as party leader so split the Conservative party that this split was a factor in its 1967 defeat.

Van Horne projected the same messianic appeal in the rural areas that Diefenbaker possessed in the 1958 federal campaign. His oratory was that of a prairie evangelist, but with northern New Brunswick colloquialisms.[25] He had the organizational skill of a Duplessis and attempted during the 1967 camapaign to paint himself as a greater wheeler-dealer than W.A.C. Bennet, another native son. He was at various times an R.C.M.P. officer, a Canadian Army officer, a barrister, a businessman, a real estate developer, executive assistant to J. C. Irving, a federal Member of Parliament, party leader, and a Member of the Legislative Assembly. Yet even this wide range of occupations did not fully reflect his personality.

"Maverick" is the term most often applied to Van Horne by both the provincial and national press,[26] and the establishment of the Conservative party. He never exhibited the typical New Brunswick attitude, "my party right or wrong"—he criticized the Diefenbaker government on the floor of the Commons while a back bencher, supported the Liberal party against the Flemming government during the 1960 provincial election,[27] and opposed Hugh John Flemming in the Royal by-election in 1960, after Flemming had been appointed to the Diefenbaker cabinet. It would appear that Van Horne did not have a strong commitment to traditional party politics, that there was a populist strain in his political attitudes. While every politician attempts to convince the voters to cross party lines, with Van Horne this effort became a virtual fixation. He stressed that everywhere in the province traditional Liberals were casting aside their old political colors to join the Van Horne party, the people's party.[28] Likewise he had the ability to draw out the non-voter, no mean task in a province where there is substantial polarization between those who are deeply committed and those who are firmly apolitical.[29]

Van Horne was elected to the House of Commons in 1955 and re-elected in 1957 and 1958, but resigned in 1960 to work in real estate development in Canada and the United States. He returned from California in the summer of 1966,[30] and immediately upon his return the political scene took on an exciting new light.

There was considerable dissatisfaction among Conservatives with the somewhat dispassionate leadership of Cy Sherwood. Sherwood had been chosen party leader in 1962, after having served unofficially in this capacity since the defeat of the Fleming government in 1960, but many in the party felt that he was not sufficiently aggressive to confront in the Assembly, let alone defeat at the polls, the personality of Premier Robichaud. The dissatisfaction within the party grew, and after a party caucus in September 1966 Sherwood resigned.[31] Richard Hatfield, a young Carleton County lawyer and businessman, scion of an old provincial family, was the first announced candidate for the vacant leadership. He was followed by Roger Pichette, a former minister in the Fleming government, and, in due course, by Van Horne.

The entry of both Hatfield and Van Horne into the leadership race was the beginning of a party split. Hatfield was the establishment choice, the man groomed by Sherwood and others for eventual leadership, the candidate of the "respectable Tories."[32] Van Horne, on the other hand, was the candidate of the frustrated, who had been chafing in opposition for six years, who felt Sherwood's leadership had been ineffective and that Hatfield was, like him, "too nice a guy."[33] But Van Horne's wheeler-dealer financial activities,[34] his support of the Liberals in the 1960 general election, his general "irresponsibility"[35] did not sit well with the traditional Conservatives, who attempted to secure the election of the more responsible Hatfield. The means by which Van Horne stifled this opposition is a classic study in political strategy and illustrates the difficulty that an opposition leadership has in keeping its troops in line without a patronage system at its disposal. Initially, a Conservative M.L.A. from Saint John, a St. Stephen businessman and former minister in the Fleming government, and two University of New Brunswick professors planned on marshalling opposition to Van Horne. Van Horne realized that the latter two had no following within the party and hence posed no threat; he went over the heads of the former two to the basis of their political support, swung the rank and file in their organizations, and forced them to capitulate. The Van Horne method of obtaining delegate support was straightforward: if the local party leaders were sympathetic to him, he had them deliver the delegates; if the leadership was opposed, he went over their heads, got the grass roots support,[36] and in that way brought most of the local party leadership into his camp.

The outcome of the leadership convention was a foregone conclusion: Van Horne won handily.[37] But the party split, with the traditional Conservatives momentarily withdrawing as the Van Horne people moved into the ascendency. The attitude of one of the professors who had opposed him was indicative: "I am a man temporarily without a party."[38] There is evidence that these dissident Conservatives either did not work or expended only marginal effort during the 1967 campaign.

Van Horne's immediate concern after winning the leadership was to secure a seat in the Assembly. Due to the death of the Liberal Health Minister, a vacancy existed in Restigouche, and Van Horne received the party nomination for the February 6, 1967 by-election. His campaign in Restigouche was a microcosm of the campaign he conducted for the October 1967 general election. It was characterized by a total lack of policy discussion and an emphasis on bread and circuses—dances, socials,

Ski-doo parties, white cowboy hats,[39] ball point pens, cigars, gimmicks galore—even George Hees riding on a fire engine with Van Horne. The Van Horne strategy was to get people to the public meetings so they could see what a fine fellow he was: a "swinger," a wheeler-dealer-manipulator, the guy who would get things done once he got to Fredericton. The Van Horne attitude toward issues and policies was that they were non-existent. Discussing campaign tactics in a television interview on March 8, 1967, his advice to his party was to:

> *Appoint a master of ceremonies, and have him rent the biggest hall he can find... provide some lively music to accommodate the spirit of the evening... if the rally begins at eight o'clock, start the music thirty minutes before that... speeches should be short, off the cuff, positive, and to the point... don't mention the name of your opponent or any other party... keep the length of the meeting to no more than ninety minutes... afterward, mingle with the crowd, shake hands, and have the musicians stick around... if the younger set wants to have a dance afterwards, let them.*[40]

Van Horne won the by-election, sat as opposition leader for one session, and suffered personal defeat as the Conservative party was defeated in the October election. In one sense the epitome of the non-issue politican, in another sense he may have made a contribution to the lessening of racial tensions with his linguistic motion in the Assembly. Van Horne, while leader of the opposition, used a legislative tactic that Robichaud had used while opposition leader of presenting motions so wide-ranging in scope that it is next to impossible for the government to vote them down. The theory behind their usage, in an Assembly where private members' bills and motions are very rarely introduced, was that a government that used its majority to vote down a motion that favored motherhood and was against sin would receive adverse public reaction. By introducing a motion calling for the recognition of French and English as the two official languages, Van Horne created a climate of acceptability for the government's Official Languages Act when it was ultimately introduced. Although the Conservative Party and the WASP of the Saint John River Valley had virtually ignored the problems of the French in New Brunswick, the Van Horne motion demonstrated an awareness, on the part of some Conservatives, of the Acadian fact.

Following his party's and his own personal defeat, Van Horne resigned his position as party leader. Upon regaining his seat in a by-election, he contested but lost the 1968 party leadership contest to Richard Bennett Hatfield whose first test by fire was the provincial election of October 26, 1970. The Liberal campaign promised a continuation of programs of social reform instituted during the past years, and the establishment of "pollution guidelines" and a guaranteed annual income.

The Conservatives, whose campaign slogan was "It's time for a change," promised a Law Reform Commission, redistribution of multi-member constituencies, and general reform of the electoral system. They also promised to create 40,000 jobs by coordinating the efforts of various agencies to attract industry to the province.

The Conservative party secured electoral victory by taking a total of six seats from the Liberals: three in Moncton, two in Sunbury and one in Edmundston. Preliminary analysis shows that in Moncton, the Acadian elite and the working-class English were voting Conservative for diametrically opposite reasons. The Acadians felt that they had received all the redress they could expect from an Acadian Premier, and that in fact an English administration might be able to implement controversial sections of the Official Languages Act (to which both parties were by this time at least officially committed) with less opposition from the English electorate. It was felt too that in the formulation of policy, Hatfield's personal interest in Acadian problems would prove superior to the traditional sympathies of his party. The working-class English voter, on the other hand, saw in the Conservative party a potential source of relief from the language policies of both the federal and provincial governments.

The policies of the federal government were a factor as well in the Liberal defeat in Sunbury county. Canadian Forces Base, Gagetown is the only large-scale employer in the county, and the town of Oromocto is a direct result of the decision of the federal government in the 1950s to locate the largest military base in the Commonwealth in Sunbury. Preliminary analysis shows that many in the area, both civilian and military, were concerned about Ottawa's present and future defence policies. The civilians were apprehensive that, after the 1967 re-ordering of military priorities, further cutbacks would place the entire local economy in jeopardy. The military population apparently felt that government pay increases had been too late and too little. In both cases, discontent with the Federal party was expressed in a sense vicariously by a rather dramatic turn against the provincial Liberals. In 1967 the Liberal majority was approximately 1.7 to 1 in Oromocto and Base Gagetown; in 1970 it was 2 to 1 in favor of the Conservatives.[41]

In most areas the traditional ethnic identifications of the parties seem to have been strengthened in 1970. The Conservatives made gains in the English areas of Albert, Carleton, Charlotte, Fredericton, Kings, York, and Saint John West and stayed constant in Saint John Centre and Saint John East. Liberal support increased in the French counties, the areas of their traditional strength.

Like the campaign of 1970, the general election of 1974 was quiet. The Liberal opposition, under the leadership of Robert Higgins, offered no substantive alternatives to Hatfield's economic policies which remained ill-defined apart from the rhetoric of bread and butter. The

Tories were returned with a safe majority of 33 to 25, again gaining ground in traditionally Liberal territory with three additional predominantly French-speaking constituencies garnered in the north.

The Hatfield government's economic policies largely have concentrated on buttressing and expanding forest-based industry and increasing the province's supply of electric energy.[42] The search for a broader, more secure industrial base eluded Hatfield as it had Robichaud during the previous decade.

In general, voter turnout in the last four elections has been higher in rural than in urban, and in French than in English areas. An explanation for the former might be the parties' greater visibility in rural areas, as well as the close association of personal and political loyalties. In rural communities, elections are significant social events, often vitalized by inducements such as two-dollar bills, mickeys of rum, or boxes of chocolates. Along with these favors, which often have the status of obligations, gratuities may be paid to people working for the party on election day, with the effect of encouraging them to bring their extended families to the polls.

The higher voter turnout among Acadian than among English New Brunswickers could be a reflection of the Acadians' sense of exclusion from the economic and social elites in the province (there is an Acadian elite in Moncton but it is strictly localized). Consequently, Acadians may have a higher incidence of voter participation both because their interest is in changing rather than maintaining the status quo, and because their access to other forms of political leverage is restricted. In Bathurst and Edmundston, for example, where the only industry (pulp and paper) is English-controlled, the heavy Acadian vote may be an attempt to counter-balance this power.

Conclusion

Politics in New Brunswick have more color than content. The politicians are less concerned with issues than with the parish pump; but this may be what the electorate wants. To an outsider, the patronage system may appear abusive; to the people it may seem to fulfill their needs more effectively than can institutionalized bureaucracies. To the democratic theorist, the imbalance between constituencies and the existence of multi-member ridings may appear unjust; to the people it may appear as the only way that an Irish-Catholic can get elected. To the urban dweller from Toronto, such election day activities as the sale or barter of votes may seem like something out of Tammany Hall; to the people. it's a few extra dollars and a lot of fun. To the urbane political scientist, the behavior in the Assembly may appear infantile; to the people it's "the boys havin' a bit of fun." To the rest of the country, politics here may appear insupportably rustic; to the people of New Brunswick their style is preferable to the mass media politics that merchandise candidates like so much soap powder. But the electoral system and Assembly are still in need of reform, great families run the political affairs of some areas, non-issue-oriented politicians and a substantial patronage system prevail. Yet the people prefer their political system the way it is. Is there anything in democratic theory that implies that even when the people are wrong they are right?

Endnotes

[2] Successive premiers have promised reform of the distribution of Assembly seats since at least 1917. The electoral map was finally changed in 1974 when 58 single-member ridings were created to replace the previous 20 ridings containing a total of 57 seats.

[3] As one Liberal put it, "They (the party leadership) stand on the mountain and throw it over—we are supposed to catch it."

[4] On one occasion the then leader of the opposition sent a dozen eggs, a bushel of apples, and a length of pulp wood to the government benches to prove a debating point.

[5] In 1967 the NDP ran three candidates in a four-member constituency, capturing 1,247 votes out of 92,579 cast. In 1970, encouraged by their recent success in Nova Scotia, the New Democrats contested 32 seats, winning 3.4% of the popular vote. In the 1974 election the NDP again failed to establish a presence in the Assembly.

[6] In 1944 the CCF ran 41 candidates, but despite capturing 68,248 votes, compared to the Liberals' 282,367 votes (37 seats) and the Conservatives' 233,301 (11 seats), it did not return a single Member. The Left tried again in 1948 but took only one-half of its 1944 total vote and, after a half-hearted attempt in 1952, disappeared from the provincial scene until the NDP contested Northumberland in 1967. The Social Credit party appeared once provincially, fielding candidates in 18 of 52 seats, took 9,490 votes and disappeared. Independent candidates have vanished as well—eight ran in 1948; by 1963 the field was down to one, with none in 1967. Drawn from Howard Scarrow, *Canada Votes* (New Orleans: Hauser Press, 1961), pp. 206 208.

[7] It is very common to think of oneself as belonging to a "Liberal family" or a "Conservative family" and to vote accordingly.

[8] Compiled from the Dominion Bureau of Statistics, *Census of Canada*, 1961.

[9] *The Daily Gleaner* (Fredericton), March 16, 1969.

[10] Also annual meetings of the Liberal Women's Association and Young Liberals, in constituencies where they exist.

[11] The frameworks of the two major parties are essentially the same.

[12] A prime illustration of the leadership role was witnessed by the author as the Liberals held their nomination meeting for Saint John City in June 1960 in the old Mayfair theatre. When the meeting had been in progress for a while, the chairman made a statement to the effect that "We're not nominating

tonight, two of our candidates are fogged in at Halifax." One naive party worker jumped to his feet and started to exclaim that he understood that it was to be an open convention, at which point the chairman bellowed, "I said we ain't nominating, now sit down and shaddup." End of dissension.

[13] From 1967 to 1974 there were two five-member, six three-member, seven two-member, and only four single-member constituencies.

[14] Chapter 6, *Acts of New Brunswick, 1961-62*; also Order-in-Council 62-185, March 8, 1962.

[15] *Report of the Royal Commission on Finance and Municipal Taxation* (Fredericton, 1963) Table 7c, Appendix 07c.

[16] Formerly known as the Maritime Loyalist Association.

[17] This is an area where the Orange Lodge still exists in its nineteenth century context.

[18] Canadian Loyalist Association, *Bulletin*, n.p., n.d.

[19] *Ibid.*

[20] The mayors of two of the three major cities were Conservatives when Equal Opportunity was introduced. Mayor Jones of Moncton was mooted in both 1966 and 1969 as a possible leader of the Conservative party. Mayor Walker of Fredericton entered the 1969 Conservative leadership race four days after being defeated for re-election.

[21] *Atlantic Advocate* (Fredericton), October, 1966, p. 32.

[22] *Report of the Royal Commission on Finance and Municipal Taxation* (Fredericton, 1963), p. 16.

[23] There was an identical response from some when Dr. Frankel recommended collective bargaining for New Brunswick public servants.

[24] The by-election on February 6, 1966, not his later by-election on November 4, 1968, which he also won.

[25] For example, his favourite remark that the Government seemed to be "dog dancing."

[26] E.g., *The Daily Gleaner* (Fredericton), November 25, 1966; *Star Weekly Magazine* (Toronto), October 17, 1966; and *The Globe and Mail* (Toronto), October 20 and 21, 1966.

[27] *The Daily Gleaner* (Fredericton), June 17 and 20, 1966.

[28] The Conservative slogan in the election campaign made no reference to the Conservative party, simply, "Van Horne for the People."

[29] In the 1963 provincial election, 15,958 voted in Restigouche, with a difference of only 360 votes between the Liberal who led the polls (three running) and the bottom Conservative (three running). In the February 1967 by-election, the Liberal candidate polled 7,000 votes, a drop of 646 votes from that polled by the top Liberal in 1963, yet Van Horne won by 2,673 votes, a net gain of over 2,000 votes, with no significant population increase in the riding. A few tombstones may have voted in 1967, but in essence Mr. Van Horne brought out 2,000 more votes than the 1963 Conservative candidates were able to do.

[30] It has been implied many times that Van Horne was brought back from California by the Irving interests, for whom he once worked, but no evidence is available to prove or disprove this allegation.

[31] The official version was that Sherwood called for a re-appraisal of the leadership, saying that he would take a few days to decide whether to re-

offer. A credible version of what happened is that party dissidents, notably the president of the York Progressive Conservative Association, succeeded, over the objections of former Premier Flemming, in having Sherwood dropped.

[32] The Hatfield slogan, "Victory with Honour," suggests the kind of support he was trying to elicit.

[33] This was the standard refrain of delegates at the time of leadership convention, particularly the day before the actual balloting.

[34] *Star Weekly Magazine* (Toronto), October 17, 1966.

[35] Tom Bell, Member of Parliament for the then riding of Saint John-Albert, nominated Van Horne at the leadership convention and when asked by the *Globe and Mail* why he had, was quoted as stating: "the mood of New Brunswick tends at the moment to be irresponsible . . . and Charlie is the guy who can fit that mood. He tends to be irresponsible . . . " The *Globe and Mail* (Toronto), February 4, 1967.

[36] Some such pressure may in fact have been brought to bear on Bell who, by temperament at least, was initially a Hatfield supporter.

[37] The official results of the balloting, although never announced, were as follows: Van Horne 458, Hatfield 135, Pichette 9.

[38] This was only one of a considerable number of defections from the party from the ranks of the respectable Conservatives.

[39] This could probably be classed as the Van Horne trademark: white felt with a blue band, on which was printed "Pour le Peuple Van Horne for the People."

[40] Provincial Affairs Telecast, CHSJ-TV, March 8, 1967: *Telegraph Journal* March 9, 1967. Van Horne's final remark in relation to the young is of some interest, for while it is unusual to see younger people at political meetings, he attracted them in droves. In restrospect, it would seem that they were there not to be politicized but rather to socialize, as it was usual for Van Horne to hire a rock group whenever he held a meeting. During the general election the Conservatives hired Don Messer and the Islanders, who were allegedly not paid for performing, and the 1969 leadership convention, which chose Hatfield over Van Horne, had to do without live music.

[41] Compiled from the Report of the Chief Electoral Officer, Twenty-Sixth General Election, p.19, and *Telegraph Journal* (Saint John), October 27, 1970. It might be suggested that the Liberal defeat in Sunbury was aggravated by the absence of a considerable number of officers and men on loan to civil authorities in Quebec during the "October crisis." The author's feeling is that if these troops had been home in time to vote, the Conservative majority would have been higher.

[42] The Bricklin episode stands in rather stark contrast to the general thrust toward resource-based government expenditures on industry. It is interesting to note that the Bricklin affair seems not to have affected the outcome of the election of 1974. Although actual closure of the Bricklin plant occurred in the months following the election, it appears to be accepted as just another episode in the Province's unsuccessful attempts to industrialize.

NEWFOUNDLAND
Plus Ça Change, Plus C'est La Même Chose

Susan McCorquodale

In 1933 the Report of a Royal Commission authorized to inquire into "the future of Newfoundland and in particular to report on the financial situation and prospects therein ..." recommended among other things that the "country should be given a rest from party politics for a period of years."[1] The Report recognized that Newfoundland was a small island caught in a world-wide depression, but nevertheless it reached the conclusion that much of the blame for the financial failure could be laid at the door of the extravagant political malpractices of successive governments during the years 1920-1931. Newfoundland, in the words of a later historian, had been "tested by the political and administrative canons of a mature political ... system such as that of England and had been found wanting."[2] Faced with the alternatives of self-government on the one hand and economic survival on the other (a choice which is really not a choice at all) the island had accepted the principal recommendations of the Amulree Commission and for the years between 1934 and 1949 party politics, at least in their most obvious manifestation, disappeared along with self-government.[3] The people of Newfoundland shared this lack of confidence in themselves and their political leaders. The most general response to the Report was a feeling of relief, stemming from a widespread conclusion that the ills of Newfoundland had at least part of their origin in the defects of party politics.[4]

These events in the 1930s stand in sharp contrast to the events of the 1940s. In this latter period "politics" returned to the island during the period when a new dynamic leader awoke the people to new political choices, culminating on March 31, 1949, when Newfoundland changed her constitutional status to become the 10th province in the Canadian Federation. "Confederation" was thus doubly a new beginning: on the one hand the province turned her back on her history as an independent nation; on the other hand, after an interregnum of 15 years the manifest garments of a modern, elected democracy were put on. This study is concerned first, with the re-establishment of party politics in Newfoundland in the post-Confederation years; and secondly, with the events of the post-Smallwood era. Briefly, however, we must explain something of the historical and political heritage Newfoundland brought to Confederation.

The Historical Background

Newfoundland's population in 1976 was just over 550,000, nearly 40 per cent being concentrated on the Avalon Peninsula at the south-east corner of the island, furthest from the Canadian mainland. There are few urban centres: St. John's had a population in 1976 of 84,000 and Corner Brook, the next largest centre, a population of 24,000. Recent years have seen a rural population changed into an urban one, but the fact remains that by Canadian standards, Newfoundland's "urban" centres are small (the average town population is only 2,056 persons).[5] A recent Report on Municipal Government estimates that 104,890 persons, just under one-fifth of the entire population, are located in 520 unincorporated communities whose average size is 190.[6]

The primary reason for this scattering of population is not hard to determine: fish. Until the 20th century Newfoundland was regarded largely as a convenient way-station, far out in the Atlantic, useful as a place to serve the "prosecution of the fishery." Today, while not as important economically, coming fourth in the Gross Provincial Product, the fishery is important socially and is apparently playing a role much like agriculture in other developing countries: acting as a sponge to absorb a growing labor force for which other economic opportunites have not opened up.

Economically, Newfoundland is a "have-not" province. The GPP is only 60 per cent of the GNP. Newfoundland's personal income per capita, while it had risen from the 56 per cent of the national average that it was in 1962, was still only 66 per cent of the national average in 1972. As a sop to provincial pride we might note that, in 1972, for the first time since 1949, Newfoundland did not have the lowest average income per capita reported in all 10 Canadian provinces. This dubious honor was achieved in that year by Prince Edward Island.[7]

Socially, Newfoundland has a population which is overwhelmingly British by ethnic origin—93.7 per cent of the people are of Anglo-Saxon or Celtic stock, and 98.5 per cent are English-speaking only.[8] Social divisions are not ethnic; they arise from religious and class antagonisms. Newfoundland has today her share of battles between "Liberals" and "Conservatives," but tied into these divisions are folk images of old battles between Protestant "establishment" and Roman Catholic "reformers" in the 19th century overlaid by liberal movements in the 20th century which were largely Protestant and finally further complicated by the alleged anti-Confederate attitudes in Roman Catholics.

THE EARLY YEARS

While present-day orators like to claim that Newfoundland is "Britain's Oldest Colony" in point of fact the legal existance of a colony was not acknowledged by Britain until 1824. Prior to that time, successive English governments had either ignored the settlers or actively sought to drive them off the island (while at the same time disputing with the French claims to the fishery). The system of representative, but not responsible government, tried out in 1824 was not a great success because tied in with the political defects were social conflicts, largely stemming from denominational antagonisms. In the early 19th century the population was approximately one-third Roman Catholic (Irish laborers for the most part brought over by the English fish merchants); one-third Anglican; and one-third non-conformist. But each denomination was not equally influential, and struggles in the political arena took on coloration from this "skewing" of the influence patterns. The antagonism climaxed in the election campaign of 1861 when three men were killed and 20 wounded.[9] Expediency dictated a solution: religious representation in administrative appointments, in the personnel of the Courts and, in fact, in all public office.[10] It was later to be reinforced by the system of public education, which is in fact to this day entirely denominational.

The 20th century opened for Newfoundland as a time of relative prosperity. Public interest in union with Canada was at a low ebb, having failed to arouse support both in the 1860s and the 1890s; the railway had been built, and in 1911 the age-old fishery disputes with France and the United States had been settled. However, the guns of August, 1914, shattered bright hopes; and before the end of the war, Newfoundland had seen over 5,000 of her men in arms and had added over $13 million to her public debt.[11]

The end of the war signaled the date from which we can trace the present-day political parties. The pre-war years had seen the rise of a new political force on the north-east coast of the island, the first genuine effort to unite fishermen into one great union. At its peak the Newfoundland Fishermen's Protective Union had about 20,000 members and between 1908 and 1932 it was very important to the social, economic and political life of the colony. It was the first such organization to stress to the fishermen that they were being robbed by the merchants and the government, that they should be proud of their calling, and that by organizing themselves into local, district and national councils they could gain the political experience which, in the absence of local government, they lacked. The leader of the F.P.U. was W. F. Coaker and in 1912 he made the decision to go into party politics by allying himself with the Liberals, at this time led by Sir Robert Bond, a former Prime Minister, a progressive who had, perhaps alone of the old-style politicians in Newfoundland, raised his eyes above internal conflicts and had sought to bring Newfoundland into the international arena. Bond and Coaker lost the election of 1912, but clearly the new force was one to be reckoned with: the F.P.U. had run 11 candidates and won with all of them and five of the seven Liberals elected had also won in "fishermen" districts.[12]

The election of 1919 saw the victory of the man who has been called the "political ancestor of J. R. Smallwood"–the Liberal, Sir Richard Squires. Squires and Coaker fought and won the election as one political party, but in actual fact once again the bloc of fishermen's seats held the balance between the 13 seats won by Squires and the 12 seats held by the opposition Conservatives. Coaker became Minister of Marine and Fisheries and introduced a new system of fish marketing (the "Coaker Regulations") which at least in the beginning stood a fair chance of winning merchant support and rationalizing a chaotic situation. Unfortunately, the bright promises failed to materialize, the steam went out of the F.P.U., and when in 1924 scandal touched Squires, the government was forced to resign, not to return again until 1928. Squires' personal victory was decisive (83 percent of the vote) and his campaign manager was one Joseph R. Smallwood.[13]

But the economic dislocations of 1929 produced new political problems and by 1931 the twin pressures of a fall in the world price of her primary product and rising public debt at home were forcing Newfoundland into disaster. In 1929 the public debt stood at $87.7 million; by 1931 it was periously close to $100 million and interest payments on the debt reached nearly 65 percent of the average revenue over the preceding years.[14] Between 1931 and 1932 the value of exports fell from $33.5 million to $26.6 million.[15] Added to which, nature itself seemed angry, for the fishery failed in three successive years. One-quarter of the population was on relief. In spite of drastic cuts in expenditure, increased taxation, and desperate searches for alternative solutions, the government in 1933 was finally forced to request help from the United Kingdom, with the results outlined at the beginning of this paper.

THE END OF THE COMMISSION OF GOVERNMENT

The British Government promised in 1934 that when Newfoundland became self-supporting again responsible government on request of the people would be restored. Economically, it was evident by 1945 that the war had made Newfoundland "self-supporting"; she had in fact a financial surplus of $40.3 million when she joined Canada in 1949.[16] As events turned out, it was to take four years and three elections for Newfoundland to decide on the future form of government and at the same time accept the leadership of the man who for the next 20 years would dominate the life of the new province.

First in June, 1946 delegates were elected to a National Convention called by the British Government to offer suggestions for a new form of government. Then came the first referendum vote on the choices put to the people. The results were:

Commission of Government—14.3%
Confederation with Canada—41.1%
Responsible Government—44.5%

It was necessary therefore to hold a "run-off" Referendum in July, 1948 and the result was victory for Confederation.

The delegates to the National Convention had been instructed to "consider the financial state of Newfoundland and make recommendations on possible forms of future government." By the time the Convention first met in September, 1946 the battle lines and the leading advocates of alternative courses had become clear: Joseph R. Smallwood, a populist politician and journalist who after 25 years had found the Cause he had been searching for—Confederation of Newfoundland with Canada; Major Peter Cashin, a maverick member of the Establishment who wished to see the island return to the proud tradition of 400 years—independence and responsible government; and Chesley Crosbie, a respected member of the Establishment who pleaded for the anti-Confederate halfway house of Economic Union with the United States.

The British Government had made it a condition of election to the National Convention that the candidates had to reside in the districts they represented. This gesture towards grass-roots democracy went somewhat against the political traditions of Newfoundland where outport constituencies were often but not invariably represented by men living in St. John's. Despite this attempt to broaden the base of politics, not one fisherman was elected, only four of the delegates had had experience in the pre-1934 House of Assembly, two were lawyers and one a former magistrate, while many of the new men were co-operative field workers or teachers.[17] From the delegates who favored the return to full self-government, together with those who wished to see the Commission of Government retained and those few who held on to the hope of economic union with the United States, the Convention was able to put together a loose majority of anti-confederates. But it was not a "party" in the accepted sense; it lacked a leader and a clear sense of what it was for rather than what it was against. Smallwood on the other hand dominated his small group of confederate supporters and together they looked and acted more like a party. They had to some extent campaigned as a group, since in 1946 the St. John's District Labour Party had been created (led by Irving Fogwill who had been a founding member in 1937 of the Newfoundland Federation of Labour)[18] and this group had campaigned strenuously for the election of the party's candidates to the National Convention. Fogwill, a union organizer, was thus one of the original "old confederates." Smallwood has said himself that at this time and during the two subsequent Referenda campaigns, the "dictator" charge so frequently to be laid at his door (unjustly) as Premier, could with greater truth have been attributed to him.

The debate over Confederation revealed the peculiar regional, class and religious nature of the battle. The center of the anti-confederate movement was in St. John's; its dominant elements were merchants and Roman Catholics. Opposed were the residents of the 1,300 small and isolated communities around the island: fishermen and loggers, largely Protestant. The roster of the key members of the Responsible Government League read like a "Who's Who" of the Establishment.[19] The Roman Catholic Archbishop of St. John's was a known and implacable opponent of union with Canada, a position not shared by his fellow bishops in Grand Falls and Harbour Grace. But Archbishop Roche authorized a series of articles in a Catholic journal which succeeded in arousing a Protestant reaction. Jamieson records that sectarian bitterness was widespread and that "the greatest issue in the history of Newfoundland public life was dominated, in the dying days of the campaign, by a full-fledged Catholic-Protestant feud."[20] The accepted mythology of the day, that somehow Confederation was a Protestant movement, ignored the fact that the vote cut across religious lines to a marked degree, that there were in fact many Protestant communities virtually solid in their support for Responsible Government.[21]

Equally stressed in the accounts of the events from 1945 to 1949 is the emergence of the mass media, in those days primarily radio, as an instrument for reaching and creating public opinion. The communications pattern developed at that time was to carry Smallwood successfully through many future electoral campaigns. He was an experienced propagandist in 1945. Initially by means of radio, then via a lively, colorful newspaper and finally by well-publicized meetings in areas he knew to be "confederate," Smallwood projected himself and his cause successfully to an audience hitherto ignored and apathetic. The National Convention had almost defeated Smallwood in 1948 by the simple expedient of refusing by 28 to 18 to put the choice "Confederation with Canada" on the ballot slips. But the daily proceedings of the Convention had been, for the full 18 months preceding, broadcast over the government-owned radio network. Throughout the island in homes, lodges and halls, people had gathered to hear the broadcasts and thousands had become deeply and personally involved with the issues: for the first time they listened to *their* politicians talking about *their* country.[22] Smallwood had during this time directed almost his every word at the microphones and to the audience beyond. He tested the potency of his link with public opinion after the negative decision of the Convention by reaching over their heads and calling on the support of the people of Newfoundland. "Within days a blizzard of telegrams descended . . . on St. John's. These contained more than 50,000 signatures all asking for the inclusion of (the) Confederation (option) . . . "[23] The British Government, responding to a plea they wished to hear, rejected the avowed function of the Convention and itself put the Confederation choice on the ballot. If we measure voter turnout alone, the campaign to awaken the people of Newfoundland was eminently successful. In 1946 only 20% of those eligible had voted at the National Convention election.[24] By contrast 88% and 84% respectively of the electorate participated in the Referenda elections.

Born at this time was another technique of persuasion that was to serve Smallwood well—wavering support could be strengthened and opposition bought off with government appointments. On a train trip across the island with delegates to the National Convention aboard, Smallwood used this technique to such good effect that "at least three delegates disembarked convinced they were to become Minister of Finance, there were also five potential chairmen of the Liquor Board and would-be Senators were as common as spruce trees."[25]

The Political Parties, 1949–1968

The results of the first Referendum had given the advocates of Responsible Government the idea that their cause was certain to win; they had led the poll 69,440 to 64,066. Support had come from St. John's, from the ancient business families, from the management of the largest papermill company—Bowaters of Corner Brook—and from the Roman Catholic Church. Their appeal had been nationalism, conservatism, and fear of economic domination. These appeals had been successful in thwarting union with Canada in 1896. They were not destined to be so in 1949. The reasons for failure lay partly in the changed circumstances produced by Newfoundland's tentative steps into the 20th century taken most clearly during the Second World War; partly the cause of failure lay in the opposition they faced—a small band of dedicated followers with a clear cause, led by a man supreme in his skill as propagandist and organizer; and partly their failure lay in themselves—overconfident, they made too many assumptions. They were the amateurs who did not look at voting patterns; they did not see that Confederation forces had breached many of the strongholds of the Responsible Government League on the Avalon Peninsula, nor that the overwhelming support in

Roman Catholic districts was bound to produce over-reaction in the Protestant areas. Roman Catholics, after all, constituted only one-third of the island's population.

The Responsible Government League and the Economic Union activists knit a clumsy joint effort against Smallwood in the seven weeks between the first and second Referenda. But the businessmen and lawyers who surrounded Cashin and Crosbie were successful merely in taking the heart out of the younger supporters of Economic Union, men like Jamieson and Stirling who alone perhaps were capable of an active, driving campaign. Moreover, opponents of Confederation were running into a situation they were to face even more acutely in the future: the comparative lack of funds. The leading men on Water Street and the paper companies were unwilling to back their cause to the same extent that Liberals in Ottawa were backing theirs. Smallwood, billing himself as spokesman for the poor outporters, had had the use of a seaplane, motor transportation and cash for the traditional outlays for beer, rum and votes. Gwyn suggests that the Confederate Association had amassed a fund of close to $150,000.00.[26] In the dying days of the Confederation battle, Smallwood fought hard to overcome the religious bigotry being aroused on all sides and he added respectability and "tone" to the cause when the newspapers made it clear that several leading citizens—a Bowring, a Baird and an Outerbridge—had seen the light. The 22,000 voters who had voted for retention of the Commission of Government were wooed with the announcement that two of the Newfoundland Commissioners, Pottle and Quinton, were now working for the cause of Confederation. (Subsequently, these men had their rewards; both joined the first provincial cabinet and one became a Senator.)

The result of the second Referendum was just under a 7,000 vote majority for Confederation; in percentages it was 52.24% in favour and 47.76% against. Canadian Prime Minister King was agreeable to calling this a "clear and beyond all possibility of misunderstanding" expression of the will of the people. Between June, 1948 and March 31, 1949 negotiations over the Terms of Union proceeded in Ottawa and on the latter date Newfoundland joined Canada. Smallwood who in 1945 had caught a glimpse of what the future might hold, had virtually single-handedly changed the course of his island's history.

While the Ottawa talks proceeded, Smallwood was taking the necessary steps through which the victorious Confederation Association "melted, thawed and dissolved itself" into the Liberal Party. In August Smallwood went to Toronto and dramatically introduced himself to the National Convention of the Liberals. In April of the next year he called a provincial Convention where some 1,500 Newfoundland delegates were called together to achieve two purposes: to select himself as leader of the Liberal Party and to choose the candidates for the first provincial election. The first was unanimously achieved (and was the last time for 20 years that the Party would officially express its confidence in him) and the second proceeded by a uniquely Smallwood method. The groups of delegates were supposedly free to elect the candidates for their respective districts. But one such nominee has recorded that first of all, Smallwood "had him down" for Bonavista South; secondly, that the delegates of the district were not all that keen on him and would have preferred a waiting "native son"; and that thirdly, it was only after Smallwood met with the delegates, reminded them they had chosen him to do an important job, and that he needed the right kind of men to help him, did they agree. Thus it was that Bonavista South—which in 1932 had defeated one J. R. Smallwood, the Squires candidate—found its candidate and elected him with a 2,000 vote majority.[27]

By turning the Confederate Association into the Liberal Party, Smallwood allied himself with a Canadian political party which had a national record of electoral success; he allied himself with his own pre-1934 Party; and he provided years of campaign oratory to the effect that since all Confederates were now Liberals, it followed that all Progressive Conservatives were anti-Confederates. In a province where an ever increasing majority became persuaded of the benefits of Confederation, the Liberals thus provided themselves with years of electoral victories.

For the anti-Confederates the choice was whether to remain a local party or to ally themselves with the national Progressive Conservatives. After the second Referendum the diehards of the League for Responsible Government and the Economic Union met in February, 1949 with J. M. Macdonnell and Richard Bell. "Out of a crew of dissidents" the Progressive Conservative Party was born. The leader of the Party, H.G.R. Mews, who within two years was out of politics and running as Mayor of St. John's, has said that his party's defeat in 1949 was not so much by men as by cheques: Old Age Pension cheques and Family Allowance cheques which appeared as promised in the two months preceeding the first provincial election.[28] The issue in that first election, as it was to be for years, was personalized; voters either supported or were opposed to Smallwood. The Conservatives changed their leadership six times in 16 years searching for an alternative personality. The first two elected leaders, J. G. Higgins in St. John's East in 1949 and 1951 and M. Hollett in St. John's West in 1952 and 1956 represented old, elite St. John's.[29] Both were Rhodes Scholars, Higgins the son of a distinguished judicial family and Hollett a magistrate for 25 years. In 1959 J. J. Greene, at the age of 31 took over the leadership. He was son and grandson of politicians (his grandfather was prime minister in 1894) and he remained leader until 1966. He resigned in order to return to his law practice and the leadership fell on Dr. N. Murphy who held it for only eight months. He had been elected in Humber East in 1962 and it was hoped that his accession to office meant a new electoral drive beyond the confines of the Avalon Peninsula. Unfortunately for the Progressive Conservatives the "Big Gun" of Smallwood himself was turned on their leader. As had been the case in 1959 when Hollett had been defeated in a direct fight with Smallwood, so in 1966 Smallwood and a young Corner Brook lawyer, Clyde Wells, running as a team in the two Humber seats defeated their respective Progressive Conservative and New Democratic opponents. Murphy's successor, Gerald Ottenheimer, was elected from St. John's East in 1966. He was young, 34, well educated (Ph.D. in Literature) and wealthy, born in Newfoundland of Swiss parentage. In 1970 Frank Moores, late of the House of Commons and former National President of the Progressive Conservative Association took the leadership of the Newfoundland party and in 1972 was elected Premier.

The Conservatives as they organized themselves in 1949 were aware of the disabilities of geography, class and religion they had inherited from the Responsible Government League. They established a formal organization with a Constitution and an elected Executive. They aimed at reinforcing their base in St. John's and then "... from this limited organization we can branch out in an attempt to get organizations in other sections of the island and then a provincial organization."[30] The trouble was that, as the leadership difficulties illustrate, the first eight years of Confederation saw the party bogged down in internecine squabbles; funds from National Headquarters were spent unproductively; and the Progressive Conservatives presented no real alternatives either in terms of policies or leadership.

In the two subsequent provincial elections after 1949 Smallwood easily gained victory. In 1956 it is alleged that he scarcely bothered to campaign and still won 32 out of 36 seats.[31] He quickly learnt the techniques of parliamentary procedure and became the master of the House of Assembly. He regularly attended all sittings of the House and he dominated debate. He began with a wave of reform legislation and created administrative machinery geared in many respects to the best models that either Ottawa or Toronto could provide. He invested heavily in education and medical care for children and those living in outports. He enthusiastically tackled the problems of economic development and industrialization. In this latter cause a lot of mistakes were made and before this initial state of the revolution was over Smallwood's chosen economist had been sentenced to four years in jail for fraud, and some $30 million had been wasted, and Newfoundland was still backward and tied to the fishery.

Zest for the political battle and a Smallwood victory for two more provincial elections came out of the federal Progressive Conservative victory in 1958. Diefenbaker and Smallwood clashed over two issues: the first arose out of the International Woodworkers of America strike against the Anglo-Newfoundland Development Company in western Newfoundland. In 1959 Smallwood enacted "the most punitive anti-labour legislation of any post-war Canadian government other than that of Duplessis"[32] and when violence resulted and the RCMP's request for additional men to maintain order was refused by the federal Cabinet, the clash was well and truly joined. Federal-provincial relations were further strained that same year over "Term 29." This was one of the original Terms of Union negotiated in 1949 and dealt with a review of Newfoundland's fiscal position once Confederation had "shaken down." A federal Royal Commission had recommended an annual grant of $8 million to Newfoundland in perpetuity, but Diefenbaker chose to make this grant only until 1962 when Newfoundland's position would be considered along with that of all other provinces. Smallwood denounced this as a violation of the Terms of Union. In August, 1959 he called an election to gain a mandate and split the Conservatives over the issue of loyalty to Newfoundland versus loyalty to a national political party—an issue which attacked them at the very roots of their origin and support. The result was the defection of prominent Conservatives and the creation of the United Newfoundland Party, a Party "dedicated to the interests of Newfoundland, a party which is not bound to the policies of any national party."[33] The United Newfoundland Party ran nine candidates in that election and won two St. John's seats. Their activities were condemned by the Progressive Conservatives as a "three-way split of the anti-Smallwood forces which would guarantee the Liberals every seat."[34] In point of fact the Liberals elected one less than at the previous election. By 1962 the United Newfoundland Party was dead. One of its leaders lamented that "had it been formed shortly after Confederation when local feelings for Newfoundland as a separate country still ran high, it probably would have had a much larger following. As it was by 1959 the intense local loyalties were beginning to fade and become vague under pressure of Confederation."[35]

The echoes of 1959 lingered into the 1962 federal and provincial elections. In the federal election Smallwood ran a personal quarrel campaign against W. J. Browne, the Solicitor-General in the Diefenbaker Cabinet as a representative of a government which had flouted the province's rights in the International Woodworkers of America and Term 29 disputes. This claim was symbolized by the appointment as campaign manager of a United Newfoundland Party member (John O'Dea) to the Liberal Party's challenger in St. John's West.[36] A study of the voting during this election suggested two points which will be dealt with in this paper: the degree to which Roman Catholics vote Progressive Conservative and the inability or unwillingness of voters in Newfoundland to distinguish between federal and provincial politics.[37]

The provincial election which followed in November 1962 has generally been accepted as a "quiet" one, enlivened to some extent at the end by the denunciation on television by a St. John's Progressive Conservative candidate of the alleged Liberal practice of handing out $5.00 grocery coupons to grateful voters. Smallwood had launched the election to gain support for a "great fishery programme, something special, something big which must be done for our fisheries. I don't know what it is (yet) but I'm going to make a strong bid to find out."[38] There appears to have been an agreement between the Progressive Conservatives and the New Democratic Party (born on the island in 1961) not to contest seats where the other had a chance. The scheme worked to the benefit of the Progressive Conservatives, where in Humber East and Grand Falls, Conservatives took the districts; and in Humber West, the Newfoundland Democratic Party in a straight fight came within 240 votes of the Liberal winner.

The result was the "worst defeat" Smallwood had yet suffered; one of his cabinet ministers was defeated and the Progressive Conservatives won seven seats, three of them off the Avalon Peninsula, and an Independent won in Labrador West thereby creating an opposition of eight, the largest yet faced by the Liberals.

In general the early 1960s were quiet years. More legislation was enacted to prevent strikes or lockouts in hospitals, but to balance such sanctions, the Newfoundland Federation of Labour for the first time in seven years was in 1963 permitted to present a brief to cabinet. The antagonisms of 1959 thus appeared to be lessening.

In 1963 when the Liberals returned to power in Ottawa, the earlier decision of Smallwood to pick a boy from Manitoba as the member from Bonavista-Twillingate (J. W. Pickersgill) began to pay off. Massive hydro developments at Churchill Falls in Labrador and at Bay d'Espoir on the island were getting started, plans were laid for the third paper mill, oil was discovered off the Grand Banks, and the Trans-Canada Highway linking the island from east to west was paved. In addition, various Centennial projects were creating employment and once again a great fisheries programme was envisioned which would require an estimated $100 million over five years. Between 1963 and 1967 Newfoundland became Ottawa's favourite province. Pickersgill used his influence to dot the island with rural post-offices, he authorized $14 million in improvements to the ferry links between the island and the mainland, he provided subsidies to bail out Eastern Provincial Airways, and transferred responsibility for St. John's Harbour and its annual deficit to the National Harbours Board.[39]

The provincial election in 1966 climaxed the mood of prosperity. Smallwood fought "the first modern election campaign in Newfoundland's history" and spent an estimated $300,000 doing it.[40] He hired a Toronto advertising company, ran a campaign based on motivational research which stressed Labrador and the hopes for the future in lieu of gratitude for Confederation. He fielded a younger team which injected needed vitality into the House and the Cabinet, and wound up killing the Conservative hopes of the previous election by taking all but three seats.

This election has since been regarded as the beginning of the end of Smallwood's dominance; it is seen as an expression of gratitude to the Premier for past efforts, a last acknowledgement of the old style of demagogic politics before the onset of a younger, better educated, urban electorate searching for a more modern political style. Smallwood had set out to transform Newfoundland society, to bring material progress to his people and to encourage their participation in their own political future. But like Coaker before him, driven by frustration and impatience, he had often taken these new tasks into his own hands, thereby robbing the islanders of the opportunity to stand alone and mature if necessary by making mistakes. This "take-over" appears to have been true for the co-operative movement, the fishermen's union and municipal government.

The Conservatives, smelling blood, regrouped themselves about their leader, Ottenheimer, at a time when they were ready for either new life or for death. One of the contributing factors in the almost complete victory of the Liberals in 1966 was the disarray of the Conservatives. Their leader, Dr. Murphy, had remained uncommunicative in Corner Brook and as always they had found it hard to find candidates (one such has recorded that he was asked to run at 11:00 p.m. on the day before nominations closed and yet managed to come within 128 votes of winning).[41] The Gander district became the one to watch in 1967. In a provincial by-election the Progressive Conservatives turned an 1,100–vote 1966 defeat into a 900–vote victory. A month later in a federal by-election the encouraged PC organization reduced the Liberal victory in Pickersgill's old seat from 6,400 votes to 1,700.

Then in June 1968 the tide for the Liberals ran out. While the rest of Canada was falling victim to Trudeaumania, Newfoundland elected Conservatives to six of the seven federal seats. This time Smallwood's pattern of fighting federal elections as if they were provincial campaigns did not work to his benefit. After 20 years, what local newspapers called the "inevitable reaction" occurred.[42] All over the island the opinion was expressed that it was time for a change. A tough budget, a cutback in capital expenditures, the discrediting of Smallwood's administration in a report on the province's economic prospects, the defection of two prominent Liberal cabinet ministers, Smallwood's questionable tactics during the election: all contributed to the Liberal defeat, aided by a resurgent Progressive Conservative party fielding aggressive candidates backed by good organization.[43] Smallwood was severely shaken by the upset, but he bounced back with an effort to revitalize the party by confirming a new constitution and leader at a convention to be held in November, 1969.

Crosbie, who had earlier left the Cabinet over the financing of the oil refinery at Come-by-Chance, now emerged as the strongest challenger to Smallwood, and one who was apparently unacceptable to the Premier. In June, 1969, in response to a petition from all but four Liberal MHAs, Smallwood postponed his retirement and decided to try to remain as leader. It was an exciting time in the province as both camps fought it out in terms of lists of committed delegates, floods of literature and well-organized campaigning: when the ballots of the 1,700 delegates had been counted, the outcome was a decisive victory for Smallwood, 63 per cent to 26 per cent for Crosbie.

In October, 1971 Smallwood fought his last campaign as leader of the Liberal Party. This was the famous "Sally's Cove" election and the results were very close: Conservatives 21 seats, Liberals 20 seats, and the balance of power held by the one seat, that won by Tom Burgess, leader of a Labrador separatist group, the New Labrador Party (NLP), which died after the 1972 election. Waiting for the courts to decide disputed elections, Smallwood did not resign as Premier until January, 1972. Frank Moores, became the new Conservative Premier, and won the "run-off" election in March 1972 against the Liberals, now led by Ed Roberts, a young lawyer and former executive assistant to Smallwood and former Minister of Health. The Conservatives garnered 60 per cent of the vote (Liberals 38 per cent, NLP 1 per cent) and 33 of the 42 seats.

The leadership of the Liberal Party was contested again in 1974 when Smallwood, now nearly 75 years old, challenged Roberts. On the second ballot Roberts won by 57 per cent to Smallwood's 42 per cent. But the latter, determined to "reform" the Liberal Party, formed a new third group and led it as the Liberal Reform Party (LRP) into the provincial election of September, 1975. The number of seats had increased to 51 and the results were:

TABLE 1

Results of the 1975 provincial election

	% of the vote	# of seats
Conservatives	45	28
Liberals	37	15
Liberal Reform	12	4
Independent	1	1
Voided		3

The history and achievements of the C.C.F.-N.D.P. in Newfoundland can be briefly told. One C.C.F. candidate ran in St. John's East in the first federal election of 1949. Of the 18,170 votes cast, he won 197 (.01%).

In all, the party engaged in 14 Federal contests in five seats between 1949 and 1965 and its highest overall share of the voting came in 1962 with 4.9%.

TABLE 2

Newfoundland Provincial Elections 1949-1975

	Percent Turnout	Total Seats	Accla-mation	Liberal Seats (% total vote)	Conservative Seats (% total vote)	Others
May/49	76	28	0	22(65%)	5(33)	1
Nov/51	58	28	5	24(63)	4(35)	0
Oct/56	59	36	5	32(66)	4(31)	0
Aug/59	68	36	1	31(58)	3(25)	2
Nov/62	57	42	2	34(58)	7(36)	1
Sep/66	64	42	3	39(61)	3(34)	0
Oct/71	88	42	0	20(45)	22(51)	1
Mar/72	79	42	1	8(38)	33(60)	0
Sep/75	72	51	0	15(37)	28(45)	5[1]

TABLE 3

Newfoundland Federal Elections 1949-1974

	Percent[2] Turnout	Liberals Seats (% total vote)	Conservative Seats (% total vote)
June/49	58	5(72)	2(28)
Aug/53	57	5(67)	2(28)
June/57	52	5(62)	2(38)
Mar/58	74	5(54)	2(45)
June/62	72	7(59)	8(36)
Apr/63	69	7(64)	0(30)
Nov/65	66	7(64)	0(32)
June/68	66	1(43)	6(53)
Oct/72	63	3(43)	4(47)
June/74	57	4(50)	3(38)

[1] Three elections voided by Supreme Court of Newfoundland.
[2] These voter turnouts are the lowest in Canada.

The story at the provincial level is much the same. The party's initial thrust came in 1956 when 10 candidates were fielded under the label of the Newfoundland Democratic Party. In contesting 13 districts during various elections, in only five was a campaign mounted more than once. During the 1962 and 1966 elections a deal was apparently made between the N.D.P. and the Progressive Conservatives in which the Conservatives agreed to contest only Humber East and to have Humber West solely contested by the N.D.P. The result was an upsurge in N.D.P. voting in Humber West. Ed Finn, the then Leader of the party, came within 240 votes of defeating the Liberal cabinet minister and won 48% of the vote. But in 1966, the N.D.P.'s candidate was opposed by Smallwood himself and its share of the vote fell to 33%. Overall the N.D.P. wins between 4 and 5 per cent of the vote. In the 1975 provincial election the party fielded only 17 candidates and averaged 12 per cent of the vote in those constituencies. In general terms the N.D.P. suffers from being too orientated to the "mainland" in leadership and policy. Moreover in the context of the Newfoundland political culture there is no place for a mass party with a progressive philosophy; to many outport voters, at least until very recent years, it was almost presumptuous to question what the "big fellows" were doing. The tradition lingers on that the political battles are fought between Liberals and Tories; third parties are regarded as intruders.

Elections and the Electoral System

Smallwood and the Liberal Party began their domination of Newfoundland electoral results in 1947. In the first referendum, out of 27 electoral districts, nine voted for Responsible Government. At the second referendum only seven districts maintained their anti-Smallwood position, and in the first provincial election in May, 1949, only four of the original nine gave their support to the Progressive Conservatives—successively lost were Bonavista South, Carbonear, Port de Grave, Harbour Grace and St. John's West (the latter four all on the Avalon Peninsula). Electorally the Liberals continued to dominate until 1971.

Until 1971 the total vote for the Liberal Party's candidates in provincial elections was never less than 58 per cent. In the 17 years between 1949 and 1966 they never had less than 80 per cent of the seats in the provincial legislature. In terms of Schlesinger's definition of party systems, Newfoundland stood as the only Canadian provincial example of a one-party system.[44] At the Federal level until 1968 the picture was no less decisive. The Liberals averaged about 60 per cent of the vote, and in three of the seven pre-1968 elections had won 100 per cent of the seats. Significantly, the "break" when it came, came first at the national level, thereby confirming Rasmussen's idea that in both the United States and Canada, the federal field has tended to be more competitive than the state or province.

We must first examine an important indicator into the political culture of Newfoundland, the drawing of constituency boundaries, before turning to the reversals of June 1968 and October 1971. In Newfoundland as elsewhere, the drawing of constituency boundaries has a considerable impact on the outcome of elections.

CONSTITUENCY BOUNDARIES

The drawing of constituency boundaries in Newfoundland has traditionally been governed not by population or geography but by religious denomination. It was the pre-1932 practice to attempt to draw boundaries so that each district would have a majority of its members adherent to one religious denomination and that the total in the House of Assembly would bear some near proportion to the overall religious balance of the Island. By 1935 this practice was running into difficulties owing to population shifts, and in fact 44% of the members represented constituencies in which there was no denominational majority.[46] When Smallwood took over in 1949 he continued with the districts as drawn by the Commission of Government. His first opportunity to redraw boundaries came in 1955 and the results clothed advantages to his own party in a new version of the need to maintain the denominational balance in the House. In the first place, the formula was changed to a "one-third, one-third, one-third" rule which was "wrong" on two counts: the population breakdown in 1961 was Roman Catholics 35.7%; Anglicans 28.5%; United Church 21.4% and others 14%; and, secondly, the traditional rule was representation strictly according to population. This meant that as the House was increased to 36 seats in 1955 the Anglicans were "entitled" to 11 seats, not the 12 seats allotted to them under the "one-third" rule; the United Church to 9; the Salvation Army to 3; and the Pentecostals to 1.[47]

Even if the new version of the rule were accepted, some peculiar things happened to at least one Roman Catholic seat. Harbour Main in the Conception Bay area of the Avalon Peninsula was in the original draft of the bill destined to end its life as the last dual riding in the province. But during the course of the debate the government announced that a twelfth Roman Catholic district was needed and that the choice had fallen on Harbour Main (a good Liberal seat). This left the many more Conservative electors in each of the predominantly Catholic districts of St. John's Centre, St. John's South and St. John's East distinctly under-represented.[48]

In 1962 when the House went up to 42 members, Mr. Smallwood congratulated himself that the balance was now 14-14-14, when in point of fact what he achieved, once again, was the under-representation of urban areas that just happened to have a tradition of Conservative voting. It should be added here that however "unfair" the boundaries, at least one geographic fact was taken into consideration. The Avalon Peninsula, with 40 per cent of the population of the island, accounted for about 40 per cent of the seats in the House—the trouble was that urban St. John's lost out to rural Bay de Verde, St. Mary's and Ferryland.

The new Conservative government implemented an election promise when they passed The Electoral Boundaries Delimitation Act, 1973.[49] Modelled on the federal statute, the Act provided for an independent commission to redraw electoral boundaries once every 10 years, increased membership in the House of Assembly from 42 to 51, and provided that each constituency was to keep within 2,500 of the average of 10,000 people per district. The Boundaries Commission reported in December, 1973, and their Report, with changes by the Government, was proclaimed in December, 1974, just in time for the September, 1975, provincial election. The changes affected 31 of the 51 ridings; some were minor while others, quite major, seemed aimed at hurting Liberals and helping Conservatives. It would seem that drawing electoral boundaries, while it has improved, has not altogether changed in Newfoundland. At least in defending the government's changes, the premier in 1974 did not refer to the denominational character of the constituencies.

The 1971 Change of Government—Why?

In 1966 the subjects of the Only Living Father's Realm voted by 62 per cent to return the Liberals to power. By the second of the twin elections of 1971 and 1972 the Liberals had seen their share of the popular vote drop to 38 per cent. What happened in Newfoundland, to the parties, to the candidates to account for this massive shift? Are the elections of 1971-72 in Newfoundland to be likened to the 1960 election in Quebec: "critical" affairs that announced a "durable electoral realignment between parties based on the activation of new or latent social and attitudinal cleavages"?[50] Or is it the case that the change of government signalled very little: that it meant rather an exchange of the outs for the ins, replaced a party based on lawyers and businessmen for one based on businessmen and lawyers?

Twenty-two years of Confederation had certainly brought visible physical, economic and social changes to Newfoundland. By any one of a number of social indices, Newfoundland's face had changed in the Confederation years: more roads per mile, more telephones, a higher proportion of the population completing Grade 11 and attending post-secondary educational institutions, a smaller proportion of the labor force engaged in primary occupations counter-balanced by a rising proportion in the tertiary or services sector of the economy.

This internal change has not altered the province's external position *vis-à-vis* the rest of Canada. Nearly one-quarter of the income received by Newfoundlanders has accrued in the form of government transfer payments. By 1972 this figure stood at rather more than twice the equivalent national ratio.[51] In terms of public spending per capita on provincial and municipal services, Newfoundland had attained a reasonable parity with the rest of Canada only by virtue of large annual infusions of federal funds and an accelerating growth in the public debt level. The federal share of total provincial current account revenues amounted to 52.7 per cent in 1954-55; 49.6 per cent in 1964-65, and is estimated at 52.4 per cent in 1974-75. If the rate of growth in the public debt is any indication, this infusion of federal money has not left the province in any favorable or surplus position. Nova Scotia apart, Newfoundland now has the heaviest burden of annual debt carrying charges in Canada.[52]

The point to stress is that although there have been undoubted changes in the personal lives of Newfoundlanders in the years between 1949 and 1975, the structure of the economy has not changed all that much. In Quebec the Duplessis years saw the provincial economy transformed from a rural, primary industry base to an urbanized, industrialized base. When the Quebec Liberals came to power in 1960 it was time for the political reality to catch up with the changed economy. But this is not the case in Newfoundland. The economy has grown and diversified, but it has not changed utterly its nature.

The fact remains that at the level of political party voting a profound change has taken place in Newfoundland. The dominance of one man and his party has been broken, whatever else may or may not have been changing in this economy. How do we account for this? How do we assess its significance? Various commentators on the Newfoundland political scene have addressed themselves to these questions. In an analysis of the Smallwood years, Copes pointed to the strategic position of the fishermen's vote in Newfoundland. However, as fishing declined as an occupation he speculated that Smallwood's political support would erode. Political forces were realigning, he argued, away from the old "religious and regional prejudices to new divisions tending towards industrial/occupational differentiation."[53] In sum, Smallwood's base of support had been from the traditional, rural segment of Newfoundland's society and as the relative importance of this segment declined, so too would Smallwood's political dominance, especially if added to this were changes in social attitudes that rejected the "paternalism and autocratic administration" of Smallwood. Thus one explanation for the changes in the political system may lie in changes associated with changes in the make-up of the labor force.

A variation on this same theme comes from another analysis of recent events in Newfoundland.[54] Matthews, a sociologist, concluded that the cleavages of religion and dependence on the fishery were still major factors in voting behavior. But he went on to argue that a "new force" was at work and that it was obvious that "urbanism is now the main force in Newfoundland politics." Using the long accepted premise that the 42 seats in the House of Assembly are divided to give 14 seats to each of the three major denominations, Matthews argued that in 1971 the districts which voted against Smallwood were urban, or Catholic, or both. These districts had been the last to support Smallwood in the confederation issue of the 1940s, and they were also the first to withdraw their support in the 1970s. Urbanism for Matthews is a generalization for the complex changes which have occurred in the society.

Both Copes and Matthews seem to take it for granted that Newfoundland is experiencing what might be called social mobilization[55] and that the P.C. victory in 1972 should be seen as giving expression to the modern forces in the society. Copes speaks of "industrial/occupational differentiation" and sees the fisherman's vote as an alliance that superseded religious cleavages. Matthews is more cautious, seeing some re-emergence in 1971-72 of the traditional alignment of party and religion, but also finding that the main force in Newfoundland politics is now that of urbanism.

A recent paper has attempted to inject some empirical evidence into these speculations.[56]

For the four elections of 1962, 1966, 1971 and 1972, polling division results were grouped to match 1971 Census Enumeration Areas. Analysis of the resulting data set has not yet been completed, but what we do have is information about a relatively large number of small (mean population 1,139) units aggregated into electoral districts, and the data are comparable across four elections spanning 10 critical years. The hypothesis being tested was whether the major swing from Smallwood Liberal dominance seen in the 1971-72 provincial elections was the result of "social mobilization" set in motion by Confederation in 1949 and reaching a critical threshold in the late 1960s.

A total of approximately 20 independent variables were selected from the census as potential indicators of "traditional" social cleavage and more recent social mobilization. Religious denomination and fishing as an occupation were obvious candidates for the former designation, while education, occupation, and size of community fell into the latter category.

The results of regression equations indicated less "new alignment" than might have been expected, given earlier analysis of these same elections. Religion, the old traditional factor in Newfoundland politics, showed up as the single most dominant variable; in fact, it increased in importance through the period of analysis. The notion that the long standing importance of religious ties is being eroded by modernization is not supported by the analysis. Explained variance in the four elections was best captured by just three variables and the resulting table is reproduced on the following page.

The variable FISH was the per cent of the experienced labor force in fishing or trapping in each of the electoral districts. The weak R^2s do not justify Copes' broad argument that the "fisherman's vote" in itself played

TABLE 4
Summary of Regression Analysis

Dependent Variable	Standardized Regression Coefficients (betas)			R^2
	%RC	HIED	FISH	
LIB%62	−.22	−.27	.10	.18
LIB%66	−.00	−.27	−.03	.08
LIB%71	−.29	−.37	.14	.31
LIB%72	−.39	−.27	.13	.30

N=400 (47 analytical units missing due to acclamations or population resettlement after 1966).

a strategic role in providing the electoral base of the Liberals. Nor does the loss of that vote account for Smallwood's downfall. In the judgment of Graesser and Wallack, much of what Copes observed to be a fisherman's vote would appear to be a Protestant and low education vote.

The variable HIED was the per cent of the population with Grade 11 or higher and turned out to be the most important in three of the four elections. The conclusion seems to be that places with higher proportions of people with Grade 11 schooling were most likely to vote Conservative. But since this variable has so similar an effect in each of the four elections, the authors suggest that its increased value in the 1971 election cannot be used to support the hypothesis that the swing to the Conservatives was due to a realignment of mobilized voters.

The regression model being used by Graesser and Wallack must not be asked to carry more of a burden than it should. The authors point out that the model is far from satisfactory statistically in that it leaves two-thirds of the variance unexplained. Measurement error may account for some, but not all, of this variance, but it is far more likely that other characteristics of the local political scene will account for much more. Specifically it is suggested that the introduction of variables such as candidate incumbency, and locality may result in higher R^2s.

In an earlier edition of this book the "conventional wisdom" explanation of voting patterns in terms of religion was tested statistically by matching the percentage of Roman Catholics with the percentage Liberal vote in each district for the 1956 and 1959 elections.[57] A correlation coefficient of -.33 was obtained; weak, but in the predicted direction: Catholic districts were disproportionately Conservative. At that time we hesitated to draw too many conclusions from these data because of the bivariant nature of the analysis. Using 1971 census data and 1971 and 1972 election results this analysis has been replicated (see table in Appendix "A"). Correlations of -.30 and -.46 for the two current elections indicate that the denominational alignment of voters has remained a background factor relatively unaffected by social change, a conclusion consistent with the Graesser and Wallack multivariate analysis.

We are left with the conclusion that no explanation of who votes for which political party in Newfoundland can ignore the importance of the traditional social cleavage, religion. It would seem that the consequences of social change in the relatively unstructured society that is Newfoundland, are in a sense being mediated by religion. In such a situation the historic links between the Conservative voting and Roman Catholicism are being reinforced because the latter is the most structured of the three major denominations. What statistical analysis of the type described above cannot get at is the manner by which religion determines or influences voting behavior. Newfoundland is as likely as the rest of Canada to be less and less influenced by the church *per se*. What is different in this province is the role of the churches in education. There are no "public" schools in Newfoundland. All schools are owned and operated by either the Roman Catholic, Amalgamated Protestant or Pentecostal churches, with large infusions of public funds and guidance. The social and political results are not fully explored in the academic literature, but circumstantial evidence suggests that co-religionists in Newfoundland interact with each other more than in the rest of Canada. They go to the same schools, they play sports together (and against other schools which are at the same time other denominations), they intermarry and they inter-dine. Opinion leaders know and are known in what is after all a relatively small population where there has been very little immigration for over 100 years. We have noted already that the economy of Newfoundland has not basically changed in modern times. The same appears to be true of the society. Or, alternatively, if social indicators show that some changes are taking place, if indeed large numbers of people are moving away from traditionalism and into a broader and deeper involvement in modern life, then it is happening slowly and it is likely to be a long time before differentiation on "modern" lines replaces differentiation of a more traditional character.

Formal party organization in both major political parties in Newfoundland is growing and in some respects should be seen as a response by the political system to a mobilized society.[58] Information as to the nature and the effect of organization, however, is less precise than that relating to voting and thus any conclusions must be very cautiously drawn. It may be that under the Tories, now that they are in government, the same informal politics goes on. The only difference now may be that it is cloaked under the guise of formal organization and thus made legitimate. Formal organization, however inactive between elections, is, as Smallwood found out, something which cannot be ignored once it is set in motion. If it does nothing else it provides both parties with a framework for intra-party competition, both at the level of constituency nominations and at the level of contests for the provincial leadership.

It is naive and illusory to conclude too hastily that a broadened political culture has arrived in Newfoundland. Many strands weave together to suggest the changing nature of the Newfoundland society: more people with higher levels of education, the "demonstration" effect resulting from increased physical and cultural contact with the mainland of Canada, the displacement of church-sponsored organizations by increased membership in fraternal organizations like the Kinsmen and Kiwanis, etc., the rise of a militant trade union in the fishery, that most unorganized of occupations. Karl Deutsch has warned us that social mobilization, while it may engender demands for much higher levels of government responsiveness and performance, may also activate hitherto latent "primordial" divisions in society, divisions based on religion or ethnicity for example.[59] No explanation of voting in Newfoundland can ignore the importance of religion. No discussion of party organization can ignore the possibility that while the players have changed, the game goes on much as before.

Another way to explore this dilemma is to discover the recruitment patterns and political experience of the men (and one woman) who currently make up the Members of the House of Assembly. If their socio-economic characteristics are more "modern" and their recruitment patterns involve active roles in the party organization, then we will have some evidence to conclude that the creation of the formal organization has had some effect on the functioning of the political system.

THE NEWFOUNDLAND HOUSE OF ASSEMBLY – JUNE 1976

The first study using structured interviews with all the Members of the House of Assembly was undertaken in June, 1968.[60] The same questionnaire was administered in June 1976 to 16 of the 36 new Members. Biographical data were obtained for all the others, 12 of whom were in the Cabinet and for whom, consequently, extensive biographical information is available. One of the new Members was not finally declared elected until after the interview period.

The size of the Newfoundland House of Assembly was increased in 1974 from 42 to 51 members. The House still sits for an average of 60 to 65 days a year. The backbenchers' indemnity has risen from $8,500 in 1968 to a flat rate of $9,856 to all members, plus a $3,500 district allowance. Added to this is a graduated scale of travel allowances that ranges from no extra amount for the 12 seats in St. John's; $1,000 extra for five seats close to the capital; $2,000 extra for eight seats readily accessible; $2,500 extra for 17 moderately remote districts; $3,000 extra for eight districts with difficult transportation links (Fortune, Burgeo, etc.,) and $4,000 for the one seat representing coastal Labrador–Eagle River. The average works out to about $15,000 per member with the usual extra allowances for whips, Leader of the Opposition, etc. The government supports the Opposition Office with a grant of about $30,000 per annum for research assistants and other office expenses.

The turnover rate of MHA's remains high–70 per cent of the members are new since 1968. The median age of the House is 45 which makes, surprisingly, the 1976 House just a little older than its counterpart in 1968, although there is a greater proportion of members who are in their 30's. The median age of the cabinet alone is also 45 years, which makes it much younger than the Smallwood Cabinet in 1968 when the median age was 51.5 years.

TABLE 5

Nfld. House of Assembly – Age at Entry (percentage)

	1968		1976
20 – 30	7		1 (n = 1)
30 – 39	25		31 (n = 16)
40 – 49	41		45 (n = 23)
50 – 59	17		13 (n = 7)
60 – 69	8		5.8 (n = 3)
Over 70	1		1(n = 1)
		Total	51

THE CABINET

The size of the Moores cabinet, 17 ministers, is almost the same as that of Smallwood in 1968, 18 ministers. These numbers are large, but given the increased size of the House of Assembly their numerical dominance is not so obvious. In a 1972 major re-organization of the executive branch of government Moores attempted to reduce the size of cabinet, but for a variety of reasons it has remained much the same.[61]

It would appear that the educational attainments of the P.C. cabinet reflect the greater educational opportunities open to Newfoundlanders in the post-Confederation era. In 1968 we found that about 40 per cent of the men who had served as cabinet ministers between 1949 and 1968 had university degrees. The figure in the Moores cabinet is nearer 60 per cent. The three principal occupations among cabinet ministers were teaching (five), law (four), and business (three).

In terms of previous political experience–a vital concern in a government which came to office in 1971 after 22 years in the wilderness–the Moores cabinet exhibits considerable experience at all three levels of government. Moores, Lundrigan and Carter had served as federal M.P.s;

Crosbie and Hickman had been provincial Liberal cabinet ministers; and six other ministers served varying periods of apprenticeship at the municipal level.

The religious balance in the Cabinet has shifted marginally, but overall maintains the traditional balance between the three major denominations.

TABLE 6

Religious Denomination, Members of the Nfld. Cabinet

	1967	1976
Roman Catholic	5 (30%)	5 (30%)
Anglican	6 (35%)	7 (40%)
United Church	6 (35%)	5 (30%)
	17	17

THE BACKBENCHERS

Comparing the occupational range and the education of the backbenchers of 1976 and of the sample we took in 1968, it is clear not only that the range of occupations is wider, but that it includes many more of what might be termed "modern" or "new" occupations in contrast to the familiar categories of business: the professions, teaching, etc. There are, for instance, two broadcasters in this "new" group, two community development officers, one town manager. Even the range within the professions is wider, including not only lawyers and physicians, but a dentist and an engineer.

TABLE 7

Principal Occupations and Level of Education of Members of the Nfld. House of Assembly, 1949-1968, and 1976

Occupation	*1949-1968 (n=72)*	*1976 (n=34)*
Professionals	37%	5 (14%)
Proprietor-Mgrs.	36%	8 (23.5%)
Teachers	11%	7 (20.5%)
Other	15%	7 (20.5%)
Unknown		2
Education		
University degree	35%	15 (44%)
Post Gr. 11 training	24%	10 (29%)
Grade 11	26%	6 (18%)
Grade 10	2%	1
Unknown	12%	2

The greatest single change is the doubling of the number of teachers on the backbenches and what can only be seen as a qualitative improvement in their educational attainment. The category "teacher" includes several principals—one district school superintendent and one supervisor of language arts for a large school board.

Overall, there has been a marked qualitative improvement in the education of the Newfoundland backbenchers and a broadening of their occupational backgrounds. They are as a group just as much of an elite, compared with the majority of their fellow Newfoundlanders, but their education and experience is broader than ever before.

In terms of religious affiliation there have been some marked changes since the calculations of 1968. For one thing the Progressive Conservatives have increased their Protestant numbers and the Liberals, while continuing to be the more "balanced" of the two parties, have markedly increased their Salvation Army numbers.

TABLE 8

Religious Affiliation of Newfoundland House of Assembly, 1949-1968 and 1976

	Liberals		*Progressive Conservative*	
	1949-68	*1976*	*1949-68*	*1976*
Roman Catholic	26%	7 (35%)	80%	6 (43%)
Anglican	35%	3 (15%)	5%	2 (14%)
Salvation Army	1%	4 (20%)	0%	0
United Church	39%	4 (20%)	5%	5 (36%)
Unknown	0	2	10%	1
		20		14

The voting strength of the Liberals come principally from rural and Protestant parts of the province, and it is from these areas that the Salvation Army draws its numerical strength. The social characteristics of the district is reflected in the social character of the MHA's (or vice versa!).

It continues to be a "rule" of the Newfoundland House of Assembly that by and large the Members will come from and live in the constituencies they represent. In 1968 when the Liberals formed the government, about 20 per cent of their Members had no personal or professional connection with their districts. This number has now dropped to about 10 per cent for both the Liberals and the Conservatives. This suggests that voters wish to know their representative personally and that political parties, aware of this, rarely parachute any candidate into a district. One example will perhaps illustrate the attitude. The only woman elected in 1975 is a Liberal from St. George's on the province's west coast. She decided to challenge the sitting Progressive Conservative when it became clear that the only nomination for the Liberals was a "stranger" (sic) from St. John's. At the last moment she threw her hat in the ring and won by 150 votes.

In 1968 we discovered that the principal avenue to election to the Newfoundland House of Assembly was municipal politics. We regard this as a remarkable finding because of the generally low level of popular support for and involvement in local government in Newfoundland. The political turmoil of the post-1969 years clearly drew many young men into politics. For nearly 45 percent of those interviewed, a period of apprenticeship on the executive of a riding association was the necessary first step in being a candidate. For about one-quarter of the new members their first taste of public office was through municipal politics. All these men were, as we might expect, "joiners," active members in the few associational groups in Newfoundland. Overall, and compared with 1968, there has been a considerable drop in the importance of being chosen by the party leader. No one in 1976 mentioned that they had waited for a "call" from the Premier and the "assignment" of a district. In this respect, at least, much had changed. In 1968 we concluded that a survey of the membership of the Newfoundland House of Assembly pointed to the traditional roles played by the members. Today little has changed. The members see themselves as delegates from their districts, tied to the people they represent by very close personal, almost kinship ties.

Conclusions

After 22 years of one-man, one-party dominance, the people of Newfoundland concluded that it was "time for a change" but what they got was not all that much change! The victory for the Conservatives in 1975 (45 per cent of the popular vote, 28 out of 51 seats) confirmed, albeit narrowly, that decision. Smallwood as leader of the third party, and calling again on the old ties of tradition and loyalty, was not able to turn back the tide of change which he himself had set in motion. But the size of his vote indicates that the traditional Newfoundlander has by no means been replaced by his more modern brother.

The Moores administration, catching the drift of the society, has set in motion its share of "conservative" changes. In particular I suggest that two of these, reform of the provincial executive administration, and reform of municipal government, will have long-reaching effects on the society.

The Conservatives came to power in January of 1972. By November of that year a White Paper was released which set in operation a major and continuing reform in the administrative branch of government. Following a modified version of the Ottawa and Ontario models, a system of

Cabinet Committees was set up and the roles of the Cabinet Secretariat and Treasury Board staff were strengthened. The objective was to relieve over-burdened ministers, to bring to complex issues more intense study and to try and ensure policy integration. The restructuring of most of the line departments and the central control agencies was done to end the *ad hoc* decision-making which seemed to characterize the Smallwood style of bureaucracy. The objective was to encourage rational decision-making, to specialize—in short, to modernize. The well-educated Newfoundlanders who had entered the provincial civil service in the 1970s were determined to end the bad old days.

A recent review of the changes, some three years later, concludes that the formation of cabinet committees has not bureaucratized the relationship between the leader and his followers.[62] It appears that while indeed modern machinery has been set in place, scale and the informality of the Newfoundland political arena have combined to prevent too radical a change. Cabinet Committees discuss and distill departmental opinion but the premier has never attempted to relieve the cabinet of the final discussion. At the departmental level there have been continuing efforts to modernize policies and legislation and the manner of doing things. A new Public Service Commission Act has strengthened the hand of that recruitment and training agency. But at the same time much goes on in the comfortable, traditional manner. Often the ties of kinship and friendship seem more important than rationality, efficiency and the search for a merit bureaucracy. Administration has modernized and improved in Newfoundland in the past five years, and our suspicion is that it will continue to do so at an accelerating rate in the future, but the Moores administration did not mean a complete break with the past.

In the past five years there has been an unprecedented interest in municipal government in Newfoundland. Since 1966, five Royal Commissions have been appointed to deal with different municipal problems. In 1970 a seven-volume Community Plan (Plan 91) was published for St. John's. In March, 1973, a federal-provincial DREE-sponsored study on the St. John's Urban Region was published. This was one of the most comprehensive planning documents ever prepared for any Canadian metropolitan region. The third and final Report of a Commission of Enquiry on this study was released in January, 1977. As indicated above, there are now over 300 incorporated areas in Newfoundland and approximately 80 per cent of the population is living under some form of municipal organization. It seems that the former reluctance to adopt local government machinery is being dissipated. An attitude survey sponsored by the 1974 Royal Commission on Municipal Government in Newfoundland and Labrador (the Whalen Commission) showed that fewer than 5 per cent of Newfoundlanders could be considered to have "official" municipal experience.[62] Contrast this with the number of MHAs with municipal experience. The survey showed overwhelming support for the extension of municipal government throughout the province. As levels of formal education rise, so too do levels of participation in civic activities. No doubt, as the Whalen Commission points out, there are negative features about the practices of local democracy. But it is widely accepted that municipal experience encourages the development of mature, efficient, self-reliant and independent citizens. We conclude that at long last the reluctance to adopt local government institutions has been broken down, and that if the Conservative Government, which has in large measure sponsored the impressive list of Royal Commissions and studies outlined above, can bring itself to enact the major recommendations of these studies, then another chain of events will have been set in motion that will further encourage the modernizing tendencies within Newfoundland society.

Traditional and modernizing values persist and exist in Newfoundland society, the end of the Smallwood years signalled another phase in the maturing of the society, but it did not mean a radical break with the past. Continuity and change continue to mark this society and most other societies. Plus ça change, plus c'est la même chose.

APPENDIX "A"

Provincial Districts, Percentage of Roman Catholics (1971) Census and Percentage of Liberal Vote

District	% of population Roman Catholic	% of Liberal vote 1971 prov. election	% of Liberal vote 1972 prov. election
Bay de Verde	36	50	39
Bell Island	60	66	49
Bonavista N	11	55	55
Bonavista S	14	53	39
Burgeo-LaPoile	4	48	43
Burin	37	43	32
Carbonear	21	50	41
Ferryland	94	49	35
Fogo	11	60	57
Fortune	32	55	44
Gander	24	37	33
Grand Falls	38	43	41
Green Bay	4	54	46
Harbour Gr.	24	53	42
Harbour Main	57	43	12
Hermitage	42	52	38
Humber E	25	34	30
Humber W	36	35	0
Labrador N	28	44	39

Labrador S	19	47	50
Labrador W	46	22	31
Lewisporte	9	46	42
Placentia E	77	58	45
Placentia W	57	67	50
Port au Port	77	41	35
Port de Grave	22	57	47
St. Barbe N	20	68	62
St. Barbe S	17	51	44
St. George's	73	44	34
St. John's C	60	29	23
St. John's E	65	30	22
St. John's EE	53	29	21
St. John's N	34	33	29
St. John's S	60	35	23
St. John's W	47	32	27
St. Mary's	98	52	30
Trinity N	7	58	48
Trinity S	12	58	47
Twillingate	1	61	58
White Bay N	16	82	84
White Bay S	28	62	56

Correlation, 1971 election = -0.30, $R^2 = 0.09$
Correlation, 1972 election = -0.45, $R^2 = 0.20$

Data prepared by Bruce Grant, Dept. of Political Science, Memorial University.

Endnotes

[1] Great Britain, *Newfoundland Royal Commission*, Lord Amultree CHMN, Cmnd #4480 (1933).

[2] MacKay, R.A., ed., *Newfoundland Economic, Diplomatic and Strategic Studies* (Toronto: Oxford University Press, 1946), p. 75.

[3] During this period the Commission of Government made efforts to informally sound out public opinion and municipal politics continues in St. John's.

[4] Perlin, A. B., *The Story of Newfoundland* (St. John's: Dicks and Co., Ltd., 1959), p. 46.

[5] Royal Commission on Municipal Government in Newfoundland and Labrador (Whalen Commission), St. John's (1974), p. 57.

[6] Ibid., p. 63.

[7] Ibid., p. 65-67.

[8] Statistics Canada, *1971 Census*. Catalogues 92:723 and 92:725.

[9] Gunn, G. E., *The Political History of Newfoundland 1832-1864* (University of Toronto Press, 1966), p. 182.

[10] The phenomenon persists. In 1962 the Hon. J. L. Cheeseman, himself an Anglican, brought to the attention of the House of Assembly that out of six senators in Ottawa not one was a member of the Church of England. "It is

rather strange," he said, "when one third of the population are Anglicans . . . It is generally considered here that seats will be proportionately distributed. The Anglicans of Newfoundland have no representative in the Senate"; St. John's *Daily News* (February 6, 1962). In 1975 the Supreme Court of Newfoundland was split into trial and appeals divisions and nine justices have served the new courts: three Roman Catholics, three Anglicans, and three United Church.

[11] Amulree Report, p. 41.

[12] Smallwood, J. R., *Coaker of Newfoundland* (London: Labour Publishing Company, 1927), p. 35.

[13] Rothney, G. O., *Canada in One World* (Toronto: The House of Grant, Ltd., 1966), p. 182.

[14] Chadwick, St. John, *Newfoundland: Island into Province* (Cambridge University Press, 1967), p. 155.

[15] Ibid., p. 155.

[16] *Newfoundland Royal Commission on Economic Prospects*, p. 419.

[17] Browne, Hon. W. J., "The Case for the Restoration of Responsible Government," *The Book of Newfoundland III* (1967), p. 127; and Gwyn, Richard, *Smallwood, The Unlikely Revolutionary* (Toronto: McClelland and Stewart, Ltd., 1972), p. 80.

[18] St. John's *Telegram* (March 7, 1967).

[19] Jamieson, D., "I Saw the Fight for Confederation," *Book of Newfoundland III*, p. 88.

[20] Ibid., p. 103.

[21] Ibid., p. 92.

[22] Gwyn, Richard, op. cit., p. 84.

[23] Jamieson, D., op. cit., p. 85.

[24] Perlin, op. cit., p. 53.

[25] Gwyn, op. cit., p. 79. Supported by Jamieson, op. cit., p. 72.

[26] Op. cit., p. 99.

[27] Russell, Ted, *My Political Memoirs*, printed in the St. John's *Telegram* (October 28, 1966).

[28] Mews, H. G. R., as quoted in the St. John's *Telegram* (January 1969).

[29] Jamieson, op. cit., p. 81.

[30] Minutes of the Executive of the Progressive Conservative Association of Newfoundland (September 12, 1950), as quoted in R. Penney, "The Progressive Conservative Party of Newfoundland—An Exploratory Study," an unpublished termpaper presented to the Department of Political Science, Memorial University of Newfoundland (1968).

[31] Gwyn, op. cit., p. 126.

[32] Gwyn, op. cit., p. 209.

[33] Statement of J. Higgins, quoted in the St. John's *Daily News* (July 21, 1959).

[34] Statement of A. D. Pittman, Corner Brook President of the Progressive Conservative Association, quoted in the St. John's *Daily News* (June 15, 1959).

[35] Duffy, A. M., quoted in Saywell, J. T. and Forster, D. F., eds., *Canadian Annual Review* (University of Toronto Press, 1962), p. 47.

[36] Perlin, George, "St. John's West," in Meisel, J., ed., *Papers on the 1962 Election.*

[37] Ibid., pp. 12 and 14.

[38] Smallwood, J. R., quoted in Saywell, op. cit., p. 47.

[39] Gwyn, op. cit., p. 287.

[40] Gwyn, op. cit., p. 281.

[41] Penney, op. cit., p. 35.

[42] Editorial, St. John's *Telegram* (June 28, 1968).

[43] Ibid.

[44] Schlesinger, J., "A Two-Dimensional Scheme for Classifying the States According to the Degree of Inter-Party Competition," *American Political Science Review,* XLIX (December, 1955), pp. 1120-28.

[45] Rasmussen, J., "A Research Note on Canadian Party Systems."

[46] Rothney, G. O., "The Denominational Basis of Representation in the Newfoundland Assembly, 1919-1962," *Canadian Journal of Economics and Political Science* (1962), p. 562.

[47] Ibid., p. 566.

[48] Ibid., p. 567.

[49] Statutes of Newfoundland, Act #44 (1973).

[50] V. O. Key, "A Theory of Critical Elections," *Journal of Politics,* Vol. 17 (1955), p. 16.

[51] *Report,* Royal Commission on Municipal Government in Newfoundland and Labrador, St. John's, Newfoundland (1971), p. 60.

[52] Ibid., p. 91.

[53] Copes, Parzival, "The Fishermen's Vote in Newfoundland," *Canadian Political Science Review,* Vol. III (December, 1970), pp. 579-604.

[54] Matthews, Ralph, "Perspectives on Recent Newfoundland Politics," *Journal of Canadian Studies,* Vol. IX (May, 1974), pp. 20-34.

[55] Deutsch, Karl W., "Social Mobilization and Political Development," *American Political Science Review,* Vol. 55, pp. 493-514. Deutsch defines "social mobilization" as the process "in which major clusters of old social, economic and psychological commitments are eroded or broken and people become available for new patterns of socialization and behaviour . . . Mannheim suggests an image of large numbers of people moving away from a life of local isolation, traditionalism and political apathy, and moving *into* a different life or broader and deeper involvement in the vast complexities of modern life," p. 495. It is this definition we are using in this paper.

[56] Grasser, Mark and Wallack, Michael, "Social Mobilization and Voting in Newfoundland." Paper presented to the Annual Meeting of the Atlantic Provinces Political Studies Association, Wolfville, Nova Scotia (October 1976).

[57] Susan McCorquodale, "The Only Living Father's Realm" in M. Robin, ed., *Canadian Provincial Politics: The Party Systems of the Ten Provinces* (Toronto: Prentice-Hall of Canada, Ltd., 1972).

[58] Wolinetz, Steven B., "Party Organization in Newfoundland: The Liberal Party Under Smallwood." Paper presented to the Annual Meeting of the Canadian Political Science Association, Edmonton, Alberta (June 1975).

[59] Deutsch, op. cit. This point is drawn in the paper by Graesser and Wallack, op. cit., p. 14.

[60] McCorquodale, op. cit.

[61] *Government White Paper on the Organization of the Public Service of Newfoundland and Labrador*, St. John's, Newfoundland (November 1972).

[62] Johnson, Ross A., "Cabinet Decision-Making Structures: Taking Issues out of Politics?" Paper presented to the Annual Meeting of the Canadian Political Science Association, Quebec City (June 1976), p. 7.

[63] Whalen Commission, op. cit., pp. 101-102 and 105.

NOVA SCOTIA Tradition and Conservatism

J. Murray Beck

Nova Scotian parties did not emerge Minerva-like from the province's rocky base. They were the products of various forces acting and reacting on each other to produce syntheses that in turn became subject to the same process of change. The analysis that follows attempts to relate the Nova Scotian party system to the broader milieus of the political and social systems, using a rough approximation of David Easton's concept of inputs and outputs.[1] First, there will be an examination of the factors—the inputs—which have gone into the shaping of the parties: then there will be a treatment of the outputs of the parties, especially as they provide political leadership and public policies.

How Nova Scotian Parties Came To Be What They Are

THE HISTORICAL ROOTS

A useful technique for bringing comprehension and order into the early period of Nova Scotia's politics is the functional approach of E. E. Schattschneider.[2] It contends that the nature of the politics and parties of a country or region is largely determined by the objectives of the dominant politicians of the day. From the granting of representative institutions in 1758 almost up to the winning of responsible government in 1848 the character of Nova Scotian politics was determined by a Halifax Compact more closely interconnected by family relationships than the Family Compact of Upper Canada. Until the close of the American Revolution a mercantile group headed by distillery merchant Joshua Mauger possessed more power than it needed to ward off the challenges of an immature assembly and to dominate the colony's politics for its own ends.[3] With the coming of the Loyalists it appeared as if something akin to parties might develop from the cleavage between Loyalists and pre-Loyalists. But once it became clear, as it did under their patron John Wentworth, governor from 1792 to 1808, that the Loyalists "were not to be denied a reasonable share of the patronage, constitutional agitation lost much of its old charm. The cleavage between Loyalists and pre-Loyalists in the Assembly melted away never to be revived."[4]

Nova Scotia continued to be dominated by an oligarchical clique of merchants and officials centered in the Council of Twelve who, in their executive capacity, held the governor in fief and, in their legislative capacity, checkmated the Assembly. Shortly after 1800, William Cottnam Tonge sought to unite the Assemblymen from outside Halifax—the country members—in support of such measures as the taxation of landlords and higher customs duties, thereby challenging the oligarchy in its possession of the major privileges that it was using to maintain its hold on government. However, Tonge's "country party" was hardly a disciplined grouping and on several occasions the Assembly adopted a middle course in preference to his extreme proposals.

The Assembly had become a much more robust body after it obtained sessional indemnities for itself in 1781 and thereby ensured the attendance of non-Halifax members on a regular basis. It even won from the prerogative-conscious Wentworth a deviation from the British practice that left later colonial secretaries aghast. The Nova Scotian financial procedure came to be that, after the essential expenses of government were met, the Assembly usurped the normal role of the executive by dividing the remaining revenues, obtained principally from customs duties, among the counties for roads and bridges, and by appointing commissioners to spend the moneys. Reluctantly the Council acquiesced in this practice, which did not interfere with the oligarchy's own interests, because the alternative would have brought the entire business of government to a halt. The result was to provide the services that the assemblymen and their constituents most valued in the manner they wanted them—without resort to direct taxation. It was no wonder that relative peace descended on the Nova Scotian scene for more than two decades and that parties did not take shape until late in the 1830s long after their appearance in the Canadas.

In the 1820s protests were directed against the political, economic, and ecclesiastical power that was concentrated in the Council of Twelve. They were sporadic assaults in areas of special concern to a few leading assemblymen, however, and not full-fledged attacks on a totally irresponsible system. By 1830 the first demands for genuine parties were being heard. They were an outgrowth of the politico-ecclesiastical radicalism of Principal Thomas McCulloch of Pictou Academy, and were made vocal by the Pictou Scribblers, especially Jotham Blanchard, in the *Colonial Patriot*. The Scribblers argued that, although the Canadas had well-developed parties to withstand misgovernment, there was "yet no *organized party against misrule* in Nova Scotia, and therefore the regularly *organized party* on its side had easy times. It is only to form themselves into a phalanx, when anyone has the effrontery to attack, and the individual assailants are soon wearied of insulated efforts."[5]

Before the struggle against the entrenched oligarchy was to be united, Joseph Howe had to become as convinced as the Scribblers of the need for a disciplined reform party, and that took 13 years to come about. Starting adult life as a "mild Tory," he is purported to have said that "the Pictou Scribblers . . . have converted me from the error of my ways"; yet in late 1830 he was still equating party with faction, and insisting that "the party to which we belong is the *Province of Nova Scotia*."[6] Five years' experience and a celebrated libel suit convinced him that the Halifax oligarchy had extended its tentacles into every nook and cranny of Nova Scotian society and intended to keep them there. No reforms were possible, he concluded, "without a majority pledged to the people, and kept in salutary awe of them in the Assembly."[7] However, he was not advocating party in the normal sense; fearing that parties would be no more than selfish factions, he was proposing a rally of the Nova Scotian people, whose representatives in the Assembly would keep a strict surveillance over the governor's advisers and the provincial bureaucracy. Largely because of Howe, the Assembly to which he was himself elected in 1836, contained, in addition to a number of "loose fish," two nascent parties—a larger one which supported his condemnation of the oligarchy and a smaller one which sustained the Council. Such was the genesis of the Reform and Tory parties of Nova Scotia.

Although Howe accepted the Durham Report as soon as he read it, he did not yet favor the disciplined parties that were needed to make Durham's major recommendations effective. In contrast, Herbert Huntington of Yarmouth—the Robert Baldwin of Nova Scotia—contended that, since there were two sides to all the major public questions in the province and since the political opinions of every public man were as well known as in England, parties ought to function in Nova Scotia much as they did in Britain. Because Howe still had no clear concept of what he expected of a party, Governor-General Charles Poulett Thomson (the later Lord Sydenham) had no difficulty in persuading him to enter into a coalition with the moderate Tory J. W. Johnston in 1840. Apparently Howe took the view that men of moderate opinions from the *two existing parties* could work together harmoniously for rational, responsible government, thereby frustrating radicals and reactionaries alike. He soon discovered that to make a strong administration something more was required

> *. . . than nine men treating each other courteously at a round table. There is the assurance of good faith—towards each other—of common sentiments, and kindly feelings, propagated through the friends of each, in Society, in the Legislature and in the Press, until a great Party is formed . . . which secures a steady working majority to sustain their policy and carry their measures.*[8]

Thus, step by step, Howe had been "induced almost against his will to don all the trappings of the typical colonial reformer of his day,"[9] including a recognition of the need for disciplined parties.

The inevitable outcome was the breakdown of the coalition in December 1843. Thereafter the great political debate hinged on the applicability of party government to the colonial sphere. The Tories would "admit of no principles or issues in colonial politics which could in any way justify two clearly defined political parties such as existed in England";[10] the Reformers conceded that the issues in Nova Scotia politics could not possess the same absolute significance as those in Britain, yet they insisted that these issues were just as important to colonials as those agitating the larger sphere were to Britons. Accordingly Howe devoted all his great energy to creating the strictly disciplined following that was needed to beat the Tories. In the election of August 5, 1847 the voters could clearly distinguish between Tory and Reform candidates in every county, and the election was largely a plebiscite on responsible government. The Reformers' majority was only 7, but the new Assembly contained none of the "loose fish" who had been accustomed to swim in any pool that chanced to be full. Parties had been needed to secure responsible government; in turn, responsible government helped to rivet party government on the province.

THE SOCIAL MILIEU

Charles Dickens watched the proceedings of the Nova Scotia Legislature in 1841 and said "it was like looking at Westminster through the wrong end of a telescope."[11] However, it was by no means certain that British institutions would ever be completely at home in their new environment. Joseph Howe, it is true, had prophesied that

> *. . . 'little things are great to little men,' and to little Provinces, and I could point to a dozen* [*past*] *questions of internal policy . . . and to a dozen* [*future*] *. . . that were or will be of just as much importance to the people of Nova Scotia, as were the questions upon which ministers* [*in England*] *have come in and gone out . . . since 1688. It cannot be otherwise in the very nature of things.*[12]

Despite Howe's optimism, few issues of substance appeared during the 1850s, and by 1855 one-time advocates of party government such as the

Acadian Recorder were saying that "at the present juncture . . . it would nonplus the shrewdest politician to invent any cogent reason for the division of the representatives of Nova Scotia into two parties, regularly organized for the annihilation of each other, in the halls of our Legislature. We are not aware of a single public question, of the least consequence to any class, being in suspense. . . . "[13]

The split of the Assembly along religious lines in 1857 and the "disputed election" of 1859—the outcome of which depended on whether half a dozen Liberals were legally entitled to sit in the Assembly—led to several years of bitter, partisan maneuvering. These events also caused the *Sun* to lament that "the game of politics is becoming a pretty expensive one, and so long as parties remain constituted as they now are, Bluenose must expect to pay for it";[14] and the lieutenant-governor, the Earl of Mulgrave, to observe that "no great political question . . . divides [the parties] . . . which should keep them in perpetual antagonism to one another. The matter in dispute is now simply one of men, not measures."[15]

Nova Scotian politics of the early 1860s was by no means moving towards the impasse of the Canadas, however; the short-term religious split bore no resemblance to the differences arising from race and religion in Canada. "The Nova Scotian parties and groups all accepted the existing social order, and agreed both upon the role to be played by government and upon the specific means calculated to provide good government. The most suitable designations for the administration and its opposition had become the Ins and the Outs; the struggle between the two was one for place, power, and the spoils of office."[16]

For a few years the question of Confederation did provide an issue that permitted a meaningful cleavage of the electorate along party lines. But Confederation also served to restrict the province's legislative field, attenuate its financial power, and reduce the possibility of provincial initiative, thereby lessening the likelihood that the parties would be clearly divided on issues in the future. As early as 1876, the *Acadian Recorder* concluded:

> *There is not, nor can there ever be, any policy dividing the people as far as local matters are concerned. The policy of the opposition will be to struggle by every means . . . to reach the treasury benches, and the policy of the Government will be to checkmate them, and retain the place and power they hold. A change of government in Nova Scotia now-a-days, would only mean changing the officials in some four or five heads of departments. . . . Hereafter the local elections will turn on purely local matters.*[17]

Prophetically, most subsequent elections hinged on the performance of one specific function: the management of the day-to-day business of government. So it has remained to this day. By 1970 however, that business was of the order of $350 million annually, and its management had itself become a meaningful issue.

Issues or the lack of them have a distinct bearing on party ideology; in turn, it is closely related to the intangible complex of beliefs, emotions, and values that comprise the political culture of Nova Scotian society. Highly pertinent to the Nova Scotian political culture is Walter Bagehot's "cake of custom," or the idea that "it is the dull traditional habit of mankind that guides most men's actions, and it is the steady frame in which each new artist must set the picture that he paints."[18] Although Bagehot had England in mind, the point he made is no less applicable to Nova Scotia.

By Confederation the general shape of the provincial community had taken form. Pre-Loyalists and Loyalists, Acadians, English, German, Scottish, and Irish had taken up their abode, and no great influx of settlers was to follow. The development of the coal and steel communities was still to come; the smaller settlements were to blossom into larger towns; but the shape of rural Nova Scotia has remained much the same to this day. An unusually large proportion of the society agreed upon a basic stock of attitudes and values. Highly significant was the antipathy towards direct taxation, especially on property. This feeling was all the more intense because the Nova Scotians' major demands on government had for so long been met through the seemingly painless imposition of customs duties.

The attitude of the public towards direct taxation was significant in engendering the Assembly's excessive caution. This explains why in the 1850s the counties and districts were permitted to decide for themselves whether to incorporate for purposes of local government. In the end none of them did; their attitude was that of the newspaper correspondent who urged that "the clarions of war should be sounded, and Taxation, Taxation, Taxation proclaimed throughout the county."[19] Even in areas settled by people whose forebears had governed themselves through the New England town meeting the antipathy was no less strong. Paradoxically, the province that was the first to gain responsible government had to have local self-government forced on it. The Conservative government of Simon Holmes imposed local self-government in 1879 to alleviate serious financial difficulties, but paid the price with defeat in the next election.

The Nova Scotians' dislike for direct taxation long prevented the adoption of a free education system through compulsory assessment. Joseph Howe advocated free education in the 1840s, but it was the Conservative government of Charles Tupper which summoned up enough courage to implement it in 1865. If newspaper correspondence is any indication, the school question might have brought about Tupper's defeat if the Confederation issue had not altogether submerged it in the election of 1867. As for the Confederation question itself, the threat of increased taxation under the new order was an important, although not the dominant, issue. Also significant was the fear of a rush into the unknown: the caution in accepting any innovation that might lead to additional taxation had grown into a suspicion of innovation itself.

This suspicion was shared by the provincial politicians. Thus Charles Tupper refused to accede to the demands of Archbishop Connolly of Halifax that Nova Scotian Catholics be accorded the same guarantee in education as those of Ontario were to enjoy. The problem was resolved in a typically Nova Scotian manner of refusing to meet the problem head-on. By convention the local authorities—first in Halifax and later in some Cape Breton communities and the larger mainland towns—would give recognition to Catholic schools within the public school system. For the politician this device had the pleasing result of completely removing a vexed question from the provincial arena.

The conservative nature of the society has caused some undesirable political practices to endure; this is particularly true of patronage. Prior to 1848, vacant offices invariably went to the hangers-on of the Family Compact and its cliques in the county towns; for a time thereafter the Reform ministry resisted the pressures to supplant the incumbents with its own partisans, but by the mid-1850s it had bowed to the clamors of its supporters for jobs. Subsequently both parties unabashedly resorted to the spoils system.

Even after Angus L. Macdonald's government set up the Nova Scotia Civil Service Commission in 1935, the situation remained much the same; the Commission served as a front behind which a Liberal administration could follow the old procedures and escape criticism. R. MacGregor Dawson said in 1945 that *"so long as the Civil Service Act is applied and interpreted as it is to-day, there is no reason to expect anything but an outburst of dismissals following a change of Government."*[20] Fortunately a trend developed after World War II towards strengthening the Commission, adding to the categories of personnel over which it had the jurisdiction, and making it more the kind of body it was alleged to be. This development took place not because public attitudes demanded it, but because partisans were less attracted to low-paid provincial offices in the ensuing period of prosperity.

In other areas patronage survives, although also in a less offensive manner than previously. For many decades politics in the rural districts was highway politics; the first—and often the only—condition for securing work on the highways for oneself or for one's team of horses or truck was support of the party in power. More recently the vast increase in highway expenditures has permitted—indeed, almost obliged—the government of the day to let its political opponents share in the benefits. In the matter of government purchases the friends of the party in office still appear to have a preference, but only under regulations that ensure the protection of the public interest.

The mores of the society are also tolerant of the evils associated with the electoral process. For many years the Liberals manipulated the electoral rolls to their own advantage, but never so brazenly as to incur the wrath of an easy-going public. Nova Scotians will tolerate only so much of this kind of thing, however, and when the Conservative party, not nearly so skilled in gauging the public attitudes, appeared to be using similar methods flagrantly to steal an election, their tactics back-fired. Certainly the Great Franchise Scandal played a part in the Conservative defeat of 1933.

Electoral bribery and corruption was being practised on an extensive scale as far back as the election of 1830. As in the other Atlantic provinces it is difficult to overcome the tradition that anything goes in politics. One observer stated as late as 1933 that the electoral process "drags . . . many of our leading citizens down to the level of gangsters."[21] Even today, "no matter how high-intentioned a candidate may be he is forced to fall in line with a system which operates on the principle that elections are not won by prayers."[22] Yet, when a prominent Conservative admitted as much during the provincial campaign of 1967, the Toronto *Daily Star* acted as if it had made a discovery; not so the people of Nova Scotia, who appeared neither surprised nor shocked. To all appearances, however, the practice of buying votes is not quite so prevalent as it once was.

The agencies of political communication have done little to break down the conservatism and caution, the tendency to cling to things of the past—even if undesirable. Rather, they have operated to maintain things as they are. It is a sad commentary on the press that it has retrogressed steadily since the 1840s when an extraordinary variety of newspapers agitated the issues of the day. So long as the Liberal Halifax *Chronicle* confronted the Conservative Halifax *Herald*, the public at least had access to province-wide newspapers that expressed the views of the major parties. Since 1949 the public has had to be content with the Halifax *Chronicle-Herald*, whose publishers express their Conservative views obliquely and seldom take stands on anything that might alienate their readers or advertisers. Its predecessor, the Halifax *Herald*, went to incredible lengths in its pro-British, anti-American stance, especially in the federal elections of 1891 and 1911; the present paper has not served the cause of national unity by its catering to the Anglo-Saxon backlash against French Canada that is all too prevalent in Nova Scotia.

The province's pressure groups normally do not work through the political parties or their members as such; they present their requests to the cabinet, in some cases through annual briefs. Sometimes the opposition takes its cue from the government's failure to meet an interest group's demands, but since the membership of these groups usually cuts across party lines, they are often reluctant to have their interests adopted by any one party. Over the years the Union of Nova Scotia Municipalities has tried so hard to maintain its nonpartisan character that it has suffered in effectiveness. The exception to the general rule is trade unionism, which has been largely responsible for any success that the Independent Labour Party, the CCF, and the NDP may have had. However, the unionists, too, are pragmatic Nova Scotians, and they support the old parties when their interests seem to warrant it. Thus Nova Scotian pressure groups barely disturb the even tenor of the party system.

The people who have provided the formal and informal leadership of the community further contribute to the conservative character of Nova Scotian politics and government. Much as John Porter has shown it to be applicable to all Canada in *The Vertical Mosaic*,[23] so in Nova Scotia an upper and upper-middle income elite, principally composed of lawyers and businessmen, has left a deep impression on the politics and parties of the province. On the two occasions in which the minority Conservative party was in such dire distress that its survival seemed in doubt, a few of these notables (to use Max Weber's term) nursed it back to health and thereby preserved an institution that the elite found congenial. The business elite has also helped to keep in office for long periods Liberal premiers whose administrations were to its liking.

Clearly this is not an environment in which the major parties are likely to espouse a meaningful ideology. "Not a Conservative leader since Confederation has, in fact, pretended to be the exponent of a conservative creed or sought inspiration from English or American conservatives, and those Liberal leaders who have attributed their own success and the province's well-being to their acting in consonance with liberal tenets were treating the intelligence of the electorate with scant respect."[24] Both the Liberals and the Conservatives are pragmatic parties that take stands on specific issues more on grounds of expediency than principle. They have often reversed the roles expected of parties bearing their names. The Liberals long resisted the introduction of universal suffrage because it could do them no good politically; the Conservatives favored it as a means of preventing the dominant Liberals from manipulating a property franchise in their own interest. Again, the Conservatives tried for more than 50 years to have a second chamber of dubious merit abolished; the Liberals tolerated it as a means of strengthening their own position.

There is also no difference between the parties in their attitudes towards social legislation. Because the Liberals were almost always in power, they enacted all the early legislation of this kind, but after the Conservatives assumed office in 1956 their record on social legislation compared favorably with that of their opponents.

> *Both the Liberals and Conservatives emphasize, however, that too much can be expected of governments and that paternal legislation is not the remedy for economic and political ills. Both hold that the duty of a government is simply to "create conditions under which its citizens can work out their own destiny." This, in fact, is the closest that either comes to having a philosophy. But although the statement appears vague and platitudinous, it is at least flexible enough to permit a government to meet the needs and desires of a small community which is not characterized by a sharp conflict of interests.*[25]

Understandably there is much to sustain the existing party system—characterized as it is by two major parties competing for public support—and little to challenge it. In David Easton's model one kind of input—demands—places a political or party system under stress, while a second type of input—supports—maintains it. In Nova Scotia there is an abundance of diffuse support fed into the system as a result of the strong ties of loyalty to the old-line parties. Because the population was static and the influx of new people small, and because caution and conservatism were the prevailing attitudes, the process of political socialization—especially as the family contributed to it—led to the state of affairs that Attorney General J. W. Longley described in 1894:

> *Under the party system whole families maintain with a sort of proud tradition an unbroken history as partisans for generations. ... A party convention will muster the same men and especially the same families it did twenty years before. Political issues may have changed, leaders may have changed and the party may have gone utterly wrong in the interval, it matters not. The old party traditions have gone on and its adherents have remained serenely blind.*[26]

The situation remained much the same until the end of World War II. Since that time—although there are no surveys to measure it quantitatively—the percentage of Nova Scotians who identify themselves as party adherents and the intensity of party identification have diminished somewhat, as knowledgable party workers will readily attest. To a high percentage of Nova Scotians, however—especially those living in areas least subject to change—the old parties continue to be endowed with a sense of legitimacy: they can still be counted on to promote the general welfare of Nova Scotians.

Rarely has the party system been confronted with demands of such an intensity, variety, and volume as to overload it, cause output failure, and threaten its collapse. The most serious threat occurred in the provincial election of July 27, 1920, when 29 Farmer-Labour candidates polled 32.3 per cent of the popular vote compared to the Conservatives' 23.3 per cent, and when 11 Farmer-Labour candidates were elected to the Conservatives' 3.

For this phenomenon to have occurred in tradition-oriented Nova Scotia, a series of factors had to be operating to the same end.[27] The first was a political vacuum: the Liberals, after 38 uninterrupted years in office, were hardly a party of initiative and vision, even in a tradition-oriented province; the Conservatives, suffering from the bad image of the Unionist administration at Ottawa, had fallen into disarray.

The economic situation made such distasteful alternatives seem even more repellent. Much of the province's industry and union activity had become concentrated in the coal and steel areas of Pictou, Cumberland, and especially Cape Breton counties. After the stimulus of the wartime boom was over, the loss of the Quebec coal market, the decline in railway construction and hence in the demand for steel, and the increase in freight rates seriously affected the province's heavy industry. A worsening situation was magnified by a steep rise in the cost of mining coal (much more pronounced than in the United States), the long, expensive haul to central and western Canadian markets, and the lack of capital resources to cope with technological changes. The Independent Labour Party of Cape Breton had been established in November 1917; later the closing of war industries and a serious wage-price squeeze in an already unfavorable economic context led to the founding of the Independent Labour Party of Nova Scotia in April 1920.

It is perhaps not surprising that labor would take concerted political action. It occurred in the heavily unionized areas—particularly Cape Breton County—where the population had not been static but had become increasingly concentrated during the preceding three decades, where there had been some immigration, and where the tenets of British trade unionism, including that of intervention in politics, were strong. However, it does come as a surprise that the United Farmers of Nova Scotia came into being barely a week later. In 1919 the Nova Scotia Farmers' Association had 269 locals in fourteen of the eighteen counties; fruit growers, dairymen, and poultrymen had associations of their own; the number of co-operative societies had risen to eighty-seven; and all these organizations had given the farmer a sense of affiliation and joint action. Still, there was nothing in these associations to indicate that a static rural population of mixed farmers with widely divergent interests could be induced to take concerted political action.

However, the same factors were operating among the farmers as among the industrial workers: a definite political vacuum, serious economic difficulties, and especially a pronounced wage-price squeeze. One of them stated the farmers' case thus:

> *The farmers of this province, fed up with doing the drudgery of production while the politicians, forgetful of their election promises,*

have been enjoying the high lights of social life at Ottawa and Halifax, have at length decided to withdraw their allegiance from the old party standards, to do their own thinking, their own organizing, and when they get into power, to do their own legislating for the benefit of a country which, in the last analysis, is mainly agricultural.[28]

Further impelling the Nova Scotian farmers into action were the United Farmer organizations in the other provinces—particularly in neighboring New Brunswick—and their recent electoral triumph in Ontario.

The Farmer-Labour group might have elected more than eleven members in 1920, but for two reasons. The first was the failure of farmers and unionists to co-operate effectively. While they did present a combined slate of candidates in three counties, the relationship between them is typified by the farmers' reaction to the delegation of unionists that appeared before the founding convention of the United Farmers of Nova Scotia: "before they had a chance to talk they were told to work longer hours."[29] The more significant factor, however, was the tactics used against the Farmer-Labour group. Before either group could get properly organized, Premier George Murray had the Assembly dissolved on June 28 and an election called for July 27. The *Morning Chronicle*, after denouncing the Farmer-Labourites as socialistic agitators, said that Nova Scotians were sensible people who had no use for alien radical ideas;[30] the Antigonish *Casket* feared that "these blockheads may persuade the people to give their quack-medicine a trial and put the clock back three thousand years";[31] and the Pictou *Advocate* warned that "the boys whose sacrifices in the war and whose bodies lie in France did not give up their lives there in order that Canada should be handed over to Socialists and Bolshevists."[32]

As quickly as the Farmer-Labour movement had mushroomed, so it collapsed. Its members made a poor showing in the legislature, and the Conservatives, who have a habit of rising phoenix-like from the ashes whenever their position as a second party is threatened, recovered quickly to become the spokesman for all discontented Nova Scotians during the early 1920s.

In contrast with the Farmer-Labour group, the CCF did not get properly organized in Nova Scotia until some years after its founding. In the federal election of 1935 the Reconstruction candidates of H. H. Stevens garnered the votes of protest and reform. They captured 13.9 per cent of the popular vote (mostly in eastern Nova Scotia and especially in industrial Cape Breton and Pictou counties), their best showing in all Canada. It was perhaps revealing of the Nova Scotian character that the radicalism the province chose to support was the mildest imaginable.

The CCF did not make a genuine start in Nova Scotia until 1937, when District 26 of the United Mine Workers of America affiliated with it; thereupon the Nova Scotian section of the CCF was organized. In 1941 it polled 7 per cent of the vote and elected three members to the legislature, all from Cape Breton County. Four years later, as a result of the disillusionment prevailing generally throughout Canada, the CCF raised its share of the popular vote to 13.6 per cent, but lost one of its seats. This was its peak, for although it (or the NDP) retained two Cape Breton County seats up to 1956 and one up to 1963, its popular vote plummeted, reaching a low of 3 per cent in 1956. Federally, Cape Breton South returned a CCF member between 1940 and 1953, and an NDP member in 1962. For the same reasons that led Cape Breton County to elect Labour candidates in 1920, it has been the only part of the province to accord significant support to the CCF and the NDP. Beginning in 1956, however, its coal miners and steel workers turned in large numbers to Robert Stanfield and the Conservatives. Thus even the members of the strongest unions in the province display the same pragmatic attitudes as Nova Scotians generally. It ought not to be surprising, therefore, that the limited success of a third party has been largely confined to one of the 18 counties. Where industrial concentration does not exist and where few outsiders have been introduced into a long established population, the hold of the old parties has not been challenged. The nature of the economy and the social structure tend to reinforce this state of affairs.

> *The economic development of the province up to now has not been such as to evoke any pronounced feelings of class consciousness, and divisions based upon class have therefore no real significance. Furthermore, there is no substantial economic group which, in the manner of the grain growers of Western Canada, is able to maintain a cohesive political existence by attributing the insecurity of its material position to dependence upon outside financial interests. For while the Nova Scotia primary producers may subsist in what Professor Macpherson describes as a state of "quasi-colonialism,"*[33] *their problems are so diffuse that combined action to improve their lot is rendered extraordinarily difficult.*[34]

In the provincial election of 1970 the NDP fared somewhat better, polling 6.7 per cent of the popular vote and electing two members in Cape Breton County, but as yet there is no evidence that this improvement in the party's fortunes is likely to continue.

THE POLITICAL MILIEU

The British parliamentary system, the federal system, and the electoral system have all left their marks on Nova Scotian parties. The first has had its usual results on party discipline. In the 1850s a few assemblymen defected from their parties on the railway and the religious issues; in the 1860s a few more left because of retrenchment and Confederation; but since 1867 defections have been almost nonexistent. Straight party votes in the Assembly became normal at an early date, and Nova Scotian party leaders have seldom been confronted with even a hint of rebellion in the party caucus.

In contrast, federalism has affected the Nova Scotian parties much more than those of most provinces. The act of union itself produced a rearrangement of the existing parties, and in the grand shuffle of supporters the anti-Confederates or Liberals fared much the better. The Confederates immediately incorporated themselves into the federal Conservative party, and like the latter assumed the name Liberal-Conservative, the designation of the Conservatives in the United Province of Canada since the 1850s. Because the Confederates could not win elective office in anti-Confederate Nova Scotia they prevailed upon Sir John Macdonald to ensconce them in lucrative federal offices.[35]

For the anti-Confederates the problem was not nearly so simple. They soon had to face the serious difficulty confronting any party that cannot fulfill a basic promise—in this case repeal of the Union. Their inability or unwillingness to adopt strong measures for the "liberation" of the province alienated their extremist followers; at the same time the Confederates were trying their best to wean away the lukewarm supporters of repeal.[36] After the anti-Confederates lost a dozen seats in the provincial election of 1871, they realized they could no longer continue to win elections simply by blaming their opponents for the fact of Confederation.

Their position in federal politics was even more difficult. To expect their members at Ottawa to remain in splendid isolation was indeed a forlorn hope. "Going up to Ottawa as red-hot Antis," complained the *Morning Chronicle*, "they have been successively wheedled, with four or five sturdy and honorable exceptions, into giving an almost unbroken support to a Government which includes Howe and Tupper."[37] Prior to the federal election of 1872, the anti-Confederate newspapers anxiously deliberated which of two courses their M.P.s should follow in the next Parliament. They agreed that, if their M.P.s were to join in any alliance at all, it would have to be with the Blake and Mackenzie party in preference to the "designing [Macdonald] faction . . . now . . . denying us an honest, vigorous and economical government."[38] But the Nova Scotian M.P.s might also maintain their independence, get all the federal moneys they could for local services, and refuse to enter into alliances until questions of principle had superseded the struggle for power in the Dominion.

Seemingly the second alternative was decided upon; apparently, too, the federal election of 1874, fought as it was on the Pacific Scandal and a return to honest government, provided the principles that were needed to seal an alliance. The eighteen anti-Confederate (or Liberal) members that Nova Scotia returned in 1874 all became faithful supporters of Alexander Mackenzie's government, and two of them entered the cabinet. The result was to complete the integration of the Nova Scotian parties into the national parties and to submerge the one issue that permitted the meaningful cleavage of the electorate along party lines.

Indirectly, however, Confederation continued to affect the parties. Because it left the Liberals with a larger core of supporters than their opponents, they entered every contest with a decided advantage over the Conservatives. The failure of federal Conservative governments until 1896 to show much concern for their provincial counterparts also assisted the Liberals substantially. Above all, Nova Scotian Conservatives had to take the blame for the unpopular fiscal and tariff policies of the national government.

Macdonald's cavalier treatment of W.S. Fielding's Liberal government led to a provincial election on the repeal of Confederation in 1886. It is difficult to determine how much a secessionist Fielding was; undoubtedly he accepted the repeal plank partly as a means of placating the extremists within his own ranks and partly as a means of putting pressure on Macdonald for additional financial assistance. How much his overwhelming victory was due to his government's record and how much to the repeal argument is impossible to tell; the federal Conservatives carried the province decisively in opposing repeal less than a year later and thereby laid the matter to rest.

Prior to the provincial election of 1890, however, the Conservative organizer, C. H. Cahan, was again bewailing the federal government's failure to consider the provincials:

> *... if Mr.* [*Charles Hibbert*] *Tupper* [*the Minister of Marine and Fisheries*] *had set himself to work to destroy the liberal-conservative party in local politics he could not have adopted methods more likely to effect his purpose than those he has pursued in his treatment of the saw-dust and lobster questions....*
> *We are really fighting a federal contest without the aid of federal leaders, federal patronage, and federal rallying cries. We have in every county the odium which the Dominion government may perchance have incurred.*[39]

Factors such as these helped to keep the provincial Liberals in power (except for the recession election of 1878) during the first part of their lengthy tenure of office extending from 1867 to 1925. Yet the margin between the parties was not such as to prevent the Macdonald federal government from winning decisively in Nova Scotia in four general elections between 1878 and 1891. This was partly due to the desire of a have-not province to support the party that it felt was likely to win a federal election, and hence assure itself of federal beneficence. Until recently at least Nova Scotia has been one of the country's more accurate bell-wethers. The existing state of affairs—Liberal at Halifax and Conservative at Ottawa—was perpetuated because, not unnaturally, the abler Liberal politicians remained in provincial politics, while the abler Conservative ones were drawn to Ottawa. Much of the Conservative success federally was due to Charles Tupper, who could always be counted on to rescue the Macdonald government from its difficulties in Nova Scotia. Yet Tupper's presence was a drawback to the provincial party, for as long as he dominated Nova Scotia Conservatism, "the [provincial] party had a 'leader' of sorts and thus it could afford, or so it thought, to accept inferior leadership on the provincial scene while it waited for the emergence of another Tupper."[40]

Ironically Tupper could do more for Macdonald in Nova Scotia than he could for himself in Nova Scotia as prime minister in 1896. It was also unusual that Fielding, as Laurier's minister of finance, could use the national policies of Macdonald, which he had previously condemned, to promote one of the country's greatest booms. Nova Scotia shared in the prosperity and responded to it by reinforcing Liberal supremacy both provincially and federally in the first decade of the century. To Fielding's chagrin, however, he could not convince his compatriots of the merits of reciprocity in 1911, even though it was specially calculated to serve their interests: the Halifax *Herald* urged them not to truck or trade with the Yankees, and latent pro-British sentiment did its work.

The character of federal—Nova Scotian relations and the nature of federal-provincial party relationships changed substantially after World War I. Not only did Nova Scotia, like the other Maritime provinces, fail to recover from the post-war recession as quickly as the rest of Canada, but its slow rate of growth compared with central and western Canada became obvious for the first time. Since then there has been continual jockeying between the old parties to have themselves recognized as the better spokesman for the provincial interest. Sometimes it has been difficult to determine whether the party or the provincial interest is foremost in their thinking.

During the early 1920s the Conservatives took over a newly formed Maritime Rights movement and used it as one vehicle, among others, to win decisive victories federally and provincially in Nova Scotia during the later years of the decade. Under the Conservatives, the movement took a peculiar twist. The Duncan Commission, a federal royal commission investigating the province's disabilities, altogether ignored the major ill, the incidence of the protective tariff, allegedly at the insistence of a Conservative government at Ottawa. For that reason a Liberal premier, Angus L. Macdonald, later appointed his own agency—the Jones Commission—to remedy the defect.

The province's most successful politicians in recent decades, Angus L. Macdonald and Robert Stanfield, sought especially to create for themselves the image of provincial defender against unfavorable federal policies. Macdonald even demanded that a federal government of his own party get out of the lesser tax fields if it expected the provinces to abandon the major ones. Stanfield, who came to be regarded as the builder of a new Nova Scotia, got credit—much to the Liberals' indignation—for the assistance provided by the Pearson government for provincial development, even though he capitalized politically on his criticism of the same administration.

Federal party leaders normally think it desirable to have governments of their own party in power in the provinces; Nova Scotian (and other) premiers are of two minds on this issue. Undoubtedly they find it more congenial to deal with a prime minister of the same political persuasion at Ottawa; but such a situation inhibits them in using the federal government as a scape-goat for provincial ills. Robert Stanfield found the Pearson government at Ottawa much less sympathetic than the Diefenbaker one, but the change at Ottawa had its compensations: it permitted him to add to his image of champion of the provincial interest. In the federal election of 1965 he was the chief Conservative campaigner in Nova Scotia, denouncing the Pearson government's treatment of offshore mineral rights and the government's application of a tight-money policy equally throughout Canada. There was more than a little truth to the lament of the Liberal national campaign director that "the Stanfield machine creamed us."[41]

How much the provincial interest has suffered in the efforts to maintain harmony between the federal and provincial sections of the old parties is not calculable. It is pertinent to wonder, however, whether Nova Scotian M.P.s and M.L.A.s have been too concerned with maintaining over-all party solidarity at the cost of safeguarding provincial interests; whether their representatives at Ottawa have been content with little more than temporary sops; and whether it would have been to the advantage of Nova Scotia to have followed the course of the Prairie provinces by returning third-party representation in strength to both the federal and provincial parliaments.

The electoral system has affected Nova Scotian parties even more than has the federal system. That effect can be seen more easily if some sort of order is brought into Nova Scotian elections through a classificatory scheme (see Table I). Perhaps most useful is the technique used by Professor Angus Campbell in classifying American presidential elections.[42] Campbell assumes that the vote cast by the electorate (or specific groups within the electorate) may be split into two parts: the normal vote division to be expected, other things being equal, and the current deviation from that norm. While at any one time there is a majority party and a minority one, short-term forces may produce large enough fluctuations from the normal vote to elect the candidate of the minority party without disturbing the basic division of party loyalties: such is a deviating election. If the fluctuations are not large enough to defeat the majority party, the election is a maintaining one. Occasionally the popular feeling is so intense that enough voters change their basic commitments and produce a new majority party: that is a realigning election.

The Nova Scotian election of 1836—the first one in which there was anything resembling party divisions—must be regarded as a realigning one since not only did it lead a substantial portion of the electorate to align itself in support of reforming principles, but it also returned a majority of assemblymen who favored reform. Although any attempt to reconstruct the party bases must be largely conjectural, Joseph Howe had good ground for boasting that much of his support came from the sturdy agriculturalist who had won his farm from the wilderness and who objected to maintaining a top-heavy, irresponsible, governmental establishment. It it no less clear that the Tories did best in the shire towns and bigger communities where the local compacts of merchants, officials, and lawyers were closely tied in with the larger compact at Halifax; the Tories' consistently better showing in the township ridings as compared with the county ones serves to confirm it. It is equally evident that, while the Tories could count on a preponderant share of the Church of England vote, the Reformers more than made up for it by the strong support they received from the Protestant Dissenters and Roman Catholics, two groups for which Howe had always shown a great deal of sympathy. The exception was the Baptists; Howe alienated this group in 1843 by his determined opposition to government grants to sectarian colleges.

On the basis of support of this kind the Reformers—in the 1850's they came more and more to be called Liberals—remained the majority party until 1867, but not decisively so. Thus the Tories, by catching their opponents unprepared in a surprise election in 1843, emerged as the larger element in a two-party coalition. Even the responsible government election of 1847 was a nip-and-tuck contest, as were the subsequent ones of 1851, 1855, and 1859. The two parties became still more closely matched as a result of Howe's break with the Catholics in 1857 and their wholesale desertion to the Tories. The conservatives won the most decisive election of the pre-Confederation period in 1863 when the Liberal government collapsed from old age and lack of leadership. But like the election of 1843, it was a deviating election, since there was no substantial change in basic voter commitment.

In contrast, the election of 1867 in which Nova Scotians divided for and against Confederation was a realigning one. "For the moment even the old shibboleths of Conservative and Liberal were discarded in favor of Confederate and anti-Confederate, and while the nucleus of the Con-

TABLE I
Classification of Nova Scotian Elections: 1836-1967

Maintaining Elections	Deviating Elections	Realigning Elections
		1836
1840		
	1843	
1847		
1851		
1855		
1859		
	1863	
		1867
1871		
1874		
	1878	
1882		
1886		
1890		
1894		
1897		
1901		
1906		
1911		
1916		
1920		
	1925	
	1928	
1933		
1937		
1941		
1945		
1949		
1953		
		1956(?)*
1960		
1963		
1967		

* The election of 1956 is shown questionably as a realigning one, since it can be argued that the realignment of political forces under Robert Stanfield was not completed until the election of 1963.

federates was Conservative just as that of the anti-Confederates was Liberal, the break in party ties was on such a scale as to create new parties in fact as in name."[43] The realignment occurred within all groups, and the net shift in the voters' party identification was sufficient to make the Liberals a much stronger majority party than they had been between 1836 and 1867. It took until 1874 or thereabouts for the situation to stabilize itself, but the Conservatives were still substantially in the minority. They remained so until Robert Stanfield's success in 1956, since their victories in 1878, 1925, and 1928 were short-lived ones resulting from recession and financial difficulties.

This is the context in which the electoral system has operated in Nova Scotia. Recently Professor Alan Cairns has suggested that in Canada's federal elections the electoral system has tended to stimulate the politics of sectionalism and has thereby contributed significantly to the evolution of the party system. Because the party leaders realize they can reap rich dividends in seats—altogether out of proportion to their parties' votes—from specific regions, they deliberately cater to such areas. The result, Cairns suggests, has been "a politics of opportunism based on sectional appeals and conditioned by one-party bastions where the opposition is tempted to give up the battle and pursue success in more promising areas."[44]

In the small community of Nova Scotia this brand of politics is hardly possible. None the less, the first-past-the-post electoral system by which a candidate with a plurality is elected has had almost as drastic results because of its usual propensity to give the winning party a disproportionately large share of the seats and the second party a disproportionately small share (see Table II). In the 22 elections between 1867 and 1953 the Liberals received only 49.8 per cent of the votes, but got 68.1 per cent of the seats; the Conservatives gained 44.2 per cent of the votes, but only 29.2 per cent of the seats. In 11 of these elections the Conservatives won eight seats or less and in only one election did they elect sufficient assemblymen of ability to conduct an efficient opposition and look like a credible alternative to the ruling Liberals.

Despite their overwhelming predominance, the Liberals' share of the popular vote never exceeded 52.9 per cent after 1911, and despite the Conservatives' minority position their popular vote fell below 38.5 per cent only twice since Confederation. The Conservatives suffered severely because their vote was quite evenly distributed across the province and because they could count no seat as safely theirs. For them the result was to produce a chronic instability of leadership such as seldom befalls a major party.

Sometimes, indeed, the Conservative leaders appeared to be playing a game of musical chairs, although not of their own will. Dr. William MacKay was Conservative House leader in the Twenty-ninth General Assembly (1886–1890), but gave way to C. H. Cahan when he was defeated in his own riding; he resumed the leadership in the Thirty-first

Assembly (1894–1897) when Cahan was rejected by his own constituents. John F. Stairs, the first elected leader of the provincial party, in contrast with the House leaders of pre-1897 days, never became a member of the Assembly although he tried to in 1897 and 1901.

TABLE II* (a)

Results of Nova Scotian Provincial Elections: 1867-1974

Year	Popular Vote			Percentage of Popular Vote		
	Liberal	Conservative	Other	Liberal	Conser-vative	Other
1867	44,339	29,095	2,182	58.6	38.5	2.9
1871	39,213	32,808	3,128	52.2	43.7	4.2
1874	37,169	29,492	921	55.0	43.6	1.4
1878	45,672	52,311	3,268	45.1	51.7	3.2
1882	49,945	45,247	1,205	51.8	46.9	1.3
1886	61,822	49,216	1,943	54.7	43.6	1.7
1890	71,202	63,720	1,407	52.2	46.7	1.1
1894	75,121	68,455	1,073	51.9	47.3	0.7
1897	84,000	67,779	968	55.0	44.4	0.6
1901	78,375	57,689	2,147	56.7	41.7	1.6
1906	84,359	66,638	7,423	53.2	42.1	4.7
1911	99,192	88,114	6,851	51.1	45.4	3.5
1916	136,315	131,844	2,215	50.4	48.8	0.8
1920	154,627	81,044	112,283	44.4	23.3	32.3
1925	161,158	270,544	12,260	36.3	60.9	2.8
1928	209,380	218,974	4,862	48.3	50.5	1.1
1933	166,170	145,107	4,805	52.6	45.9	1.5
1937	165,397	143,670	3,396	52.9	46.0	1.1
1941	138,915	106,133	18,583	52.7	40.3	7.0
1945	153,513	97,774	40,271	52.7	33.5	13.8
1949	174,604	134,312	33,618	51.0	39.2	9.8
1953	169,921	149,973	25,765	49.1	43.4	7.5
1956	159,656	160,996	10,690	48.2	48.6	3.2
1960	147,946	168,023	31,686	42.6	48.3	9.1
1963	137,873	191,128	14,076	39.7	56.2	4.1
1967	142,945	180,948	18,371	41.8	52.8	5.4
1970	174,943	177,986	26,724	46.1	46.9	7.0
1974	206,648	166,388	58,122	47.9	38.6	13.5

Perhaps the story of Charles E. Tanner best illustrates the oscillating fortunes of a Conservative leader in Nova Scotia. First elected to the Assembly in 1901, he assumed the House leadership of a contingent of two, and was later proclaimed leader of the provincial party. He was re-elected to the Assembly in 1906, thereby becoming the first Conservative leader since 1886 to retain his seat. He found his position as leader so unrewarding, however, that he ran federally in 1908. He failed to get elected and then could not win back his provincial seat. The election of 1911 returned him to the Assembly with ten followers; five years later he gave the Liberals a good fight, but—as was almost to be expected—he lost out personally. He had had enough; shortly afterwards he accepted a more secure resting place in the Senate. His successor, W. L. Hall, suffered an even more unkind fate: he lost his seat in 1920 and was deposed as leader just before the great Conservative triumph of 1925.

After eight years on the government benches, the Conservatives went through a similar, although shorter cycle. Their leader, Gordon S. Harrington, lost his seat in 1937, and his successor, L. W. Fraser, could not get elected in either 1941 or 1945. On the latter occasion the Conservatives, for the first time, won no seats at all. "I can no longer lead this party hopefully," said Fraser, "and that leaves me only one course to follow."[45] For such sentiments, which might have been echoed by most of his predecessors, the electoral system was substantially responsible. By returning to the legislature only a corporal's guard of members from a party that normally polled at least two-fifths of the vote, that party was left lacking in leadership, low in morale, and deficient in organization. Only a deep-seated tradition of party identification enabled it to survive at all.

More recently the Liberals have been administered a milder dose of the same medicine. Their leader was defeated in 1960 and 1963, and while Gerald Regan won his seat in 1967, his party's 41.8 per cent of the vote gave it only 13 per cent of the seats. Under these circumstances the Liberals were having the same difficulties that the Conservatives once experienced in maintaining morale and rebuilding their organization. Obviously the electoral system has had a potent effect on both the working of the legislature and the nature of the parties and provincial politics.

How Nova Scotian Political Parties Have Affected the Political and Social Systems

A political system must, above all, provide leadership and make decisions for the society, and political parties play a key role in performing both functions. Since the Nova Scotia House of Assembly has—indirectly at least—been a major decision-maker on the provincial level, its composition is of special significance. Of 1089 assemblymen elected between 1867 and 1974, two were Independents, 11 were Farmer-Labourites, 16 were CCF or NDP, and the rest were members of the old parties—657 Liberals and 403 Conservatives. The practices that the parties use to nominate their candidates are therefore crucial and are closely connected with party organization per se.

The conversion of the casual party meetings of the 1840s into organized conventions took place in stages and by no means uniformly throughout the province. During the 1860s, shortly after dissolution the unofficial party leaders in the shiretowns would send circulars regarding a nomination meeting to their friends in the outlying districts. In 1871 the Conservatives of Pictou introduced a significant innovation: "All those in attendance at the nomination meeting from a specific polling district chose one person from among themselves—a *delegate* so-called—to sit on the committee which proposed the candidates."[46] In the federal and provincial elections of 1874 the practice was extended to other counties and in 1878 it was a commonplace. The election of 1871 was also noteworthy for an occasional reference to the nomination gatherings as *conventions*. By 1878 this term—an American importation—was in common use and by 1882 it was employed almost exclusively. However, bona fide conventions would be largely a myth as long as the parties had no organization until just before an election.

February 4, 1878 was therefore a red-letter day for party organization. On that date the Liberals established the Reform Association of Halifax and organized themselves on a permanent basis, not only at the county level, but also at the ward and polling district levels. This permitted them to introduce another significant innovation in August 1878: "a convention consisting solely of delegates accredited by the organization in the wards and polling districts selected the party's candidates in an inner room, while the members of the Reform Association and their friends gathered in a larger outer room to await their determination."[47] Perhaps it was understandable that the Liberals contrasted these procedures with the undemocratic ones used by the Tories in the same county: "The wire pullers get together in some garret in the city and cook up their ticket. Then . . . as a matter of form, they invite gentlemen to come in from the rural districts. . . . What a farce!"[48]

Actually the Conservatives of Halifax had set up a Liberal-Conservative Association in July 1874 in response to Charles Tupper's argument that a party without organization tended to be a multitude of scattered atoms. The Association did little to build up an organization at the grass roots, however, and it was not until 1882 that it could hold a convention similar to that convened by its Liberal counterpart in 1878. Before similar conventions could be held outside Halifax, the county and local organizations had to be established on a firmer basis, a development that took place spasmodically over the next decade or two. In the case of the Liberals a great spurt of organizational activity followed Laurier's visit to Halifax and the founding of the Nova Scotia Liberal Association in December 1890; within two months county organizations were set up in Richmond and Guysborough for the first time.

The county and local organizations of the Conservatives—a weak and dispirited party—came into being more slowly. As late as July 1896, the

Halifax *Herald* declared them "not fit even to choose delegates to a general convention," and Peter Aucoin has written of the party:

> *... it was such a nebulous thing that it is questionable if it should be called a party at all. It had no provincial organization and no rules regulating party membership, the nomination of candidates, the selection of a party leader, or anything else for that matter.... In essence, the party was the loosest association between notables in Halifax and in the other counties.*[49]

Accordingly, under the urging of their national leader, Sir Charles Tupper, the Conservatives took steps in October 1896 to "reconstruct, remodel, re-equip and infuse some hurrah into the party."[50] Borrowing the designation of their English counterpart, the National Union, they established the Liberal-Conservative Union of Nova Scotia and thereby equipped themselves with an extra-parliamentary apparatus similar to that of the Liberals.

In both parties the relationship between the parliamentary parties and their mass organizations has varied over time and it is hardly true to say—as R. T. McKenzie states of British parties—that a healthy balance has existed between the two, ensuring all the more that the parties have been highly useful adjuncts of liberal democracy. During the long tenures of Liberal premiers George Murray and Angus L. Macdonald, which included most of the period between 1896 and 1954, these two figures dominated the extra-parliamentary organization as much as they liked; indeed, there is more than a suspicion that Macdonald let the organization decay in his later years. Nevertheless, the Liberal party workers attributed their almost continuous success to superior organization on both the provincial and county levels, and, because the lower echelons of the party helped to allocate the local patronage, the Liberals had no trouble in maintaining a coherent organization at the polling district level.

Normally the Conservatives had nothing comparable to this. Between elections their only activity was the annual meetings of the provincial and constituency associations; their organization at the polling district level was nonexistent, or at least quiescent in most counties.

> *Yet, when an election* [was] *called, they* [were] *usually able to enlist a sufficient number of the old faithful to provide at least the semblance of a contest in every constituency. Generally their only solace after the counting of the ballots on election night* [was] *to register surprise at the size of their popular vote despite the strength of the contending forces.*[51]

Twice, in 1920 and in 1945, the Conservatives lost their position as second party in the legislature, and it took a few notables to save the party and effect a resurrection; undoubtedly the fear that the Conservatives might be supplanted by a radical alternative spurred them into activity. On the second occasion it was Robert Stanfield, president of the Young People's Conservatives, who directed the re-organization of the party that made him its leader two years later. By maintaining that organization in fighting trim, he was ready to take over the province when the opportunity arose in 1956. Normally, however, the experience has been that strength in party organization has been more effect than cause, that nothing succeeds like success, and that a party in opposition experiences a loss of morale and weakened organization. Yet, when the

TABLE II* (b)

Results of Nova Scotian Provincial Elections: 1867-1974

	Seats			Percentage of Seats		
	Liberal	Conservative	Other	Liberal	Conservative	Other
1867	36	2		94.7	5.3	
1871	25	13		65.8	34.2	
1874	24	14		63.2	36.8	
1878	8	30		21.1	78.9	
1882	24	14		63.2	36.8	
1886	29	8	1	76.3	21.1	2.6
1890	28	10		73.7	26.3	
1894	25	13		65.8	34.2	
1897	35	3		92.1	7.9	
1901	36	2		94.7	5.3	
1906	32	5	1	84.2	13.2	2.6
1911	27	11		71.1	28.9	
1916	30	13		69.8	30.2	
1920	29	3	11	67.4	7.0	25.6
1925	3	40		7.0	93.0	
1928	20	23		46.5	53.5	
1933	22	8		73.3	26.7	
1937	25	5		83.3	16.7	
1941	23	4	3	76.7	13.3	10.0
1945	28		2	93.3		6.7
1949	28	7	2	75.7	18.9	5.4
1953	23	12	2	62.2	32.4	5.4
1956	18	24	1	41.9	55.8	2.3
1960	15	27	1	34.9	62.8	2.3
1963	4	39		9.3	90.7	
1967	6	40		13.0	87.0	
1970	23	21	2	50.0	45.7	4.3
1974	31	12	3	67.4	26.1	6.5

* Sources for Tables II(a) and (b): Up to 1886, newspaper election reports: since 1886, appendices to *Journals of the Nova Scotia House of Assembly* and *Returns of General Election for the House of Assembly*, (Halifax: Queen's Printer).

scent of victory is in the air, there is no dearth of volunteers to fight the opposition party's election battles. Generally the organization of the Liberals and Conservatives can be said to be democratic in the sense that no one who wishes to participate in their affairs is likely to be denied the opportunity.

Such is the organizational apparatus that chooses the old parties' candidates for the Legislature and the premiership. When Conservative Premier E. N. Rhodes and Liberal Premier Angus L. Macdonald entered the federal cabinet in 1930 and 1940, the party rank and file did not participate in the choice of their successors. However, these were exceptional circumstances; it seems certain that neither party will in future choose a leader through means other than its provincial association assembled in a leadership convention. Of the seven such conventions held by the Conservatives, only the one that chose Robert Stanfield in 1948 involved a contest for the leadership. In contrast, four of the five Liberal conventions—all held since 1930—have had contests. The one held in 1954 was too much of an exercise in democracy, for it produced a religious cleavage and left wounds that took a long time to heal.

Both parties have had difficulties—although of a different kind—in maintaining an appropriate relationship between the "brass" and the "grass." As recently as 1964, there have been spirited contests for election to the executive of the Nova Scotia Liberal Association; in that year a young "ginger group" demanded more aggressive direction of the party's affairs. For the Conservatives the problem has been to secure greater involvement of the rank and file in party concerns. To that end in recent years they have had the members of the provincial cabinet—the directors of the corporation—subjected to questioning by the ordinary membership—the shareholders of the corporation—at the annual meeting of the provincial association.

At the constituency level the Conservative party organization was so weak prior to the 1950s that in many constituencies it was impossible to convene a delegate convention. In the rare case in which a nomination was contested, the party ran the risk of having an unsuitable candidate foisted on it by an open convention. Since the revitalization of the Conservatives neither of the old parties has had to run that risk. Although contested nominations are by no means the rule, they have become much more common since the mid-1950s.

Whom do the conventions nominate as possible assemblymen and potential political leaders? Anyone who seeks to establish that one party's conventions select candidates who are different from those of the other party in philosophy or in any other respect is pursuing a will-o'-the wisp. To the onlooker in the Legislature's public galleries, the elected candidates, like members of other provincial assemblies, appear to be a rather mediocre lot; however, their lack of oratorical ability often conceals their good common sense. Almost invariably they are local men: the candidature of an outsider is likely to raise questions, and the parties have seldom resorted to carpetbaggers except in the absence of a suitable local candidate. From the earliest days of the Assembly one-fifth to one-third of its members have been lawyers, and in recent Assemblies the proportion is tending to be even larger. In earlier years the number of general merchants often rivalled that of the lawyers, but today the non-lawyers among the assemblymen are of diverse occupations—farming, lumbering, contracting, medicine, journalism, manufacturing, finance, and insurance. As in the Parliament of Canada, trade unionism is poorly represented. On the whole the members come largely from the middle and upper-middle income groups, but none the less they reflect—perhaps too accurately—the tradition-oriented political culture.

From the assemblymen come most of the true decision makers, the premiers and cabinet ministers. In Nova Scotia the premiers have had an even greater influence than is normal, simply because four of them—William Stevens Fielding, George H. Murray, Angus L. Macdonald, and Robert L. Stanfield—held the premiership for 66 of the 83 years between 1884 and 1967. (It would have been 71 years if Macdonald had not entered the federal cabinet during World War II.) Each stamped something of himself on the character of his administration.[52]

Contrary to the ways of British political parties—especially the Conservative party, in which the leader and prime minister normally "emerge" after proving their mettle in the Commons—these four Nova Scotians took over the party leadership, and sometimes the government, almost sight unseen. Fielding had been an assemblyman and executive councillor for less than two years before he became premier; Murray had made three unsuccessful attempts to be elected to the Commons or Assembly before he took over the premiership and at the time he formed his government he was serving in the cabinet as a member of the Legislative Council; Macdonald assumed the premiership months before he sat in the Assembly; and Stanfield became Conservative leader the year before he was elected to the legislature.

Each of the four provided a different type of leadership, although it may be stretching a point to call it leadership in the case of Murray. By his own admission, he "refused to place himself in the vanguard of public opinion and to persuade it to accept policies which he conceived to be conducive to the provincial interest."[53] As he put it, "new ideas cropped up from time to time, and it was the duty of the government to discern the wishes of the public and to meet these wishes as occasion demanded."[54] To innovation of any kind, he put his inevitable question: Has it been tried elsewhere and with what success? "Under him the Ontario statute book became the utmost limit to which Nova Scotia might hope to aspire in many matters."[55] This philosophy pervaded Nova

Scotian government for 27 years (1897–1923); it left the statute book deficient in legislation appropriate to the nascent positive state and left the administrative machinery obsolescent.

In contrast, Fielding, Macdonald, and Stanfield sought, in different contexts, to ensure that the climate was favourable for provincial development to take place. Although Fielding's premiership (1884–1896) fell within the period of laissez-faire government, his was the first Nova Scotian administration to assume "the initiative in all the most important measures of the session."[56] With some truth he could be credited with "waking-up [Nova Scotia] from a Rip van Winkle sleep"[57] for he undertook, among other things, an extensive programme of building roads and bridges as capital projects, and induced outside interests to develop the provincial coal resources.

Under Angus L. Macdonald "the Liberals secured once more the Fielding type of leadership."[58] In the early years of his premiership, at least, he insisted that no government ought to be content with the mere routine of administration and that all its departments should give real leadership in their respective spheres. On his assumption of office in 1933, despite the impoverishment of the provincial finances, he proclaimed the Old Age Pensions Act, which his Conservative predecessors had left dormant on the statute book, and initiated an ambitious programme of hard-surfacing the main highways. While the Macdonald of post-1945 days was more reluctant to assume new initiatives, he had already acquired the image of willing innovator.

The philosophy of Robert L. Stanfield was that Nova Scotians should forget the days when they were content to attribute all their ills to sinister forces in central Canada and seek to raise themselves by their own bootstraps. It was a basic function of government, he contended, to provide the climate and incentives needed to promote economic development. Despite his reputation for caution, his administration advanced $200 million for the establishment of secondary industries and the name "Stanfield" became inseparably associated with "the new Nova Scotia."

How are the four premiers' long tenures of office to be explained? Obviously Murray's is the most difficult. In part it is to be accounted for by the attitude of his Conservative opponents, whose philosophy differed little from his and who concentrated all too much on destructive criticism to oust him from office. But it was due much more to Murray himself: in him were combined a pleasing affability that made him personally attractive and the political subtlety of a Mackenzie King. While the performance of the brokerage function is much less exacting in Nova Scotia than it is on the national level, Murray did have to moderate class interests at a time when the province was first experiencing serious clashes between capital and labour. His maxims were infinite caution and political expediency. On the platform he abstractly espoused the interests of labor and the masses, but he candidly admitted that his policy was to secure the greatest possible development of the province by making the burden on capital as light as possible. By going into social legislation as little as possible and by accepting the protective tariff he convinced the corporate world that nothing was to be gained by upsetting his government. The outcome was that he managed to avoid alienating the labor vote until 1920, while enlisting the tacit support of even Conservative businessmen.[59]

The success of the other leaders stems in part from their concept of leadership, but there are other factors as well. Fielding inherited the government when the opposition was in disarray, and he quickly and solidly established himself and his party in a position of pre-eminence. Perhaps his goatee did "cover the closest mouth in politics,"[60] but his facility with a trenchant phrase, his logical and incisive speech, his ability to reduce financial complexities to a single formula understandable to the layman, and the impression he created of fairness and integrity all won him public respect. His defence of Nova Scotian interests against the brusque treatment of John A. Macdonald and his success in promoting provincial development served further to create the attractive image that withstood all his opponents' attacks.

Macdonald and Stanfield riveted themselves on the province for many of the same reasons, but not with the same facility. The former took over a party in good health and within three years used recession and the Great Franchise Scandal of 1933 to gain power. Stanfield had more formidable difficulties to overcome, especially in reorganizing a party devoid of representation in the legislature and in eroding the support of such a majestic father figure as Angus L. Macdonald. The latter's death in 1954 accelerated his progress toward victory. The convention to choose Macdonald's successor split along religious lines and the new premier, Henry Hicks, followed a courageous, if politically unwise, course in proceeding with far-reaching changes for the financing of education that substantially increased municipal taxation. Both factors affected the election of 1956: the first caused the Liberals serious losses among the Catholic voters in eastern Nova Scotia, but the second may have tipped the balance in a close election by producing Conservative majorities in western Nova Scotia. It is perhaps true that "Stanfield grows on one," because it took three elections to produce the massive realignment of voters that ensured his political domination of the province.[61]

By 1963 Stanfield, like Macdonald, had inspired the trust and confidence of the people—indeed had created a rapport with them—and had won the good opinion of the business community. Both men succeeded in impressing themselves on the public mind as defenders of the provincial interest against unwarranted or unreasonable federal action; both were regarded as vigorous proponents of a better Nova Scotia; both were strongly partisan, yet managed to create the impression that they stood above politics; both performed the leadership function without riding roughshod over deeply implanted tradition or imposing heavy additional taxation. However, their relations with their parties were different; Macdonald, who relied more on his personal strength maintained a distance between himself and his party; under him Liberal slogans proclaimed that "All's well with Angus L." In contrast, Stanfield, the party man, led a team and Conservative advertisements referred to "A Stanfield Government" or "The Stanfield Team." Personal qualities also became part of the public image of both men. In Macdonald's case it was sentimentality —the poor boy who worked his way through college and ultimately became premier—his Scottish name and ancestry: "it was when he 'put on his kilt' that one rich facet of his personality was revealed. Then we could expect the felicitous phrase, the reverent communing with the bards."[62] In Stanfield's case it was his humility: the rich man who drove an unostentatious Volvo and who walked two miles to work from his home in the south end of Halifax.

Is there something in the Nova Scotian character that makes the people feel more secure when they have a father figure presiding over their destinies? Other provinces, especially Quebec and Ontario, have similarly experienced long tenures of office, although not extending over such protracted periods as Nova Scotia. It seems likely, therefore, that an accidental coincidence of personalities and circumstances, rather than peculiarities of the provincial character, account for the Nova Scotian phenomenon. Because the major parties have not differed markedly in ideology, the voter has tended all the more to emphasize the leader. David Easton might say: the outputs from Nova Scotian parties—through their impact on society generally—have contributed to the emergence of new inputs, especially in the form of diffuse support (leaders with attractive images and the like), that tend not only to maintain the party system as it is, but also to preserve the existing balance of the major parties over long periods.

The major Nova Scotian parties, as performers of functions, display little out of the ordinary. As connectors they bridge the gap between the people in society and their political and governmental systems. Their raison d'être is the expectation that they will be called on to perform the function of manager-operator of the government. To that end they act as nominators—in modern Nova Scotia no candidate who is not the nominee of a political party has a hope of being elected; as broker-mediators —in a province where ethnic, religious, and class differences are not pronounced the task of reconciling interests is much less exacting than at the national level; and as organizers—like their national counterparts the old-line parties in Nova Scotia do more to organize the electorate for victory at the polls than to organize support for coherent schemes of public policy.[63]

A substantial, though decreasing, number of Nova Scotians have a high sense of party identification; for them a party has considerable capacity to influence their behaviour simply because it exists, no matter what is done in its name by the leadership. By the process of perceptual distortion they simply ignore or explain away what is objectionable in party activity; thus the parties' "*being* as well as *acting* as important."[64] The tendency of a father figure to become the symbol of the party reinforced the phenomenon.

If the Engelmann and Schwartz typology of parties[65] is applied to Nova Scotia, the Liberals and Conservatives are broad-based, cadre parties of electoral success with governmental experience. More explicitly, they have a wide measure of support across ethnic, religious, and class lines; their local associations do not have "the populist notion of possessing the right to direct the destinies of the party";[66] they are highly pragmatic and oriented to political success rather than to principles; they are highly pragmatic and oriented to political success rather than to principles; they have governed the province and have provided leadership and decisions on a day-to-day basis, although the Conservatives have acquired most of their experience since 1956. In contrast, the CCF/NDP—the only other party that has had more than a transient existence—falls into the type of "mass" party of principle with a restricted base and no governmental experience.

It can be argued that Nova Scotians would have benefited from experimenting further with a party of the second type. However, the point is surely academic, since the political culture of Nova Scotia almost guarantees that the conditions necessary to bring such a party to power would have to be altogether catastrophic in nature. The existing parties may be a case of Tweedle-Dum and Tweedle-Dee, but nothing yet in the offing challenges their existence. As Lord Bryce said of their American counterparts, they "continue to exist, because they have existed. The mill has been constructed and its machinery goes on turning, even when there is no grist to grind."[67]

The events of the 1960s continued to demonstrate the meaninglessness of party ideology. During these years the Conservative governments of Robert Stanfield and G. I. Smith used $200 million of public money to promote industrial development, and, although they had not intended it, the province found itself the owner of a heavy water plant, a steel mill, and a stereo-television factory. Gerald Regan, the Liberal leader, could say that "Premier Smith is too much of a socialist for me," and the management (or, as the Liberals alleged, the mismanagement) of provincially-owned industries became a major political issue. In fact, it was a prime factor in undermining the Smith government and in bringing the Liberals to power in October 1970.

The 1970s appear to have brought with them a somewhat greater resilience in the political culture, and under conditions of demonstrated need the provincial politicians can, probably more than heretofore, make changes of substance with less likelihood of doing serious political injury to themselves.[68] But only within limits, for when, in 1974, the Royal Commission on Education, Public Services and Provincial-Municipal Relations recommended a radical restructuring of local governments and their functions, it was too potent a medicine for Nova Scotians to take. Change will take place in municipal government but only in a piece-meal fashion within the existing structure. In 1976 the provincial Conservative party gave itself a written constitution for the first time, but, not unexpectedly, its contents did little more than incorporate existing practice and provided only a limited leadership review. All in all, the only significant change in the working of the parties has been that, with the renascence of Conservatism, a one-and-a-half party system has been converted into a genuine two-party system. Yet even it cannot be taken for granted, for with the passing of the Stanfield era, there is at least the possibility that the Conservatives could be seriously weakened and that the Liberal Gerald Regan might establish a mastery over the province no less strong than that of Fielding, Murray, Macdonald, and Stanfield.

Endnotes

[1] See, for example, David Easton, *A Systems Analysis of Political Life* (New York: John Wiley & Sons, Inc., 1965).

[2] See E. E. Schattschneider, "United States: The Functional Approach to Party Government," in *Modern Political Parties*, Sigmund Neumann, ed. (Chicago: The University of Chicago Press, 1956), pp. 194-198.

[3] For a full treatment of early Nova Scotian parties, see M. Gene Morison, "The Evolution of Political Parties in Nova Scotia: 1758-1848" (M.A. thesis, Dalhousie University, 1949).

[4] J. Murray Beck, *The Government of Nova Scotia* (Toronto: University of Toronto Press, 1957), p. 29.

[5] *Colonial Patriot* (Pictou), February 20, 1830 (italics in original).

[6] *Novascotian* (Halifax), October 28, 1830 (italics in original).

[7] Howe to Blanchard, October 26, 1835, quoted in J. Murray Beck, "Joseph Howe: Mild Tory to Reforming Assemblyman," *Dalhousie Review*, XLIV (Spring 1964), 52.

[8] Howe to Falkland, April 3, 1843, Howe Papers, Public Archives of Canada, VI, 39.

[9] Beck, "Howe: Mild Tory," p. 56.

[10] Beck, *Government of Nova Scotia*, p. 80.

[11] Charles Dickens, *American Notes and Pictures from Italy* (London: Macmillan and Company, 1903), p. 18.

[12] J. A. Chisholm, *The Speeches and Public Letters of Joseph Howe* (Halifax: The Chronicle Publishing Company, 1909), I, 361.

[13] *Acadian Recorder* (Halifax), January 20, 1855.

[14] *Sun* (Halifax), April 17, 1861.

[15] Mulgrave to Newcastle, April 3, 1862, *Journals of the Nova Scotia House of Assembly, 1863*, Appendix 11, Civil List, p. 6.

[16] Beck, *Government of Nova Scotia*, p. 111.

[17] *Acadian Recorder* (Halifax), May 9, 1876.

[18] Walter Bagehot, *The English Constitution* (London: Oxford University Press, 1928), p. 8.

[19] *Novascotian* (Halifax), October 6, 1856.

[20] R. MacGregor Dawson, *Report on the Civil Service*, No. XVIII of the *Report of the Royal Commission on Provincial Development and Rehabilitation*, Section 15 (italics in original).

[21] See speech of R. H. Murray as reported in the *Chronicle* (Halifax), September 27, 1933.

[22] Beck, *Government of Nova Scotia*, p. 265.

[23] John Porter, *The Vertical Mosaic: An Analysis of Social Class and Power In Canada* (Toronto: University of Toronto Press, 1965), especially ch. 13.

[24] Beck, *Government of Nova Scotia*, p. 156.

[25] *Ibid.*, p. 157.

[26] *The Week*, XI (January 5, 1894), 126-127.

[27] Some of the material on the Farmer-Labour groups came from the papers of A. A. MacKenzie and D. A. Sutherland written for the seminar in Nova Scotian politics and government at Dalhousie University.

[28] *Herald* (Halifax), January 30, 1920.

[29] *Morning Chronicle* (Halifax), April 15, 1920.

[30] *Ibid.*, July 3, 1920.

[31] *Casket* (Antigonish), July 8, 1920.

[32] *Advocate* (Pictou), July 23, 1920.

[33] C. B. Macpherson, *Democracy in Alberta* (Toronto: University of Toronto Press, 1953), pp. 245-247.

[34] Beck, *Government of Nova Scotia*, p. 169

[35] *Ibid.*, p. 154.

[36] *Ibid.*

[37] *Morning Chronicle* (Halifax), July 8, 1872.

[38] *Ibid.*, January 8, 1872.

[39] C. H. Cahan to John S. D. Thompson, March 28, 1890, Thompson Papers, Public Archives of Canada, Item 12017.

[40] Peter C. Aucoin, "The Conservative Leader in Nova Scotia: Selection and Position in a Minority Party" (M.A. thesis, Dalhousie University, 1966), p. 64.

[41] For details of the campaign see J. M. Beck, "The Electoral Behaviour of Nova Scotia in 1965," *Dalhousie Review*, XLVI (Spring 1966), 29-38.

[42] Angus Campbell, *et al.*, *Elections and the Political Order* (New York: John Wiley & Sons, Inc., 1966), ch. 4.

[43] Beck, *Government of Nova Scotia*, p. 154.

[44] Alan C. Cairns, "The Electoral System and the Party System in Canada," *Canadian Journal of Political Science*, I (March 1968), 75.

[45] *Chronicle* (Halifax), February 22, 1946.

[46] J. M. Beck, "The Nomination of Candidates to Nova Scotia," *Dalhousie Review* XXXVI (Winter 1957), 365.

[47] *Ibid.*, pp. 365-366.

[48] *Acadian Recorder* (Halifax), August 20, 1878.

[49] Aucoin, "Conservative Leader," p. 66.

[50] *Morning Chronicle* (Halifax), October 16, 1896.

[51] Beck, *Government of Nova Scotia*, p. 161.

[52] Some of the material on the four premiers comes from the papers of Mary Ellen Clancey, Allan Dunlop, David Flemming, Frank Hennessey, A. A. MacKenzie, and J. W. O'Brien written for the seminar in Nova Scotia politics and government at Dalhousie University.

[53] Beck, *Government of Nova Scotia*, p. 161.

[54] *Debates and Proceedings of the Nova Scotia House of Assembly*, 1906, p. 114.

[55] Beck, *Government of Nova Scotia*, p. 201.

[56] *Acadian Recorder* (Halifax), April 27, 1885.

[57] *Ibid.*, March 9, 1894.

[58] Beck, *Government of Nova Scotia*, p. 162.

[59] *Ibid.*, pp. 166 and 167.

[60] Joseph Schull, *Laurier* (Toronto: The Macmillan Company of Canada, Ltd., 1966), p. 188.

[61] See Peter Aucoin, "The Stanfield Era: A Political Analysis," *Dalhousie Review*, XLVII (Autumn 1967), 400-409.

[62] *Casket* (Antigonish), April 22, 1954.

[63] See the functions of parties as outlined in Neil A. McDonald, *The Study of Political Parties* (New York: Doubleday & Company, Inc., 1955), pp. 22-6.

[64] *Ibid.*, pp. 21 and 22.

[65] See F. C. Engelmann and M. A. Schwartz, *Political Parties and the Canadian Social Structure*. (Toronto: Prentice-Hall of Canada, Ltd., 1967), pp. 3-14.

[66] *Ibid.*, p. 243.

[67] James Bryce, *The American Commonwealth* (New York: Macmillan Co., 1907), II, p. 24.

[68] J. Murray Beck, "The Evolution of Municipal Government in Nova Scotia: 1749-1973," A study prepared for the Nova Scotia Royal Commission on Education, Public Services and Provincial-Municipal Relations, September 1973, p. 59.

ONTARIO*
The Dominant Province

Norman Penner

By every standard Ontario is and always has been the first and foremost "have" province in Canada. In population, industry, resources, revenues, foreign investment, and even in agriculture, Ontario is ahead of every other province.[1] So bountiful have been Ontario's blessings, that one of its more ebullient premiers was moved to suggest that God must be on his province's team.[2]

Certainly, Ontario has been favored with superb natural advantages: the lower St. Lawrence and Great Lakes waterways, proximity to the most heavily industrialized regions of the United States, abundant mineral resources including the world's largest nickel deposits, some of the best agricultural land in Canada, to mention the most conspicuous.

The manufacturing industry, the commercial centers, the big cities, the large mass of people are mainly crowded into the southwest corner of Ontario from Peterborough to Windsor. Within 300 miles of Toronto, the bulk of Canadian manufacturing takes place.[3] This is due in large measure to the proximity of this region to the U.S. auto industry which duplicated itself in the areas in Canada closest to it, to the easy access the steel industry has had to coal and iron sources,[4] and to the availability of water resources which gave that region an early start in the development of low-cost hydro-electric power.[5] The same area contains rich agricultural land and accounts for most of the farm production in Ontario of hay, feed grain, fruit, vegetables, tobacco, and sugar beets. These basic factors have a cumulative effect, in locating the main commercial, retail, wholesale, and financial institutions close to the manufacturing plants. The rapid and steady growth of population creates a large concentrated market, which in turn attracts more population and industry. In this prosperous belt, there are 14 large urban centers with a combined population of over 4.25 million or 20 per cent of the popula-

* My thanks to Professors Simon McInnes and Graham White for their helpful criticism and suggestions.

tion of Canada.[6] The old rivalry between Montreal and Toronto is definitely being decided in favor of Toronto, the process having been accelerated by the exodus of head offices from Montreal to Toronto during the past decade.

On the other hand, the Ontario North which comprises the vast territory from Sudbury to Manitoba, Hudson Bay, and the Western borders of Quebec, is a region that contrasts sharply with Southern Ontario. It is different in topography, lying inside the pre-Cambrian Shield, abounding in rocky terrain, small mountains, fresh water lakes, and vast forests. Its population, approximately one-tenth of the rest of Ontario, is principally engaged in mineral extraction, cutting and hauling timber, producing pulp and paper, fishing, trapping, tourism, and some agriculture. In all, Ontario is Canada's most complete province economically. Except for oil, natural gas, and coal, which it lacks, Ontario comes close to the description by one of its pioneer industrialists who boasted in 1900 that "Ontario possessed all the essential requirements of a self-sufficient industrial state."[7] Indeed for an industrial state, it also lacks access to the ocean, but as long as Quebec is in Confederation, this deficiency has not been noticed.

These superb advantages, which stem from the accident of location, have been utilized by Ontario politicians and capitalists to give the province economic supremacy if not domination within Confederation. It was the only province that really wanted Confederation, and its spokesmen took the lead in negotiating, cajoling, and ultimately in forcing it on largely unwilling partners.[8] This enthusiasm paid off in the end because Ontario has been "the chief beneficiary" of the Confederation arrangement."[9]

Politically this arrangement gave Ontario "rep. by pop." which it had wanted but could not get under the Act of Union. Ontario was bound to dominate the House of Commons by controlling the largest single bloc of members. The division of powers in the B.N.A. Act was at the outset satisfactory to Ontario, because the centralization of finance, trade, and tariffs, would, in effect, make the economic life of the new Dominion dependent on the business elite of Central Canada, while the provincial control of property assured the Ontario businessmen the opportunity to fashion provincial policies to aid and promote the development of capitalist enterprise.

The close identity between government and business had already been established prior to Confederation. Speaking of the Province of Canada, D. G. Creighton puts it this way:

This would continue to be the guiding "principle" of the Dominion and the *modus operandi* of the province of Ontario. Thus what had been basic to the political culture of the business elite in the Province of Canada became the same for the elites who now dominated the new central government. The two elites, to the extent that they were different, merged in their conception of the national and provincial interest. More often, however, they were the same people seeking and obtaining policies and practices that would advance their cause, from whatever level was appropriate. If there was a dispute between the governments, they learned how to play what one historian calls "the dominion-provincial game,"[11] to their own advantage.

The pattern of government assistance to business after Confederation was established by the munificent financial support given to the CPR: the outright cash and land grants, the handing over of hundreds of miles of existing railroad built by others, tax exemptions, some of them in perpetuity, and monopoly privileges. Innis called this deal an example of "the acquisitiveness characteristic of eastern Canada."[12] It worked to the benefit of capitalists mainly situated in Montreal and Toronto, and it helped make central Canada the economic center of the Dominion.

But the major measure of government assistance to business was the tariff policy adopted by the Canadian Government in 1878. Ontario has been the promoter and chief beneficiary of these high tariffs. Under this protection, Ontario industry grew both in Canadian controlled enterprises and by encouraging American industries to establish branch plants on the Ontario side of the tariff walls. This latter aspect of protectionism has resulted in Ontario having the highest percentage of foreign ownership in practically every category, with manufacturing in the forefront. Non-resident owned companies in Ontario now represent at least 70 per cent of Ontario's corporations taxable income.[13]

Successive Ontario governments did not lag behind the federal governments in assistance to industrial development and the business elite. This program was highlighted by the development of hydro-electric power as a publicly-owned provincial resource. This enabled private industry to purchase electric-power at a far lower cost than would have been possible under private ownership. It was a key factor in the industrial growth and supremacy which Ontario has achieved. The discovering of rich mineral deposits in Northern Ontario and their subsequent exploitation brought forth programs of social overhead capital in the form of provincial railways and highways, as well as legislation to protect and promote these resources. As a result of these measures, this region with its vast storehouse of wealth was subordinated to the control and direction of the Toronto business community which made the North a major hinterland for Southern Ontario's manufacturing and Commerce.[14]

The municipalities too were caught up in the policy of state aid to industrial development, giving enormous concessions and property tax exemptions to new business locating in their jurisdiction. This was particularly true of cities and towns in Southern Ontario, and much of it was directed at attracting American branch plants into that area.[15]

As Innis has pointed out, the development of the American connection, largely through provinces like Ontario and Quebec which had the resources that U.S. industry sought, created "a division" between the pull of the North-South trade and the transcontinental East-West axis on which Canada was founded.[16] Yet as far as Ontario was concerned there was no contradiction, because the province benefitted from both trading patterns.

Its spokesmen successfully fought every attempt made in the rest of Canada to weaken or undermine the policy of high tariffs. But when they wanted an exception to be made to benefit an Ontario industry, they promoted and secured free-trade in automobile manufacturing.

In the federal-provincial arena, Ontario's has been a powerful voice. Under Mowat and for a long time after, Ontario was at the head of the provincial rights movement. In collaboration with Mercier, of Quebec, Mowat initiated the first conference of provincial premiers in 1887 and there laid down 22 grievances which the provinces adopted against the BNA Act and the practices of the federal government vis-a-vis the provinces. Mowat fought for and secured important Privy Council decisions that enlarged the scope of provincial powers, as well as Ontario's boundaries. Yet Ontario jealously guarded its own revenues against any proposal that involved redistribution of taxes from the richer to the poorer provinces. This reached its apotheosis during and immediately after the work of the Rowell-Sirois Commission when the Liberal Premier Hepburn and the Tory leader Drew fought against what the former called making Ontario "the milch cow for the rest of the Dominion."[17] From Frost on, however, the Ontario Government has accepted the policy of tax sharing, albeit with some continuing protest.[18]

In Ontario every class and group known to modern capitalist society is represented: working class in primary and secondary industries, and in construction; farmers, prosperous and marginal; small and big capitalists, financiers, industrialists, entrepreneurs, retail kings, wholesale distributers, rentiers. Among them are further distinctions as between those who are part of the American branch plant network, others whose interests are in Canadian enterprises; some who look to the east-west axis, the original trading pattern in Canada, and those who are motivated by the north-south pull. There are those whose interests do not go beyond the provincial borders, others whose commercial dealings are national and international. A significant portion of the economic rulers of Canada live and work in Toronto; this is now rapidly increasing as a result of the exodus of head offices from Montreal mentioned above.

Within its provincial boundaries, Ontario is therefore a composite cross-section of a highly developed capitalist society, with all the tensions, conflicts, and political divisiveness which flow from that. While Ontario is still only a province, it is the dominant one, vitally concerned with both federal and provincial policies, and it is difficult if not impossible to draw sharp lines between Ontario provincial and federal politics, or between its political culture and the rest of English-speaking Canada which Ontario has influenced so markedly.

The dominant political culture of Ontario—generally accepted over the years by both the provincial Conservative and Liberal parties—is a compendium of ideas, social and political values, and practices which have the force and impact of tradition and history. Ontario—and before Confederation, Canada West and Upper Canada—was the principal environment in which Canadian conservatism developed. This point is made tellingly in a paper by Sidney F. Wise:

> *From the seeds of early Toryism, with its deep hostility towards democratic and republican values, had sprung, by the decade before Confederation, a dominant set of political values of sufficient sharpness and intensity to provide the ingredients for a transcontinental nationalism. From this point of view, it is hardly surprising except to a modern developmentalist, that the chief impulse for national integration should have emerged from the irrational pressure cooker of Upper Canadian politics, and that the leader of the integration movement should have been the true heir of early Toryism, the Conservative John A. MacDonald. In significant respects, Confederation was a triumph of Upper Canadian "imperialism," its slogan "peace, order, and good government," came directly out of the conservative lexicon; and the manner of its attainment, through negotiation and legislation rather than popular ratification, was entirely characteristic of the undemocratic and elitist Canadian political style.*[19]

The undemocratic and elitist political style of Canadian conservatism, has been moderated by the reform tradition in Ontario and by pressures over the years from farm and labor movements, but the essential features remain. A specific Canadian characteristic of conservatism has been the way in which the business elite used the State to further its needs and protect its interests. The Tories from the outset became identified as the spokesmen for "the business conservatives"[20] who were prepared to go to great lengths "in mortgaging the public credit,"[21] and for whom there was "nothing doctrinaire" about the concept of using "public credit to supplement and eventually to replace private capital."[22] The reformers at first fought against this, but after their defeat in 1837, and the ascendancy of Baldwin and particularly George Brown as the reform leaders, opposition to this "conservative tradition" disappeared. The unity between the Ontario Conservatives and the Grits that made Confederation possible, came about as a result of the enthusiasm of both groups over the possibilities of utilizing the public purse to finance the economic development of Canada which as businessmen they would control. George Brown was just as enthusiastic over this prospect as was John A.

Macdonald, when he exclaimed in the *Globe*: "It is an empire we have in view and its whole export and import trade will be concentrated in the hands of Canadian merchants and manufacturers if we strike for it now."[23]

Ontario has been the most British of the provinces and this has been just as much a political as an ethnographic description. Both parties have shared in this orientation in federal and provincial politics, although on balance it would appear that the Conservatives have benefitted more, especially when a particular issue arose in federal elections which had pro-British connotations as was the case of reciprocity in 1911, conscription in 1917, Byng versus King in 1925. The Ontario Conservatives took the lead on these issues and this was reflected in Tory sweeps in Ontario in those campaigns. In the 1911 campaign a number of prominent Liberals in Toronto supported the Conservatives and in 1917 the majority of the Ontario Liberal party headed by its provincial leader N.W. Rowell deserted Laurier and became part of the Unionist coalition. In the federal campaign of 1949 it was the Liberals who benefitted from the cry which the *Toronto Star* emblazoned on its front page: *Keep Canada British! God Save the King*! as a result of the Conservative leader George Drew forming an alliance with the anti-British Camillien Houde, Mayor of Montreal.[24] In provincial politics there was never any serious division on that question. If anything there has been some sharp competition between the two old parties to demonstrate which had the greater devotion to the Crown and the Flag. This was certainly the case at the outbreak of World War II when both Hepburn and Drew outdid each other in proclaiming their loyalty to the Empire, in criticizing Mackenzie King for his alleged lack of an equal amount of patriotic fervor, and in denouncing two university of Toronto professors whose loyalty was said to be in doubt.[25]

Ontario has regarded itself as the mirror of the nation—and in many respects that is true, precisely because of its overwhelming preponderance in all the things that matter for a nation. Ontario identifies nation and province in a way that no other province can or does. Consequently it is not surprising that much of the current regional discontent in Canada is directed at Ontario as well as the federal government, as indeed it has been in the past.[26]

The Ontario Political Party System

Ontario has the only provincial legislature in which the three major federal parties are represented in strength. Wilson and Hoffman in the first edition of this volume, characterized the status of the three parties as follows:

> *The fact is that for nearly thirty years beginning with the election of 1943, the system in Ontario has been characterized by competition between three electorally strong parties, and it has now developed to a stage where any one of them might reasonably expect to take power at the next election. It is in short, a pure three-party system.*[27]

The three elections held since that was written—1971, 1975, and 1977—repeat the general pattern that was begun in 1943 and confirm the statement quoted above.

All provinces started their political lives after Confederation with provincial replicas of the federal parties. Only the Maritimes have retained this two-party system with the original parties. The Liberals and Conservatives of Ontario experienced early challenges to their political monopoly in 1894, 1919, and 1923 from farmer and farmer-labor parties, but except for 1919 when a farmer-labor government was elected, only the Liberals and Conservatives have held office. Yet the appearance of a third party in 1943 which has held a solid base of support ever since, has changed basically the party system in Ontario provincial politics.

Mowat's long tenure in office set a pattern which most subsequent Conservative regimes in Ontario have been careful to follow. He used the provincial budget to aid industrial resource development, he enacted a modest program of reform legislation, he took care to see that there was always something in the pot for the farmers, and he defended and extended provincial powers. The Conservatives under Whitney took office in 1905 and followed that path, with one major innovation. They began the process of making hydro-electric power a public utility and thereby gave the state a positive and interventionist role in the economy. Both parties in their conduct of office were careful, within limits, not to antagonize any significant section of the electorate, although this was not always easy or possible to do. The revolt of the farmer and trade unionists in 1919 was due in the main to national policies and international events in the aftermath of the war.[28]

But that changed during the 1930s. Conservative Premier George Henry followed in Ontario the same kind of policies that R. B. Bennett was using nationally to suppress the unrest, particularly in the labor movement, over depression conditions.[29] In the face of this, Hepburn in the 1934 election campaign made protection of labor's rights a key plank in his election appeal, and as a result won a majority of working class votes in the urban ridings.[30] But in 1937, by attacking the auto workers of Oshawa, he declared war on the new industrial unions being organized under the CIO. His attacks did not succeed in stopping or even slowing down the phenomenal growth of the huge industrial unions, but eventually did result in "the decline of Liberalism in Ontario."[31] The labor votes which had been such an important element in the Liberal victory of 1934 went in 1943 in almost equal numbers to the CCF. It won 34 out of 50 urban ridings.[32] The provincial Liberal Party never recovered from this setback in urban Ontario.

The success of the CCF in winning labor support was not fortuitous. It resulted in part from the conscious decision of an important group of leaders in the Ontario CCF with the support of the national secretary David Lewis, to make organized labor the special target of CCF efforts. While J. S. Woodsworth did not overtly oppose this orientation, neither did he push it. In a letter addressed to Woodsworth in 1938, Herbert Orliffe, Ontario provincial secretary of the CCF stated the problem bluntly. "Ontario", he wrote "has an industrial population greater by far than that of the western provinces.... This makes the question of the Trade Union Movement and its support more important to the CCF in Ontario than in the western provinces.... The CCF has been fairly static in the industrial communities of Ontario.... It needs, therefore, to use the vernacular, 'a shot in the arm' to change the static position into a dynamic one." He went on to discuss the problem involved in winning trade union support. One was that the CCF was identified in the minds of many international trade union officers as a partisan of the national trade unions whose center was the All-Canadian Congress of Labour. If a choice had to be made, according to Orliffe the CCF should choose without any equivocation both of the international unions, the A.F.L. and C.I.O. The CCF should change its constitution to allow trade union affiliation, even if in so doing it ran the risk of having some of these unions entering the CCF with their Communist leadership intact. But Orliffe was quite emphatic in his prognosis that the CCF would never get anywhere in Ontario if it did not link up with the trade union movement.[33]

This did become CCF policy in Ontario. The party sent prominent members into the fledgling CIO unions to help organize them, as the Communists were already doing.[34] It also recruited many of the local officers into the CCF. The dilemma which concerned Orliffe of choosing between the international and national unions, was partially resolved by the merging in 1940 of the CIO's Canadian branches with the national unions in a new trade union federation, the Canadian Congress of Labour, with some help from the CCFers inside both the CIO and the ACCL. This paid off when the 1943 Convention of the CCL endorsed the CCF as its "political arm." It was indeed a significant breakthrough for the CCF on its way to becoming a more labor-based party.

But the success of the CCF during this period was not due entirely to Ontario circumstances. In fact these circumstances owed a great deal to a world upsurge in the expectations of people concerning the shape of the post-war world. As the war against fascism was entering its most crucial phase, with the prospects of victory already dimly visible on the horizon, there began to grow in all the allied countries the demand for a better world, vaguely but persistently identified as socialism, the welfare state, full employment, or the consumer society. The CCF throughout Canada stood to be the political beneficiary of these expectations, with the Gallup polls recording at regular intervals a steady escalation in support for the CCF.

But the CCF was not going to be allowed to remain the sole custodian of the idea of the welfare state. The Conservative Party federally—now renamed the Progressive Conservatives—and most of its provincial parties, and the Liberal government under Mackenzie King entered with dispatch into the domain of social reforms. George Drew fought the 1943 provincial election—his first as Ontario Conservative leader—with his famous 22-point platform, as exuberant in its outlines of a provincial welfare state as anything the CCF had proposed, promising economic and social security from the cradle to the grave. This platform undoubtedly played a role in the Conservative victory, and without it the CCF might well have become the government at that time. But though the platform had been designed in part to accomplish that partisan political aim, the 22 points set Ontario firmly if sometimes slowly on the road to a welfare state. Moreover this platform included proposals for recognizing the rights of labor and codifying them, a far cry from Drew's earlier endorsement of Hepburn's anti-labor position. The 22 points signified that the Ontario Progressive Conservative Party had now taken a new look at the twentieth century and had become a liberal reformist party. It was as though Drew had read Mackenzie King's *Industry and Humanity* which Hepburn had abandoned and King himself had ignored, and by embracing it, set the pace for the federal Liberals to follow!

In his interesting survey of 30 years of uninterrupted Conservative power in Ontario starting with Drew, Jonathan Manthorpe points out that in putting the 22-point program into practice over these years, the successive Conservative governments have stretched perhaps to its limit the allegiance of "their rural power base."[35] Nevertheless they have kept this traditional base while winning new support in the cities, including a large share of the labor vote.

The Progressive Conservatives have been able to stay in power principally by adhering to this program, as the Liberals have done federally. Moreover they have been aided, again like the federal Liberals, by a period of steady growth in the GNP and consequently in government revenues, a prosperity which has favored Ontario more than any other province.

But other factors and devices have been employed to keep the PCs in power. One of the most surprising is the frequency with which they change leaders. It is not usual for a party that is winning elections to do this, yet the Conservative Party has dumped leaders while they were still premiers. We can only speculate as to how much this affected the party's political longevity, or whether it was a thought-out practice, but since it is associated with continued success, Conservative party organizers are entitled to think there is a causal relationship between this practice and the positive results.

Although there have been few major scandals, there have been some, yet these have not affected the stability of the government or its success at the polls. But there have been enough suggestions of conflict of interest to leave a very strong implication that the major business interests on Ontario are supporting the PCs with ample funds to run their campaigns and maintain active year-round organizations in every constituency. Indeed it would be strange if a party that has held power for so long, and with so many favors to dispense, did not get abundant funds from the corporations. They support the party financially because they support its main policies. There has grown up over the 30 years of Tory power a *cameraderie* between the leading government figures and those in business. They mix socially. They are part of the same exclusive clubs and organizations. They are part of the establishment. It is a natural relationship between the dominant business representatives of the financial and industrial interests in the economic heartland of Canada and the dominant political spokesmen represented there.[36]

As a result of over 30 years of one-party domination, certain powerful advantages accrue to the governing party. According to Schindeler's thorough study of Ontario government, "members of the civil service are found equating the Government with the majority party and seeing themselves as servants of the party instead of as servants of the administration."[37] He could have gone further to point out that under a government that has been in power for such a long period, the party itself loses a great deal of its role. It becomes merely a collector of funds, and at the constituency level exists to provide the infantry for election battles.

Schindeler makes a good point when he describes how under prolonged one-party dominance "the principles of parliamentary government which liberalism produced exist now only as myths."[38] One of the most conspicuous examples of this is the "continual shift of power and responsibility away from the legislative branch to the executive."[39] He says this tendency is "more pronounced in this province than at either Ottawa or Westminister."[40]

The political problem which every PC government in Ontario has faced since the emergence in 1943 of a strong social democratic party, is that it cannot allow the initiative on social reforms to pass to the NDP. It has to be "progressive" as well as "conservative," and this problem is particularly acute when the government is a minority one with the NDP as the official opposition. A proper balance between the two characteristics of the Ontario P.C. is however not easy to maintain, particularly in periods of economic downturn, and there are some signs that serious differences in the Ontario P.C. Cabinet have developed on this question. According to a seasoned observer of Ontario politics, Premier William Davis was faced in 1977 "with a growing concern among his Cabinet ministers that the government has drifted too far to the political left in its policies," and that "several ministers are questioning whether they should remain with a government that does not reflect their own philosophical beliefs."[41]

It was partly in response to these pressures that Davis called a new election in June 1977 less than two years after the last one. But while he increased the Tory vote from 36 per cent to 39 per cent and the seats from 51 to 58, he did not get the majority he sought. (See Table I).

The Ontario Progressive Conservative party has a broadly based electoral support coming from all areas of the province and covering the various classes and strata. Yet in the past two elections it has dropped its percentage of the popular vote to below 40 per cent, the only times this has happened since 1943. It has also dropped to below 60 seats. Some of these losses have taken place in Metro Toronto and in Northern Ontario mainly to the benefit of the NDP. Other losses have been in rural areas and these have gone to the Liberal Party. Whether these losses which took place in 1975 and for the most part were repeated in 1977, are signs of a fatal illness setting in for the government remains to be seen. It has now equalled the record set by the Mowat-Hardy-Ross Liberal Governments which ended in 1905 after 34 years in office.

As has been pointed out by Wilson and Hoffman, the longevity of the Conservative regime in Ontario is due in some large measure to the fact that the opposition to it is split between two strong parties—the Liberals and the NDP.

The Liberal Party of Ontario remains for a substantial number of voters, the alternative to the Tories. Its vote increased from 1971 to 1975 from 28 per cent to 34 per cent and then dropped two percentage points in 1977, while at the same time regaining from the NDP its position as the official opposition. In every election in 34 years except the 1943 disaster, the Liberals have received more votes than the NDP and in most cases the difference has been substantial.

The Liberal Party of Ontario owes its position to a number of factors. First of all is its long history and tradition which parallel those of the Conservative Party. It shares with the Conservatives an ideological similarity which distinguishes it in the voters' minds from the NDP. To these voters the Liberals are the "safe" alternative to the NDP. It also shares with the Conservatives a strong rural base which the NDP does not possess. In addition, the Liberal Party has specific areas of strength—

among Roman Catholics and French-Canadians—and a definite lead among certain ethnic groups,[42] although some recent NDP gains among Italian voters have been at the expense of the Liberals.

But the Liberal strength in Ontario provincial politics is due in large measure to its association with the federal Liberals and their success in Ontario. While on some issues the provincial Liberals find it convenient and necessary to take a position different from that of the federal government, they are constantly haunted by the memory of the disaster they suffered when Hepburn did this too often and too much. It may be true that voters prefer a different party in provincial office from the one occupying federal power, or at least a party that will exercise independence vis-à-vis Ottawa, but the federal Liberal party for most of this century, has been the preferred party in Central Canada, and this has rubbed off on its provincial counterparts in Quebec and Ontario.

The CCF and its successor the NDP have changed the character of Ontario provincial politics. They have upset the traditional two-party system, and by so doing exercise a strong influence to bring about social reforms which the two old parties have had to recognize. It could be said, with some truth, that the Conservatives became "Progressive" in response to the upsurge in CCF support in the 1940s.

The CCF-NDP owed its initial electoral success to the support of organized labor. The NDP continues to enjoy that support and this accounts in the main for the strong showing which it makes in urban industrial centres and in the North. Because its main strength is concentrated in relatively few geographic areas, the NDP is able to win a greater seat distribution than the Liberals, for a smaller percentage of the popular vote.

In analysing the 1967 election Wilson and Hoffman made this observation:

> *A careful analysis shows that the most prominent increases in the NDP vote occurred mainly in areas of working-class concentration and that the variation in the size of the increase in these cases was almost entirely accounted for by those which were previously weak drawing level in 1967 with those where the party had already established a commanding position. As urbanization, industrialization, and union organization extend further throughout Ontario, destroying the more traditional influences on the vote of religious affiliation and ethnic origins, this pattern of change may be expected to occur with greater frequency, pointing to a much stronger competitive position for the NDP across the province in the future.*[43]

The following three elections have confirmed that analysis, and produced certain nuances which are important. One is that the NDP support is growing among white collar as well as blue collar workers and this shows up in the increase in the party's fortunes in the Ottawa area. In 1975 and 1977, the NDP won four ridings in Metro Toronto in which the Italian and black working class votes were decisive. In three of these ridings, Italian-speaking candidates of the NDP were elected. The Conservatives continue to get the bulk of the votes of recent immigrants from Central and Eastern Europe, but they are not nearly as decisive in Toronto now as are the Italian, and Caribbean New Canadians.

But in spite of these successes, the NDP leadership confronts the problem of how to go beyond their present support to break through to traditional Liberal and Conservative areas.

It is quite clear that the main NDP leadership believes that it must move closer to the centre, to make it part of what Gerald Caplan, author of the history of the Ontario CCF, and once Stephen Lewis's principal assistant, calls "the political culture's mainstream."[44] His assessment of the "failure" of the CCF is that it was too far removed from this Ontario mainstream. Desmond Morton, author of a recent history of the NDP and likewise an important policy-maker for the party, makes the same criticism.[45]

It is because this perception is held by most of the NDP leaders, that they became so disturbed by the origin and rapid development of the "Waffle" movement within the Ontario NDP. It was thought that the radical stance of the Waffle would alienate public opinion in Ontario, which is essentially conservative. This estimation was not borne out in the ridings where Waffle candidates ran in 1971. They improved the previous vote of the NDP, and the percentage of this improvement over the 1967 vote was on the whole better than most of the NDP candidates. However inasmuch as the Wafflers ran as NDP candidates in only seven ridings in the province, this result may reflect the particular cases of a small sample. Nevertheless those ridings were quite diverse and covered a general cross-section of the urban ridings of Ontario. But at any rate the Waffle is now dead and those of its members who remained in the NDP, have made their peace with Stephen Lewis, Ontario's NDP leader.

After a brief flirtation with nationalism, albeit of a lesser degree than that demanded by the Waffle, the NDP federally and in Ontario, moved away from that issue after the Waffle left the party. The official position of the NDP as contained in the so-called "marshmallow" resolution, moved by David Lewis at the 1969 Winnipeg Convention to offer a moderate nationalist alternative to the Waffle Manifesto, remains on the record. But it is not perceived by the party to be an issue now, and therefore has been put in limbo, perhaps to be revived in the future, if the need arises. The NDP once again has turned its whole attention to the traditional "bread and butter" issues which are felt to be of more concern to the voters than ideological ones. It is impossible to establish a causal connection between the rejection of the Waffle and the increased vote of the NDP in the 1975 elections. At least it did no harm.

Similarly with certain other issues which concern the NDP leadership, they feel that the long standing policy of the party on nationalization, and particularly the resolution it adopted under Waffle pressure to nationalize energy distribution in Ontario, is an acute embarassment, and was detrimental to the NDP in the 1977 elections.

It is out of this same desire to move beyond its present support that the NDP has sought in various ways to demonstrate its independence from the organized labor movement by not identifying too closely with certain issues that the trade union movement considers very important, such as the wage and price guidelines. There is no easy way of judging the effect of trade union support on the NDP either positively by increasing the percentage of workers who vote NDP or negatively in the sense of frightening middle-class voters. Nevertheless the NDP is perceived by most Ontarians to be a labor party or the party most sympathetic to labor's claims, and often an issue does arise which makes it possible to see the effects of this image. Thus when the NDP took up very strongly a campaign to show the connection between poor working conditions in the uranium and nickel mines and the incidence of fatal or serious lung diseases, it had a strong impact on the mining communities in Northern Ontario and was undoubtedly a factor in the increase in votes and seats which the NDP registered in the 1975 election in that region.

Wilson and Hoffman in trying to project the future political situation in Ontario wrote that "the province has entered a transitional phase—where both the electorate and the legislature reflect a more nearly equal division of opinion. . . ."[46] The three elections which followed show a transition—but a very slow one. Nevertheless the opposition vote has moved to 60 per cent and this continues to threaten the future of the Conservative government. Its response to this is to hold to policies that narrow the gap between it and the NDP. It is in the interest of the Conservatives not to provoke any sharp cleavage as they began to do in 1975 when they proposed a cutback in expenditures on social welfare and health. Sensing the impact of this on public opinion, the Conservatives withdrew most of their proposals, but there is no doubt that as the economic situation continues to deteriorate, the PCs will re-introduce similar policies. At that point we may see a breakdown in the centrist positions of the Tory government and a shift to a right-left electoral struggle.

At the same time the difficulty in projecting the immediate future prospects in Ontario provincial politics is compounded by the emergence of an issue which while not provincial, is of great concern to Ontario: the possibility of the separation of Quebec. Ontario which gained the most out of Confederation would be the hardest hit by its breakup, and this is realized by the three parties in the Ontario legislature. From the positions they have enunciated, there are no basic differences in their approach. But as the crisis in Confederation deepens, the provincial government, by projecting itself more and more as an important factor in the debate and negotiations, will benefit politically.

The three-party system is likely to continue for a long period, although the strengths of the different parties will alter. But to project a defeat for the Progressive Conservative Party of Ontario in the next period is as impossible a task as to suggest which of the other two parties will replace it when that happens.

TABLE I

Ontario Election Results 1943-1977

		P.C.s		LIBS		NDP	
	SEATS	%	SEATS	%	SEATS	%	SEATS
1943	90	36	38	31	16	32	34
1945	90	44	66	30	14	22	8
1948	90	41	53	30	14	27	21
1951	90	48	79	32	8	19	2
1955	98	49	84	33	11	17	3
1959	98	46	71	37	22	17	5
1963	108	48	77	35	24	16	7
1967	117	42	69	32	28	26	20
1971	118	44	79	28	20	27	19
1975 dissolution	118		77		22		20
1975	125	36	51	34	36	29	38
1977	125	39	58	32	34	28	33

Endnotes

[1] The latest figures available are for 1973: Ontario with one-third of Canada's population, is first with 51 per cent of the nation's manufacturing, 27 per cent of cash receipts from farming, 35 per cent of construction, 40 per cent of metallic mineral production, has the highest income per capita which is 27 per cent over the national average. (*Canada Year Book*, 1975).

[2] Neil McKenty, *Mitch Hepburn* (Toronto: McClelland and Stewart, 1967), p. 161.

[3] Francois-Pierre Gingras in "Ontario" in Bellamy, Pammett, Rowat, eds. *The Provincial Political Systems* (Toronto, 1976), p. 32.

[4] Pierre Camu, Z.W. Sametz and E. P. Weeks, *Economic Geography of Canada* (Toronto: Macmillan Company of Canada Ltd., 1964), pp. 202-203.

[5] *Ibid.*, p. 140.

[6] Brantford, Burlington, Guelph, Hamilton, Kitchener, London, Niagara Falls,

Oakville, Oshawa, Peterborough, St. Catherines, Sarnia, Metro Toronto, Metro Windsor.

[7] Francis Hector Clergue, quoted in *The Politics of Development*, H. V. Nelles (Toronto: Macmillan Co. of Canada Ltd., 1972), p. 56.

[8] Peter B. Waite, *The Life and Times of Confederation, 1864-1867* (Toronto: University of Toronto Press, 1967), p. 323.

[9] Desmond Morton, in *Government and Politics of Ontario*, Donald C. MacDonald, ed. (Toronto: Macmillan Company of Canada Ltd., 1975), p. 5.

[10] D. G. Creighton, *British North America At Confederation* (Ottawa, 1963), p. 15.

[11] Nelles, *op. cit.* p. 107.

[12] Harold Adams Innis, *A History of the Canadian Pacific Railway* (Toronto: University of Toronto Press, 1971), p. 291.

[13] *Foreign Direct Investment In Canada* (Gray Report) (Ottawa: Information Canada, 1972), p. 23.

[14] H. V. Nelles, *op. cit.* p. 118.

[15] See Thomas William Acheson, *The Social Origins of Canadian Industrialism, A Study In the Structure of Entrepreneurship, 1879-1911.* (Unpublished Ph.D. manuscript, University of Toronto, 1971). Also Tom Naylor, *The History of Canadian Business 1867-1914* Vol. 2 (Toronto: James Lorimer, 1975), pp. 147-149.

[16] Harold A. Innis, "Great Britain, the United States, and Canada" in *Essays In Canadian Economic History*, H.A. Innis and M.Q. Innis, ed. (Toronto: University of Toronto Press, 1956) pp. 394-412.

[17] Neil McKenty, *op. cit.* p. 159.

[18] See Ontario Economic Council and Joe Martin, *The Role and Place of Ontario in The Canadian Confederation* (Queen's Printer, Ont.: 1974).

[19] Sydney F. Wise, "Conservatism and Political Development: The Canadian Case", in *The South Atlantic Quarterly*, Vol. LXIX, No. 2, Spring 1970, pp. 242-243.

[20] S. F. Wise, "Upper Canada and the Conservative Tradition" in *Profiles of A Province*, Edith G. Firth, ed. (Toronto: Ontario Historical Society, 1967), p. 23.

[21] *Ibid.*, p. 29.

[22] *Ibid.*, p. 30.

[23] Quoted in Donald Creighton, *Dominion of the North* (Toronto: Macmillan Company of Canada, 1966), p. 292.

[24] See James Murray Beck, *Pendulum of Power* (Toronto: Prentice-Hall of Canada, Ltd., 1968). pp. 120-135, 136-148, 163-176, 259-275.

[25] Neil McKenty, *op. cit.* pp. 186-229.

[26] See David Jay Bercuson, ed. *Canada and the Burden of Unity* (Toronto, 1977).

[27] John Wilson and David Hoffman, "Ontario—A Three-Party System in Transition" in Martin Robin, ed. *Canadian Provincial Politics* (Toronto: Prentice-Hall of Canada, Ltd., 1972).

[28] Wilson and Hoffman, *op. cit.* p. 212.

[29] See Desmond Morton, "Aid to the Civil Power: The Stratford Strike of

1933" in *On Strike*, Irving Abella, ed. (Toronto: James Lorimer, 1974), pp. 79-91; also, Neil McKenty, *op. cit.*, p. 49.

[30] Gerald L. Caplan, *The Dilemma of Canadian Socialism* (Toronto: McClelland and Stewart, 1973), p. 67.

[31] Irving Abella, "Oshawa 1937" in *On Strike*, I. Abella, ed. (Toronto: James Lorimer, 1974), p. 125.

[32] G. Caplan, *op. cit.* pp. 104-105.

[33] Herbert Orliffe to J. S. Woodsworth, M.P., January 31, 1938. (In *MacInnis Papers*, Special Collections, University of British Columbia.)

[34] See I. M. Abella, *Nationalism, Communism and Canadian Labour* (Toronto: University of Toronto Press, 1972).

[35] Jonathan Manthorpe, *The Power and the Tories*, (Toronto: Macmillan Company of Canada Ltd., 1974), p. 9.

[36] There are interesting examples of this in Manthorpe's book, and in Neil McKenty's biography of *Mitch Hepburn* we see how this worked when the Liberals were in power.

[37] F. F. Schindeler, *Responsible Government in Ontario* (Toronto: University of Toronto Press, 1969), p. 265.

[38] *Ibid.*, p. 260.

[39] *Ibid.*

[40] *Ibid.*, p. 261.

[41] Jonathan Manthorpe, *Toronto Star*, January 14, 1977.

[42] Wilson and Hoffman, *op. cit.* p. 218.

[43] Wilson and Hoffman, *op. cit.* p. 234.

[44] Gerald L. Caplan, *op. cit.* p. 68.

[45] Desmond Morton, *NDP: The Dream of Power* (Toronto: A. M. Hakkert Ltd., 1974). See the "Foreword" by Gordon S. Vickert, Secretary, New Democratic Party of Ontario, pp. v-vi.

[46] Wilson and Hoffman, *op. cit.* p. 238.

PRINCE EDWARD ISLAND
Big Engine, Little Body

Frank MacKinnon

Prince Edward Island has one of the largest governments in the world and this fact determines the nature of its party politics. The province is 140 miles long and from 3 to 35 miles wide, and its population is 110,000. Yet is has a lieutenant-governor, a premier, a cabinet of 10, a legislature of 32, a chief justice and 6 other supreme court justices and 3 provincial court judges, and all the fashionable government departments, boards, and commissions. The number of politicians and civil servants per population, per square mile, and per dollar earned or spent is immense.

In this sense the Island reflects Canada as a whole, for the nation has 11 sets of governmental institutions to handle the affairs of only 24 million people. In some parts of the world governments of similar size would be sufficient for several hundred million people.

Prince Edward Island is the smallest partner in a huge federation, and, like Tasmania in Australia and Rhode Island in the United States, it is relatively so small that it is easy to question whether or not it should be a separate province. Size is not the major issue, however, in assessing political, economic, and social units, especially when the unit concerned is a distinct geographic entity with a tradition of its own. There is no evidence that man has been any happier or life more fruitful in very large units than in very small ones. And little places have their own role to play and their own characteristics to develop among the varied international, national, and local political organizations designed to administer the affairs of men. The politics of Prince Edward Island illustrates, not so much public life in miniature, as the staging of a large production in a tiny theatre. It has played for over two centuries and, if the plot is complicated and the price high, both participants and spectators have had a grand time.[1]

The Development of Parties

Prince Edward Island's politics have been lively since its government was established in 1769. The first party activities were the result of personal and group rivalry in government, church, and militia. The population was only 271 when the government was set up, yet right from the start officials vied for what little power and influence there was. Churches struggled for ascendancy over each other, and the militia sought glory in an establishment where a shot was never fired in anger. The families of officials wanted to translate favorable connections in the mother country or political position in the colony into social prestige and dynastic distinction. People soon sorted themselves into political, denominational and social categories, and, because these categories were too numerous for a small and isolated colony, they exaggerated their own importance and quarrelled bitterly. The resulting turmoil threatened the very existence of the colony.

Another source of party politics was the land question. The British government, when it took over the Island from the French in 1763, had no definite plans for its administration. After much discussion and a survey, the authorities divided the Island into 67 lots and distributed them to persons who had some claim on the Crown. These landlords were expected to bring out settlers and develop their holdings: in return they would receive "quit rents" from the settlers. This scheme hampered the Island's development for a century. Most absentee land proprietors were unwilling or unable to do much for their distant holdings; the settlers were not secure on land they did not own and often were unable to pay rent for it or unwilling to improve it. The settlers had all the problems of homesteading without the stimulus of ownership. As a result the Islanders early developed the habit of looking to distant authorities for action and money.

By 1800 group rivalries and land problems were the source of most political activity. The first organized political party, called the Club of Loyal Electors, appeared in 1810. Led by J. B. Palmer, who held several political offices, and joined by a number of American Loyalists, it was organized to oppose the proprietors and gain control of the Assembly at election time. The party had branches throughout the colony and held meetings to rally supporters and promote discussion on public issues, particularly the land question. Palmer was a friend of Governor J. F. W. DesBarres and was therefore able to exercise influence. Some officials were suspicious of the group, however, and, as a result, DesBarres instructed Attorney General Charles Stewart to make a report on it. Stewart reported that the group was a "self-created permanent political body ... for the purpose of controlling the representation of the people in the House of Assembly, as well as the appointment of public officers.... This same society have had the temerity of more than insinuating that they could procure a dissolution of the General Assembly of the Island, whenever it suited their views." Stewart concluded that a group with such revolutionary ideas "is highly illegal and unconstitutional and ... ought to be discountenanced and suppressed."[2] The Loyal Electors stirred up considerable interest, but lost much of their effectiveness when DesBarres retired in 1813. Governor C. D. Smith would not tolerate them and they were forced to work secretly. The party then became just another faction, unorganized and with shifting platforms and personnel.

The conflicts involved in the relations between Governor, Executive Council, Legislative Council, Legislative Assembly and courts which were common to all the colonies were in full operation in Prince Edward Island during the struggle for responsible government from 1830 to 1851. The Assembly was kept in the background in its early years, partly because the other institutions wished to retain their powers and partly because the Assembly took a long time to attract enough able members to exert any influence. Organized party activity in the Assembly, as distinct from early temporary liaisons centered around current grievances, developed after 1832 when the Assembly advocated separation of the Executive and Legislative Councils, inclusion of members of the Assembly in the executive Council, regular sessions of the Assembly (which had been called together only at the will of the lieutenant-governor), and respect from other institutions for the traditional rights and privileges essential to any parliament. These reforms were encouraged by the Colonial Office, but several governors and the family compacts kept delaying their enforcement. After the two Councils were separated in 1839 and two members of the Assembly were appointed for the first time to the Executive Council, reform leaders proceeded to the real issue of responsible government—the ultimate control of public affairs, especially finance, by elected members of the Assembly instead of the governor and his advisers.

The alignment of politicians into conservative and liberal or reform parties took place in much the same way as in the other colonies. There was no outright rebellion, but each year the sessions of both houses became increasingly bitter as each side became organized. Local officials spared no accusations or strong language in reporting the activities of their opponents to the Colonial Office. Even the governor was rebuked by Gladstone for using "sarcastic and contemptuous language," instead of "that calm and measured tone" necessary to official business.[3] Deadlock between executive and legislature, the refusal of supply, and rising public support for the reformers, together with instructions to the governor from the Colonial Office which ordered reform, led to the implementing of responsible government in 1851 and the assumption of office by the Liberals under George Coles. This was the first government to take office because it had the confidence of the Assembly.

Prince Edward Island got responsible government later than the other colonies because her government and legislature did not include a sufficient number of able men. This lack was evident in both the Executive and Legislative Councils where family connections and denominational representation were obvious determinants in appointments. Governor Ready had reported in 1827 that there was no one of wealth, talent, respectability, weight, or consequence in the upper chamber. There was little improvement by 1845 when Governor Huntley showed open contempt for members of the Assembly and their capacity for public affairs.[4] Nevertheless reform could not be prevented and the decisive factor in granting it to the Island was the example of reform in the other colonies.

Events soon proved, however, that even in 1851 the Island was not ready for responsible government. Political turmoil, legislative chaos, and bad management resulted in incredible governmental spectacles from 1851 to 1873. In that period there were no less than 12 governments, and the province was in a continuous state of electioneering. Public careers were brief, so brief that, because the title of "honourable" was then given for life to cabinet members, the number of citizens with that title reached scandalous proportions. Competent men were discouraged from entering politics by the upheaval, while the main cause of it was the lack of able leaders.

The issues were also a major contribution to the political troubles. Denominational struggles were the chief problem because they introduced so much bitterness into politics. The control of the schools by churches and clergy, the allocation of public funds to denominational institutions, the teaching of the Bible in the classroom, the incorporation of the Orange Lodge, and clerical interference in political matters were regular subjects of legislative wrangling and public discussion. As a result of the acrimony involved, they were the main issues that toppled governments, ended political friendships, and ruined personal careers. Less emotional, but still troublesome, were discussions of land reform, especially proposals for the confiscation of proprietors' estates. The rights of both landlord and tenant were vigorously championed and riots and raids were common. As Confederation approached, questions of union and independence kept the political pot boiling furiously. There were controversial issues in all the colonies, of course, but within the narrow confines of Prince Edward Island they were particularly intense.

These problems clearly affected the party system. When responsible government first began public men were divided for a short while into "liberals" and "conservatives." There was an opportunity to develop these groups into alternating governments and oppositions formed on teamwork and personal association. But disputes over denominationalism, land reform, and union cut through party lines to such an extent and in such varying ways that it was impossible for any leader to hold enough of his colleagues together long enough to form a workable party. Both sides were loose and shifting associations of interest groups based on weak and temporary compromises. In this period when most colonies were developing industry and communications Prince Edward Island was instead over-occupied with politics. The resulting bad government hampered the growth of the province for decades and was a legacy which future administrations never overcame and which many of them simply continued.

Church politics and union issues became so severe in 1870 that a one-party government could not be formed because there were no stable parties. J. C. Pope finally put together a coalition by getting its members to sign a pledge to drop these issues; in addition he focussed official and public attention on an interesting diversion—a railroad. The Prince Edward Island Railroad was supported with enthusiasm and it was built on a grand and expensive scale with extensions, branch lines, and patronage to please everyone. This escape was an illusion, however, because the Island could not afford a railway. Money ran out, debentures were unsaleable, and the Island went bankrupt. The old issues were soon revived, temporary political associations dissolved, and government disintegrated. The only alternative was Confederation.

When the Island entered Confederation in 1873 its "liberal" and "conservative" parties were little more than temporary debating teams with convenient names. Various attempts were made to organize them; John A. Macdonald personally contacted his local friends and Alexander Mackenzie was able to attract all the new province's M.P.s to his side during the Pacific scandal crisis. It appeared that federal politics would stimulate local party stability. Fresh controversy broke out in 1876, however, when the school question split the legislature in two: Protestants formed a coalition government, and Roman Catholics formed the opposition. Politicians soon realized that this alignment was a source of chaos; after the passing of the Public School Act of 1877 they drifted back once more into liberal and conservative groupings.

From this point the firm development of modern political parties on Prince Edward Island began. Two of the disrupting issues had been settled; union by Confederation, the land question by the Land Purchase Act of 1875 and accompanying arbitrations and federal financial assistance. Denominational problems were eased temporarily by the Public School Act and by the simple expedient of covering them up. Larger issues appeared as Island politicians participated in national affairs. Provincial Liberal and Conservative parties soon realized that, with the many diversities in the electorate, they could not rigidly reflect one viewpoint but would have to represent the varying viewpoints of those whose votes they sought. They also wanted close associations with federal politicians in order to obtain concessions and patronage. Consequently, the development of local parties followed closely the growth of their federal counterparts. This association with federal parties has had one remarkable result: the Island has always elected governments of the same political allegiance as the government in Ottawa.

The Political Setting

Prince Edward Island parties function within a gigantic governmental structure and relatively small constituencies. The legislature consists of 32 members (increased from 30 in 1965), representing 16 two-member constituencies. The cabinet comprises 10 members (increased from 9 in 1966). Thus almost one-third of the legislative branch is made up of executive members—a large portion by any standard of administration. If the party in power were to have a bare majority, cabinet ministers would comprise no less than ten-sixteenths of the government side of the house. The cabinet therefore dominates both the caucus and the legislature, and a larger than normal amount of debate and decision-making takes place, in fact if not in form, in the cabinet rather than in the legislature. Each opposition party has complained bitterly about this, and the consequent lack of information and discussion—for example, the disputes about developing industry in Georgetown from 1965 to 1968 and economic improvement plans since 1968.

The 16 constituencies, necessarily small in area, vary in the number of voters from 7,000 in fifth Queens to 1,500 in fifth Kings in the 1974 election. This arrangement encourages highly localized contests and concentration on minutiae which would go unnoticed in larger areas. The paving of an extra mile of road, the giving of some benefit to a family, or the recognition of the services of a party worker—always factors anywhere—can easily become important issues in a tiny constituency. The pressures of his voters on a candidate are very great, and without question they limit his perspective both when he is a candidate and when he holds office.

Politics is carried on, therefore, with a high degree of informality and politicians are much closer to the people than are their counterparts elsewhere. It is not difficult for members of the legislature to maintain a substantial acquaintance among the voters. They are never more than a short drive from their constituencies and can attend local functions readily. House members who are lawyers, doctors, and merchants maintain political contact through their professional occupations because politics on the Island is generally only a part-time occupation—even for members of the cabinet. It is difficult to attend many functions on the Island without seeing at least one member, and the attendance of cabinet ministers is common.

In Prince Edward Island there is great interest and participation in the activities of party organizations. Everyone knows everyone else in a given area and the voters are labelled house by house and one by one. With few exceptions all citizens are interested and most of them know, or have met or seen, the candidates and the party officials. This intimacy affects party workers and supporters in three ways. Some view party activities as a normal adjunct to the business of government; these people keep Island politics going because they understand the significance of what they are doing. Others regard politics as great sport. It is their hobby; they have a good time. They approach it in much the same way as they would any other contest. They work at it assiduously, mainly at election time, but they do not take it too seriously. Still others take local politics too seriously. Being a Liberal or Conservative is of almost religious significance; anyone who is not with them is a political heathen. The first category gets the business done. The second provides the interest and color. The third, influential in small contests, is always a source of problems and a barrier to progress. One troublesome result of intense politics is, said one authority in 1970, "the easy way people in one party come to believe evil things about people in the other party. Good citizens are distrusted, disbelieved, discredited, disclaimed and disarranged just because they belong to the opposite party," which attitude is "one of the main reasons for the lack of progress in the province."[5]

The significance of effective organization is increased by the relatively small number of voters and the small majorities. There is an average of about 2,000 voters for each member of the legislature, and majorities of less than 50 are common. Workers and candidates cannot take for granted the will of the constituents, even to the point of not calling on a family, neglecting to speak in a district, or ignoring a request for patronage. In one sense this intimacy is democracy at its best because the wishes of the "grass roots" readily find expression. In another sense it is a serious drawback to the Island's government because it is easy for a politician to make unwise decisions and unrealistic commitments in an effort to secure the small majority. Under these circumstances powerful or selfish interest groups can impose their will with devastating effects.

Party organizations therefore feel they must make many concessions to pressure groups. Denominational ones are the most powerful. They are feared the most because of the bitterness that can occur in a small area, and because of the tendency of ecclesiastical interests to precipitate or paralyze official action by threatening to intervene in controversial matters and to thwart the democratic process by use of "gentlemen's agreements" rather than open discussion. Church rivalries are obvious in all Island affairs and whether an individual is Catholic or Protestant is taken far more seriously than in most other provinces. The school system divides many citizens from Grade One, and the parish, social, and political systems maintain the division. In party organizations the result is obvious in the selection of officers, the awarding of patronage, and the appointment of judges and senators. The "turn" is evident in almost all appointments—now a Catholic, now a Protestant. This practice, on top of political patronage, has a damaging effect on government, because it often supersedes qualifications. For example, appointment of an official is often made from only a quarter of the persons eligible after political and denominational affiliations have been considered. The weak appointments that result have been depressingly obvious for many years.

Another powerful, but far more constructive, pressure group is the agricultural organization, such as the Federation of Agriculture, the Women's Institutes, and associations concerned with various activities such as potato growing and dairy farming. The dominance of agriculture on the Island assures its importance in both parties. The dependence of other industries on agriculture prevents a large gap from developing between their interests and those of the farmers.

It is surprising that the small size of the province and its constituencies and the close relationships among its social and political agencies have not minimized the principle of representation of interest groups in public organization. On the contrary this principle has been emphasized to the point where it has become undemocratic and grossly inefficient. The problem of pressure groups is evident throughout the province; they insist on their "rights" in the tiniest constituency and the smallest committee. Patronage and public works are carefully distributed by county and by district. Excellent appointments and projects are often sacrificed because authorities are prevented from taking an Island-wide view of their responsibilities. For example, it is difficult to get local authorities to understand that a major concentration of capital and effort for one industry in one area is often more productive for all than their piecemeal distribution over a number of districts. The latter results in a host of inefficient small economic projects and no really effective industry. Most governmental projects in the province are difficult enough to carry out, but it is even more difficult to rally general support for them from the numerous interests that oppose them or insist on some compensatory advantage. In fact political as well as financial costs are attached to almost everything the Island government does and much provincial politics is devoted, not to actual government, but to the interplay that results from over-emphasis of the representation principle.

This over-emphasis sharpens the acquisitive instincts of Islanders.

The politics of acquisition and the consequent maneuvering are common in all federal systems. It is quite natural for the smallest partner to demand its share and to be determined to have the privileges enjoyed by the larger partners. The Island has acted in this manner in its federal-provincial relations and to an even greater extent in its internal politics. The efficiency of government depends substantially on the way it makes use of the ability, money, effort, and time that society can reasonably devote to public business. Only a limited proportion of these resources can reasonably be devoted to the mechanics of administration and politics; the major part must go to the services necessary to society. Herein lies one of the serious problems of Island politics: because the mechanics of politics is so extensive in the Island's large system, the process of "getting" for limited advantage too often displaces the process of "doing" for the benefit of all. Every district that wants something because another district has something, every denomination that will not tolerate an advantage to another unless it gets a favor, and every organization and individual that puts a price on its citizenship add to the getting process and too often subtract from the necessary doing process. For example, the money spent on the construction of many miles of unnecessary paved highway would have paid for many valuable services that the Island has been forced to do without; and the appointment of people of doubtful competence to responsible positions merely because they belonged to a particular denomination or came from a particular district has deprived the Island of much ability and cost it many mistakes.

The high cost of politics on the Island has one compensation. Everyone is interested and the opportunities for participation and patronage are numerous. The large number of organizations in the province provide many forums for political discussion and stepping stones to public life Governmental officials and institutions are not distant phenomena seen only by a small portion of the citizenry; they are in the immediate neighborhood. Gilbert and Sullivan described this kind of situation in "The Gondoliers":

> *"And Party Leaders you might meet*
> *In twos and threes in every street*
> *Maintaining, with no little heat,*
> *Their various opinions."*

In one sense officials suffer the disadvantage of working in full view of everyone, but in another sense there is a very real and strong link between government and citizens which is a source of the pride and interest without which a democracy cannot thrive. There are difficulties no doubt—

> *"Yet the duties are delightful, and the privileges great;*
> *But the privilege and pleasure*

That we treasure beyond measure
Is to run on little errands for the Ministers of State."

Party Organization

The intimacy of the political setting in Prince Edward Island makes party organizations highly personal. There is, therefore, a tendency to interpret the rules to conform to local practice and to the circumstances of the moment. If no one is interested in an annual meeting it can be permitted to lapse; an ineffective committee can be ignored; a rule can be interpreted with elasticity to permit or justify an action.

Both parties have provincial organizations. The officers are chosen, if possible, from the leaders of the district associations. An annual meeting is held but it is usually of interest only just before an election or when it is combined with a convention to select candidates. Both parties have women's organizations but their functions are largely social; the ladies make their major contributions through the main associations. Recently young people's political clubs have flourished with the rising interest of youth in public affairs and especially with the lowering of the voting age to 18 in 1967. There are student political clubs in the university and in some larger high schools. It is already an interesting question whether a young person, who joins a club because his friends do regardless of his family's political affiliation, may change his mind when he becomes older.[6]

Both parties changed their intermediate organizations after the federal redistribution of 1964. The old Prince, Queens, and Kings county associations were replaced by associations for the new federal districts: Egmont, Malpeque, Hillsborough, and Cardigan. These associations operate for both federal and provincial elections and are expected to include representatives of provincial districts; indeed, the Conservative constitution makes this mandatory in the selection of directors.

Most of the business of the provincial organizations is handled by an executive committee consisting of the officers, past presidents, representatives of provincial district and federal constituency organizations, and representatives of the women's and youth groups. Other committees handle special details such as finance, membership, and publicity. This apparatus works with sporadic efficiency. By and large it is lively before and quiet after an election and it is much more active when the party it supports is in power. Each of the district and constituency groups has a similar organization.

The poll organization is the basic unit of the party machinery and it maintains the closest contact with the voters. There are 292 polls in 250 polling divisions on Prince Edward Island. For each poll organization there is a poll committee with a chairman and secretary and from 5 to 20 members (depending on the size of the poll), all selected by an advertised annual meeting of party members in the poll. The duties of this unit include organizing party workers at election time, scrutinizing voters' lists, canvassing voters, arranging transportation to the polls, and assisting the candidates. The organization also sends delegates to meetings and conventions of the party and shares in the work of the larger groups. All poll organizations are active at election time; between elections some are dormant, but some keep busy by maintaining contacts with members and voters, handling patronage and distributing information.

The most spectacular work of the party organizations is in the planning and staging of ordinary conventions, leadership conventions, annual meetings, and political meetings. A large portion of the constitution of each party is devoted to these gatherings, which provide the best illustration of how the party machinery works.

The party convention is both the focal point for publicity, celebration, and propaganda and the instrument for the selection of candidates. It has always been the occasion for rousing party expressions of self-confidence and, occasionally, high jinks. Today, however, with the attentions of television, radio, and the press, it has also become a highly organized and efficient machine for impressing the public as well as for getting business done. Conventions must he held often enough to serve these purposes and yet infrequently enough to allow party enthusiasm and public interest to accumulate. The district conventions are usually held in the months immediately prior to an expected election. The provincial convention is held when a party leader must be chosen, when a leader needs an expression of confidence, or when the benefits of a major publicity effort are required.

At the 32 district conventions which take place within a few weeks party leaders speak on the issues of the day, extol one another's virtues, and receive votes of confidence from their supporters. Attending the conventions are chairmen of committees, five-man delegations from poll meetings who vote on official matters, and other party members who participate in the business and enjoy the proceedings. Resolutions are passed and sent to appropriate authorities. Party leaders often make special announcements in order to get a headline in the press reports of the proceedings, which inevitably attract less attention as the many conventions take place. The effectiveness of these gatherings depends on the ability of the organizers, on whether the constituency concerned is sure, doubtful, or a lost cause, and on the extent of the contest for nominations.

Candidates for nomination are subject to the judgment of officers, chairmen, and other voting delegates who were previously selected by poll meetings. The five delegates from each poll are selected sometimes without a contest, perhaps from the members of the poll committee, and sometimes after bitter rivalry among supporters of particular candidates for nomination. The "packing" of delegations is common and persons working on behalf of candidates must watch the proceedings carefully from the very first poll meetings. At the convention the delegates are assiduously wooed by the candidates and their supporters. The delegations sometimes vote as a body; usually, however, they vote as individuals.

The procedure at conventions varies widely and is often informal. Nominations can be made from the floor or by a nominating committee. Movers and seconders sometimes make elaborate speeches and sometimes they content themselves with a simple declaration. Those named accept with alacrity and pride, although occasionally someone who is nominated as a tribute gracefully declines. If there are only two nominees (perhaps the sitting members) there is no contest and they receive acclamations. If more than two persons are named there are one or more ballots, with the person receiving the lowest number of votes dropped at each one. The winners are declared elected to resounding cheers, the losers spring forward to declare the vote unanimous, and the wives of the winners are led up to the podium for congratulatory embraces. This last procedure, which was not common in earlier days when wives usually stayed home or at the back of the hall, developed slowly as women's interest in politics increased and as press and television photographers came to play an important role in covering conventions. Eventually every political meeting included women as officials and delegates. In 1970, the first woman was elected to the legislature, and in 1974 two were successful. A woman was appointed to the cabinet in 1970 to be followed by another in 1974.

The provincial convention brings together federal and provincial sitting members, defeated candidates, members of the executive, and district, constituency, and poll delegates from all parts of the province. It is a rousing affair held in a coliseum of appropriate size. The media and the public take a lively interest and music, entertainment, decorations, and refreshments entice and please the crowd. It is the party's biggest opportunity, short of an election, to relay its messages to the public, and also the chance for candidates to vie for the leadership.

This procedure replaced the practice followed in Island politics until 1950 of always selecting party leaders in the caucus. Whether a party was in power or in opposition, its sitting members in the legislature made the selection, even at times when this group was very small. Occasionally there was an obvious successor to a retiring leader, and the transition was made with ease. Often there were several aspirants and much maneuvering took place in the limited confines of the caucus. Indeed one man's vote often determined the winner, as it did in 1943 when J. W. Jones secured the Liberal leadership after a bitter contest in which the retiring

Premier, T. A. Campbell, opposed his selection.[7] Although the winner was never repudiated by the party, the process by which he won often caused dissatisfaction. This occurred particularly with respect to commitments he might have had to make to individual colleagues in the process of securing support, to the fact that the party had little or no voice in making the choice, and to the sitting members' advantage over other possible candidates. The caucus occasionally found it difficult to support a controversial leader whom, perhaps, one member might seek to undermine, or to dispose of a leader whose effectiveness was over and who would not resign.

Whatever the shortcomings of the convention, its voice is clear and final. Such a voice was necessary in 1950 when the Conservatives held their first convention to select a leader (R. R. Bell replaced W. J. P. MacMillan) and in 1961 when the Liberals held their first convention to confirm the leadership of the incumbent (A. W. Matheson was challenged by J. W. MacNaught). The mere demand for a convention forced a decision to be made on a difficult party problem—in the one case delayed retirement and in the other internal rivalry. Although the problems remained, the leadership was clearly designated by the convention, something the caucus was unable to do. Nevertheless, W. J. P. MacMillan never seemed to accept the fact that R. R. Bell had replaced him. The result was disunity resulting from divided leadership and the ability of the Liberals to play one Conservative faction against the other in the legislature. Both parties now follow the practice of selecting their leaders by convention. Premier A. B. Campbell was the first Liberal leader and Opposition Leader Melvin McQuaid the fourth Conservative leader to be so selected. It is significant that Mr. Campbell had been in the legislature for just a few months and W. R. Shaw and his successor George Key were without a seat when they were chosen party leaders, while Mr. McQuaid had been a member of the House of Commons.

The constitution of the Prince Edward Island Liberal Association now provides that the Executive Committee of the party shall call a leadership convention "whenever it becomes necessary to select a Provincial Leader" and a provincial convention "at such time and place as the circumstances may warrant," in any case at least once every four years. Voting delegates comprise all former and sitting Liberal members of the Senate, House of Commons, and provincial legislature, "non-elected" Liberal candidates in the most recent federal and provincial elections, the president and officers of the provincial, constituency, women's, young Liberals', and university Liberals' organizations, the presidents of the district associations, and five poll delegates from each official polling division. The Executive Committee is specifically charged with the arrangements of the convention.

The Conservative party constitution is in some ways more flexible.

For instance it is not specific about procedure for leadership conventions although the actual procedure is similar to that of the Liberals. Conservative voting delegates include candidates nominated for a coming election; only if there are no such candidates are the candidates of the last election included.

The formal provisions for holding conventions tell only part of the story. No one expects the clarion call of untrammeled democracy to come out of such gatherings. In preceding weeks there is much manipulating of opinion and bargaining for commitments, as leadership candidates work tirelessly in the glare of publicity. In a close contest every sentence in a nomination speech, every handshake, every interview with the press, and every conversation in a back room, may contribute to victory or defeat. Nothing must be taken for granted. Skulduggery must be expected and countered; one candidate lost by a narrow margin in a recent convention because some of the voting delegates supporting him were taken "out back" by his opponents and treated with refreshments until after the ballots were cast. Most of all, however, the candidate must present an image for the occasion that will impress the viewers on television and the multitude in the hot, noisy auditorium for whom he must perform in the demanding glare of spotlights and with the restricting limitations of microphones.

There are two kinds of political meetings that take place at election time. One is the great rally of party faithfuls and interested or curious citizens in a district where there is a lively contest. At this type of meeting a battery of prominent speakers and crowd-pleasing entertainment are provided in a packed hall as background for the exhortations of candidates and enlightenment of public opinion. The other kind of meeting is the much quieter, perhaps dreary, gathering, held in an area that the party has given up for lost. Speakers and candidates know there is little cause for enthusiasm in such an area and listeners must be coaxed to attend. The speeches and the routine are much the same in all meetings. Those who must accompany candidates expect to hear the same ideas repeated again and again, and the press reporters generally find it increasingly difficult, as the campaign progresses, to glean some fresh news for their readers.

These kinds of meeting are comparatively modern on the Island. Until 40 years ago the joint political meeting was common. Representatives of both sides filled the halls to capacity to hear opposing candidates debate the issues of the day under the watchful eye of an independent chairman. These were lively meetings highly charged with excitement and always interesting and newsworthy. Candidates had to speak in the presence of their opponents who had a chance to present the other side of the arguments. The candidates' supporters cheered and the opponents' supporters booed; hecklers tested speakers' patience and their ingenuity.

Today's meetings present only one side and cheering predominates. While the older, more rowdy, meetings favored the debaters and penalized the shy candidates, it can be argued that democracy has lost something important in the change.

Another major factor in party activities is the altered position of the newspapers. Until recently *The Guardian* was Conservative and *The Patriot* Liberal. Each reported on platforms, candidates, and meetings in a partisan manner, and its editorials praised one side and criticized the other. Those who read only one paper got a slanted interpretation of political events; but those who read both got not only both sides of issues but also an enormous amount of news because there was stiff competition between the papers. In addition, the newspapers provided continuous practice in assessing the relative significance of conflicting opinions. Today the papers are owned by one syndicate. Advertising displaces the long reports and speeches. Television competes for the political news. The biased thunder has gone from the editorials. *The Guardian* is now independent with a Conservative slant; *The Patriot* is independent with a Liberal slant; it takes a major issue to increase the slant. Whether or not this change has been a good one for the newspapers' readers is debatable. Certainly for the parties it has removed a formidable weapon for defending virtue and fighting political opposition.

An important factor in all this political activity is the limited number of citizens served. No other group of 110,000 people in Canada has so many party gatherings and so much political machinery. Socially there is no question of the amount of fun Islanders have with their politics. Psychologically party politics offers a release for the Islanders' energies and their combative instincts. It brings Islanders together as few other activities can do, and continuously reminds them of their responsibilities as citizens. It is also evident, however, that, as often happens where there is too much of a good thing, politics is overdone on the Island to the detriment not only of other activities but of politics itself. While recognizing the advantages of the political machinery, we should now examine the issues with which it deals and the efficiency with which it operates.

The Political Issues

No issues clearly divide the Liberals and Conservatives in Prince Edward Island. No theory, no policy, and no political action can be identified with either party; each has advocated and opposed everything, depending on whether it was the party in power or in opposition at the time.

Third parties have played no significant part in Island politics. Independent, Progressive, CCF or NDP candidates have never posed a threat and have no effective organization. With one exception (J. A. Dewar, who sat as an Independent from 1919 to 1923), no one from any of these groups has ever won an election and almost all have lost their deposits. Agriculture has always been the dominant industry. The wishes of the rural population have been major factors in party strategy, and the farm vote is well represented in both main parties. There is no big business and industrial labor is not numerous. Consequently there has been no area of political interest with which third parties could identify themselves. Because both parties have appealed to the same electorate for a century and the issues debated in the legislature have changed little in that time, variations in party politics have not been encouraged.

The issues that the parties dispute in elections and in debates in the legislature, that cause most maneuvering within the parties, and that influence directly the administration of government fall into a few main categories: denominationalism, transportation, federal-provincial relations, patronage, public works, and agriculture, in roughly that order. In the past decade industrial development has also been a lively subject for discussion.

Denominationalism plays such a large part in Prince Edward Island politics that it might well be said that the Island has four political parties: Liberal, Conservative, Catholic, and Protestant. Everyone is publicly labeled from the moment of birth or entry into residence, and his approach to public affairs is clearly dictated by his allegiance. The history of Island politics has shown the major role of denominationalism. Today, in almost every phase of public activity, ecclesiastical interest and inter-church rivalry are powerful forces and major obstacles to be reckoned with by anyone seeking to inaugurate any policy or project. More public business has been disrupted by church politics than by any other single issue. This problem alone has done more than anything else to add to the cost and uncertainties of governmental business. The denominational issues are of two kinds: actual disputes over education and social services in which churches have a direct interest, and hidden maneuvering—apparent in most matters—concerning ecclesiastical advantage in securing money, patronage, or power. Some of the arguments, fear of arguments and reprisals, compromises, and gentlemen's agreements that have been caused by denominationalism have been open. However, because of the bitterness of earlier days, which almost ended government in the Island, most denominational forces now operate underground. As a result, the legislature avoids the subject and the public does not have an opportunity to hear the arguments and discuss them intelligently—no matter how much money is allotted to fulfilling a denominational wish, no matter how good a project is that is being obstructed by denominational opposition, and no matter how inept might be a denominational appointment to a public office. Church politics is the one force exempt from the democratic process in Prince Edward Island.[8]

Transportation is of interest to everyone on an island that must communicate and trade with the mainland. It is also a major source of jobs, contracts, and political influence at the local level. Both parties feature it in all their manifestos and every legislative session is concerned with it. When the Island entered Confederation the British North America Act guaranteed "efficient and continuous communication with the mainland" to be provided by the federal government, and since then the Island has seen to it that Ottawa has lived up to this promise. The ferry services and the trans-Canada highway have always been topics for debate. The provincial opposition party can always find something wrong with these services and every government has featured in its propaganda its efforts to get still better transportation agreements than did its predecessors. In recent years the causeway has been a *cause célèbre*; its varied implications provide endless sources of fascinating discussion.

For its size and population the Island now has the finest network of roads of any province in Canada. It has built, and must maintain, approximately 2,000 miles of excellent paved highway and 3,500 miles of secondary roads. Building additional roads is one of the provincial government's main tasks and each administration carefully indicates what it has done or will do in this area of development. Paving is the best vote-getting process there is and each district must get its share. Many of the Island's roads are vital arteries of commerce; others, however, must be among the least travelled ones in Canada. No one can afford to call a halt and road-building proceeds until, as some people joke, the Island might sink beneath the weight of concrete.

Railways have been the cause of much discussion in Prince Edward Island as they have been throughout Canada. The federal government took over the bankrupt Prince Edward Island Railway at Confederation and the line eventually became part of the CNR. It has never paid its way, but it has been an essential part of Island commerce. Although today, with competition from airlines and truck transports, its business is dwindling steadily, the Island will not part with it. Politicians protest vigorously any curtailment of its services. Whether or not there should be a railway on the causeway is a choice subject for debate.

Finance is a normal source of discussion in any government. The Island as the smallest province, demands a share of the nation's funds commensurate, not with its size and population—for the Island could not live on a sum based on such proportions—but with its status as a province. For this reason the Island has always resisted per capita and matching grant arrangements; provincial officials have debated at great length among themselves and with federal authorities regarding suitable financial agreements. Because the provincial government has nearly always been of the same political allegiance as the federal government, the opposition party has been able to use provincial finance as a potent weapon of attack.

The fact that two-thirds of the provincial government's revenue now comes from Ottawa in the form of miscellaneous grants and payments puts the local treasury in the role of an agent for the distribution of federal funds. This role weakens the local taxpayers' understanding of their own financial responsibility. The Island government finds it difficult to say, "If you want you must pay;" the answer from the taxpayers would probably be, "Why are you not getting more from Ottawa?" The role of agent also enables the provincial government to excuse its own lack of action or mistakes by blaming the federal government for not giving it enough money. Furthermore, the channeling of federal funds such as university grants through the provincial treasury instead of direct to institutions greatly increases the power of the provincial government over those institutions and puts them in a position of complete dependence on the government and on its ability to raise money and make good decisions. This procedure further diminishes the taxpayers' understanding of public finance. In the case of the university, for example, it tends to encourage the interpretation of educational policy by the limited interests of local administration and politics with a resulting weakening of the national interest or the interest of the university itself. These difficulties, which are experienced to a varying degree in all provinces, are particularly evident on the Island because of the high dependence on federal funds and the relative inability of the smallest province to dictate terms to Ottawa or to relieve the overwhelming pressures of local politics on public finance.

Patronage in Prince Edward Island is an unusually large encouragement of political participation, party loyalty, and attention to the government's wishes. The governorship, 10 judgeships, 4 senatorships, a speakership, and the 10 cabinet posts are attractive dignities. Many positions in the province are at the disposal of the government. It is always apparent what firms and individuals are currently in favor as suppliers of goods and services. As the constitution of the Liberal party directs, "The Patronage Committee shall keep records of service and contributions of party supporters and shall make recommendations for patronage benefits." What is unique about this arrangement is the extent to which the large amount of patronage in a small population enhances the power of the provincial government, increases the proportion of political activity motivated by the hope of patronage,[9] and limits severely the independence and judgment of politicians and citizens who must rely too much on the government's favor.

Public works are a major interest of both parties and a lively cause of controversy. The parties as well as the public have widely encouraged public works despite the fact that the population is the same as it was a century ago, and the productive capacity of Island industry has not increased relative to that of the nation or relative to the amounts spent on public works. The parties do not argue about whether or not public works are justifiable—politically no one wants to say "No" to demands in small places—but why there are not more of them. Consequently one does not travel far in the province without being amazed at the amount of public works for 110,000 people. The wisdom of supplying and maintaining so many of them is inevitably questioned when one notes the less politically popular services that are not adequately provided. The wisdom can be questioned further because of the scattered and marginal benefits of public works. With the compartmentalization of politics into districts, it is difficult to encourage works of a more general and often more efficient and productive nature, which would benefit the whole province and raise its industrial capacity.

As agriculture is the main industry, it is always an important subject of dispute and it generally prevails over other considerations. Both parties must go out of their way to do things for the farmers whose support they must have. What debate there is is usually on how much the government has done and how much the opposition can blame the government for drops in prices or production of farm products.

The Island has a strong tradition of education, and provision of educational facilities is itself not a subject of dispute. The real issues of education have been denominationalism and the need for public works because they, rather than actual educational needs, have so often dictated whether or not institutions, facilities, or services should be provided or obstructed in a particular district or for a particular group or for the province as a whole.

Fortunately for local politics, broader issues periodically enlarge the scope of party interests because the provincial party machinery is also used for federal politics. Because of the Island's status as a province, its officials participate in national governmental and party activities and conferences to a much greater extent than the province's size and population would otherwise warrant. This participation contributes to the officials' appreciation and enjoyment of public life as it compensates for the limiting responsibilities of local politics by providing a wider sphere in which to offer opinions and talents.

All these issues combined in the 1960s to make a major change in the administration, the economy and the fortunes of the province, and, by the end of the decade, even to alter profoundly its system of responsible government. Both parties and most of the pressure groups were involved. The Conservative government of W. R. Shaw embarked on a food processing and shipbuilding project in Georgetown which failed because of ministerial inexperience and interference, bad management and singularly naive attempts at business planning, all of which were subsequently investigated and condemned by a royal commission. The resulting financial disaster, which was inherited by the Liberals under A. B. Campbell in 1966, drained the local treasury. The causeway, which had already begun, had committed whatever special funds the federal government could reasonably be expected to spend on the Island. Nevertheless the provincial government proceeded to negotiate a new project of its own with Ottawa in the form of a comprehensive development plan. It got the plan but the causeway was immediately stopped and abandoned and the federal government saved a great deal of money in the deal. These successive events were criticized severely in the national press and the Island lost much of the good will and sympathy which it had long enjoyed. Despite the already large number of institutions and officials on the Island the federal government sent an enormous task force to Charlottetown. This group literally took over the government and the development plan proceeded to embrace every aspect of Island life. Opposition politicians raised a storm over the extent of the takeover, the competence of the planners, the transfer of power from ministers and civil servants to the planners, the size of the resulting bureaucracy, the lack of information, the by-passing of the legislature, and, in general, the loss of responsible government. The affair caused speculation elsewhere on the consequences of this unusually detailed intervention of the federal government in provincial jurisdiction.

In the period 1970-76 the development plan involved still more control from Ottawa, and, within the province, greatly increased centralization of effort in the provincial government. The implications continued to be discussed annually in the legislature and many of them were described in reports from appraisers of projects.[10] The main question was whether the effort would result in permanent productive assets which would generate employment and revenues of long-term value, or whether it would result simply in temporary consumer benefits and an ultimate inability of the province to pay back the large loans from the federal government. One result was clear: the ample federal funds available for the provincial government to distribute, and the powers which accompanied their dispersal, vastly increased both the government's intervention in every aspect of Island life, and the dependence on the government of politicians and officials seeking advancement and of citizens seeking benefits. Meanwhile the Conservatives, led by four leaders in a decade, were able to make little impression on these momentous events.

The Efficiency of the Machine

The duty of a democratic government to perform certain functions is generally understood by the people. Less understood is the cost of administering these functions and of maintaining an expanding political and official establishment. Prince Edward Island provides an example of the high cost in money and effort of political overhead. It also illustrates how individual and community effort and responsibility decrease as a large government takes over an increasing proportion of the activities of the society.

The large system and the rewards of politics on Prince Edward Island encourage active political affiliations and close associations with government. Almost anyone's party label is known. Governmental patronage is important in many careers. Because government is so omnipotent and close to the people there is a great tendency toward the "let the government do it" attitude. Whole communities depend exclusively on public enterprises. The benefits are obvious in a social service age, and the democratic theory of people and their government being close to each other is more than adequately honored. The result of this process, however, is the inclusion in governmental activities and the civil service of a large number of people interested and experienced in, and occupied with, purely political activities as distinct from actual government. The work performed by them regardless of need, in response to purely political demands or in the hope of attracting political support, comprises an ever increasing part of the government's programme to the point where much of the work is a waste of time and money and overshadows more important functions. Furthermore, as this work grows the supply of able people in the small Island society who are available for government service diminishes and the government must call on less competent people.

Another result of the large political emphasis in government administration is the discouragement of imaginative private enterprise by the desire of the government to concern itself with every phase of activity that may bring it credit and by the inertia among people who look to the government for action rather than act themselves. There is every sign that the Island is far behind other provinces in non-political activity, especially in industry. When the government itself has attempted to fill the gap by engaging in industry, it has been unsuccessful because governmental personnel have been unable to provide industrial leadership and the government could not resist the temptation of running industry by political standards. The fiasco in Georgetown in the 1960s, for example, was a hopeless mixture of business and politics brewed by people who tried food processing and shipbuilding without knowing very much about either. The loss in 1969 of the causeway to the mainland which had been approved and commenced was another example: the provincial government demanded too much of the taxpayers of Canada by seeking an expensive federal economic improvement plan at the same time. Because of its dominant position the Island government finds it difficult to acknowledge its inability to handle major projects and to permit initiative and leadership from non-political sources with non-political motivations.

Probably the most serious effect of the large political system on personnel, however, is the fact that dominant government alone cannot attract and hold able people. Where there is too much emphasis on the political standard of measurement, too much looking inward at itself by the government rather than outward at other thriving enterprises, and too much concern with maintaining the establishment for its own sake, good people leave. The Island exports a dangerously large portion of its able young people; the dominance of politics is among the main reasons. It must be emphasized that this statement is not a reflection on the nature of politics but on the amount. In abnormally large quantities politics discourages other enterprise, and imposes its methods and interests on them. Important as it is, politics or politically supported activity is not everyone's preference as a career or as a means of promoting a career or an enterprise.

The justification for a government in Prince Edward Island and the efficiency of political, social, and economic life in the province would be greatly increased if the size and functions of the government were cut by at least one-third. The reason is the operation of Parkinson's Law. Work, Parkinson said, expands in importance and complexity, not with its real significance, but with the time to be spent; and the number of officials is not related to the quantity of the work.[11] The Prince Edward Island government exemplifies Parkinson's Law and the desires of officials to seek control, multiply subordinates, engage in paper work, make work for one another, and, ultimately, to discourage or prevent non-political enterprise.

A partial solution to the problem, often found elsewhere but not yet sufficiently tried in Prince Edward Island, is the separation of party politics and civil service administration from some public enterprises. Parties and their activities are essential to the selecting and changing of governments and to the process of making public officials responsible to the people. But they are not always essential or desirable in the direct operation of public business. It is not always possible to keep them out of public business in the larger systems. It is far more difficult to make the separation in the smaller ones. Nevertheless the emergence everywhere of the public trusts has provided a combination of public enterprise and professional initiative that neither civil service nor party personnel has been able to give to the management of essential services. Despite some weaknesses, most of these trusts have worked well. It is significant that Prince Edward Island had to wait until 1964 to get its first trusts—an industrial corporation, a university, and a centennial commission—the first public organizations in the province to be free, at least initially, of party politics and departmental management.

The administrative aspects of governmental expansion do not concern us here. The political aspects can never be removed in any democratic government. In Prince Edward Island they tend to be too obvious because governments are so close to, and so dependent on, the party process and the powerful pressure groups. Governmental involvement in some project or function however suitable or necessary that involvement may be, can be demanded and often implemented simply because it sounds well in a platform or pleases an interest group. Every such involvement increases the establishment and decreases the scope for and initiative of non-political enterprise. The point has been reached where the amount of administration and politics is too large in relation to what it does for the people of the Island and to the province's production in goods, services, and social amenities.

Having ministers of the Crown, for example, is of course essential to the Island's parliamentary system. It is also useful to political parties in power by providing titled leadership in political processes. But 10 of them, all with portfolios and deputy ministers, is difficult to justify when the actual business each handles amounts in significance to little more than that looked after by a clerk in a city or county elsewhere. Moreover competent ministers are scarce because the number of elected members from which a premier must choose his colleagues is so small. Under the circumstances it is too easy for ministers to get into mischief or take themselves too seriously by getting into activities that they are not supposed to handle or for which they do not have enough competence. Until the 1940s premiers distributed almost all the portfolios among a few senior ministers and retained other colleagues as part-time ministers without portfolio. Politics made it impossible to maintain this distinction, however, as portfolios increased in number and were divided among all the chosen. As each minister and deputy expanded his organization and looked for more to do, the cabinet inevitably got involved in minutiae and had less time for the general executive functions for which it was intended. Political organizations and the public, in turn, expected and demanded this attention to minutiae, the process spiraled, and matters of real significance were neglected. "We have a cabinet of 8 members and a presiding officer!" said Hon J. D. Stewart, Minister of Tourist Development and Municipal Affairs and Provincial Secretary, in the legislature in 1964. "Too large, too cumbersome, too voluble—the same as this House—[Laughter]—too many squeaking wheels. Let us be sensible for goodness sake. Let us get down to size; let us cut this unwieldy thing to a workable size; not more than five members and a presiding officer."[12] "This," said Opposition Leader and former Premier A. W. Matheson, "is good, sound advice."[13] Yet two years later the cabinet was increased by another minister.

If the legislature, cabinet and civil service and the functions they perform were reduced by at least one-third, all three would undoubtedly work better and more efficiently. Political party organizations would in turn be reduced in size. Their units would work in larger areas and with large issues. Because their contacts with voters would be less parochial, the issues would be more worthy of their effort. Because their contacts with elected representatives and ministers would be with fewer men with more to do, their leadership would be stronger. With less patronage to look for, politicians would likely be more independent of the govern-

TABLE I

Party Tenures of Office with Years of Formations of Governments and Names of Premiers

Liberal	1851	George Coles
Conservative	1854	John Holl
Liberal	1855	George Coles
Conservative	1859	Edward Palmer
Conservative	1863	John H. Gray
Conservative	1865	J. C. Pope
Liberal	1867	George Coles
Liberal	1869	Joseph Hensley
Liberal	1869	R. P. Haythorne
Conservative	1870	J. C. Pope
Liberal	1871	R. P. Haythorne
Conservative	1873	J. C. Pope
Conservative	1873	L. C. Owen
Coalition	1876	L. H. Davies
Conservative	1879	W. W. Sullivan
Conservative	1889	Neil MacLeod
Liberal	1891	Frederick Peters
Liberal	1897	A. B. Warburton
Liberal	1898	Donald Farquharson
Liberal	1901	Arthur Peters
Liberal	1908	F. L. Haszard
Liberal	1911	James Palmer
Conservative	1911	J. A. Mathieson
Conservative	1917	A. E. Arsenault
Liberal	1919	J. H. Bell
Conservative	1923	J. D. Stewart
Liberal	1927	A. C. Saunders
Liberal	1930	W. M. Lea
Conservative	1931	J. D. Stewart
Conservative	1933	W. J. P. MacMillan
Liberal	1935	W. M. Lea
Liberal	1936	T. A. Campbell
Liberal	1943	J. Walter Jones
Liberal	1953	A. W. Matheson
Conservative	1959	W. R. Shaw
Liberal	1966	A. B. Campbell

ment, and more motivated by service than reward. A greater number of necessary non-governmental enterprises might well be encouraged. As for the citizens, politics might take up a little less of their lives and perhaps make way for a desirable increase of their initiative in other directions. This initiative should encourage what the Island needs most and what government cannot provide—new business, new industry, new and improved methods in primary industries and in production as well as in the arts and in cultural and educational leadership and research. These alternatives to political, and often non-productive and non-essential, activities would develop the province because they are productive, provide more rewarding employments, and train and attract able young people by giving them challenging opportunities. In turn the government itself will become more significant as the province becomes more self-sufficient.

The Island has all the physical assets to enable its people to lead a varied, interesting, and rewarding life. Its government gives it an identity and prestige of which its people are proud. But just as too much power may render dangerous a vehicle which it propels, a surfeit of politics on the Island may make unstable the democracy which it serves and ultimately cause the Island to lose its government altogether. While the nation itself is discussing constitutional change, the Island might well consider the advisability of overhauling its own system after 200 years of operation.

The Island is a tribute to the flexibility of the British type of constitution which permitted it to be established and equipped as a political unit. It is a tribute to Confederation which enabled so small a place to be a full partner and allowed it to be treated with generosity and even affection. It is an interesting laboratory of politics where a long experiment has been conducted on the consequences of permitting man's political actions and associations to overshadow and permeate all other aspects of his society while at the same time retaining many essentials of democracy. As in all laboratories, there is noise and smell from time to time, but everyone is occupied and the results are always interesting, sometimes even startling. And, in the valuable tradition of laboratories, may not the Island's political apparatus indicate with reasonable accuracy what can happen, in similar circumstances, in larger constitutional installations?

Endnotes

1 For a general description of Prince Edward Island government and politics see Frank MacKinnon, *The Government of Prince Edward Island* (Toronto: University of Toronto Press, 1951), and the author's yearly summaries in *The Canadian Annual Review*.

2 Charles Stewart to J. F. W. DesBarres, Oct. 18, 1811, Prince Edward Island Papers, Public Archives of Canada, A25, p. 247.

[3] Gladstone to Governor Henry Vere Huntley, June 30, 1846, Prince Edward Island Papers, Public Archives of Canada, G16, p. 459.

[4] Ready to Lord Bathurst, June 12, 1827, Prince Edward Island Papers, Public Archives of Canada, A44, p. 97; Huntley to Lord Stanley, April 22, 1845, Prince Edward Island Papers, G48, p. 204; and Huntley to Gladstone, April 17, 1846, Prince Edward Island Papers, G48, p. 284.

[5] J. Elmer Murphy, Editor, *Summerside Journal—Pioneer*, in *The Guardian*, June 16, 1970. See also *The Guardian*, June 4 and 5, 1970 for a discussion of "smear campaigns" in the legislature.

[6] The formal details of party organization are set forth in the constitution of the Prince Edward Island Conservative Association dated September 1966 and that of the Prince Edward Island Liberal Association dated November 1967.

[7] The Jones-Campbell rivalry remained a longstanding one of particular interest. In 1935 the Liberals under W. M. Lea won every seat in the legislature, partly because of depression problems and an unbelievably inept Conservative campaign. Premier Lea died in 1936 to be succeeded by Thane A. Campbell. Without an official opposition, the legislature developed one itself —a group of dissident Liberals under the leadership of J. Walter Jones, who had once been a Progressive. Jones' opinion of Premier Campbell was not high, and the premier and his supporters resented the open breaches of party discipline. After Jones became premier much ill-feeling remained among the Liberals to enliven the administration during complex, and often controversial, post-war governmental activity, while the crushed and quarrelling Conservatives posed no threat. Nevertheless, the government came alive for a decade under Jones who, despite an unpredictable nature, unorthodox methods, and an impatience with party patronage, achieved much and was by far the ablest Island premier of this century.

[8] The determination of Premier J. Walter Jones to end the scandalous prohibition and divorce situations in the period 1945-9, together with a long dispute in 1951 over the seating of Anglican clergymen at head tables at public functions, and numerous refusals of church-related patronage by Jones, caused him much difficulty. He was only able to settle the first matters by playing off against each other Catholics who opposed a divorce court but favored more sensible liquor laws and Protestants who wanted the divorce court but opposed new liquor laws. Diehards on both sides, including many in the Liberal party, never forgave him for this ploy, or for his ultimate reluctance to discuss government business with church leaders.

[9] A slogan, from the First Kings by election of 1966 which broke a tie between the parties in seats won in the general election of that year, became famous: "If it moves, pension it; if it doesn't, pave it."

[10] Chapters on P.E.I. in *Canadian Annual Review*, 1974-75.

[11] C. Northcote Parkinson, *Parkinson's Law* (New York: Ballantine Books, Inc., 1957), pp. 15-16.

[12] *Speeches of the Prince Edward Island Legislative Assembly*, 1964, March 17, 1964, p. 456.

[13] *Ibid.*

QUEBEC "Heaven is Blue and Hell is Red"

Vincent Lemieux

Historical Background

An old Quebec legend attributes the above saying, used as the chapter title, to a priest who, from his pulpit, exhorted his parishioners to vote for the Conservative party, known as the "Bleus," rather than the Liberals, known as the "Rouges." Many Quebec voters have never regarded these parties in terms of heaven and hell. Nevertheless, the old rivalry between the two major parties dominated the provincial scene from 1867 to 1970.

The most constant characteristic of provincial party politics in Quebec, until the 1970 election, was the two-party system. From time to time a third party or a splinter group from one of the two major parties threatened to disrupt the system traditionally dominated by Conservatives and Liberals or Union Nationale and Liberals, but such parties have never been successful. The most serious threat occurred during the 1930s when the Action Libérale Nationale, a dissident wing of the Liberal party, joined forces with the Conservatives. In 1936, this alliance became the Union Nationale party. The Conservative representative from Trois-Rivières, Maurice Duplessis, became the leader of the new party and held this position until his death in 1959. In 1944, 1948, and 1966, respectively, the nationalist Bloc Populaire, the Créditiste Union des Electeurs, and the independentist Rassemblement pour l'Indépendance Nationale and the Ralliement National tried unsuccessfully to gain a toehold in the Quebec Parliament. In 1944, however, the Bloc Populaire did manage to gain four of the 91 seats, but the Créditistes in 1948 and the independentists in 1966 did not elect a single representative. In 1970, the Créditistes got 12 of the 108 seats, and the Parti Québécois seven of them. In the eyes of observers the two-party system has come to an end.

The difference between the two major provincial parties has never been as extreme as the difference between heaven and hell. Nevertheless, the parties' ideologies and policies through the years reveal differences that have been virtually constant. There have been three lengthy phases from 1867 to 1970, that point out these differences.[1] In the initial period, which lasted until Laurier's victory in 1896, the two big provincial parties confronted each other for the most part on nationalist and religious issues. At the beginning of this period, the Conservatives were the Confederation party in Quebec, as they were in all of Canada, with only one extremist wing of the Liberal party opposing them on this issue. Disputes of a religious nature often overshadowed the nationalist squabbles. There were elements in the Liberal party who wanted separation of church and state as well as greater individual freedom in religious education. This movement was opposed by most of the Catholic bishops in Quebec, who gave their support to the Conservatives. Nevertheless, throughout this entire period the provincial Quebec Liberals, together with the Quebec Liberals in Ottawa, proved to be more provincialist than the Conservatives. During this era the Liberal opposition was most active in 1886, after Riel's execution and the accession to power of Mercier's "Parti National." Mercier drew support from the Liberals, the National Conservatives, and the Ultramontanes. The last-named, who advocated an alliance between the Church and the State with the Church dominating, had always been in the Conservative ranks, and their battles with the Rouges of the Liberal party raged through the second half of the 19th century. For this group to find itself with Mercier's Liberals was indicative of the times. Although the Conservatives defeated Mercier in 1892, it was the last time this party achieved a victory in Quebec provincial elections. From 1897, immediately following Laurier's victorious appearance on the Canadian scene, the provincial Liberals took over the government and held power until 1936. This long tenure forms the second phase of Quebec provincial politics.

It is interesting to note that during the entire second period the Quebec voters consistently preferred the Liberals to the Conservatives at the Federal level. Ottawa became the norm for the provincial vote. The provincial Conservatives suffered from the federal Conservatives' policies, which antagonized the nationalistic feelings of the Quebec voters. The religious quarrels of the 19th century had died away; furthermore, the two parties hardly differed on economic and social issues until Taschereau became premier in 1920. His government systematically encouraged the industrialization of Quebec through private enterprise. However, opposition to this policy came more from the nationalists than from the Conservative party, which had no organized basis on which it could conduct an effective offensive against the Liberals.

It took the smell of corruption coming from a regime that had lasted too long and, even more, the economic crisis of the 1930s to finally defeat the Liberal government. Yet the final blow was delivered by a splinter group from the Liberal party, the Action Libérale Nationale, which, allied with the Conservatives, left no more than a majority of six out of the 90 seats to the Liberals in 1935. The two opposition parties then formed the Union Nationale party, which crushed the Liberals the following year. The special characteristics of this period made economic and social matters as important as, if not more important than, the national question in the struggle between the opposition and the Liberals. In 1939, however, with the threat of war, the Liberals regained control of the government. The federal ministers from Quebec had forcefully intervened in the campaign, threatening to resign if the Union Nationale were re-elected. Their resignations, they claimed, would leave the field wide open for the imperialist conscriptionists. Nevertheless, the federal Liberals called the conscription vote and, in the view of the Quebec electorate, bore a stigma for bolstering the cause of centralization of power during the war years. The Union Nationale took advantage of this situation and got elected by a narrow margin in 1944; they stayed in power until 1960. They managed to do this by directing all their campaigns against the Ottawa Liberals with whom the provincial party was closely identified. Little by little, the Quebec Liberals came to rely on social and economic policy. Finally, they took advantage of the successive deaths of Duplessis and Sauvé as well as the end of the Liberal reign in Ottawa and gained power by a small majority in 1960 elections. They won again in 1962, but in 1966 the Union Nationale gained a slight edge over the Liberals in terms of the number of seats won, even though they obtained only 40 per cent of the popular vote compared to 47 per cent for the Liberals.

In 1970 the Union Nationale was reduced to 20 per cent of the vote and to 17 seats, against 45 per cent of the vote and 72 seats for the Liberals, the P.Q. and the Créditistes capturing the remaining votes (35 per cent) and seats (19 out of 108). In 1973, it was a landslide: the Liberals got 102 seats with 55 per cent of the vote, and the P.Q. only 6 seats with 30 per cent of the vote. Two seats were gained by the Créditistes and more by the Union Nationale.

Finally, another new party emerged at the end of 1975, under the leadership of Jérôle Choquette a dissident Liberal, and Fabien Roy, a dissident Créditiste, two members of the National Assembly. This party was named le Parti National Populaire. Because of the lack of data on this new party, it will be ignored in the following sections of this chapter.

From any point of view, 1936—the year the Union Nationale party was formed—and 1970, were two of the most important turning points in provincial politics and in the history of Quebec provincial parties. For the systematic study of Quebec provincial parties, only this recent period (1936-76), which opened with the end of the 39-year Liberal reign, will be considered. After party ideologies and policies are examined, a study will be made of the electoral supporters. Another section will be devoted to the social structure and organization of parties. In the last, most general section, the Quebec provincial party system will be reviewed, giving particular emphasis to recent changes.

Party Ideologies and Policies

In Quebec, as elsewhere, the main objective of all political parties is to obtain enough votes to gain political power. To reach this goal, parties must present ideologies and policies that will persuade a sufficient number of voters to vote for them.

In view of this, a great distinction can be made between the external ideologies and policies and the internal ideologies and policies of Quebec provincial parties. We define external ideologies and policies as those referring to Quebec's position in the Canadian federal system. By internal ideologies and policies, we mean those referring to groups and communities inside Quebec.

EXTERNAL IDEOLOGIES AND POLICIES OF PROVINCIAL PARTIES

Since 1936, and even earlier, at least one of the Quebec provincial parties has attached a great deal of importance to its external ideology and policy. It was noted earlier that until 1936 the Liberal party was the more provincialist and the more autonomist of the two parties. The situation was reversed after 1936 with the formation of the Union Nationale, a strictly provincial party. The Liberals and their leader Adélard Godbout became identified in the war years to follow with conscription and federal centralization of power. In the election of 1944, 1948, 1952, and 1956, the Union Nationale successfully exploited the conflict between its autonomist policy and the Liberal position of centralization. The longer the federal Liberals stayed in power in Ottawa, the easier this task became. Furthermore, the Quebec Liberal members in Ottawa were unable to restrain themselves from intervening in the provincial electoral campaigns. The Union Nationale used this fact to identify provincial Liberals with those in Ottawa. Another factor that aided the Union Nationale was that Godbout, the leader of the provincial Liberal party, was succeeded by Georges-Emile Lapalme, who had been one of the federal members of Parliament.

The Ottawa Liberals (who were identified with those in Quebec) were not only accused of over-centralization; they were also reproached for their excessive generosity to African and Asian countries, since it was felt that this had not been in the best interests of Quebec. In 1956, when Polish eggs were flooding the Quebec market, the Union Nationale widely circulated a denunciation blaming the federal government for its complicity in the matter.

This situation lasted until the late 1950s, when the Conservatives defeated the federal Liberals. The Union Nationale could hardly identify the provincial Liberals with an Ottawa government that favored centralization, when the government there was a Conservative one. Paul Sauvé, Duplessis's successor as leader of the Union Nationale, even began negotiating with Ottawa in order to resolve such problems as subsidies to Quebec universities. Duplessis's attitude toward negotiation with Ottawa had always been completely negative.

During the 1950s the provincial Liberals had had little success in bringing the debate with the Union Nationale to any ground other than that of federal-provincial relations. But when they took over the government in 1960 and found themselves dealing with a Conservative government in Ottawa, they were in a good position to formulate their own autonomist philosophy and to practice a policy of guerrilla warfare against Ottawa. They did this, however, in a more positive fashion than had Duplessis, by accepting the principle of negotiation. In their negotiations, the young specialists recruited by the Liberals displayed a degree of competence that had not been customary in Quebec spokesmen.

It is true that from 1963 the Quebec Liberal government had to deal with a Liberal government in Ottawa. However, in 1964 there was a separation in the Liberal party structures—between the Quebec provincial federation and the Quebec wing of the national federation—that left the provincial Liberals plenty of room to maneuver in their dealings with Ottawa. This separation was a sign of the times, as was the formation of the two independentist parties, the Rassemblement pour l'Indépendance Nationale and the Ralliement National. As an indication of the political trend, in the provincial election of 1966 all four parties involved advocated a nationalist philosophy. Both "third parties" proclaimed themselves as independentist parties. The Union Nationale's new slogan was "Egalité ou Indépendance" ("Equality or Independence"), taken from the title of a book by the party's leader, Daniel Johnson.[2] The Liberals proposed to continue the battle they had started six years earlier for greater sovereignty for Quebec.

Daniel Johnson died in September 1968, and was succeeded by Jean-Jacques Bertrand, whose leadership was confirmed by a convention of the Union Nationale in June 1969. Jean Lesage retired from politics at the end of 1969, and Robert Bourassa was chosen as Liberal leader by a leadership convention in January 1970. At the same time two new parties appeared. The Parti Québécois was created at the end of 1968 and soon absorbed the Rassemblement pour l'Indépendance Nationale and the Ralliement National to form a unified independentist party under the leadership of René Lévesque, a dissident Liberal. The Ralliement Créditiste decided in 1969 to enter provincial politics and in January 1970 selected Camille Samson as leader of the new provincial party.

The appearance of new parties and leaders led to new positions with respect to external (or constitutional) questions. The Liberals assumed a strong federalist position, in opposition to the Parti Québécois. The Ralliement Créditiste gave a moderate support to federalism and the Union Nationale gave Ottawa four years to develop a federal constitution acceptable to Quebec; if, at the end of that time, Ottawa proposals were unsatisfactory, the question of independence for Quebec would be put to the people in a referendum.

In 1975, the Parti Québécois proposed its own idea of a referendum. It would be used, it was decided, if a P.Q. government was forced to do so because of a deadlock in its negotiations with the federal government. The Union Nationale, on the other hand, ceased to speak of a referendum. The new Parti National Populaire advocated constitutional arrangements more favorable for Québec, and the Liberal Party remained, with the Ralliement Créditiste, the more federalist of the five parties.

INTERNAL IDEOLOGIES AND POLICIES OF PROVINCIAL PARTIES

Concerning external ideologies and polices, the Quebec provincial parties have been distinguished from each other by the degree to which they favor nationalism. The distinctions between these parties have not been so evident in their internal ideologies and policies. It is particularly difficult to refer to them as being right or left, assuming these terms represent ideologies and policies designed either to maintain or to reduce the differences between individuals and between groups of a society. Since 1936 neither one of the two parties has had a policy that has been at all constant in terms of right or left.

The measures taken by the Union Nationale from 1936 to 1939 and after 1944 with the intention of improving the standard of living of the farmers (extending the supply of electrical power in rural areas, liberalizing credit, etc.) can be considered leftist, since they reduced the difference between this class of Quebec society and other more favored classes. Similarly, the campaign of the Union Nationale in 1962 to raise the minimum salary of the province's workers to $1 per hour and to reduce the taxes of low-wage earners can also be considered leftist. In spite of these measures (or electoral promises) one cannot disregard the fact that under Duplessis the Union Nationale was also a party clearly anti-union and very sympathetic to the economic and financial interests that filled its electoral coffers.

Since 1936 the Liberals have not been much different in this regard. It can be noted, however, that in the 1966 convention the radical wing of the party fought with some success to permit publication of party finances. In the 1950s, as in the 1960s, the Liberal party was consistently more favorably disposed to unionism than was the Union Nationale.

Whether or not this was due to the fact that the party happened to be in power at the time, the Union Nationale, nevertheless, brought to a vote all the laws that to some degree restrained the freedom of Quebec unions. The Union Nationale was also in power when the workers of Asbestos and Murdochville were clubbed by the provincial police.[3] In contrast, the Liberals have been committed to the return of a certain amount of union liberty and to measures as bold as the right of civil servants to strike. The Liberal government of 1939 to 1944 and, even more, of 1960 to 1966, was different from the Union Nationale government since it paid less attention than the Union Nationale to certain groups or specific areas that had been surpassed by technical progress or, in more general terms, that did not benefit from the modernization available to other groups or areas of society.

All of this indicates that although there are differences in the ideologies and particularly in the policies of the two major Quebec provincial parties, the parties cannot be accurately defined as being left or right. The differences refer rather to the conception that each party has of its role in government as well as to the means it employs to achieve this involvement.

In general, then, the Liberal party is more interventionist than the Union Nationale, in the sense of favoring not a police state but a state that dispenses goods and services. From 1944 to 1960, the annual expenditures of the Province of Quebec increased from slightly less than $100 million to slightly less than $500 million; during a period only one-third as long—that of 1960 to 1966—expenditures increased from less than $500 million to more than $1 billion. This was largely due to the Liberal party's social welfare measures designed to serve society in general. The Union Nationale has been more concerned with specific areas and classes that have been the most deprived, either economically or culturally. Because of this, the Union Nationale has been more electorally-minded than the Liberal party.

Without exaggerating the differences between the two parties, several concrete illustrations will nevertheless point out that these differences are real. Nationalization of electrical power is a good example, since it was an issue throughout most of the period under study here.[4] In the early 1930s Dr. Philippe Hamel started the fight to establish a public commission on electricity, but the nationalization of all the electrical companies was not accomplished until after the 1962 provincial election. Until 1939 the two parties talked much about the "electricity trust," and certain steps were taken to remedy the situation. However, it was not until the end of the Godbout regime, in March 1944, that Hydro-Québec was formed as a provincial hydro-electric commission by nationalizing the Montreal Light, Heat and Power Company.

During the debate over nationalization the arguments used by each side illustrate the differences between the two parties. The Liberals talked of rate reduction for the small consumer, of the public interest (i.e., of the entire population), of an economic and social equilibrium, and of the industrial and commercial development of the province. Seldom did they refer to specific classes of society other than farmers and settlers who stood to profit from the installation of electric power in rural areas, which nationalization would make possible.

Duplessis, who saw in nationalization a "state capitalism resembling Bolshevism," admitted that rural electric power was a pressing need. But, according to him, the only way to proceed was to establish farmers' cooperatives. Eighteen years later Daniel Johnson, the Union Nationale leader, also opposed the nationalization of electric companies as proposed by the Liberals. He was in favor of partial nationalization only as the means most likely to reduce the rate and improve service. He asserted that the Union Nationale had first to improve the situation of the less favored classes. He stated during his campaign in 1962: "What the province really needs is not nationalization of electricity, but full employment and a more humane policy which gives more to those who are in need and less to those who are prosperous."[5]

This position of the Union Nationale was substantially different from that of the Liberal party which, even more than in 1944, talked of industrial development, of the general building up of the number of employed, of gaining control of the economy, and of the well-being of Quebec. (When René Levesque, the chief promoter of nationalization, spoke of those who would gain by this step, he referred to farmers and to families residing in the isolated areas of Quebec. However, he concerned himself as much, if not more, with the engineers and technicians of Quebec who would also benefit, and with the population in general, the consumers, the taxpayers—classes significantly less specific than those to whom the Union Nationale appealed.)

Some of the same distinctions are found in the social policies of the two parties and in their policies regarding subsidies to agencies receiving aid from the state. Duplessis opposed social measures coming from Ottawa not only because he maintained they were anti-constitutional, but just as much because he was opposed to the ideology that inspired these steps. As he said, "The best system is that which depends the least on the State." The Union Nationale government adopted certain social measures and did not overlook the subsidization of organizations such as municipalities, school boards, and co-operatives. But these measures and subsidies were usually restricted to categories or organizations representing the least favored elements of the population, or else they were not statutory.

In opposition, the Liberals proposed, from 1950 onward, more universal or statutory social policies and subsidies to state-assisted organizations. These were put into effect from 1960 to 1966. For example, hospitalization insurance became effective a few months after their 1960 victory, and standardization of subsidies to municipalities and school boards was realized a short time later. After the Union Nationale returned to power, health insurance became a problem. The Liberal party was in favor of a universal plan as proposed by the Castonguay Commission; the Union Nationale government avoided taking a definite position on this question.

In nearly every area of governmental activity, differences of this nature can be observed between the Liberal party and the Union Nationale. Between 1944 and 1966 the most interventionist and most collective features of the Liberal ideology and policy were apparent in the domain of education. After the Liberals came to power in 1960, a total reform of the entire school system was started. The Union Nationale government had occupied itself for the most part with the building of schools and with non-statutory subsidies to school boards. Similarly, a difference between the two parties can be noted in the area of municipal affairs. The Lesage government talked of a voluntary merger plan to be followed, if necessary, by an obligatory plan for the municipalities. The Johnson government, which succeeded the Lesage government in 1966, did not discuss the matter further. Again, on the matter of highways, the Liberals gave top priority to the construction of superhighways; the Union Nationale always gave precedence, at least in certain public declarations, to rural and regional highways.

These differences between the internal objectives of the Union Nationale and the Liberals can be seen most clearly by comparing the Duplessis regime from 1944 to 1960 with the Lesage regime of 1960 to 1966. The differences are less distinct in the period 1936 – 1944 and even less before 1936. When the Union Nationale returned to power in June 1966, these differences again diminished, just as differences concerning the external objectives of Quebec began to fade at this time.

There are at least two causes for the rapprochement that developed between the ideologies and the policies of the two major Quebec provincial parties. The first and unquestionably the more important is concerned with the strengthening of the Quebec public administration, specifically the strengthening of its higher management. In 1960 the Lesage government began to recruit specialists from Quebec universities and from the federal public administration. Some of them became deputy ministers or directors-general; others acted as advisors to the premier. Except in a few instances, they retained their positions after the 1966 Union Nationale victory. They continued to influence ministerial policies and, in the case of the advisors to the premier, general government policy. This resulted in a parallelism, in several areas, between the policies of the two governments.

The greatest correspondence between the two parties can be found in the ministries and in those areas well equipped with specialists. The most obvious case is that of the Ministry of Education, where the Union Nationale continued the Liberal policies. It is also evident that the similarity between the Liberal and Union Nationale governments in their policies towards Ottawa was largely due to the fact that some civil servants in the Department of Intergovernmental Affairs (previously the Department of Federal-Provincial Affairs) and some advisors had served under both governments.

On the other hand, the policy of the Union Nationale differs the most from that of the Liberals in the ministries whose senior administrations had not been strengthened by the Lesage government. In the area of municipal affairs, for example, the Union Nationale quickly made a break from the merger plans of the preceding government.

A second cause for the similarity between the two parties was the Union Nationale's desire to modernize their party. In the final years of the Duplessis regime, the Union Nationale party came to be associated more and more, in certain centers, with political corruption as well as with anti-unionism. Furthermore, the party was accused of designing its policies mainly (if not exclusively) to win votes. The Union Nationale government that was elected in 1966–in particular its leader, Daniel Johnson–made great efforts to erase this image of the old Union Nationale. It declared itself against patronage; it moved closer to the intellectual and university community, particularly at the party convention in March 1965; it wished to involve interest groups in the preparation of the electoral program of 1966; and it gave certain guarantees to the labor unions. Meanwhile, the Liberals marked time after their great activity in the early 1960s and fell into disfavor among several sections of the population. The result was that the programmes of the two parties, which were very different in 1962, were much less so in 1966, and that the policies of the Union Nationale government corresponded in many areas to those of the Lesage government.

But in any case, the Union Nationale remained less interventionist, or at least slower to intervene, than the Liberal party. It also continued to prefer specific rather than collective means, or at least it sought, more than the Liberal party, for ways to make collective measures more specific.

In the 1970s the differences between the internal ideologies and policies of the Liberals and of the U.N. have remained vague, with some hesitations in both of those parties between an interventionist and a non-interventionist style of government. A more contrasted style in the management of public affairs was adopted by the new parties, the Parti Québécois and the Ralliement Créditiste. The first of them has a neat tendency to promote a more encompassing public sector, in contrast with the Créditistes who are opposing such a tendency and advocating for a strong autonomy of the private sector.

These differences can be seen in many cases, from 1970 to 1976. It was exemplified, among other cases, when Bill 65 was presented by the Liberal government, with the intention to create a regional level in the management of social affairs and to make more democratic the administrative boards of hospitals, social agencies, etc. The Créditistes were opposed to such a move; they rather favored a greater financial support to the already existing decentralized institutions. The U.N. has about the same position as the Liberals, but its recommendation was for more incremental changes. The P.Q. deputies for their part were in favor of more power to be delegated to the regional level and of a greater democracy in the make-up of the administrative boards. These two positions by the P.Q. implied a greater intervention by the government in the operation of social affairs.

These different points of view are related to other factors we are going to consider now, namely the differences in the electoral supporters of the parties, as well as the differences in their social make-up and their organization.

Electoral Supporters of the Parties

The electoral supporters of the parties showed distinct characteristics from 1936 to 1966, and again in 1970 and 1973. First, the geographic distribution of each party's supporters will be examined. Concerning this, the result of the disproportion of the electoral districts will be noted. An examination of socio-economic characteristics of the electorate will follow. The last part of this section will comprise a brief study of the stability of the electorate since 1936.

TERRITORIAL FOUNDATIONS OF THE PARTIES

If Quebec is considered in terms of 10 large electoral areas, distinctions can be noted in the support each region has given to the two main provincial parties from 1936 to 1966. Table I gives the total number of elections held from 1936 to 1966 within the constituencies of each region, and the number of these elections won by the Liberals. The areas can be rated according to Liberal strength on the basis of the proportion of elections the Liberals have won in each area.

From 1936 to 1966, the Liberals found their strongest support in the metropolitan area of Montreal, as well as in three other areas: Côte Nord, Nord-Ouest, and Bas Saint-Laurent-Gaspésie. The first two have been populated relatively recently. Conversely, the Union Nationale has its strongest base in the areas where the population has been settled the longest and where the movement of the population has been relatively slight for the past 50 years.

The Liberal party has, since 1939, obtained greater support from the

TABLE I*

Proportion of elections won by Liberals from 1936 to 1966 in 10 regions of Quebec.

District	Total Number of Elections	Liberal Victories	Ratio
Côte Nord	9	6	.67
Métropolitain (Montréal)	149	98	.66
Nord-Ouest	41	19	.46
Bas Saint-Laurent-Gaspésie	63	25	.40
Montréal (non-Métropolitain)	198	74	.37
Cantons de l'Est	63	23	.37
Québec	170	58	.34
Saguenay-Lac Saint-Jean	32	9	.28
Trois-Rivières	81	17	.21
Outaouais	36	7	.19
TOTAL	842	336	.40

*Source: Reports of the Quebec Chief Electoral Officer and the Canadian Parliamentary Guide.

cities than it has from the rural areas. This is illustrated by the party's great strength in the metropolitan area of Montreal. This theory can be applied not only at the regional level, but also at the levels of the constituencies and the municipalities, and even at the individual level.

Jean Hamelin, Jacques Letarte and Marcel Hamelin[6], as well as Paul Cliche[7], have shown in their studies of the provincial elections that from 1944 to 1956 the Liberals had greater success against the Union Nationale in urban rather than in rural constituencies. This was less clear in 1960, although the Liberals won in 29 of the 48 constituencies where city-dwellers constituted more than 60 per cent of the population, and in only 22 of the 47 constituencies where city-dwellers constituted less than 60 per cent of the population. In 1962, however, the Liberals won in 37 of the 48 most urban constituencies, and in only 26 of the 47 least urban. In 1966 the Union Nationale won in only one-third of the 39 constituencies that were more than 80 per cent urban; on the other hand, they won in 42 of the 69 other constituencies, or in two-thirds[8]. In most studies of the provincial constituencies of Quebec the same phenomenon has been established: rural localities are generally more favorable to the Union Nationale than are urban localities and, conversely, the Liberals have stronger support in urban rather than in rural localities[9].

Finally, polls taken before the elections of 1960, 1962, and 1966 have confirmed this difference at the individual level. In the three elections, except perhaps in 1960, there was a very clear relation between the degree of urbanization in the voter's area of residence and the voter's attitude to the Liberal government. This is well illustrated, for example, in Table II, which contains figures taken from a poll made before the 1962 election.

The territorial foundation of the Parti Québécois is about the same as that of the Liberals, and conversely the territorial foundation of the Créditistes has more in common with that of the Union Nationale.

The seats gained by the P.Q. in 1970 and 1973 were located mainly in the regions where the Liberals had the best performance from 1936 to 1966.

TABLE II*

Attitudes to the Liberal government in 1962, relating to the degree of urbanization of place of residence.

	Place of residence			
	Montreal	Other cities	Towns	Rural municipalities
Percentage of voters favoring the Liberal government	62	57	56	35
Total number of cases	299	273	95	80

*Source: Groupe de Recherches Sociales, Les Préférences politiques des électeurs québécois en 1962, Montreal 1964.

Most of those seats were gained in the metropolitan area of Montréal, one was gained in the Côte-Nord, and another in the Saguenay-Lac Saint-Jean.

For their part the Créditistes have won in the following regions: Nord-Ouest, Cantons de l'Est, and Québec. As shown in Table I these regions were, generally speaking, more favorable to the Union Nationale, than those where either the Liberals or the P.Q. gained seats.

THE EFFECT OF THE DISPROPORTION OF ELECTORAL DISTRICT

The great inequality in the number of voters in each provincial constituency has favored the Union Nationale since 1939. Twice, in 1944 and 1966, they won more seats than the Liberals even though they obtained a smaller percentage of the vote.

The elections of 1952, 1956, and 1960 provide a good illustration of the effect that the disproportion in the electoral map has had on the election results. In 1960 the Liberals obtained almost the same percentage of votes as the Union Nationale received in 1952 and 1956, and the latter obtained almost the same percentage as the Liberals had received in these two elections. Nevertheless, in 1952 and in 1956 the Union Nationale won 68 and 72 seats, respectively, compared to 23 and 20 won by the Liberals. In 1960 the Liberals won only 51 seats compared to 43 for the Union Nationale.

The most extreme result of the inequality of the electoral map occurred in the election of 1966. The Liberals received 47 per cent of the popular vote but won only 51 seats. The Union Nationale received only 40 per cent of the popular vote but won 55 seats. The disparity in the electoral map—even more than the third parties, which hurt the Liberals

TABLE III

Relationship between socio-economic characteristics of electoral constituencies and Liberal victories in these constituencies from 1956 to 1966.

	1956	1960	1962	1966
Liberal proportion of victories in all constituencies.	.22 (20/93)	.54 (51/95)	.66 (63/95)	.47 (51/108)
Liberal proportion of victories in constituencies where non-French Canadians comprise more than 20% of the population.	.43 (10/23)	.58 (14/24)	.75 (18/24)	.84 (26/31)
Liberal proportion of victories in constituencies where those with at least a secondary education represent more than 40% of the adult population.	.47 (9/19)	.65 (13/20)	.95 (19/20)	.77 (24/31)
Liberal proportion of victories in constituencies where professional people, administrators, and technicians make up more than 15% of the labor force.	.29 (12/42)	.60 (25/42)	.86 (36/42)	.56 (30/54)
Liberal proportion of victories in constituencies where the average salary for men is more than $3,000.	.26 (11/43)	.62 (28/45)	.84 (38/45)	.57 (34/60)

*Sources: Canada Census (1961), Reports of the Quebec Chief Electoral Officer, and the Canadian Parliamentary Guide.

more than they did the Union Nationale—accounts for these lopsided results. The situation is clarified by noting that the Union Nationale was victorious in 20 of the 30 constituencies with less than 20,000 voters and in 27 of the 49 constituencies with between 20,000 and 40,000 voters, but won in only eight of the 29 constituencies with more than 40,000 voters![10]

Still in 1970 the electoral map was favoring the Union Nationale, helping it to get more seats than the other two opposition parties (the Ralliement Créditiste and the Parti Québécois) and, consequently, to be elected as the official opposition. The Union Nationale was victorious in 12 of the 28 constituencies with less than 20,000 voters, but in none of the 30 constituencies with more than 40,000 voters. This party got only 10 per cent of the registered voters in these constituencies, versus 31 per cent of voters in the constituencies of less than 20,000 voters. The Parti Québécois was victorious in none of these small constituencies and was supported by only nine per cent of the registered voters in them, but in the larger constituencies, those of more than 40,000 voters, it was supported by 24 per cent of the registered voters and got four seats.

SOCIO-ECONOMIC CHARACTERISTICS OF THE ELECTORATE

To demonstrate the city-dwellers are generally more inclined to the Liberals and to the P.Q. than to the Union Nationale and to the Créditistes, and that the opposite is true in more rural areas does not present the complete picture. Socio-economic categories must be examined to determine whether or not there are significant differences in party support along these lines. An accurate analysis of these differences requires a detailed statistical study of successive public opinion polls. Unfortunately, none were made before the late 1950s. In this section we will use the polls made after this date to study the socio-economic characteristics of the electorate, first from 1956 to 1966, and then in 1970 and 1973.

In Table III several relationships are revealed at the constituency level between the results obtained by the Liberals in 1956, 1960, 1962, and 1966 and the socio-economic characteristics of the electorate, based on certain data from the 1961 census.

It is apparent that there is a positive relationship between each of the four variables utilized and Liberal victories from 1956 to 1966. The Liberals won proportionately more victories in constituencies where these variables—non-French-Canadian population, levels of education, number of professional and skilled people, and average salaries—were higher than in the province as a whole.

Among the four variables, the one concerned with educational background seems to maintain the strongest positive relationship with Liberal victories. Three times out of four—in 1956, 1960, and 1962—it ranked first in Liberal proportion of victories. In 1966 it ranked second, behind the ethnic variable. This fact is worthy of note, as the ethnic variable constantly increased in its Liberal proportion of victories from 1956 to 1966. The three other variables decreased in this proportion in 1966, after steadily increasing from 1956 to 1962.

In 1956 the ethnic and educational variables appear to have played more important roles than the others. In 1960 the four variable factors had almost equal importance. In 1962 the educational variable dominated, while in 1966, as in 1956, the ethnic and educational variables seem to have been equally important factors.

These relationships at the constituency level are apparently just as applicable in the case of individual voters. The following data cannot feasibly be presented in a single table, because the statistical categories differ from one election to another[11].

The ethnic variable will be treated first. According to a poll made on the eve of the 1960 election, whereas only 43 per cent of the voters of Montreal intended to vote for the Liberals, 50 per cent of those who were not French-Canadian intended to do so. Just before the 1962 election 78 per cent of the English-speaking voters of Montreal favored a Liberal government, compared to only 58 per cent of the French-Canadian voters. Outside of Montreal, this percentage was 55 per cent of the English-speaking and 53 per cent of the French-speaking population.

It is even more probable that a voter with a high level of education will support the Liberal party. Just before the 1960 election, 53 per cent of the voters with less than nine years of schooling intended to vote for the Liberals, as opposed to 37 per cent of the voters who had more education. The 1962 figures appearing in Table IV are even more indicative of this trend, which may have been accentuated by the fact that the Liberals were then the governing party.

Concerning occupations, the data show that on the eve of the 1960 election, 41 per cent of professional people and managers preferred the Liberals to the Union Nationale, compared to 34 per cent of the skilled workers. Just before the 1962 election, 58 per cent of the voters were satisfied with the Liberal government. The proportion was 76 per cent among professional people and highly specialized technicians, 67 per cent among office workers and salesmen, and 65 per cent among salaried executives. This is in contrast to only 43 per cent of the laborers and domestics, 49 per cent of skilled workers, and 51 per cent of small proprietors and small businessmen. Again in 1966, according to a poll that found 57 per cent of the electorate intending to vote for the Liberal party, 75 per cent of the white-collar workers who expressed their preference intended to vote for the Liberals, compared to only 50 per cent of the laborers.

Finally, according to the results of the polls used, there is a strong probability that a Liberal party supporter will have a high rather than a low income. In 1962, while 58 per cent of the voters were satisfied with

TABLE IV*

Percentage of voters favoring the Liberal government, according to number of years of education (1962)

	0 to 4 years	5 to 8 years	9 to 12 years	13 years and over
Percentage favoring the Liberals	46	52	58	72
Number of cases	76	372	276	90

*Source: Groupe de Recherches Sociales, Les préférences politiques des électeurs québécois en 1962, Montreal, 1964.

the Liberal government, this proportion was only 46 per cent of those whose declared net income did not exceed $3,000, but it was 65 per cent of those whose declared net income was over $5,000. In 1966, more than 90 per cent of the voters earning over $8,000 intended to vote Liberal, compared to only 50 per cent of those whose income did not exceed $3,000.

It can be concluded that on both the constituency and the individual levels there was a pronounced relationship from 1956 to 1966 between the socioeconomic factors of ethnic origin, education, occupation, and income and the vote for the two main provincial parties of Quebec. Generally, there is a greater likelihood of finding support for the Liberal party if the voter or the constituency is one with a high level of education, occupation, and income. There is also a greater likelihood of finding Liberal supporters among non-French-Canadians or in constituencies where there is a relatively large number of voters who are not French Canadians.

In the 1970s these relationships have changed with the emergence of two new parties, the Parti Québécois and the Ralliement Créditiste, and the subsequent evolution affecting the Liberal party.[12]

Let us first try to describe the Creditistes. Very few of them are English speaking, they are spread throughout all age groups, and they include less educated people, farmers, small businessmen, and skilled and unskilled workers. The movement is almost nonexistent in Montreal.

Like the Ralliement Créditiste, the Parti Québécois is heavily French speaking. Its supporters are much younger and more educated, though. Its occupational background is more ambiguous, though it seems to get greater support from students, white collar workers and French speaking professionals.

The occupational outlook of the two parties' supporters is quite revealing, if related to some changes that took place during the Quiet Revolution. In the 1960s the gap between the average income of those in the liberal professions and all other professions widened. The sole group whose average income declined is the farmers. To them the Quiet Revolution was more of a setback than anything else, which partly explains the Ralliement's relative popularity among them. Likewise the small businessmen, who also joined the Ralliement in fairly large numbers, saw their relative situation worsened in the 1960s. The situation of skilled and unskilled workers is less clear, but if we take into account the fact that Ralliement Créditiste supporters come from outside Montreal, the same pattern probably holds. On the other hand, the best supporters of the Parti Québécois—students, teachers, civil servants, white collar workers and the professionals—improved their relative situation during the same period. It would thus seem that the Quiet Revolution is an important reference point in the Quebecois' mind. Its assessment has an impact on the voters' choice.[13]

For their part the Liberals have continued to receive massive support from the English-speaking electorate, but otherwise their socio-economic support showed no salient characteristics. They are strong in all age groups and in all educational groups, but in the occupational groups their greatest strength lies in categories like administrators, businessmen or salesmen whose situation did not worsen during the 1960s but who feel themselves threatened by Québec independence.

STABILITY OF THE ELECTORATE SINCE 1936

It was demonstrated earlier that since 1939 support for the Liberal party has been stronger in cities than it has been in rural areas, and that the opposite has been true for the Union Nationale. On the other hand, the Liberals' long domination before 1936 was primarily due to their massive rural support. At that time the Conservatives did much better in the towns than in the country.

This indicates that the elections of 1935, 1936, 1939, and 1944 were elections of realignment in some constituencies. On the one hand, several constituencies on the Island of Montreal that had been Conservative strongholds until 1939 turned to the Liberals in the 1939 election and remained faithful to them afterward. This was the case, for example, with the wealthy English-speaking areas of Notre-Dame-de Grâce, Outremont, and Westmount. On the other hand, the Union Nationale took over the rural constituencies around Montreal and Quebec, which had remained faithful to the Liberals until 1939 or 1944, and held on to them afterward almost without exception.[14]

In 1944 and 1948 two important third parties affected the votes polled by the two main parties. In 1944 the Bloc Populaire, a nationalist party, ran candidates in 91 constituencies. With André Laurendeau as its leader, the party obtained 15 per cent of the vote and elected four members. In 1948 the Union des Electeurs, a créditiste party, ran candidates in 92 constituencies. The party received nine per cent of the vote, but none of its candidates was elected. The Union des Electeurs' strongest concentration was in the city of Quebec and its environs, as well as in the Cantons de l'Est, the Nord-Ouest, and in Saguenay-Lac St-Jean. By contrast, the Bloc Populaire was primarily a Montreal party and, in general, more urban than the Union des Electeurs.

In 1948 the Liberals won in only eight constituencies out of 92 and were reduced to holding little more than the Island of Montreal. In 1952, following the Union Nationale's anti-union position taken at the time of the Asbestos strike, the Liberals won back several constituencies in Montreal and in other areas where union workers were relatively numerous. Most of these constituencies were retaken by the Union Nationale in 1956, although that year they lost several constituencies with half-urban and half-rural populations—in Abitibi and Bas Saint-Laurent, as well as some rural constituencies with a relatively high proportion of English-speaking people.

The Liberal victory in 1960 was largely due to the party's ability to regain some rural constituencies, particularly poor rural constituencies with a high proportion of farmers. It was pointed out earlier that the classification of electoral supporters on the basis of the urbanization of their area of residence is not as clear for the election of 1960 as for the preceding or later elections. Also, in 1962 and 1966, with the Liberal party in office, the variables of occupation and income seem to have been more significant than in 1960. This indicates some neutralization, in 1960, of the socio-economic differences between the two parties' supporters and, in particular, a temporary return of some farmers to the Liberal party. A public opinion poll made before this election also indicates that 38 per cent of the farmers intended to vote Liberal, as opposed to only 35 per cent of all the voters.

On the other hand, in 1962 and 1966 the percentage of farmers favorably disposed to the Liberals was clearly smaller than the percentage of all voters who favored that party. According to polls made for the Liberals, these percentages were 40 and 50 per cent, respectively, in 1962. In 1966 57 per cent of the voters intended to vote for the Liberals, but only 51 per cent of the farming population intended to do so.

These percentages and others cited indicate how large the differences were in 1962 between the two parties' supporters. Never—before 1936 or after—has there been such a contrast between the two parties. In 1962 the Liberal party was largely the party of city-dwellers, non-French Canadians, educated people, people with high occupational levels, and people with high incomes. Conversely, the Union Nationale party was supported just as strongly by the rural population, people of little education, people with low occupational levels, and people with low incomes.

The contrast was less in 1966, although the opposing factors continued to remain important. At least one of them will be emphasized again —the one concerning non-French Canadians who supported the Liberal party, and the French Canadians who were more disposed than in 1962 to the Union Nationale. Two third parties, one independentist—the Rassemblement pour l'Indépendance Nationale (RIN)—the other independentist and créditiste—the Ralliement National (RN)—obtained respectively 7 per cent and 3 per cent of the votes cast in 1966. Some of the data suggest that the RIN supporters resembled those of the Liberals, other than English-speaking liberals, who would not be expected to back a separatist party. There is on the other hand a great similarity between the RN supporters and those of the Union Nationale.

According to a public opinion poll taken before the 1966 election, only 4 per cent of the voters questioned indicated an intention to vote for the RIN, but the proportion was 6 per cent of those with an income between $5,000 and $8,000, 9 per cent of the young people between 18 and 24, and 25 per cent of the student population. According to the same poll, 13 per cent of those questioned indicated they would vote for the RN. It was the choice of 25 per cent of skilled workers, only 6 per cent of white-collar workers, and only 2 per cent of those with an income over $8,000.

In this period the electoral stability of the Union Nationale was apparently greater than that of the Liberal party. Except for the 1936 election, in which the Union Nationale obtained 57 per cent of the votes cast, its success has varied from 52 per cent in 1956 to 38 per cent in 1944. This is a fluctuation of only 14 percentage points, compared to a variation of 21 percentage points in the Liberal vote during the same period. The Liberals obtained 57 per cent of the vote cast in 1962, but only 36 per cent in 1948. The Liberals' portion of the vote dropped from 57 per cent in 1962 to 47 per cent in 1966; at the same time, the Union Nationale's percentage only changed from 42 to 40. From 1936 to 1966, the votes polled by third parties seem to have affected the Liberals much more than the Union Nationale. This, among other things, explains the greater electoral instability of the Liberals in these 30 years.

In view of this greater stability of the Union Nationale from 1936 to 1966, the results of the general elections of 1970 and 1973 were quite astonishing. One may speak of realigning elections, as were the elections from 1935 to 1944. The Union Nationale, who got 40 per cent of the vote in 1966 and whose the lowest score during the previous 30 years was 38 per cent (in 1944), was reduced to 20 per cent of the vote in 1970, and to five per cent in 1973. At the same time the Liberals got 45 per cent of the vote in 1970, and then 55 per cent in 1973, their highest since 1962. The Liberal Party now appears as the more stable of the old-line parties in provincial politics, as it has been for a long time in Quebec federal politics.

The polls indicate that the Union Nationale was losing its supporters to each of the other parties: many nationalists to the Parti Québécois, many in the rural or semi-rural areas to the Ralliement Créditiste, and a great number to the Liberal Party, among the owners or business people. As an aging party the Union Nationale was also losing its supporters to death. Many of the young people who supported it with passion in the 1930s or 1940s ignored it in the 1970s, and the rejuvenation of the party was very weak in the interim fifties and the sixties. The Union Nationale was rooted in a political generation and it is passing over with its generation.

Social Structure and Organization of the Parties

The differences established between the Quebec provincial parties in terms of their electoral supporters can also be found in the social characteristics of their members. Since precise data is not available concerning general party membership, this study will be limited to the candidates and members of the legislature, who typify only the leaders of the parties. This will be followed by an examination of the structures of the party organizations and finally, the function of these organizations in their relations with the voters. As in the preceding sections this analysis will bear upon the 1950s and 1960s, with some complementary data on the 1970s.

CHARACTERISTICS OF THE CANDIDATES AND ELECTED MEMBERS

Generally, the successful candidates from 1936 to 1956 had less formal education than those after 1956. Likewise, there were more manufacturers and businessmen and also farmers and workers among the successful candidates during these 20 years than there were afterward. Since 1956 the proportion of legislative members who were professionals and also semi-professionals—particularly those from the educational sectors—has increased at the expense of the manufacturers, businessmen, workers, and farmers. Finally, it is not surprising to learn that the number of elected members born in medium-sized Quebec cities, as well as in the metropolitan areas of Montreal and Quebec, has been steadily increasing[15]. When classified on the basis of these characteristics, the candidates and elected members of the Liberals and the Union Nationale from 1956 to 1966 form two rather different groups.

It can be seen from Table V that the differences between the two parties' candidates correspond exactly to the differences already noted between their electoral supporters. Like the Liberal voters, the Liberal candidates generally have more education than the Union Nationale candidates and belong to occupational categories that are higher up the social ladder than those of the Union Nationale candidates. There were more key figures in the Union Nationale who were born in localties with a population under 25,000 than there were in the Liberal party. This difference corresponds to the support that the Union Nationale received from rural areas, which was much greater than its support from cities.

Table V illustrates other differences between the parties. The fact that 30 per cent of the elected Union Nationale candidates had been mayors, compared to 14 per cent of the elected Liberal candidates, illustrates the greater local basis of the Union Nationale party. However, this difference does not appear between the parties' defeated candidates. Generally, the characteristics of the defeated candidates of both parties resemble each other more than do those of the elected members. Concerning the levels of education and occupation categories, the characteristics of the elected and defeated candidates of the Union Nationale resemble each other more than do those of the elected and defeated Liberal candidates. This indicates that those voting for the Union Nationale pay less attention to the socio-economic status of the candidates.

A recent study gives some information on the characteristics of the candidates in the 1970 general election.[16] It shows that the P.Q. is the party with the greatest proportion of candidates having a university education (about 65 per cent), followed by the Liberal Party (about 55 per cent), the Union National (less than 50 per cent) and the Ralliement Créditiste (only 25 per cent). The Liberal Party and the Union Nationale have many more professionals among their candidates than the two other parties, while the P.Q. has one out of three candidates coming from the educational professions. Farmers and workers are as numerous among the R.C. candidates as among the three other parties combined.

In as much as previous or current activities are concerned, the UN continues to recruit many candidates among mayors or aldermen at the municipal level (about 35 per cent). In this respect, the Liberals come second, the R.C. third, and the P.Q. fourth, with only five per cent of its candidates with such an experience. Half of the Liberal candidates are actual or former members of the Chamber of Commerce. This proportion is about 35 per cent among the U.N. candidates, less than 15 per cent for each of the other parties.

OFFICIAL AND NON-OFFICIAL PARTY STRUCTURES

The official structures of the Quebec provincial parties have not developed evenly. In 1955 the Liberals' constituency associations united to form the Quebec Liberal Federation. The Union Nationale did not start to build any official structures until 1965, and these are not fully developed. The Parti Québécois has had official structures since its beginning.

TABLE V*

Characteristics of candidates and elected members of the Liberal and Union Nationale parties from 1956 to 1966.

	Liberal Party		Union Nationale Party	
	Percentage of elected candidates	Percentage of defeated candidates	Percentage of elected candidates	Percentage of defeated candidates
PLACE OF BIRTH				
Localities of less than 2,000 inhabitants	28	41	37	28
Localities with a population between 2,000 and 25,000	29	23	40	27
Localities with a population over 25,000 (excluding Montréal and Quebec)	12	23	13	28
Unknown	2	1	4	8
LEVEL OF EDUCATION				
Having a university education	62	50	54	50
Having no more than a secondary education	30	41	33	37
Having no more than an elementary education	1	1	6	5
Unknown	7	8	7	8
OCCUPATIONAL LEVEL				
Professionals	59	40	48	38
Semi-professionals	8	12	7	10
Manufacturers and businessmen	26	39	34	43
Employees and workers	2	3	3	2
Farmers	4	6	7	4
Unknown	1	–	1	3
PUBLIC CAREERS				
Former Mayors	14	15	30	16
Former members of Chambers of Commerce	46	49	40	47

*Source: Robert Boily, "Les candidats élus et les candidats battus," in *Quebec élections provinciales au Québec: 1956-66*, Vincent Lemieux, ed. (Québec: Les Presses de L'Université Laval, 1969).

There are some in the Ralliement Créditiste, but they are rather symbolic.

In establishing official structures, the Union Nationale has limited itself to a National Council, defined as the directive agency of the party.

This council is formed of all Union Nationale M.P.s and of three representatives (one man, one woman, and one youth) from each electoral constituency in the province. It is managed by a committee consisting of the party leader, five M.P.s and five other members chosen from the representatives of the constituencies. In October 1965, the directors of the National Council approved a project to establish a constitution uniting the constituency associations. However, these associations took little account of this project.

The Union Nationale resolved at their March meeting to hold a party convention at least every two years. Nevertheless, no convention was subsequently held, with the only exceptions in 1969 and 1971. It was also suggested at the March 1965 meeting that the Council appoint several committees to assist it in its work. However, they have not been established; the only two committees that actually seem to function are the policy committee and the finance committee, both created as a result of the 1961 convention. This convention, at which Daniel Johnson was elected party leader, was the first one held by the Union Nationale.

The Union Nationale has in its Quebec offices, some permanent employees who work primarily on party organization and strategy. There are also some employees who work directly for the party leader.

The official Liberal party structures are much more complex than those of the Union Nationale, and are often duplicated by non-official ones. The Quebec Liberal Party is built on the foundation of constituency associations, each with its own executive council. There are 23 regional groups of constituency associations. The constituency associations are also represented in the party's general council. Local constituency associations organize conventions to elect their officers. Furthermore, the regional groups each form 8 permanent committees—women, youth, financial, ethnic groups, organizational, information, legal, and policy committees.

The same committees are found at the provincial level The principal officers of the Liberal Party at this level are the president, the secretary, and the treasurer, who are elected for one year with the possibility of a one-year extension. Together with the provincial party leader and three of the party's M.P.s they form an executive committee which, between the meetings of the steering committee, administers party business. The steering committee is composed of about 60 members. In addition to the executive committee members, there are 10 M.P.s, the presidents of the 23 regional groups, and the presidents and the secretaries of the 8 permanent provincial committees.

The general council is an even larger organization where the members of the steering committee join all the other Liberal M.P.s, the presidents of each constituency association, plus a woman and a youth from each of the 23 regional groups.

The official structures of the Quebec Liberal Party are obviously quite complex. They require many elective posts and managerial or consultant organizations, many meetings, assemblies, and conventions. It is evident that these structures have not been considered as a tool for winning elections. This is why in many localities and in many constituencies there has not been much concern with official structures, which are duplicated by less official structures organized specifically with the electoral contests in mind. This is a cause of conflict, or at least some tension, which is not found in the Union Nationale.[17]

For example, in many cases the chief organizer of the constituency is not the president of the constituency association. Sometimes he does not even belong to the executive council of these associations. In spite of the fact that all requests coming from Liberals should be made to the associations rather than to the deputy or the administrations, influential party members frequently approach these officials, whom they can influence more than the officers of the associations. Furthermore, in nearly all cases the regional groups exist only on paper, and most Liberals ignore them.[18] In any case, to understand the party organizations' functions, the study of official and non-official structures must be integrated.

The official structures of the Parti Québécois are organized at three levels, as in the case of the Liberal Party. First there is the constituency level, with a general assembly and an executive council. Then there is the regional level, with a regional convention (once a year), a regional council and a regional executive council. Each constituency is represented by 24 delegates to the regional convention, and the regional council is formed by the presidents of the constituency associations, the deputies or the candidates of these constituencies, and the chairmen of the regional committees. Only the delegates can vote in these regional councils.

Third, there is the national level, with a convention, a council and an executive council. The convention is convened every two years. In the Liberal Party this convention is held every year. The members of the P.Q. national council are: the members of the executive council, the presidents of the constituency associations, three M.P.s, delegated by the M.P. council, the presidents at the regional level, and, without the right of voting, all the other M.P.s, all the official candidates of the party, and a delegate from each constituency. The executive council has the following membership: the president, the vice-president, and the treasurer of the party, the program advisor ("counseiller au programme"), two M.P.s and nine councillors. Note that the M.P.s are not eligible for the positions of treasurer, program advisor or councillor, so that the non-M.P.s are sure to be in a majority on the executive council.

As we have said earlier the official structures of the Ralliement Créditiste are rather symbolic. They are observed if there is no problem in doing so, but if there is, the structures are easily manipulated by the dominant group in the party.

All the parties convene leadership conventions to elect their leader. At the constituency level, the candidates are selected by all the members within the Parti Québécois. Within the Liberal Party this procedure is possible, plus an alternative one where the candidate is selected by delegates. It is the same within the Ralliement Créditiste, but there is another possibility: the selection by the central organization of the party. In the UN the two procedures usually observed are the selection by delegates or the selection by the leader.

THE PARTY ORGANIZATION IN ACTION

The party structures rather faithfully reflect what has been noted about the ideologies and policies of the parties and the characteristics of their supporters. It is not surprising that the parties which are more interventionist in provincial politics and the ones with greater support in urban and middle-class circles have more developed official structures. Conversely, it is not surprising that greater importance is given to non-official structures in the parties less interventionist and with a more popular basis.

These differences are evident if one observes the structures in operation. The parties then appear to be organizations pursuing definite goals through their ideologies and policies. The most important goal is to gather enough votes to be able to form the government. Our study will be limited to this goal around which, in former governmental parties such as the Union Nationale and Liberal parties, all other goals gravitate. It can be seen how integrated, in pursuit of this goal, are the phenomena discussed in the three main sections of this study: the ideologies and policies of the parties, the characteristics of their electoral supporters and, finally, the social composition and the structures of the parties.

In the past, the major provincial parties of Quebec always exploited the voters' traditional identification with either the "parti bleu" or the "parti rouge." Unfortunately, statistics are not available on the proportion of voters who continue to identify themselves in such a way. But it is sure that the parties' organizations will be able to rely less and less on attempts to retain the traditional vote. Multiple factors including urbanization have gradually weakened partisan traditions, particularly since the end of the 1950s. The astonishing success of the Créditistes in the federal elections of 1962 and 1963, as well as the three changes of regime at the provincial level in 1960, 1966 and 1970, indicate the erosion of the partisan traditions that contributed to the electoral stability of the 1940s and 1950s at both provincial and federal levels. When speaking of this situation, the election organizers agree more and more that partisan traditions are no longer important and that the vote has become increasingly unpredictable.

Whether it is a cause or an effect of the weakening of partisan traditions, candidates nominated by the parties frequently have almost no party experience. These candidates obviously do not arouse traditional identification with the party they represent. This lack of party identity was already noticeable in several of the Union Nationale candidates in the elections of 1966, and with more than one eminent minister of the Lesage Cabinet.

The party organizations have made material appeals to the voters, such as the distribution or promise of various goods and services that depend on government action. It is well known that in Quebec some of these goods and services have traditionally been distributed to voters as patronage. This patronage, which reached its peak under the Duplessis regime, was not limited to employment in public offices. Contracts, purchases, subsidies, and pensions also led to relationships of patronage between the parties and the voters. Moreover, as Quinn has illustrated,[19] in addition to individuals, there were municipal councils, school boards, factories, and co-operatives who profited from patronage. The governing party was thus assured the support of the local elite directing these organizations.

It cannot be said that all political patronage has disappeared in Quebec. The Liberals, for instance, were accused (not without reason) of having replaced "small" patronage with "big" patronage, involving powerful individuals who contributed large sums to the party's coffers.[20] However, the Salvas Commission, the reform of the civil service, and the new electoral law in Quebec have drastically limited party patronage during election campaigns. Therefore, the use of such means to win electoral support is becoming increasingly dangerous for the parties.

The party organizations have also exploited appeals of a symbolic nature in their attempts to win elections. But in Quebec, as elsewhere, the proliferation of TV exposure has modified the political impact of these attempts. TV has given a more specific image to politics, portraying it as part of daily life. In this way, it has turned away some of the myths surrounding politicians, who in the past were only seen during electoral campaigns, when they were making speeches and participating in other activities that were not part of daily life.

In response to this new challenge, public relations men have tried to build "images" of the leaders, with limited results.[21] The political prestige of Jean Lesage lasted only 6 or 7 years, that of Daniel Johnson (interrupted by his death), of Jean-Jacques Bertrand, and of Robert Bourassa even less.

The Party System of Quebec

In the late 1950s and the early 1960s the party system of Quebec started to undergo radical changes. These were determined by general changes in the political environment and, more specifically, in the Quebec political system following the Quiet Revolution.

For about 60 years, from the end of nineteenth century to the late 1950s, the party system of Quebec was relatively stable in spite of the creation of the Union Nationale in 1936 and the accompanying disappearance of the Conservative party. A close examination indicates, as noted earlier, that after 1936 the two main parties somehow exchanged some of their positions without causing basic changes in the system itself. The only apparent change was that one of the two provincial parties, the Union Nationale, was not affiliated with one of the two big federal parties.

This study indicates no basic changes in the Quebec party system resulting from the 1936 turning point. Just as before 1936, there was an autonomist governing party and an opposition party that was less autonomist or completely federalist. After 1936, as before, the party in power had the monopoly on patronage and did not fail to exploit it for electoral goals. This explains the governing party's successes in rural areas; these areas, which strongly supported the Liberal party before 1936, started after this date to support the Union Nationale just as strongly. Finally, after 1936 there were not any major modifications in the social composition of the parties or in their organization. These parties had no official structures; they were dominated by members of parliament and were for the most part groupings of election workers. The incentives offered to these election workers and to the voters were the traditional incentives referred to earlier: identification with the party and its leaders, goods and services obtained by way of patronage, and abstract ideologies on the internal and external problems of Quebec.

The Bloc Populaire in 1944 and the Union des Electeurs in 1948 threatened the stability of the system. Hindered by the electoral system and, more basically, by the temporary character of the economic and political situation to which they were responding, their threat was short-lived.

This stability of the party system is also explained by the very conservative character of the parties' actions and, even more, by the apparent stability of the society in which the parties found themselves. During the first half of the twentieth century the successive governments of Quebec enacted very few important laws capable of changing the face of society. Moreover, neither the electoral map nor the electoral law underwent important modifications during this period, except for some amendments to the law enacted by the famous Bill 34, which changed the election rules in favor of the governing party.

Although Quebec society, as early as the 1920s, was in fact beginning to change considerably, these changes remained hidden for a long time by political resistance, especially by the dominating ideologies created by the political parties in their resistance to social change. This state of affairs was upset by what has been called the Quiet Revolution. This is not the place to make a detailed analysis of this phenomenon. However, it can be stated that, of the social agents who started this "revolution" and saw it through its initial stages, none exerted more influence than the Quebec Liberal party and the government it formed after its victory in 1960.

At least 5 important series of measures that the Lesage government brought about have greatly contributed to the transformation of the party system in Quebec. These measures were not adopted solely because of the action of the Lesage government. It is evident that several of them originated with and were supported by the public and forces other than the Liberal party. Nevertheless, at one time or another during the process of decision-making that led to the adoption of these measures, the role of the governing party was decisive. These 5 series of measures, which have already been mentioned in this study, are the following:

(1) The reform of the civil service started by the Union Nationale government of Paul Sauvé produced a strengthening of the higher management of public administration. After a few governmental delays, this reform led to trade unionism in the civil service and also to a new labor code permitting civil servants to strike.

(2) When this new labor code and the famous Bill 60 creating the Ministry of Education were being considered, the government not only allowed but also solicited the intervention of the interest groups concerned. The Lesage government established new rules that made possible the inclusion of interest groups within the processes of political decision-making.

(3) Under the Lesage government major political measures were adopted, such as hospitalization insurance, the reform of the education system, the reform of the civil service, the nationalization of electric power, and the construction of superhighways. By these general political measures, wealth was more collectively distributed among the electors, and the general level of scholarship in the province was raised.

(4) In the sphere of federal-provincial relations, the Lesage government, continuing the action started by Paul Sauvé, entered into close negotiations with Ottawa. The Lesage government had the assistance of small teams of specialists from inside as well as outside the ministries. These negotiations, which ended with important gains for Quebec, have contributed in a complex and still rather obscure fashion to the development of separatist movements and parties. At least 3 factors favorable to this development can be indicated. These factors are linked with government action, although the results were not anticipated by the government. Firstly, the advantages that were obtained in the negotiations have resulted in a desire to obtain much more. Secondly, there have been obstacles over which the government stumbled in its negotiations with Ottawa. As a result of these obstacles, it has been argued, no further pro-

gress is possible in the reform of the Canadian political system. Lastly, the ideological arguments exploited in this struggle with Ottawa have created a climate favorable to the expression of independentist arguments. Certainly other more fundamental factors are behind the rise of independentist movements in Quebec, but those just listed cannot be ignored.

(5) Finally, the Lesage government enfranchised the young people between 18 and 21 and introduced amendments that have considerably modified the electoral laws of Quebec. In particular, by the strict control of electoral spending the governing party, which usually has more money to spend on elections, lost the advantage it once had over the opposition party. The new law, however, was designed to keep third parties at a disadvantage. The Lesage government was less aggressive in reforming the electoral map and satisfied itself with the creation of 12 new constituencies in metropolitan regions and another in the Saguenay-Lac Saint-Jean region. This timidity proved fatal to them on June 5, 1966.

These measures and their consequences have produced radical transformations in the Quebec party system, the results of which cannot yet be determined. The most obvious of these transformations is in the increase in the number of parties. Increased activity between Quebec and Ottawa, as well as the Quebec political situation since the late 1950s, have led to the appearance of new parties, which unlike the third parties of the 1940s seem as if they will remain for a long time on the provincial political scene.

These measures have also produced a rapprochement between the two old parties in regard to their external ideologies and policies. From the end of the nineteenth century up to the late 1950s one of the two main provincial parties of Quebec was relatively autonomist and the other relatively federalist; in the 1960s, this distinction no longer applied. The two parties were both autonomist and have proposed greater powers for Quebec within the Canadian Confederation.

This neutralization of the differences between the external ideologies and policies of the two parties has made more evident the differences between their internal ideologies and policies. These differences, although never very noticeable, had been taking shape since the early 1950s with the accession of Georges-Emile Lapalme to the Liberal Party leadership. When the measures referred to earlier were adopted by the Lesage government, these differences became more apparent. Those measures, however, were also due to pressure from senior civil servants and from government advisors for greater state intervention and for measures more general than those that had characterized the Duplessis government.

At the same time, the socio-economic differences between the supporters of the two parties became more apparent in the late 1950s and the early 1960s. Exact figures are not available on earlier periods, but it would be surprising if the polarization of a socio-economic order within the electorate would be as evident before the 1950s as after.

The 1966 election ended this polarizing movement, and even initiated a rapprochement between the internal ideologies and policies of the two parties. On the one hand, the Union Nationale's proposed programme was somewhat similar to that of the Liberals. On the other hand, there was opposition to the Liberal programme as evidenced by the public attitude to some of the Liberal policies (on education in particular). The Liberals did not present any general proposals in their platform that were as significant as those proposed in 1960 and 1962. Furthermore, as noted earlier, an analysis of the 1966 vote, compared to that of 1962, reveals a lessening of socio-economic differences between the parties' supporters.

After being returned to office in 1966, the Union Nationale proved hesitant, not knowing how to deal with a society that had undergone such sweeping changes. At the end of four years it, too, succumbed to the numerous contradictions inherent in its policies, many of which had either been prepared by the preceding government or were conceived by technocrats in the public service.

On the constitutional question the party returned after the death of Daniel Johnson to a position somewhat similar to that taken by Duplessis. Jean-Jacques Bertrand spent more time in accusing Ottawa of centralization than in devising means of assuring the autonomy of Quebec, which was replaced during the election campaign of 1970 by a four-year time limit for restructuring Canadian federalism; but it had already alienated many voters, who preferred the Parti Québécois clearly independentist platform or the equally clear federalist position of the Liberal Party.

At that time the stage was set for the major oppositions which hitherto have defined the Quebec party system in the 1970s and which are direct consequences of the so-called Quiet Revolution. The Liberal Party is clearly federalist in matters of external ideologies and policies and it is now a reluctant interventionist in matters of internal ideologies and policies, except as governmental intervention is apt to promote economic development or social order. The Parti Québécois is clearly independentist, but the other parties—The Union Nationale, the Ralliement Créditiste and the new Parti National Populaire—are much less interventionist in internal matters, as they are rather sceptical towards the changes initiated during the Quiet Revolution. All of them defined themselves as more nationalist than the Liberal Party, but they are opposed to independence for Québec.

Postscript

In mid-October, 1976, Robert Bourassa announced that a general election would be held on November 15. Officially, the rationale for this early election was the necessity for Bourassa to get, in his own words, a clear mandate in the approaching negotiations with the federal government about constitutional matters. But one can presume that the real reason was the declining popularity of the Liberal Party, as revealed by the polls, and serious internal stresses in the party over Bourassa's leadership.

The opposition parties and the press had no difficulty in showing that it was impossible for Bourassa to get a clearer mandate than in 1973, when he captured 102 of the 110 seats. More generally the Liberals had many problems during the campaign. Bourassa did not succeed in selling his platform: the constitutional debate with Trudeau, the threat for the Quebec economy represented by the P.Q. plan for independence, the responsibility of the unions in the recent strikes in the public sector, etc. In many places Bourassa was booed and sometimes he lost his temper with the P.Q. "bums," as he called them.

The Parti Québécois campaign was greatly facilitated by the loss of popularity of its main opponent. The P.Q. was very skilful in telling the voters: choose a new government first, then look at independence later by way of a referendum.

It is significant to consider the occupations of the two parties' candidates. The differences between them are linked to those observed in the former parts of this chapter (see Table V).

TABLE VI*

Occupations of the two main parties candidates, in 1976

	Parti Liberal (N)	Parti Québécois (N)
Professionals	26	25
Businessmen	48	25
New middle class*	27	42
Workers	5	10
Farmers	4	8
Total	110	110

*Teachers, technicians, public servants, etc.

* Source: André Bernard, *Quebec: elections 1976* (Montréal, Hurtubise HMH, 1976), p. 82

Businessmen are twice as numerous in the Liberal Party, but the new middle class, and particularly the teachers, are more numerous in the Parti Québécois. Even if the workers and the farmers are under-represented in both parties, there are two of them in the Parti Québécois, for each one in the Parti Liberal.

Polls made during the campaign showed the Parti Québécois in advance of the Liberals, but to many voters and observers a P.Q. victory did not look possible. So the election returns, on the evening of November 15, were astonishing (see Table VII).

TABLE VII

Votes and seats captured by the parties in the 1976 general election in Quebec

	Votes (%)	Seats (N)
Parti Québécois	41	71
Parti Libéral	34	26
Union Nationale	18	11
Ralliement Créditiste	5	1
Parti National Populaire	1	1
Others	1	0
	100	110

*Source: Report of the Quebec Chief Electoral Officier.

The evolution from 1973 to 1976 was very consistent in the case of the 4 main parties. In almost every riding the Parti Québécois and the Union Nationale did better than in 1973; on the contrary the Parti Liberal and the Ralliement Créditiste were declining everywhere.

The Quebec voters were dissatisfied with the Bourassa government because of high unemployment, harsh strikes in the hospitals, agricultural problems, and loose administrative practices. Bourassa, a highly popular figure in 1970 and 1973, became isolated from the voters, surrounded as he was by image-makers and political councillors who put too much confidence in the so-called "silent majority." He was defeated in his own riding of Mercier, in Montreal, and soon resigned as the Parti Liberal leader.

About 10 per cent of the Liberal voters of 1973 went to the Union Nationale, and another 10 per cent to the Parti Quebecois. Most were relatively young people, so the Liberals appear now as an aging party, with its greatest strength among non-French Canadians and people in business occupations.

Two-thirds of the new voters supported the Parti Québécois, whose support comes largely from electors born after 1940, who voted for the first time in the 1960s. But it seems that many of them and of the older voters gave their vote to the P.Q. as the best way to change the government. During 1977, many of them still did not seem ready to vote for independence in a referendum.

The voter turnout was the highest in the Quebec history, 85 per cent of the registered electorate, one per cent more than in 1970, the previous record.

As for the proposed independence referendum, one cannot predict its result. It is the author's opinion that the Parti Québécois cannot win without a crisis context. Whether the federal government will generate this crisis, or whether the Levesque government will be able to induce such a crisis, remains to be seen.

Endnotes

[1] A similar division into three periods, as well as a more detailed study, can be found in Jean Hamelin et al., "Les élections provinciales dans le Québec", *Cahiers de Géographie de Québec*, October 1959-March 1960, pp. 5-207. See also Herbert F. Quinn, *The Union Nationale: A Study in Quebec Nationalism* (Toronto: University of Toronto Press, 1963), and André Bernard, *La Politique au Canada et au Québec* (Montréal: Presses de l'Université du Québec, 1975) ch. VII.

[2] Daniel Johnson, *Egalité ou Indépendance* (Montréal: Editions Renaissance, 1965).

[3] On the Asbestos strike and its significance in the political evolution of Quebec, see Pierre E. Trudeau et al., *La grève de l'amiante* (Montréal: Les Editions Cité Libre, 1956).

[4] For a brief study of the various campaigns for the nationalization of electricity from the early 1930s to 1962, see Claude Boileau, "Les partis provinciaux du Québec et le problème de la nationalisation de l'électricité" (M.A. Thesis, Université Laval, 1966).

[5] *Le Devoir* (Montréal), September 20, 1962, p. 1.

[6] Hamelin et al., "Les élections provinciales dans le Québec".

[7] Paul Cliche, "Les élections provinciales dans le Québec, de 1927 à 1956", *Recherches sociographiques*, July-December 1961, pp. 343-365.

[8] In these three elections (1960, 1962, and 1966) the percentages of urban voters by constituency have been established from the census figures of 1961.

[9] See, for example, Michel Chalout, "Les études locales et régionales", in *Quatre élections provinciales au Québec: 1956-66*, Vincent Lemieux, ed. (Quebec: Les Presses de l'Université Laval, 1969).

[10] On this subject see Vincent Lemieux, "Les effets imprévus de la loi et de la carte électorales nouvelles", *Socialisme 66*, October-December 1966, pp. 107-118.

[11] In the following the results of three polls have been used. These were made on behalf of the Liberal party of Quebec before the elections of 1960, 1962, and 1966. The results are contained in the following reports: Groupe de Recherches Sociales, *Les électeurs québécois. Attitudes et opinions à la veille des élections de 1960*, Montréal 1960; Groupe de Recherches Sociales, *Les préférences politiques des électeurs québécois en 1962*, Montréal, 1964; Société de Mathématique Appliquée Enc., *Evolution du Québec*, Montréal, 1966 (confidential).

[12] For more data on the 1970 and 1973 general elections, see Vincent Lemieux et al., *Une Election de Réalignement* (Montréal: Editions du Jour, 1970) and Daniel Latouche et al., *Le Processus Electoral au Québec* (Montréal: HMH, 1975). See also Richard Hamilton and Maurice Pinard, "The bases of Parti Québécois support in recent Québec elections", *Canadian Journal of Political Science*, March 1976, pp. 3-26.

[13] These last three paragraphs are excepts from André Blais et al., "The

Emergence of New Forces in Quebec Electoral Politics", in *Canada: a Sociological Profile*, W. E. Mann ed. (Toronto: Copp Clark, 1971).

[14] For more details see Vincent Lemieux, "L'analyse hiérarchique des résultats électoraux", pp. 167-191, in *Le Quotient électoral vrai* (Québec: Les Presses de l'Université Laval, 1973).

[15] The data on the elected and defeated candidates of the two parties are taken from Robert Boily, "Les candidats élus et les candidats battus", in *Quatre élections provinciales au Québec: 1956-66.*

[16] Jacques Rivet et Hugues Laplante, "Les Candidats vus par eux-mêmes", *Le Soleil* (Québec), April 25, 1970, p. 26.

[17] See Paul-André Comeau, "La transformation du parti libéral québécois", *Revue canadienne d'Economique et de Science Politique*, August 1965, pp. 358-367.

[18] This situation exists at least in Bas St-Laurent-Gaspésie, as shown in Michel Chaloult, *Les partis politiques dans le territoire-pilote*, Bureau d'Aménagement de l'Est du Québec, February 1966.

[19] See Herbert F. Quinn, "Administrative and Electoral Practices under the Union Nationale", in *The Union Nationale.*

[20] On this, and more generally on political patronage in Quebec see Vincent Lemieux and Raymond Hudon, *Patronage et Politique au Québec: 1944-1972* (Sillery: Boréal Express, 1975).

[21] On this, see Jacques Benjamin, *Comment on fabrique un premier ministre québécois* (Montréal: Editions de l'Aurore, 1975).

SASKATCHEWAN
Parties in a Politically Competitive Province

John C. Courtney and David E. Smith

Political parties in Saskatchewan have both generated and reflected the color and the intensity of the province's politics. Since the creation of the province in 1905, individuals and groups have organized, sustained and utilized various political parties for protective as well as representational purposes. Cognizant of the division of powers inherent in Canadian federalism, Saskatchewan voters have not hesitated to change their party allegiances from one election to another and from one level of government to another. Indeed, parties themselves have joined in the game on more than one occasion by dissociating themselves from their Ottawa namesakes in order to prove to the electorate their worth as protectors of the province's interests. Federalism has made this form of politics possible; protection of economic interests has made it necessary.

The History of the System

Whatever other influences may have been prominent in the development of Saskatchewan politics, the farmer and the federal system must be given prime recognition. Any historical survey of the province cannot fail to focus upon their contribution to the distinctive features of Saskatchewan's political system. Given a one-crop economy, the significance of the farmer is hardly surprising; his opinions and his policy demands are bound to shape the political society. What is surprising about the Saskatchewan farmer, however, is his continued opposition to direct action in politics. The differences between the politics of Saskatchewan and those of other Prairie provinces are largely traceable to the Saskatchewan farmer's rejection of direct political action and to the fact that all provincial parties since 1905 have found it profitable to cater to him.

More surprising, however, has been the federal system's contribution to the development of the province's political system. Although it is hardly unexpected to find national politics affecting provincial developments to some degree, the federal contribution in Saskatchewan has been sustained and continuous. Federal government is widely accepted as a "method of dividing powers so that the general and regional governments are each, within a sphere, co-ordinate and independent."[1] Such a definition, by stressing division of powers, implies that the two levels of government enjoy a greater degree of independence than has been the case in Saskatchewan for the past seventy-odd years. Intergovernmental dependence, which has been notable during this period, may therefore be explained less by constitutional or legal ties than by common political interests.

Thus, while federalism introduces an additional dimension to the political system by providing two levels of government instead of one and by establishing between them a series of countervailing pressures, it also introduces a mechanism to resolve the conflict between centralizing and decentralizing forces—the national party system. This is not to say that national parties in a federal system do not experience conflict generated by the federal experiment. Indeed, one of the theses of this chapter is that much of the history of Saskatchewan politics can be understood only in terms of such intraparty conflict. Partisanship has clearly been a characteristic of Saskatchewan politics. In 1905 the territorial tradition of nonpartisanship was discarded; in 1917 an opportunity to return to nonpartisanship was rejected; and after 1930 the founders of the Co-operative Commonwealth Federation eschewed the example of UFA group government in Alberta for traditional party politics.

THE INTRODUCTION AND OPERATION OF THE ORIGINAL PARTY SYSTEM

Before 1896 nonpartisan politics prevailed in the Northwest Territories. After that date and until 1905 the national two-party system appeared in federal contests but was excluded from territorial politics. The reasons for the delay were simple. There was little dispute about the Territories, goals and a general conviction that, in dealing with Ottawa, these goals could be achieved more quickly and completely if members of the Assembly spoke with a single voice. On local matters some distinction was made between "government" and "opposition" members, but it was neither rigid nor enduring.[2] Federal political distinctions became manifest at the local level only as the Territories were about to achieve provincial status, when the Laurier government revealed the sections of the Saskatchewan and Alberta Bills relating to the educational rights of minorities and federal retention of natural resources.[3] Both provisions were attacked by the territorial premier, F.W.G. Haultain, a nonpartisan territorially but a Conservative federally, as derogations of provincial rights.

What is significant is that federal issues—the perennial religion-school question and a potentially contentious natural resources policy—were injected into provincial politics. Neither issue had been current in the Territories before 1905, but in that year the former was to help bring Liberal governments to power in Saskatchewan and Alberta and the latter was to become a principal object of attack for the new Conservative opposition.

The demands for unity inherent in Canadian federalism in 1905 induced the central government to seek friendly administrations in the new provinces. Initially it seemed that Ottawa would be only partially successful, since Haultain, territorial premier for eight years and a supporter of autonomy, was the logical choice as premier of one of the provinces. However, his vow to raise the school question in Saskatchewan and Alberta and his public denunciation of the Autonomy Bills in by-election campaigns on behalf of the Conservative candidates in Ontario gave the federal Liberals reason to ignore him.[4] Normally, the federal government has no role to play in the selection of a provincial premier, for it is the Lieutenant-Governor's task to seek out the leader of the party that commands the greatest support in the legislature. However, in this instance the Lieutenant-Governor had to determine which leader, Walter Scott of the Liberals or F.W.G. Haultain of the Conservatives, would likely command support of a majority in the yet-to-be-elected assembly. In making this choice, the new Lieutenant-Governor of Saskatchewan, A. E. Forget, who had also been Lieutenant-Governor of the Northwest Territories between 1898 and 1905, appears to have used "the personal discretion of the Crown . . . frankly and openly in the interests of the central government and the Liberal party."[5] In his defence he could point to the results of the 1904 federal election in the Territories when seven Liberals and only three Conservatives were elected to parliament. Later, after December 13, 1905, he could also point to the success of Walter Scott's Liberal government in securing 16 of the 25 seats (see Table I), but by then the Liberals' accession to power had been accomplished by the Lieutenant-Governor's action.

There seems little doubt that Forget's sentiments were disposed toward the Liberals. However, it is less certain that he acted under the direction of Ottawa. Whether he did or not is less important than the fact that the discretionary power of the Lieutenant-Governor, so often derided in Canadian political literature, in this instance proved determinant. The Lieutenant-Governor was originally envisioned by the Fathers of Confederation as a federal officer. Despite the office's evolution in quite an opposite direction in other provinces before 1905 and in Saskatchewan afterward, at that time and in that province Mr. Forget acted as a federal officer. The imprint of federal politics was thus stamped unavoidably on Saskatchewan's first government and, naturally, on its first opposition.

Anticipating later political development, Saskatchewan's first opposition sought temporary refuge in a special provincial organization. Until 1911, when the federal and provincial Conservative organizations were merged, the opposition actually referred to itself as the Provincial Rights party. This strategy of separation, from 1905 to 1911, reflected the personal views of F.W.G. Haultain before he was appointed to the bench in 1912, but it also proved to be a strategic move.

Since most of the electorate was composed of farmers, and a large number of them wheat farmers, their interests had to be given first consideration by any government. The Liberal government of Walter Scott (see Table II for a list of Premiers of Saskatchewan) acknowledged the farmers' importance by actively soliciting the views of their provincial organization, the Saskatchewan Grain Growers' Association, and by co-opting SGGA personnel into the cabinet.[6] On the basis of this consultation it regularly introduced legislation favored by the farmers; the best example, but by no means the only, was an act passed in 1911 that incorporated and helped finance the Saskatchewan Co-operative Elevator Company.[7] In return for this solicitude, the farmers reciprocated by eschewing direct political action and favoring the Liberals with their votes.

The farmers' attachment to the Liberal party, both federally and provincially, was natural on other grounds as well. The vast majority of them had immigrated to Saskatchewan in the early 1900s from Ontario, the United States, the British Isles, and Central Europe. In such a situation "the Liberals held trump cards. They were the government in office at a time when hopes were high, conditions buoyant. Many newly enfranchised voters of 1905 had no political tradition and were persuaded to vote for the same party that federally offered homesteads and a new life."[8]

One casualty of this goodwill between the farmers and the provincial Liberal government was the opposition party. There was little it could offer as an alternative to the government other than a more efficient administration. Following the 1905 election this was exactly what the Conservatives, as the Provincial Rights party, did offer, although they usually elaborated their campaigns with general attacks on partisanship and demands for provincial control of resources.[9] While their platform was not likely to dislodge large numbers of Liberal supporters, it did provide a single focus of opposition, independent of Conservative sentiment, for all who opposed Saskatchewan's Liberal government. To the extent that it accomplished the task of monopolizing the opposition, the Provincial Rights party until 1911 and the Conservative party afterward functioned as the principal minority party or "moon," to use Samuel Lubell's solar analogy of the American party system.[10] That Saskatchewan politics differed this early from other prairie provincial politics—for example, politics in Alberta—is evidenced in this monopoly of opposition in the former province and its dispersion in the latter.

THE ORIGINAL PARTY SYSTEM UNDER ATTACK

The first six years of the province's political history were marked by the entrenchment of the Liberal government. In the view of one scholar, "gerry-mandered representation, the work of the partisan civil services, energetic development policies and sensitivity to the wishes of the provincial farm organizations and the women's suffrage and temperance movements, kept the Liberal party in power" in both Saskatchewan and Alberta.[11] Furthermore, the provincial Liberals in this period also benefited from federal patronage. The first major disturbance to this pattern of politics occurred when the Conservatives defeated the Liberals in the federal election of 1911. Since the Saskatchewan Conservatives had spent so much energy attacking an unsympathetic and meddling federal government, they might have been expected to benefit from this change in federal political fortunes. To some extent they did, since they and their supporters became the recipients of federal patronage. However, these gains were more than offset by the federal Conservatives' image as a high-tariff party, opposed to the policy of reciprocity with the United States that was widely supported in the West. Nevertheless, the provincial Conservatives could find some solace in the results of the 1911 federal election. For the first time since the province's autonomy the provincial Liberal government lacked the support of a sympathetic federal government. According to the Lubell thesis, if the farmers switched their allegiance from the Liberal government, the minority party would be the chief beneficiary. After 1911, therefore, it was clear to the Liberal leadership that the farmers must be kept loyal at any cost or they would alter the existing party system.

The vulnerability of that system became apparent in 1916 and 1917 with the spread of the Non-Partisan League to Saskatchewan from North Dakota.[12] Overtly the League was not particularly successful. In the provincial election of 1917 only one successful candidate was nominated by the League (he also was nominated by local Liberals and Conservatives as well) and when the legislature met he took his seat with the Liberals. The League's influence lay in its theory of nonpartisanship, which deprived the Conservatives of their principal election plank, and in its practical successes in North Dakota, which challenged the achievements of the Liberal party. The League quickly realized that it could not duplicate its earlier electoral victories by the same methods it had used in the United States. In particular, the presence of party discipline and the absence of the direct primary meant that its candidates had to enter Canadian politics as nominees of a third party. Under the single-member-district, simple-plurality-vote electoral system the procedure of entering third-party candidates would almost certainly be unsuccessful unless the new party could attract a wide following among the organized farmers. In articulating many of the farmers' demands and in depicting itself as the political arm of the SGGA, the League presented the first real threat to the Liberal party's monopoly of farmer support. Although it failed to capture the farmers' organization, it did infuse them with a new militancy for direct political action. In Saskatchewan this militancy led to an even closer liaison, in personnel and views, between the SGGA and the Liberal government.

The Non-Partisan League's attack on the original party system of Saskatchewan was crucial to that system's later disintegration. It was particularly destructive since it coincided with renewed strains in federal politics. In 1917 the national Liberal party split between Laurier and Unionist Liberals on the question of forming a coalition government with the Conservatives. The provincial Liberals, who felt they had to choose between the two national Liberal factions, recognized that their choice was complicated more by consideration of their personal loyalty to Sir Wilfrid Laurier than by their concern for the effects of coalition on party organization. For many Liberals, including such prominent Saskatchewan figures as George Langley, W. R. Motherwell, A. P. McNab and G. A. Bell, the Conservative party was so tainted by big business that coalition would amount to guilt by association for the Liberals in the West. For others such as J. A. Calder, former Liberal provincial Minister of Railways and now Unionist Minister of Immigration and Colonization, union was necessary for better administration of the government's war policy including the implementation of conscription.[13] Premier W. M. Martin was concerned that coalition would associate Liberals with the Borden government's discriminatory War-time Elections Act, which prejudicially affected the voting rights of many British subjects of German and Austro-Hungarian origin who had entered Canada since 1902. There were more than 32,500 of these people in Saskatchewan in 1916.[14]

Within two weeks of the announcement of Union Government, Mr. Calder announced that a National Government Association of Saskatchewan had been formed under his direction. Calder was the recognized head of the Saskatchewan Liberal party machine; with his knowledge of provincial politics and with Conservative financial contributions the cause of Union Government seemed assured.[15] It was Calder's own opinion that "Liberalism in its truest and broadest sense [would] not suffer" from the experiment. This was an optimistic judgment. Federal party lines, which for over a decade had separated provincial parties, were blurred, and consequently party distinctions in the province were further weakened.

Another federal event, in part related to conditions arising from the war and in part derived from earlier grievances, influenced provincial political development. A national farmers' movement began to take definite shape in 1918, when the Canadian Council of Agriculture adopted a programme entitled the "New National Policy" which included a renewed demand for reciprocity with the United States in the trade of farm products. Response from farmers' organizations was favorable to political action, especially after the new Liberal leader, W. L. Mackenzie King, indicated that he did not concur completely with their demands for revision of the tariff. This was followed by farmer successes in federal by-elections in the East and the West and was capped by the victory of the United Farmers of Ontario in the 1919 general election in that province.[16]

THE FARMERS IN SASKATCHEWAN POLITICS

These wartime and post-war developments weakened traditional party allegiances in the West and at the same time presented the farmers with the alternative of direct political action to secure their policy demands. It was safe to predict that once the farmers were confident of success in federal contests, they would turn their sights on provincial politics as well. Because of their long-time close association with the SGGA, the Saskatchewan Liberals were particularly sensitive to the effect farmer unrest would have on their electoral fortunes. They were also aware that their vulnerability arose from their association with the federal Liberals, whose trade policies were unpopular with the farmers. Since there seemed little chance of altering these policies to make them more palatable to the western farmer, the alternative was for the Saskatchewan Liberals to dissociate themselves from the federal party. They did this in 1919 and the following year extended their "dissociation" to all federal parties. In the words of Premier Martin: "I will not be responsible for the organization nor for the policies of any federal political party."[17] What the Provincial Rights party had done from 1905 to 1911 was now to be duplicated by the Liberal party.

This break was in response to a potential threat. At its annual convention in 1920 the SGGA debated a motion to establish a provincial political organization that would nominate and support independent candidates. The convention finally resolved to appoint a committee to draft a provincial political platform for submission to local and district conventions and to the next annual convention. However, little interest was shown in this proposal afterward. In 1922 the annual convention of the Association further resolved to create a committee to assist provincial constituencies wishing to organize for direct provincial political action. That year the Grain Growers nominated an "Independent" candidate to run in a by-election but he was defeated by a Liberal. In 1924 the resolution of two years earlier was rescinded by the annual convention and the Association's interest in direct political action ceased.[18]

The organized farmers' threat to the supremacy of the Liberal government was thus checked five years after it had appeared. The government's ability to control farmer unrest in this period illustrated several important features of Saskatchewan politics. Obviously, it proved that dissociation from federal politics was possible. In this particular instance it allowed the Liberals to assume the role of "real" spokesmen for the farmers. As such they could attack other parties, including the farmers' movement, for their federal alignments. It became increasingly embarrassing for the farmers, and later the Provincial Progressive Association, organized in 1924, to denounce the old Liberal sin of federal connections when at the same time they advocated provincial support for the federal Progressives. An example of the difficulties that could arise occurred in 1921 when J. A. Maharg, president of the SGGA and provincial Minister of Agriculture, resigned from the Martin government because the Premier was supporting a local Liberal candidate in the federal general election. The Premier defended his action claiming he was not opposed to individual support of federal candidates but only to provincial party support of federal parties. The Premier stated that Mr. Maharg had resigned "because he could not force me and the whole of the Government into a position where we were to be a cog in the machine of a Federal political party."[19]

The organized farmers' failure to establish a separate political organization at this time was also due to objections to the scheme raised by the leaders of the SGGA.[20] They were convinced that there was no practical alternative for the farmers to the policies offered by the Saskatchewan Liberals. As evidence of their support for these policies, a number of prominent SGGA officers co-operated with the government. Mr. Maharg's acceptance of the post of Minister of Agriculture was one example; another was the appointment of Maharg and J. B. Musselman, the Association's recently-retired secretary, to the executive of the government-supported Saskatchewan Co-operative Elevator Company in 1922. Both men feared that any attempt to transform the SGGA into a political party might destroy its existing unity on economic matters. It was their belief that the farmers should try "to build up an organization which would unite, within its ranks, the largest percentage of farmers, through which they could work effectively in raising their industry."[21]

This attitude, which was generally held by the leaders of the Saskatchewan farmers, was significant not only for political developments in the province in the early 1920s but also for developments a decade later, when the Co-operative Commonwealth Federation was founded. In rejecting direct political action by the farmers, the Saskatchewan leaders were also rejecting the theory of group government then being expounded by Henry Wise Wood of the United Farmers of Alberta. Wood's thesis was that economic groups or classes were the basic units of politics; that traditional parties ignored this truth because they sought support from whoever would give it by compromising principles and balancing interests; and that, as a consequence, traditional parties lacked a unifying principle save subservience to "plutocracy."[22] The conclusion of his analysis was that democracy, which he defined as absence of exploitation of man by man or class by class, could never be achieved until group government was introduced.

The theory appealed to many western farmers because it appeared to substantiate many of their prejudices about eastern financial control of the traditional parties. In Alberta the UFA entered politics directly and refused to co-operate with any established political group that did not subscribe to Wood's theory. The size of the organization, the concentration of its vote outside of the cities, and the malapportionment of the province's constituencies in favor of the rural areas guaranteed its electoral victory. By refusing to follow the UFA's example and act as a tightly knit group based on occupational interests, the Saskatchewan farmers may well have denied themselves similar electoral success. However, their decision made possible the continuation of partisan politics in the province. The decisions made by the farmers of Alberta and Saskatchewan in the 1920s are a major cause for the different political evolutions of those provinces to the present day. By deciding to enter politics directly, the UFA destroyed the Alberta Liberal party both as a governing and opposition body; by refraining from direct political action, the SGGA helped preserve the Saskatchewan Liberal party.

Of course, the SGGA's decision of 1924 did not bind all farmers. Throughout the remainder of that decade some farmers flirted with proposals for a party of their own in provincial politics. Yet there was never widespread agreement in support of the idea. Such political activity as did occur, as in the Provincial Progressive Association, was characterized as much by demands for governmental and electoral reform as by promotion of particular farmer interests.

The results of the 1925 provincial election, in which the Liberals won 51 of the 63 seats, indicated the strength of that party. Furthermore, the actions of J. G. Gardiner, who became premier in 1926 when C. A. Dunning went to Ottawa, demonstrated a return to the old style of politics. According to one observer, Gardiner was a machine politician who made no distinction between federal and provincial politics.[23] No attempt was made to hide renewed connections with the federal Liberal party and, indeed, Mr. Dunning's policies as premier appear to have made him suspect of Progressive sympathies in his successor's partisan eyes.[24]

The vitality of the rejuvenated Liberals was tested in 1929 and for the first time in 24 years was found wanting. Part of the explanation for the Liberal defeat rested in the faulty operation of its party machine,[25] but there were several other reasons for failure. Most significantly, the issue of religion in the public schools was elevated, partly through Ku Klux Klan agitation, into a major sectarian conflict.[26] The Liberals, as may be seen elsewhere in this chapter, have traditionally received support from large numbers of Roman Catholic voters. Therefore, if non-Catholic voters were to indicate their religious prejudices politically, it was bound to affect adversely the Liberal party. That the issue was a major one may be gauged by the new government's speed in amending the School Act to forbid religious emblems and religious dress in the schools.

Other issues in the campaign were fairly typical of previous elections; for example, the opposition candidates pressed for a more progressive policy of natural resource development. It is ironic that on the eve of the Depression the Conservatives included in their platform a plank "to solve the problem of seasonal unemployment." The results of the election gave the Liberals the largest number of votes and the largest number of seats but denied them a majority in the legislature. Refusing to give their support to the Liberals, the newly elected Independent and Progressive members pledged to co-operate with the Conservatives in a new government on the condition that the Conservatives agree to "civil service reform, retention of the identity of each group and freedom in the matter of Federal politics."[27]

The latter two requirements indicated that the old issue of partisan politics was very much alive. This was true throughout the life of the Cooperative Government led by J.T.M. Anderson, a Conservative. Outside the legislature many Progressives disavowed the action of their Progressive assembly members. These members eventually became disenchanted with the experiment, particularly after the formation in 1932 of the Farmer-Labour party, for whose programme they felt considerable empathy. The Conservatives also found themselves split over the question of co-operation; many "true-blue" Conservatives opposed the Premier's willingness to countenance such diverse support. As the Depression and drought grew more severe, the Premier sought a coalition of all parties, including the new Farmer-Labour party. However, the Liberals and the leaders of the new party were alive to the value of partisan distinctiveness and refused to join a government that now seemed destined for defeat.[28] Added to the provincial burdens of the Conservatives was the unpopularity of their federal counterparts. At no time in Saskatchewan history were federal partisan attachments so disastrous for a party in power as in the provincial election of 1934.[29] The Conservative party, the traditional second party of Saskatchewan politics, was discredited along with its non-partisan allies. The party's complete defeat, indicated by its failure to elect a single Conservative in a provincial general election until 1964, marked the end of one of the two original parties as well as the end of the short experiment with co-operative government.

In the election of 1934 the Liberal party presented the Saskatchewan voters with a practical partisan alternative to the co-operative experiment of quasi-partisan politics. The success of the Liberals in that election may be seen as reaffirmation of faith in partisan politics. This interpretation of the election results is in no way modified by the support given the new Farmer-Labour party. That party, from the time of its inception, also eschewed non-partisanism. These developments once again distinguished Saskatchewan markedly from Alberta, where non-partisan politics became further entrenched by the victory of Social Credit in 1935.

THE NEW PARTY SYSTEM: 1934–1975

The new party system that appeared after 1934 was again a two-party system, but was now composed of two quite dissimilar parties. The Farmer-Labour party had been formed in 1932 in the depths of the Depression and, to a large extent, was a product of the agrarian discontent of the previous decade. The United Farmers of Canada—Saskatchewan Section, which had been formed in 1926 from a union of the Farmers' Union of Canada and the Saskatchewan Grain Growers' Association, resolved in 1931 to enter politics directly. Their decision was largely determined by the worsening economic conditions in Saskatchewan. But it was also influenced by the fact that the Liberal party, the traditional friend of the Saskatchewan farmer, was out of office; even if the economic situation had not been so bad, the old arguments against direct political action used by Musselman and Maharg in the 1920s would therefore have carried less weight. A new political force in the cities had also appeared in the form of the Independent Labour party led by M. J. Coldwell. Thus, in 1932, it was possible for the two groups, farmer and worker, to unite in a new political party.

An equally important difference between this period and the 1920s was the founding of a new national political party, the Co-operative Commonwealth Federation, shortly after the Farmer-Labour party had been established. Since the CCF was founded as a federation of occupational groups, it rejected the rigid theory of group government enunciated by Henry Wise Wood. Indeed, the farmer and labor groups that met at Calgary in August 1932, and the same groups with representatives of the League for Social Reconstruction that met at Regina in July 1933, believed that federal and provincial electoral success would be denied to any organization that so restricted its appeal.

Thus, when the Farmer-Labour party presented itself to the Saskatchewan electorate for the first time in 1934, it tried to attract support with its distinctive socialist programme from as wide a spectrum of the electorate as possible. In this endeavor it enjoyed the backing of a national party organization. But the Farmer-Labour party also had the important advantage of being a Saskatchewan party, originating from the efforts of provincial groups and continuing to possess considerable local autonomy. The wisdom of this strategy was confirmed in the results of the election. While in terms of legislative membership the party was small, it had the satisfaction of winning 24 per cent of the popular vote and, with the rout of the Conservatives in the 1934 election, of becoming the sole opposition party in the Legislature. Those who deserted the Liberals, for whatever reason, had only one place to go.

From its emergence in 1932 until its victory in 1944, the new organization acted as a true political party. Its two principal tasks were to attract as much support as it could from the Liberals and to prevent the rise of a challenger to its monopoly of the opposition. To better carry out these tasks the party decided, shortly after the 1934 election, to change its name to the Co-operative Commonwealth Federation–Saskatchewan Section, thereby emphasizing its national character within a provincial context. The following year the UFC "instructed the political directorate [of the party] to formulate plans for setting up a distinct political organization" and thereby removed the image of the party as spokesman solely of the farmers.[30] The party also began to play down its programme of government ownership in favor of government planning. By the time of the 1938 election the CCF party appeared to have established a permanent role for itself as the legitimate, practical alternative to the Liberals in Saskatchewan politics.

That election affirmed the CCF in this role. The most outstanding feature of the contest was the invasion of Saskatchewan by Alberta's Premier Aberhart and his cabinet in an attempt to bring Social Credit to the province. As it happened, only two of the 41 Social Credit candidates nominated were elected, compared to 10 of the 31 CCF candidates. But more important than numerical strength was the image of respectability the CCF achieved during the election campaign. The Liberals turned the full weight of their attack against Social Credit, equating it with dictatorship and charging it with trying to make another "Manchukuo out of Saskatchewan."[31] They warned the public against being duped into supporting "Independent" or "Unity" candidates whose politics were unknown and therefore suspect. In an atmosphere so hostile to Social Credit, the CCF gained seats, stature, and legitimacy. The CCF were commended, albeit indirectly, by the Liberals.

Given the disastrous economic conditions confronting the Liberal government and the difficulty of finding practical solutions, the appearance of Social Credit favored the incumbents by allowing them to focus on a secondary but diverting issue. The results of the election confirmed the wisdom of this ploy, for the Liberals were returned with only a slightly decreased majority. However, these returns warned of future problems for the party. The Liberals tended to do best in areas where farmers were still dependent on federal and provincial relief payments;

the CCF picked up support from farmers who had enjoyed good crops in the last harvest.[32]

In the period between 1938 and 1944 the effects of federal Liberal policies on wheat prices and the availability of farm labor did little to help the popularity of the provincial Liberals. The CCF gained stature through its effective criticism of federal and provincial Liberal policies and from the caliber of its parliamentary and legislative membership. In 1943 the one-year extension of the life of the legislature elected in 1938 signaled more clearly than any act of the CCF the imminent defeat of the Liberals.

The CCF's success in 1944, when it came to power with 50 of the 55 seats, was due to events—drought, depression, and war—and their accompanying frustrations more than to popular support for socialism. The Saskatchewan electorate decided that it was "time for a change" and the CCF presented the only alternative to the Liberal party. The aftermath of victory, therefore, was not a revolution in the province's institutions. The CCF's campaign had concentrated on restoring the province's economy, breaking the Liberal machine, and introducing greater social service benefits; it did not concentrate on nationalizing industry or collectivizing land. What new government ownership there was, was only an extension of governmental activity prevalent in Saskatchewan since 1905. It was hardly surprising then that the new Government failed:

> *to replace the present capitalist system, with its inherent injustice and inhumanity, by a social order from which the domination and exploitation of one class by another will be eliminated, in which economic planning will supersede unregulated private enterprise and competition, and in which genuine democratic self-government, based upon economic equality will be possible.*[33]

The CCF victory in the 1944 election signified the emergence of the new party system. Since that date the Saskatchewan CCF-NDP has generally modified its earlier advocacy of public ownership, although a programme launched by the NDP government in 1975 to enable it to gain majority control of the potash industry in Saskatchewan indicated that doctrinaire socialism was by no means a thing of the past. Whenever possible, the CCF had stressed its distinctive provincial heritage throughout its existence. Only following the 1967 election did it decide to change its name to the New Democratic Party—Saskatchewan Section, having retained the name "CCF" for some six years after the CCF was replaced by the NDP nationally and in the other provinces. The new party system thus bore many of the marks of the old. The Liberal party, which regained power in 1964 and held it until 1971, continued the old practice of wary allegiance to the federal party and its policies. Two parties, more or less equally matched, dominated the provincial political scene and vied for office from 1934 to 1975. For their part, the Progressive Conservatives continued their political wandering until 1975. In the election of that year, and in subsequent by-election victories, they gained enough support to suggest that Saskatchewan political alignments may be about to shift once again. Social Credit, after a repeat performance of 1938 in 1956, has become a spent force.

The Political Culture

Political culture has been defined as the "attitudes, beliefs, values, and skills which are current in our entire population, as well as those special propensities and patterns which may be found within separate parts of that population."[34] The Saskatchewan political culture has been influenced by a British political heritage, an ethnically diversified population (see Table III), an agricultural economic base, and a numerically preponderant rural electorate. The overwhelming and continuing importance of these factors, since 1905, helps to explain the simplicity of that culture.

Substructures, "particular [sets] of political orientations . . . distinguishable from others in the system," are not readily apparent in the province.[35] The traditionally close association between the farmer and the government has made permanent conflict between the two unlikely. Similarly, the acquiescence of early Liberal governments in the farmers' demands for public regulation of the economy accustomed the citizens to active government; as a result later transfers of power between "free-enterprise" and "socialist" governments have failed to precipitate major reversals of policy.[36] The principal source of whatever separateness there is in the political culture of Saskatchewan has resulted from the considerable isolation of the non-Anglo-Saxon groups from the province's political system, but even this feature of Saskatchewan politics seems to be changing.

In 1905 the federal government endowed the province with an institutional structure that was basically British and that reflected the values of the dominant ethnic group. There was no question then as to whether this was the appropriate heritage for Saskatchewan and there has been general acceptance since that the province would pattern itself after the Westminster model. Since 1905 not only the structure but also its personnel has been predominantly Anglo-Saxon. However, the status of the various ethnic groups has been changing. One indicator of this alteration has been the membership of the Legislative Assembly.[37]

Until 1938, with the exception of the small CCF contingent of 1934, 60 per cent of all legislative members were Anglo-Saxon in ethnic origin; indeed, nearly three-quarters of the Conservative, Progressive, and Independent members of the legislature were drawn from this "charter" group. By 1964 less than 40 per cent of the M.L.A.s could be so classified; for the first time in the province's history this group was under-represented according to its proportion of the total provincial population. Except for the election of 1929, when race and religion were particularly contentious issues, the Liberal contingent has never been so British-oriented as that of other parties. From the first, the Liberals have been ethnically heterogeneous; in turn, French, German, Scandinavian, Ukrainian, and Dutch representatives have found a place in Liberal ranks before appearing elsewhere. It is revealing of the different rates of cultural assimilation for the various ethnic groups that members from the groups mentioned appeared in the CCF ranks, starting in 1938, in the same sequence.

Throughout its history the Saskatchewan Liberal party has also included within its ranks a greater variety of religions and frequently a greater variety of Protestant denominations than any other governing party. Between 1905 and 1929, when the Liberals were drawing, among others, Roman Catholics and even Swedenborgians, the Conservatives drew solely Anglicans, Methodists, Presbyterians, and United Church adherents; later, in 1964, when Liberal membership in the legislature was 35 per cent Roman Catholic and also included Saskatchewan's first Jewish member, the CCF party still drew 50 per cent of its legislative membership from such Protestant denominations as the Baptist church and United Church.

One observer has noted the high correlation between Liberal party support and Roman Catholic voting patterns in the 1929 election, when religion in the schools was a key issue.[38] He has traced a similar affiliation of Roman Catholics for the Liberal party in later elections and has interpreted their support as being partly a rejection of the socialist policies of the Farmer-Labour and CCF parties. Despite this correlation, the CCF has been far more heterogeneous in terms of religious representation than was the Conservative party. Moreover, this heterogeneity has been increasing; Roman Catholic members in the legislative ranks of the CCF have almost tripled in number since 1944.

Other features of religious representation in the legislature have been an over-representation of the United Church and the denominations that comprise it, an under-representation of Lutheran adherents and, in recent years, an increasing under-representation of the Anglican community. Of the religions in the "Other" category in Table IV, the most under-represented have been the Greek Orthodox and Ukrainian (Greek) Catholic. Adherents of these religions have accounted for at least 8 percent of the declared faiths in Saskatchewan since 1931. However, only five Greek Orthodox members have sat in the legislature, all in the CCF ranks and all elected since 1944; only two Ukrainian (Greek) Catholics, Liberals elected in 1934 and 1948, have sat in the legislature.[39]

The agricultural base of Saskatchewan's economy is one of the most notable features of the province's life. In 1971, 32 per cent of the total male labor force was classified as having an agricultural occupation, as compared to 15 and 14 per cent in Alberta and Manitoba, respectively. In the last three decades the ratio of Saskatchewan's work force employed in the agricultural and non-agricultural sectors of the economy has reversed: where in 1941 two-thirds of the employed males worked in agriculture, in 1971 only one-third was so employed. It is understandable, therefore, that concern for agriculture should be traditional in the political life of the province. Consequently, it is surprising that agricultural occupations, according to occupational distribution in the province as a whole (see Table V), have been under-represented in the legislature. It is even more surprising to contrast the Liberal and CCF ministries of Saskatchewan. In the former the professions have traditionally counted for at least 50 per cent of the occupations of cabinet members; in the latter agriculture has always ranked first.[40]

This stress on agriculture is crucial to an understanding of Saskatchewan politics not only because of the large percentage of the electorate involved in the occupation but also because of the lingering scars that remain as evidence of the agricultural catastrophe that befell the province 30 years ago. In their discussion of political socialization and the process through which an individual acquires political attitudes, Almond and Powell state: "Certain events and experiences may leave their mark on a whole society. A great war or a depression can constitute a severe political trauma for millions of individuals who may be involved."[41] The result of such experiences is that people, large numbers of them, may "acquire new conceptions of the role of politics in their lives and new goals for which they may strive."[42]

It hardly seems an exaggeration to say that this was true of Saskatchewan in the 1930s when the principal industry of the province collapsed. In the words of one observer in 1933:

> *The Ford car has become a horse drawn vehicle, the rural telephone system is breaking down with staggering losses in the number of subscribers each year. Farm products (where there have been crops) supply an ever larger part of the farm diet. Clothing constitutes a problem of the first magnitude; it has been estimated that it would take $30,000,000 to restore clothing to pre-depression standards. The unrepaired houses aggravate a winter fuel problem which has always been acute on the prairie plains.*[43]

One of the most important derivatives of this agricultural economy has been the predominantly rural nature of the society, at least until the most recent census. By 1971 that feature of Saskatchewan society was clearly in the past. For the first time in its history, the province could boast of a majority of its population (54 per cent) living in urban centres (see Table VI). Not only have the past 50 years been characterized by a gradual rural-to-urban shift, but perhaps as many as 500,000 people have moved out of the province altogether during that time span. In the 1930s and 1940s, and again in the early 1970s, the population of Saskatchewan actually decreased. It has now levelled off at approximately 925,000, virtually the same figure as that recorded in the 1931 census.

One notable effect of migration has been on the age structure of the population. There is a "growing concentration of older people in the small villages and towns, of very young people in rural areas, and of middle-aged people in the cities."[44] The political implications of these demographic changes are suggested in the returns of the last two provincial elections. Until 1975 every party that succeeded in forming a government had to carry a substantial number of rural seats. In 1967 the Liberals took 28 of the 45 rural seats and in 1971 the NDP captured 34 of 44 rural seats (the number having been reduced by one through redistribution). But in 1975 when the NDP won 39 of the 61 seats in the legislature, it was successful in only 24 of the rural ridings. In contrast, it won 15 of the 20 constituencies in the four major cities, thereby showing not only a significant shift in the base of NDP support, but an overall decline in importance of the rural areas of the province. Thus it appears that the rural electorate, with its special concerns relating to the problems of an aging and declining population dependent upon an agricultural economy, has become much less essential to the electoral success of a Saskatchewan party than ever before in the province's history.

Today the political culture of Saskatchewan remains essentially unchanged from earlier decades. The institutions are still British, although the personnel are less so. Agriculture continues to predominate after repeated but generally unsuccessful attempts to attract industry. Even increased natural resource exploitation has yet to lessen the province's overwhelming dependence on wheat. To realize the impact the drought of the 1930s still has on the minds of the people, one has only to note the expressions of concern and, indeed, of fear that accompany prolonged dry spells in the summer. The migration of people, ideas, and tastes between farm, town, and city may have disguised the sharp contrasts of earlier periods; it has not eliminated them.

The Nature of the System

Given the agricultural, one-crop base of the province's economy, which would imply a similarity in economic outlook throughout the province, it is perhaps surprising to discover that a competitive two-party system has developed in Saskatchewan. In spite of the single, dominant industry, with its acute vulnerability to climatic conditions, business cycles, and sudden changes in the international demand for wheat, the people of Saskatchewan have not developed a single-party system. There have been, it is true, prolonged periods of one-party dominance: for example, from 1905 to 1929 when the Liberals were in power, and from 1944 to 1964 when the CCF was in power.

Yet by using the measurement of popular vote rather than the number of seats won in the legislature, which has the effect of removing at least some of the bias of the plurality electoral procedure, a truer gauge of party competition is made possible. In 10 of the 18 elections between 1905 and 1975 at least 80 per cent of the popular vote was cast for the two major parties (see Table VII). In 8 of the 18 elections there was a spread of only 10 percentage points or less between these parties (see Table VII).

The competitive basis of Saskatchewan party politics is even more striking when one compares it with Alberta. The two provinces were created at the same time under similar circumstances, and both had similar economic bases. In only 6 of Alberta's 18 elections, compared to 10 of Saskatchewan's 18, has at least 80 per cent of the total popular vote been cast for the two major parties (see Table VII). In one-half of Alberta's elections, compared to only three of Saskatchewan's, the spread between the first and the second parties has been more than 25 percentage points (see Table VIII). The median and mean figures presented in Table IX further support the contention that the Saskatchewan party system has been more competitive than the Alberta system. If it can be assumed that party competition, partisan preference, and political involvement are directly related to voter turnout, as it is fair to assume they are,[45] then the Saskatchewan party system is one of active participation centering around keen competition. Its voter turnout figures are consistently high. This is particularly obvious when contrasted to both Manitoba and Alberta (see Table X). Thus, the absence of single-party dominance and the continued existence of competitive party politics have been traditional characteristics and must now be regarded as essential components of the party system of Saskatchewan.[46]

How can the obvious difference between the Saskatchewan, Manitoba, and Alberta party systems be accounted for? The ability of the provincial Liberal party to deal effectively with dissent for nearly all of the province's first 40 years must rank as a factor of considerable importance. On the one hand, the Liberal party's ability to control farmer unrest during the 1920s meant that the theory of group government propounded in Alberta by Henry Wise Wood was inappropriate to Saskatchewan politics. That machine politics aided in sustaining the Liberal government during this period further indicates the considerable power enjoyed by the Liberal party in the first 25 years of the province's history.[47] On the other hand, the dominance of the Liberal party from 1905 to 1944 and, subsequently, of the CCF from 1944 to 1964 made non-partisan and coalition politics, such as the Bracken-Garson-Willis-Campbell variety in Manitoba, both unthinkable and unnecessary in Saskatchewan.[48] The electorate and the parties in Saskatchewan obviously lacked interest in adopting the experiments in parliamentary democracy found in the neighboring provinces. By so doing they helped to promote rival party politics in the province.

Furthermore, in Saskatchewan the need and desire for co-operative action and involvement has been greater than in either Alberta or Manitoba. Professor John Archer has stated:

> *The rapidity of settlement and the immensity of the area settled in Saskatchewan was quite unique. The harsh environment, the physical labour required, the need for shelter, water and food, the immensity of the prairies, the never resting wind, the richness of the soil, the littleness of one human in such a setting—these factors led to the gradual evolution of a native philosophy in Saskatchewan. It was not like Manitoba—where settlement was older and the farm land confined to a relatively small area in the south. It was not like Alberta where a strong ranching industry dominated the south and the lure of the Peace River country drew off the restless to the north. In Saskatchewan—English and Estonian, Scot and Slav, American and Armenian, everyone was subject to the same prime factors of hardship, loneliness, cold, drought, fire, frost and hail at the same time. Necessity dictated that each help the other. The wind blew just as chill over the sidehill dug-out of the Norwegian newcomer as it did over the sod shanty of the Minnesota Swede. The prairie fire licked as hungrily around the frame shack of an English remittance man as it did at the log shack of his Galician neighbour. There was the same urgency to get grain threshed before the winter. There was the same need for companionship, for roads, for schools. There were the same dark threats against monopoly and profit mongering when good wheat brought poor prices and disputed grades.*[49]

To a large extent, residents of Saskatchewan have been forced to participate in the management of their own affairs and to co-operate with each other in social, economic, and political endeavors. By the mid-1940s, as Professor S.M. Lipset found, there were between 40,000 and 60,000 different elective posts in Saskatchewan to be filled by the 125,000 farmers. In other words, there was one elective position available for every two or three farmers.[50] This vitality of Saskatchewan politics has expressed itself in other ways as well. One of the studies requested by the federal government's Committee on Election Expenses (1966) discovered that the proportion of people in Saskatchewan who were party activists or opinion leaders or who were aware of fund-raising activities was greater than the proportion in any other province.[51]

By virtue of political participation and involvement, Saskatchewan voters over the years have become aware of various issues, policies, candidates, and parties, as well as their alternatives. Provincial politics has been carried out within a framework of discussion, debate and competition. The very nature of that discussion and debate, beginning in the 1930s and continuing for the succeeding three decades, has forced both the voters and the parties to identify themselves ideologically. Thus, a large portion of the electorate has actively supported the various political parties. By 1975, at the time of the provincial election, one out of every 10 voters was a card-carrying member of one of the province's two major parties.[52]

The Bases of Party Support

The search for electoral support by the two major parties in Saskatchewan has led both the CCF/NDP and the Liberals to seek support from as large a segment of the total population as possible and as a result avoid adopting rigid positions centering around firm doctrines. While the commitment to social reform, economic planning, and government ownership of certain industries has been greater in the CCF/NDP than in the Liberal party, the latter has, with exceptions, been sufficiently aware of the need for electoral support to favor a good deal of positive legislative action. In at least one election (1964), the Liberals in fact appeared to be ideologically to the left of the CCF on a number of social issues.[53] It is, of course, one thing for a party to be progressive or leftist on the hustings; it is quite another matter to be so when elected to power. Although the CCF introduced much in the way of socialized health, welfare, and rehabilitation services and established a number of provincially-owned enterprises when it first came to power in 1944, not too many years passed before the socialists substantially modified a number of their party's policies so that they might broaden rather than restrict their electoral appeal. In point of fact

> *distinctive features of C.C.F. policy from the time it assumed office in 1944 until its defeat by the Liberals twenty years later did not represent the sharp departure from the practices of its predecessors or of neighboring provinces which was sometimes pictured. Enthusiasm and a reforming spirit were evident, administrative innovations*

occurred, there was early socialistic experimenting, changes were made and new policies and services introduced; but these occurred within the framework of the existing economic and social order. Neither the claims of its supporters nor the charges of its opponents of the replacement of the old social order by a new one were fulfilled.

In an era of increasing government activity and participation, C.C.F. performance showed a difference more in degree and in timing than in kind.[54]

On the whole, the impression created by the parties' active solicitation for support as well as their legislative records in Saskatchewan is one of moderate democratic socialism versus a peculiar Prairie variety of liberalism. Yet, in spite of such differences as there are between the two parties, there has developed over the years a characteristic unpredictability about the positions they have assumed on various issues of substantial importance. Just as the Liberal party has tended to be illiberal and anti-intellectual on certain issues, so has the CCF shown a strange penchant for conservatism in certain matters. Just as the provincial parties have shown at times a marked tendency toward dissociation from their federal counterparts (the Conservatives from 1905 to 1911, the Liberals under Martin and Dunning, the CCF as distinct from the NDP from 1961 to 1967, and the "Saskatchewan Liberals" under Ross Thatcher),[55] so have the leaders themselves worked against the very principle they advocated by moving freely between federal and provincial politics. Of the 10 premiers of the province, 6 have sat as M.P.s either before or after serving as party leader in Saskatchewan; two of those 6 became federal cabinet ministers, two ran for the national leadership of their respective parties, and one was successful (see Table XI). All this leads one to believe that Saskatchewan politics has been as much a politics of personalities as of parties. The truth of this characteristic of Saskatchewan politics is found in the fact that many people in Saskatchewan have tended to identify themselves as being, for example, "Douglas CCFers," "Thatcher Liberals," "Diefenbaker Conservatives," or "Blakeney Socialists."

In terms of federal-provincial voting patterns the Saskatchewan voter has shown himself to be a free agent. Certainly the emphasis appears to have been more on personalities and issues than on party doctrine and ideologies. Therefore, to attempt to explain the provincial party system and provincial voting patterns by referring to federal party politics would be futile. The 193,000 Saskatchewan voters who elected 17 Progressive Conservative M.P.s in 1965, felt no particular attachment to the provincial Conservative party in 1967 when all 41 of that party's candidates failed to get elected and the total vote for the party came to only 39,000.

The federal Liberals' inability to elect a single M.P. in Saskatchewan in 1965 came at a time midway between the provincial Liberals' successes in the Saskatchewan elections of 1964 and 1967. The NDP provincial government was re-elected in 1975 less than a year after the defeat of all but two NDP candidates running for the federal parliament. In short, provincial party politics have exhibited an extraordinary detachment from the federal system, in no small part because many recent provincial politicians have, like W. M. Martin before them, deliberately eschewed formal organizational and supportive links with their federal counterparts. The words of Ross Thatcher, spoken during the 1967 provincial election, aptly demonstrate this feature of Saskatchewan politics: "I say to my Conservative friends and to my Social Credit friends—if you are for private enterprise, then look at the Liberals. Cough a couple of times, but put your X in the Liberal column. We do it for you federally. You do it for us provincially."[56]

The differences between the two major parties have been as much a matter of the type of voter supporting one party in preference to another, as they have been a matter of ideological distinctions. The following have tended to give more support to the Liberals than to the CCF/NDP: those with above-average incomes; the more prosperous farmers; voters under 45 years of age; sales, managerial, and professional occupational groups; Roman Catholics, Anglicans, Jews, and Mennonites; and those with at least three years' secondary school education. Alternatively, the following have given more support to the CCF/NDP than to the Liberal party: individuals with below-average incomes; the less prosperous farmers; voters 55 years of age and over; laborers, craftsmen, and transportation and service workers; United Church members, Presbyterians, and Lutherans; and those with less than three years' secondary school education.[57] The type of electoral support received by each of the two major parties helps to explain the more conservative position of the Liberal party and the more liberal position of the CCF/NDP on public issues. The original liberal-conservative dichotomy of Saskatchewan politics has been preserved in the progressive liberalism of the CCF/NDP and the newly-found conservatism of the Liberals.

However, the results of the 1975 election suggest that the traditional two-party system of provincial politics may well be at an end. There is no question but that it has been fundamentally altered in the short-run. The Progressive Conservatives garnered more than a quarter of the popular vote in 1975, their largest in nearly 50 years. In so doing they clearly hurt both the other parties. Under their newly-chosen leader, Dick Collver, the Progressive Conservatives elected seven members to the provincial legislature—the most since J. T. M. Anderson's success in 1929. The 1975 election was an impressive three-way fight. The NDP, Liberals, and Progressive Conservatives had full slates of candidates; the turnover of

MLAs (46 per cent) was the largest since 1917 in an election in which the government was sustained; and in terms of popular vote all three parties were within a 12 percentage point range. This combination of events is unprecedented in the province's history. It could well be the basis of a fundamental partisan realignment. Post-1975 political events lend support to the contention of the Progressive Conservatives that a realignment of political forces has begun and that the PCs may eventually replace the Liberals as the only alternative to the NDP. The Conservative legislative caucus has, since the 1975 election, gained two new members through by-election victories in former Liberal seats, as well as two other members through defections from the Liberal caucus. As of the end of 1977, the two parties sitting in opposition to the NDP government have an equal number of members (eleven apiece)—the first time in Saskatchewan's history that the opposition was so divided.

Conclusions

During its seventy-odd year history, Saskatchewan has undergone several fundamental changes. The rapid settlement and growth of the early twentieth century was followed by considerable depopulation, changing the province from the third largest in 1931, with 9 per cent of the Canadian population, to the sixth largest in 1971, with 4.3 per cent of the nation's population. The optimism generated by the favorable prospects for wheat production prior to and following World War I was challenged severely by the events of the 1930s and was realized only by the large wheat crops and foreign sales of wheat during the 1950s and 1960s. The fluctuations of that market in the 1960s changed Saskatchewan first from a "have-not" to a "have" province with the third highest per capita income in Canada and then back again. In the 1970s pressure to exploit natural resources has prompted the Blakeney government, in keeping with its socialist philosophy, to assume an active role in the development of the oil and potash industries. Remaining constant against this background of economic unpredictability have been the continuing decline of the rural population, the rapid consolidation of farms and the increasing efficiency of agriculture generally.

The demographic and social developments of Saskatchewan's history have had a profound effect on the politics of the province. Political parties, understandably, have searched for ways of utilizing—indeed, of maximizing—these developments for their own purposes. Initially the Liberal party was eminently successful in drawing into its ranks the major disputants in Saskatchewan politics. This absorptive capacity of the Liberal party lasted throughout most of the first four decades of provincial history. More recently both of the province's successful parties have acted as compromising agencies, though this was less characteristic of the Liberals under Mr. Thatcher than it was previously. Consequently the Liberals' concern for individualism and "free enterprise" has not been so great as to keep them from accepting at least some radical solutions to the problems faced by Saskatchewanians; the CCF/NDP for its part, has chosen a moderate position and has assumed the role of the radical, socialist innovator less frequently than the more doctrinaire European parties on the Left. In short, both of Saskatchewan's major parties have proven themselves to be, in varying degrees and with varying emphases, power-oriented, principle-shunning, compromising entities. It remains to be seen whether the Progressive Conservatives, now that they are once again a significant force in Saskatchewan politics, will share these characteristics.

As compromising political agencies the successful Saskatchewan parties have chosen not to become identified with any one group or section of society, but have sought consciously to obtain support by way of broadly based electoral appeals. They have divorced themselves, when necessary, from their federal counterparts by establishing separate organizations, adopting distinctive names, and withholding support or endorsement of federal candidates.

Party politics in Saskatchewan has been active, intense, and, for a good part of the province's history, highly competitive.[58] Political participation and involvement are higher in Saskatchewan than in any other province, especially striking when compared to the Alberta and Manitoba participation rates. With few exceptions, partisan politics infuses every issue in Saskatchewan, whether it be the marketing of a particular agricultural commodity, the establishment of a government-operated medical care insurance programme, or the proposed nationalization of the potash industry. Party politics has at the same time served as one of the few links between the various groups of people throughout the province. The population—a good part of which is still composed of first- and second-generation Canadians—contains so many different ethnic and religious groups, is so sparsely distributed throughout the province and is so removed from other Canadians, that very few institutions or activities play any role in drawing the various individuals and groups together. Such uniting influences as there are might include, at the very most, the agricultural industry, winter sports, education, and politics. One of the few things common to all residents of Saskatchewan has been the political process; they have not failed to use it in seeking solutions to their many problems.

TABLE I*

The Popular Vote and Legislative Seats Won by Parties in Saskatchewan Provincial General Elections, 1905-75

			Liberal		Conservative		CCF/NDP		Social Credit		Others	
Election	Total Popular Vote	Total Number of Seats	Percentage of Popular Vote	Number of Seats	Percentage of Popular Vote	Number of Seats	Percentage of Popular Vote	Number of Seats	Percentage of Popular Vote	Number of Seats	Percentage of Popular Vote	Number of Seats
1905	34,057	25	52	16	47	9	–	–	–	–	–	–
1908	58,302	41	50	27	49	14	–	–	–	–	–	–
1912	87,632	54	57	46	42	8	–	–	–	–	1	–
1917	187,635	59	57	51	36	7	–	–	–	–	7	–
1921	180,955	63	52	45	3	2	–	–	–	–	45	6
1925	247,764	63	51	50	18	3	–	–	–	–	30	10
1929	361,268	63	46	28	36	24	–	–	–	–	18	11
1934	429,620	55	48	50	27	–	24	5	–	–	1	–
1938	440,273	52	45	38	12	–	19	10	16	2	8	2
1944	397,117	52	35	5	11	–	53	47	–	–	1	–
1948	492,906	52	31	19	8	–	48	31	8	–	5	2
1952	537,962	53	39	11	2	–	54	42	4	–	1	–
1956	551,698	53	30	14	2	–	45	36	21	3	1	–
1960	679,243	55	33	17	14	–	41	38	12	–	–	–
1964	666,497	59	41	33	19	1	40	25	–	–	–	–
1967	411,109	59	46	35	9	–	45	24	–	–	–	–
1971	444,003	60	43	15	2	–	55	45	–	–	–	–
1975	451,023	61	32	15	28	7	40	49	–	–	–	–

*Source: Evelyn Lucille Eager, "The Government of Saskatchewan" (Ph.D. Thesis, University of Toronto, 1957), p. 344; statements of election results for 1960 and 1964, issued by the Chief Electoral Officer for Saskatchewan, *Star-Phoenix* (Saskatoon), October 12, 1967 and June 24, 1971; and *Report of the Chief Electoral Officer, 1975* (Regina, 1975). The percentages may not add up exactly to 100 due to rounding. The decrease in total popular vote in 1967 is accounted for by the replacement of multi-member constituencies in Regina, Saskatoon, and Moose Jaw by single member constituencies and the lowest provincial voter turnout in four decades.

TABLE II

Premiers of Saskatchewan 1905-71

Premier	Term of Office	Governing Party
Walter Scott	1905-16	Liberal
W. M. Martin	1916-22	Liberal
C. A. Dunning	1922-26	Liberal
J. G. Gardiner	1926-29	Liberal
J. T. M. Anderson	1929-34	Co-operative*
J. G. Gardiner	1934-35	Liberal
W. J. Patterson	1935-44	Liberal
T. C. Douglas	1944-61	CCF
W. S. Lloyd	1961-64	CCF
W. R. Thatcher	1964-71	Liberal
A. E. Blakeney	1971-	NDP

* Composed of Conservatives, Progressives, and Independents.

TABLE III*

Percentage Distribution of the Population of Saskatchewan, by Ethnic Group, 1901-71

	1901	1911	1921	1931	1941	1951	1961	1971
Anglo-Saxon	43.9	54.7	52.9	47.5	44.4	42.3	40.4	42.1
French	2.9	5.2	5.6	5.5	5.6	6.2	6.5	6.1
German	12.9	14.4	9.0	14.0	14.5	16.3	17.1	19.2
Dutch	0.4	0.6	2.2	2.7	4.0	3.6	3.2	2.0
Scandinavian	1.6	7.1	7.7	7.9	7.7	7.5	7.3	6.3
Ukrainian	1.2	4.5	3.7	6.9	8.9	9.4	8.5	9.2
Other	37.1	13.5	18.9	15.5	14.9	14.7	17.0	15.1

*Source: Dominion Bureau of Statistics, *Census of Canada, 1961* (Ottawa, Queen's Printer, 1966), Vol. 7.1-6, Table 3, and Statistics Canada, *Census of Canada, 1971*, catalogue 92-762 (AP-11), Table 2.

TABLE IV*

Percentage Distribution of the Population of Saskatchewan, by Religious Denomination, 1901-71

	1901	1911	1921	1931	1941	1951	1961	1971
Anglican	17.7	15.5	15.4	13.8	13.2	11.5	10.3	9.4
Baptists	2.7	3.8	3.1	2.5	2.2	1.9	1.8	1.6
Lutheran	6.8	11.6	12.2	12.4	11.8	11.0	10.3	9.8
Methodist	13.3	16.2	13.4	–	–	–	–	–
Presbyterian	18.0	19.9	21.5	7.4	6.2	4.0	2.7	2.2
Roman Catholic	19.6	18.6	19.6	20.7	22.6	24.1	26.3	27.9
United Church			0.4	26.5	25.9	29.8	32.1	29.9
Other	21.9	14.4	14.4	16.7	18.1	17.7	16.5	19.4

*Source: Dominion Bureau of Statistics, *Census of Canada, 1961* (Ottawa: Queen's Printer, 1965), Vol. 7.1-11, Table 1, and Statistics Canada, *Census of Canada, 1971*, catalogue 92-763 (AP-12), Table 1.

TABLE V*

Percentage Distribution of the Male Labor Force in Saskatchewan, 15 Years of Age and Over, by Occupation, 1911-1971

	1911	1921	1931	1941	1951	1961	1971
Agricultural	67.3	70.9	66.6	67.4	56.4	43.2	32.3
Non-Agricultural	32.7	29.1	33.4	32.6	43.6	56.8	67.7

*Source: Dominion Bureau of Statistics, *Census of Canada, 1961* (Ottawa: Queen's Printer, 1964), Vol. 3.1-1, Table 3, and Statistics Canada, *Census of Canada, 1971*, Vol. 3, part 3 (Bulletin 3.3-9), Table 7.

TABLE VI*

Numerical and Percentage Distribution of Rural and Urban Population in Saskatchewan, 1901-71

Year	Total Population	Rural No.	Rural %	Urban No.	Urban %
1901	91,279	85,687	93.9	5,592	6.1
1911	492,432	412,930	83.9	79,502	16.1
1921	757,510	629,888	83.2	127,622	16.8
1931	921,785	734,664	79.7	187,121	20.3
1941	795,992	705,254	78.7	190,738	21.3
1951	831,728	580,710	69.8	251,018	30.2
1961	925,181	527,090	57.0	398,091	43.0
1971	926,240	435,610	47.0	490,630	53.0

*Source: Dominion Bureau of Statistics, *Census of Canada, 1961* (Ottawa: Queen's Printer, 1963), Vol. 7.1-2, Table 1, and Statistics Canada, *Census of Canada, 1971*, Advance Bulletin, Catalogue 92-755, (AP-4), Table 3.

TABLE VII

Vote Cast for Two Major Parties in Saskatchewan and Alberta, 1905-75

Percentage of Popular Vote	Number of Elections: Saskatchewan	Number of Elections: Alberta
50-54	0	1
55-59	0	0
60-64	3	1
65-69	0	3
70-74	2	2
75-79	3	5
80-84	3	2
85-89	1	1
90-94	2	2
95-100	4	1
Total	18	18

TABLE VIII

Spread in Percentage Points between Popular Vote for Each of the Two Major Parties in Saskatchewan and Alberta, 1905-75

	Number of Elections	
Spread in Percentage Points	Saskatchewan	Alberta
1-5	5	2
6-10	3	2
11-15	3	3
16-20	2	1
21-25	2	1
26-30	2	3
31-35	0	5
36 and over	1	1
Total	18	18

TABLE IX

Percentage of Total Popular Vote Cast for the Two Major Parties in Saskatchewan and Alberta, 1905-75: Median and Mean

	Percentage of Popular Vote (18 elections each)	
	Saskatchewan	Alberta
Median	82	76
Mean	83	76

TABLE X*

Percentage of Voter Turnout in Saskatchewan, Manitoba and Alberta Provincial Elections, 1932-75

Saskatchewan		Manitoba		Alberta	
Year	Percentage	Year	Percentage	Year	Percentage
1934	85	1932	73	1935	83
1938	84	1936	66	1940	75
1944	81	1941	50	1944	69
1948	83	1945	56	1948	64
1952	83	1949	54	1952	59
1956	84	1953	60	1955	68
1960	84	1958	61	1959	64
1964	85	1959	66	1963	56
1967	78	1962	61	1967	63
1971	83	1966	64	1971	73
1975	81	1969	64	1975	61
		1973	78		
		1977	77		
Mean	83		64		67
Median	83		64		64

*Sources: Howard A. Scarrow, *Canada Votes: A Handbook of Federal and Provincial Election Data* (New Orleans: The Hauser Press, 1962), pp. 214-223; Chief Electoral Officer, Province of Saskatchewan, Regina; Clerk of the Legislative Assembly, Province of Alberta, Edmonton; Professor T. Peterson, Department of Political Science, University of Manitoba, Winnipeg; *Star Pheonix* (Saskatoon), June 24, 1971, and June 29, 1975; Edmonton *Journal*, March 27, 1975; and *Winnipeg Free Press*, June 12, 1973, and October 12, 1977.

TABLE XI

Provincial Premiers of Saskatchewan And Their Prior and Subsequent Involvement in Federal Politics

Premier	M.P. Previously	M.P. Subsequently	Federal Cabinet Minister	Federal Party Leader
Walter Scott	X	–	–	–
W. M. Martin	X	–	–	–
C. A. Dunning	–	X	X	–
J. G. Gardiner	–	X	X	–
J. T. M. Anderson	–	–	–	–
W. J. Patterson	–	–	–	–
T. C. Douglas	X	X		X
W. S. Lloyd	–	–	–	–
W. R. Thatcher	X	–	–	–
A. E. Blakeney	–	–	–	–

Endnotes

[1] K. C. Wheare, *Federal Government*, 4th ed. (New York: Oxford University Press, 1965), p. 10.

[2] The government and politics of Saskatchewan have been studied by Evelyn Lucille Eager, "The Government of Saskatchewan" (Ph.D. Thesis, University of Toronto, 1957), and David E. Smith, *Prairie Liberalism: The Liberal Party in Saskatchewan* (Toronto: University of Toronto Press, 1975).

[3] *Statutes at Large*, 4-5, Edward VII. c. 3 and c. 42 (1905), "An Act to establish and provide for the government of the Province of Alberta (Saskatchewan)."

[4] *The Leader* (Regina), June 28, 1905, p. 5. In late May and early June, Mr. Haultain, along with R. B. Bennett and other prominent Conservatives, campaigned in the federal by-elections of London and North Oxford in Ontario. The Autonomy Acts for the new provinces were principal issues in these campaigns. See *The Leader*, May 31, 1905, p. 4; and June 14, 1905, pp. 1 and 4.

[5] John R. Saywell, *The Office of the Lieutenant-Governor* (Toronto: University of Toronto Press, 1957), p. 106.

[6] This relationship existed from territorial days when W. R. Motherwell, later the first minister of agriculture in Saskatchewan, was one of the founders of the Territorial Grain Growers' Association. Other government personalities prominent in the Association and the Saskatchewan Co-Operative Elevator Company until the 1920s were C. A. Dunning, George Langley, Charles Hamilton, and John Maharg, all of whom were ministers of agriculture in this period.

[7] Paul F. Sharp, *The Agrarian Revolt in Western Canada* (Minneapolis: University of Minnesota Press, 1948), p. 39.

[8] John H. Archer, "The Political Development of Saskatchewan" (Saskatoon: University of Saskatchewan, mimeo., 1960), p. 9.

[9] These perennial issues, discussed in both electoral and legislative debates, are noted by J. Castell Hopkins in *Canadian Annual Review* (Toronto: The Annual Review Publishing Company). See, for example, *Canadian Annual Review* (1913), p. 637; and *Canadian Annual Review* (1920), p. 795.

[10] Samuel Lubell, *The Future of American Politics*, 2nd ed., rev. (New York: Doubleday and Company, 1956), pp. 210-218.

[11] Denis Smith, "Politics and the Party System in the Three Prairie Provinces, 1917-1958" (B.Litt. Thesis, Oxford University, 1959), p. 15. A decade later during the provincial general election of 1921 Premier Martin reiterated the value of patronage in the civil service: "We have a Civil Service Commissioner whose duty it is to provide for appointments in the Civil Service, but I do not hesitate to say that in the filling of the more important positions the responsible head of the Department affected makes the selection." *Canadian Annual Review* (1921), p. 811.

[12] The electoral activities of the Non-Partisan League and its entrance into Canada are described in Sharp, *Agrarian Revolt*, chs. 5 and 6.

[13] *Canadian Annual Review* (1917), p. 615.

[14] Dominion Bureau of Statistics, *Census of the Prairie Provinces, 1946: Population* (Ottawa: King's Printer, 1949), I, 247.

[15] Smith, "Politics and the Party System," p. 38. See also *Canadian Annual Review* (1917), p. 615.

[16] W. L. Morton, *The Progressive Party in Canada* (Toronto: University of Toronto Press, 1950), pp. 82-85.

[17] *Canadian Annual Review* (1920), p. 755.

[18] For a review of the SGGA's discussion of this topic at its annual conventions from 1920 to 1924, see *Canadian Annual Review* (1920), pp. 722-776; (1921), pp. 779-780; (1922), p. 782; (1924), pp. 417-418.

[19] *Canadian Annual Review* (1921), p. 794. For further on the same topic, see also *Canadian Annual Review* (1923), p. 715.

[20] For further on the farmers' flirtations with provincial politics, see F.W. Anderson, "Farmers in Politics, 1915-1935" (M.A. Thesis, University of Saskatchewan, 1949), pp. 62 ff.

[21] *Canadian Annual Review* (1924), p. 418.

[22] Wood's distinctive theory of group government is presented in: C. B. Macpherson, *Democracy in Alberta: Social Credit and the Party System*, 2nd ed. (Toronto: University of Toronto Press, 1962), ch. 2; William Kirby Rolph, *Henry Wise Wood of Alberta* (Toronto: University of Toronto Press, 1950), pp. 63-66. For the opinion of Saskatchewan farmer leaders on this theory, see *The Grain Growers' Guide*, November 26, 1919, p. 16; December 17, 1919, p. 18.

[23] Professor Smith quotes John Dafoe as saying of Gardiner that he was "a political anachronism—a survival of a stage of political development—which we have definitely passed in the West. I doubt whether he can be modernized." Smith, "Politics and the Party System," p. 185.

[24] *Ibid.*, p. 186.

[25] Escott M. Reid, "The Saskatchewan Liberal Party Machine Before 1929," in *Party Politics in Canada*, 3rd ed., Hugh G. Thorburn, ed., (Toronto: Prentice-Hall of Canada, Ltd., 1972), p. 29.

[26] The Ku Klux Klan and its operation in Canada is discussed in Patrick Kyba, "Ballots and Burning Crosses—The Election of 1929," in *Politics in Saskatchewan*, Norman Ward and Duff Spafford, eds. (Toronto: Longmans Canada Ltd., 1968), pp. 105-123.

[27] *Canadian Annual Review* (1928-29), p. 469. It was also part of the agreement that the Government would not resign or threaten to resign except on a direct vote of want of confidence. See Eager, "The Government of Saskatchewan," p. 289.

[28] Only one Liberal, Charles McIntosh, crossed to the Government side of the legislature. He was offered the portfolio of natural resources. Saskatchewan law until 1936 required newly appointed ministers to stand for re-election in their constituencies. Between 1905 and 1936, only two of 19 such by-elections were contested, one of which was McIntosh's candidacy in Kinistino. He lost to an officially endorsed Liberal. For further discussion of the projected coalition, see *Canadian Annual Review* (1933), pp. 239-241.

[29] "The Gang's All Here," *Canadian Forum*, XIV (August 1934), p. 420.

[30] *Canadian Annual Review* (1934), pp. 284-285.

[31] Helen Orpwood, "The Saskatchewan Election," *Canadian Forum*, XVIII (August 1938), 136. See also *The Leader-Post* (Regina), May 16, 1938, p. 1; May 19, 1938, p. 9; June 8, 1938, p. 5.

[32] Smith, "Politics and the Party System," p. 300; Orpwood, "The Saskatchewan Election," p. 137.

[33] Such was the party's purpose as stated in the opening paragraphs of the Regina Manifesto of 1933.

[34] Gabriel A. Almond and G. Bingham Powell, Jr., *Comparative Politics: A Developmental Approach* (Boston: Little, Brown and Co., 1966), p. 23.

[35] *Ibid.*, p. 63.

[36] This is not to say that changes in government have not occasioned some conflict. For the effects of the change in 1944 on the civil service, see S. M. Lipset, *Agrarian Socialism* (Berkeley: University of California Press, 1950), ch. 12. For the effects of the change in 1964 on the civil service, see Norman Ward, "Regina Changes Guard," *Canadian Forum*, XLIV (September 1964), pp. 127-128; and Meyer Brownstone, "Another View on the Saskatchewan Government," *Canadian Forum*, XLIV (December 1964), pp. 198-200. See also Professor Ward's reply to Mr. Brownstone, *Canadian Forum*, XLIV (January 1965), pp. 228-229.

[37] For a detailed study of the membership of the Legislative Assembly, see David E. Smith, "The Membership of the Saskatchewan Legislative Assembly: 1905-1966," *Saskatchewan History*, XX (Spring 1967), pp. 41-63.

[38] Andrew J. Milnor, "Agrarian Protest in Saskatchewan, 1929-1948: A Study in Ethnic Protest" (Ph.D. Thesis, Duke University, 1962), pp. 60, 62.

[39] These figures do not include new members elected since 1967.

[40] The legislators' occupations were derived from their nomination papers, where possible. Otherwise, reference was made to the *Canadian Parliamentary Guide*.

[41] Almond and Powell, *Comparative Politics*, p. 65.

[42] *Ibid.*

[43] G. E. Britnell, "The Depression in Rural Saskatchewan," in *The Canadian Economy and Its Problems*, H.A. Innis and A. F. W. Plumptre, eds. (Toronto: Canadian Institute of International Affairs, 1934), pp. 109-110.

[44] James A. Munger, *Housing and Environmental Conditions in the Prairie Provinces* (Saskatoon: Canadian Centre for Community Studies, 1966), p. 30.

[45] Howard A. Scarrow, "Patterns of Voter Turnout in Canada," in *Voting in Canada*, John C. Courtney, ed. (Toronto: Prentice-Hall of Canada, Ltd., 1967), p. 107; and Angus Campbell, et al., *The American Voter* (New York: John Wiley, 1960), pp. 96-110.

[46] The point has also been made that farmers who produce for international markets, such as wheat farmers, and farmers who are subjected to economic pressures which they cannot control have both a high rate of organizational activity and a high turnout at the polls. S. M. Lipset et al., "The Psychology of Voting: An Analysis of Political Behavior," in *Handbook of Social Psychology*, Gardner Lindzey, ed. (Reading, Mass.: Addison-Wesley Publishing Co., 1954), II, pp. 1128-1129.

[47] Reid, "The Saskatchewan Liberal Machine," p. 49.

[48] For a discussion of the non-partisan and coalition tradition of Manitoba, see Murray S. Donnelly, *The Government of Manitoba* (Toronto: University of Toronto Press, 1963), pp. 46-70.

[49] Archer, "Political Development," pp. 14 and 15.

[50] Lipset, "The Psychology of Voting." p. 200.

[51] Committee on Election Expenses, *Studies in Canadian Party Finance* (Ottawa: Queen's Printer, 1966), pp. 43, 45, 47, and 135.

[52] According to the figures released at the outset of the 1975 election by the Chief Electoral Officer, and in keeping with the requirements of the revised *Election Act*, the Liberals claimed 31,801 paid-up members and showed a bank balance of $343,811, while the NDP claimed 28,103 members and $65,062. For their part, the Progressive Conservatives claimed an even 10,000 members and a bank overdraft of $408.

[53] Norman Ward, "Saskatchewan in 1964: Two Comments," in *Voting in Canada*, pp. 187-188. The Liberals in 1964 campaigned on an extension of medicare to include major drug costs, for example. Once they assumed office the Liberals abandoned some of the progressivism they had assumed on such issues during the campaign and no legislation was introduced to cover drug costs. During the 1967 election Mr. Thatcher stated he would agree to including drug costs in medicare only on the condition that approval be given by the electorate of Saskatchewan through a plebiscite. This case in particular illustrates the ability of the parties to say one thing but do another.

[54] Evelyn Eager, "The Conservatism of the Saskatchewan Electorate," in Ward and Spafford, *Politics in Saskatchewan*, p. 15.

[55] During the 1967 provincial election the Liberals campaigned on the slogan "Vote Saskatchewan Liberal," while the CCF urged support on the basis of being "Saskatchewan's OWN Party."

[56] *The Globe and Mail* (Toronto), October 5, 1967, p. 7.

[57] The information contained in this section has been drawn from Lipset, *Agrarian Socialism*. ch. 8; David E. Smith, "Questionnaire Response, Voter Turnout and Party Support," in *Voting in Canada*, pp. 115-124; and Courtney and Smith, "Voting in a Provincial General Election and a Federal By-Election: A Constituency Study of Saskatoon City," *Canadian Journal of Economics and Political Science*, XXXII (August 1966), pp. 338-353.

[58] Fewer than 100 votes separated the winner from the next highest candidate in 8 constituencies in 1967, 5 in 1971, and 4 in 1975.